ICSE Exams 2026

AF814185

All in one®

HISTORY & CIVICS

Class 9

Authors
Adhishree Neurgaonkar
Kamlesh Singh

arihant
SUCCESS AND NOTHING LESS

ARIHANT PRAKASHAN
(School Division Series)

ADMINISTRATIVE & PRODUCTION OFFICES

Regd. Office

'Ramchhaya' 4577/15, Agarwal Road, Darya Ganj, New Delhi -110002
Tele: 011- 47630600, 43518550; Fax: 011- 23280316

Head Office

Kalindi, TP Nagar, Meerut (UP) - 250002, Tel: 0121-7156203, 7156204

SALES & SUPPORT OFFICES

Agra, Ahmedabad, Bengaluru, Bareilly, Chennai, Delhi, Guwahati, Hyderabad, Jaipur, Jhansi, Kolkata, Lucknow, Nagpur & Pune.

PO No : TXT-XX-XXXXXXX-X-XX

Published By Arihant Publications (India) Ltd.

For further information about the books published by Arihant, log on to www.arihantbooks.com or e-mail at info@arihantbooks.com

Follow us on

PRICE ₹320.00

PRODUCTION TEAM

Publishing Managers	Cover Designer	Inner Designer
Mahendra Singh Rawat & Keshav Mohan	Salman Shaikh	Ankit Tyagi
Project Head	**Page Layouting**	**Proof Reader**
Shivam Gupta	Sundar Bisht	Priya Kumari

Index *cum* Study Planner

CIVICS

HISTORY

One Book- Endless Features

to Help you Succeed

Chapter Outlines

At the start of each chapter, all the topics of the chapter have been listed, so that students may know what they are going to study.

CHAPTER

01

Our Constitution and its Features

SYLLABUS

Our Constitution Definition of Constitution-date of adoption, date of enforcement and its significance.

Features Single Citizenship, Universal Adult Franchise, Fundamental Rights and Fundamental Duties, Directive Principles of State Policy (meaning), Welfare State.

Quick Revision

At the end of each chapter, Quick Revision is given. It contains crux of the chapter in pointer form that provides the quick revision of the whole chapter.

Complete Theory in Each Chapter

Each chapter has Complete, Easy to Understand and Simplified theory covering latest syllabus. Theory is developed in such a way that it suitable for all types of learners.

QUiCK Revision

- The Constitution of any country is a comprehensive document, which contains laws and rules by which a country/nation is governed.
- The Constitution was enforced on 26th January, 1950.
- The first meeting of the Constituent Assembly was held on 9th December, 1946.
- The Chairman of the Drafting Committee was Dr BR Ambedkar.
- The Constituent Assembly took 2 years 11 months 18 days to complete its historic task of drafting the Constitution for Independent India.
- The Constitution was made, enacted and adapted by the Constituent Assembly.

Definition and Meaning of the Constitution

The Constitution is a comprehensive document of any country, which contains laws and rules through which a country/nation is governed. It is also known as fundamental law of the land because it is supreme in all the documents of governance.

The main objective of the Constitution is to ensure the welfare of its citizens through good governance. It regulates the position and powers of the three organs of the government i.e. the Legislative, the Executive and the Judiciary.

Check Your LEARNING...

1. The first meeting of the Constituent Assembly was held in which year?
2. Write two significance of the Indian Constitution.
3. Who described the Preamble as the Political Horoscope of the Constitution?
4. What do you mean by fraternity?

Check Your Learning

A set of 3-5 Questions given in between the text, helps students to remain connected with the text while studying. They can instantly assess themselves for their understanding.

One Book- Endless Features

to Help you Succeed

Chapter Practice

Chapter Practice have all types of questions that are asked in the examinations such as Multiple Choice Questions, Short Questions and Structured Questions.

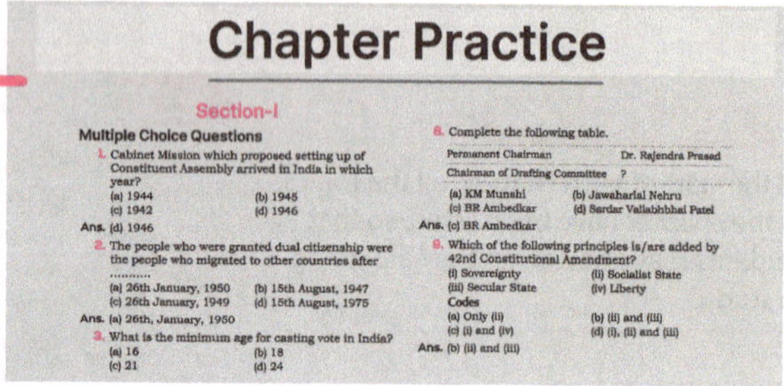

Chapter Practice

Section-I

Multiple Choice Questions

1. Cabinet Mission which proposed setting up of Constituent Assembly arrived in India in which year?
(a) 1944 (b) 1945
(c) 1942 (d) 1946
Ans. (d) 1946

2. The people who were granted dual citizenship were the people who migrated to other countries after ....
(a) 26th January, 1950 (b) 15th August, 1947
(c) 26th January, 1949 (d) 15th August, 1975
Ans. (a) 26th, January, 1950

3. What is the minimum age for casting vote in India?
(a) 16 (b) 18
(c) 21 (d) 24

8. Complete the following table.

Permanent Chairman	Dr. Rajendra Prasad
Chairman of Drafting Committee	?

(a) KM Munshi (b) Jawaharlal Nehru
(c) BR Ambedkar (d) Sardar Vallabhbhai Patel
Ans. (c) BR Ambedkar

9. Which of the following principles is/are added by 42nd Constitutional Amendment?
(i) Sovereignty (ii) Socialist State
(iii) Secular State (iv) Liberty
Codes
(a) Only (ii) (b) (ii) and (iii)
(c) (i) and (iv) (d) (i), (ii) and (iii)
Ans. (b) (ii) and (iii)

Sample Question Papers

To make students practice of examination in real sense, there are 5 Sample Question Papers at the end. All these Sample Questions Papers are exactly prepared on the latest syllabus & pattern of examination.

Chapter Assessment

It is the Assessment exercise for the complete chapter. With this exercise, students can access their understanding of the chapter and can prepare for it accordingly.

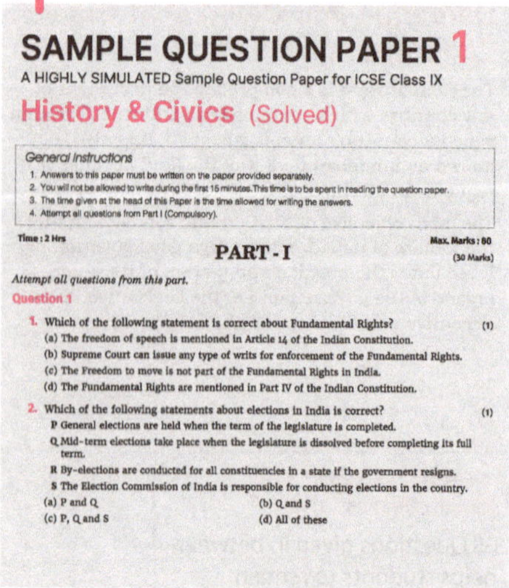

SAMPLE QUESTION PAPER 1

A HIGHLY SIMULATED Sample Question Paper for ICSE Class IX

History & Civics (Solved)

General Instructions
1. Answers to this paper must be written on the paper provided separately.
2. You will not be allowed to write during the first 15 minutes. This time is to be spent in reading the question paper.
3. The time given at the head of this Paper is the time allowed for writing the answers.
4. Attempt all questions from Part I (Compulsory).

Time : 2 Hrs Max. Marks : 80

PART - I (30 Marks)

Attempt all questions from this part.

Question 1

1. Which of the following statement is correct about Fundamental Rights? (1)
(a) The freedom of speech is mentioned in Article 14 of the Indian Constitution.
(b) Supreme Court can issue any type of writs for enforcement of the Fundamental Rights.
(c) The Freedom to move is not part of the Fundamental Rights in India.
(d) The Fundamental Rights are mentioned in Part IV of the Indian Constitution.

2. Which of the following statements about elections in India is correct? (1)
P General elections are held when the term of the legislature is completed.
Q Mid-term elections take place when the legislature is dissolved before completing its full term.
R By-elections are conducted for all constituencies in a state if the government resigns.
S The Election Commission of India is responsible for conducting elections in the country.
(a) P and Q (b) Q and S
(c) P, Q and S (d) All of these

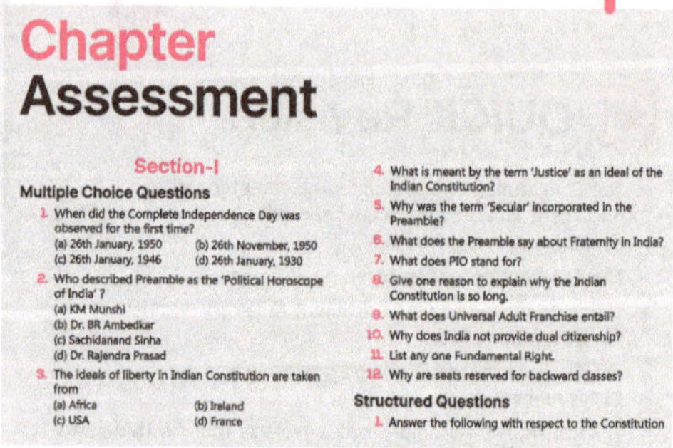

Chapter Assessment

Section-I

Multiple Choice Questions

1. When did the Complete Independence Day was observed for the first time?
(a) 26th January, 1950 (b) 26th November, 1950
(c) 26th January, 1946 (d) 26th January, 1930
2. Who described Preamble as the 'Political Horoscope of India'?
(a) KM Munshi
(b) Dr. BR Ambedkar
(c) Sachidanand Sinha
(d) Dr. Rajendra Prasad
3. The ideals of liberty in Indian Constitution are taken from
(a) Africa (b) Ireland
(c) USA (d) France
4. What is meant by the term 'Justice' as an ideal of the Indian Constitution?
5. Why was the term 'Secular' incorporated in the Preamble?
6. What does the Preamble say about Fraternity in India?
7. What does PIO stand for?
8. Give one reason to explain why the Indian Constitution is so long.
9. What does Universal Adult Franchise entail?
10. Why does India not provide dual citizenship?
11. List any one Fundamental Right.
12. Why are seats reserved for backward classes?

Structured Questions

1. Answer the following with respect to the Constitution

Latest Course Structure

There will be one paper of two hours duration carrying 80 marks and an Internal Assessment of 20 marks.

SECTION A : CIVICS

An elementary study is required of this section without verbatim study of the Constitutional Articles in detail.

1. Our Constitution

Definition of Constitution - date of adoption, date of enforcement and its significance.

Features: Single Citizenship, Universal Adult Franchise, Fundamental Rights and Fundamental Duties, Directive Principles of State Policy (meaning), Difference between Fundamental Rights and Directive Principles, Meaning of a Welfare State.

2. Elections

Meaning; Composition and functions of Election Commission of India; Direct and Indirect election; General election; Mid-term election and By-election.

3. The State Legislatures

The Legislative Assembly and the Legislative Council. Meaning of Unicameral and Bicameral Legislatures, term, composition, qualification for membership, powers and functions.

SECTION B: HISTORY

1. The Harappan Civilisation

Sources: Great Bath, Citadel, seals, bearded man, dancing girl, dockyard, granaries, script. Urban planning, trade, art & craft, and its decline.

2. The Vedic Period

Sources: Names of the four Vedas and importance of epics.

Early Vedic Period- Social Organisation- Family, Position of the king; Rig Vedic Assemblies- Sabha, Samiti, Vidhatha. Brief comparative study of the position of women in Early and Later Vedic society.

A brief comparison between the economy of Early and Later Vedic Period.

The four class divisions, the four Ashramas and the education system.

3. Jainism and Buddhism

Sources: Angas, Tripitikas and Jatakas (brief mention). Causes for their rise in the 6th century B.C. Doctrines- Jainism-Tri-ratnas, Karma, Equality, Moksha Buddhism- The Four Noble truths, The Eight-fold path, Nirvana.

4. The Mauryan Empire

Sources: Arthashastra, Indika, Ashokan Edicts, Sanchi Stupa. Names of the kings in chronological order and administration; Ashoka's Dhamma - Principles and Impact

5. The Sangam Age

Sources: Tirukkural and Megaliths. Society – Position of women Economy - Agriculture and Trade

6. The Age of the Guptas

Sources: Account of Fa-hien; Allahabad Pillar Inscription. Names of the kings in chronological order; administration; Contribution to the fields of Education (Nalanda University), Science (Aryabhatta), Sushrutha (medicine) and Culture (works of Kalidasa, Deogarh temple).

7. Medieval India

(a) The Cholas

Sources: Inscriptions; Brihadishwara Temple. Names of the kings in chronological order and administration; Chola art.

(b) The Delhi Sultanate

Sources: Inscriptions; Qutab Minar. Names of the dynasties in chronological order Alauddin Khilji – Market Regulations, Deccan Expedition, Measures against nobility, Military reforms, Revenue reforms Muhammad Bin Tughlaq-Transfer of capital, Token Currency, Taxation in Doab, Plan of conquests.

(c) The Mughal Empire

Sources: Ain-i-Akbari, Taj Mahal, Jama Masjid and Red Fort.Names of the kings in chronological order. Babur- The three battles waged to consolidate his empire. Akbar-Rajput Policy, Steps towards integration, social and educational reforms, mansabdari system.

(d) Composite Culture

Factors responsible for composite culture, principles of the Bhakti and Sufi movement impact of composite culture, impact of the Bhakti Movement, the Sufi Movement and Christian missionaries.

8. The Modern Age in Europe

(a) Renaissance

Definition, causes (capture of Constantinople, decline of Feudalism, new trade routes, spirit of enquiry and invention of the printing press) and impact on art, literature and science (Leonardo Da Vinci, William Shakespeare and Copernicus). Consequences of Renaissance.

(b) Reformation

Meaning, Causes of reformation (dissatisfaction with the practices of the Catholic Church and new learning); Martin Luther's contribution, Counter Reformation.

(c) Industrial Revolution

Definition of the term. Causes of Industrial Revolution, meaning of capitalism and causes for the rise of capitalism, meaning of socialism and causes for the rise of socialism.

CIVICS

CHAPTER

01

Our Constitution and its Features

SYLLABUS

Our Constitution Definition of Constitution-Date of Adoption, Date of Enforcement and its Significance.

Features Single Citizenship, Universal Adult Franchise, Fundamental Rights and Fundamental Duties, Directive Principles of State Policy (meaning), Welfare State.

Definition and Meaning of the Constitution

The Constitution is a comprehensive document of any country, which contains laws and rules through which a country/nation is governed. It is also known as fundamental law of the land because it is supreme in all the documents of governance.

The main objective of the Constitution is to ensure the welfare of its citizens through good governance. It regulates the position and powers of the three organs of the government i.e. the Legislative, the Executive and the Judiciary.

Making of the Indian Constitution

The Constitution of India came into force on 26th January, 1950. The **consensus**[1] for creating the Indian Constitution evolved during the freedom struggle. In 1946, Cabinet Mission arrived in India which proposed setting up of Constituent Assembly.

The drafting of the Indian Constitution was done by the members of Constituent Assembly which were elected indirectly by the Provincial Legislative Assemblies.

Composition and Functions of the Constituent Assembly

In 1946, the total strength of the Constituent Assembly was 389. Out of these, 292 members were from British India, 93 from princely states and 4 from commissioner's provinces. The Constituent Assembly held its **first meeting** on 9th December, 1946 presided by **Dr Sachidananda Sinha**.

On 11th December, 1946, Dr Rajendra Prasad was elected as a Permanent Chairman of the Constituent Assembly. The Constituent Assembly was divided into a number of committees. The most important among them was the **Drafting Committee**. This committee was set-up on 29th August, 1947 under the chairmanship of Dr BR Ambedkar. The Assembly took 2 years, 11 months and 18 days to pass the Constitution.

1. **Consensus** It refers to a general agreement.

The draft of the Constitution was published on 21st February, 1948 and submitted to President of the Constitutional assembly. The draft of the Constitution was discussed clause by clause by the Constituent Assembly since 4th November, 1948. The second reading of the draft was started on 15th November, 1948 and gets completed on 17th October, 1949 which was followed by third and final reading that was started on 14th November, 1949 and gets completed on 26th November, 1949.

Adoption and Enforcement of the Constitution

The Constituent Assembly adopted the Constitution on 26th November, 1949 after detailed discussions. On this day, the members of the Constituent Assembly signed hand-written copies of the document (one each in Hindi and English).

On 26th January, 1930 **Purna Swaraj** or Complete Independence Day was observed in the country due to which the date 26th January, 1950 was selected to enforce the Constitution. Since then, this day is observed as the Republic Day every year. At the time of enforcement, the Constitution had 395 Articles, 22 Parts and 8 Schedules.

Significance of the Constitution

- It aims for social, economic and political justice for all people of the country.
- It ensures freedom of thought and expressions, freedom of faith, freedom of belief and worship.
- It strives for equality of status and opportunity for all individuals irrespective of religious beliefs.
- It promotes a sense of brotherhood among all citizens.
- It aims at the unity of the nation being the hallmark of the efforts of the government.

Contribution of Dr BR Ambedkar to the Indian Constitution

- He prepared text of the Constitution that provided constitutional guarantees and protection to a number of civil liberties for individual citizens. These include freedom of religion, the abolition of untouchability, rights for women and a system of reservation of jobs for members of Scheduled Castes and Scheduled Tribes in the government services.
- He made the Indian Constitution flexible, workable and strong which can keep country united in the situation of both peace and war.
- He proposed a strong centre to maintain administrative discipline and territorial integrity.
- He incorporated Directive Principles and Right to Constitutional Remedies to protect the Fundamental Rights of the individuals.
- He incorporated single citizenship, single judiciary and equality in fundamental laws to unite Indian society.

The Preamble

The Preamble is an introduction to the Constitution which tells us about the source, the object and the ideals of the Constitution. Objective Resolution introduced by Pt Jawaharlal Nehru on 22nd January, 1947 became the basis of the Preamble. This resolution proposed to make India a 'Sovereign Democratic Republic'. Due to its significance, Preamble is considered as the soul and spirit of our Constitution.

KM Munshi had described the Preamble as the 'political horoscope of the Constitution'. For a long time, the Preamble was not considered as the part of the Constitution, but the Supreme Court of India ruled in the Kesavananda Bharti case (1972-1973) that the Preamble is the part of the Constitution.

Original Form of the Preamble

"We, THE PEOPLE OF INDIA, having solemnly resolved to constitute India into a

SOVEREIGN SOCIALIST SECULAR

DEMOCRATIC REPUBLIC

and to secure to all its citizens:

JUSTICE, social, economic and political;

LIBERTY of thought, expression, belief, faith and worship;

EQUALITY of status and of opportunity;

and to promote among them all

FRATERNITY, assuring the dignity of the individual and the unity and integrity of the Nation;

IN OUR CONSTITUENT ASSEMBLY ,

this twenty-sixth day of November, 1949, do

HEREBY ADOPT, ENACT AND GIVE TO OURSELVES THIS CONSTITUTION."

Note *The words printed in the capital letters in the Preamble stress the importance of the words in the context of the New India dreamt by the fathers of the Constitution.*

Main Principles/Ideals in the Preamble

- **Sovereignty State** This principle says that India is neither a dependent nor a **dominion**[2] of any other nation. There is no authority above it and it is free to conduct its own internal and external affairs.
- **Socialist State** The Constitution had a socialist content in the form of certain Directive Principles of State Policy but the term 'Socialist' was added by the 42nd Amendment in 1976 . This principle aims to end poverty, ignorance, disease and inequality from the society.
- **Secular State** The term 'Secular' was also added by the 42nd Constitutional Amendment Act. It implies that all religions have equal respect and recognition from the state. All individuals in our country are free to practise the religion of their choice.
- **Democratic State** The word 'Democratic' implies that the people of India elect their government by a system of Universal Adult Franchise, popularly known as One Man One Vote. Every Citizen of India who is 18 years of age and above has right to vote and right to be elected.
- **Republic** The term 'Republic' is used for a nation where people are governed by elected representatives. India is a Republic state. Here, power of governing is not a hereditary right.
- **Justice** The term 'Justice' in the Preamble includes three distinct forms i.e. social, economic and political. Social justice denotes the equal treatment of all citizens without any social distinction based on caste, colour , race, religion, sex and so on. Economic justice denotes the no-discrimination between people on the basis of economic factors. Political justice implies that all the citizens have right to have their political opinion/views untill they are not against the interests of the nation.
- **Liberty** The term 'Liberty' implies freedom of thought, expression, belief, faith and worship. The idea of liberty has been taken from the French Revolution (1789-1799). India is a liberal state where all citizens have liberty under laws.
- **Equality** The idea of 'Equality' has also been taken from the French Revolution. The Preamble secures to all citizens of India, equality of status and opportunity. As per Article 15 of Indian Constitution, any discrimination by the state on the basis of religion, caste, sex or place of birth is illegal.
- **Fraternity** The term 'Fraternity' means a sense of brotherhood. The Constitution promotes this feeling of fraternity by the system of single citizenship. The Preamble declares that fraternity has to assure two things, the dignity of the individual and the unity and integrity of the nation. The ideal of fraternity is also taken from the French Revolution (1789-1799).

Changes Made in the Preamble

In 1976, according to the 42nd Constitution Amendment Act, 'Sovereign Democratic Republic' was changed to 'Sovereign Socialist Secular Democratic Republic'. This amendment emphasised on the words Secular and Socialist, to make the intentions of the Constitution clearer.

Check Your LEARNING...

1. The first meeting of the Constituent Assembly was held in which year?
2. Write two significance of the Indian Constitution.
3. Who described the Preamble as the Political Horoscope of the Constitution?
4. What do you mean by fraternity?

Features of the Constitution

The Constitution of India is a legally **sanctified**[3] document that lists the basic principles of the governance of the state. The Constitution of India has several salient features that distinguish it from the Constitutions of other countries.

Some of these are

Written and Lengthy Constitution

Indian Constitution is a written document. It is one of the most lengthy and detailed Constitutions of the world. Written Constitutions are based on laws enacted by a representative body of the people elected for this purpose. The framers of the document have written all the relevant information about the working of the Legislature, the Executive and the Judiciary. There is information about Citizenship, Fundamental Rights, Directive Principles of State Policy, relations between Centre and State, Public Relations and Public Services, etc.

2. **Dominion** It refers to the supreme authority.
3. **Sanctified** It refers to make official.

A lot of amendments have been made in the original Constitution, over a period of time. Originally, it had 395 Articles, 22 Parts and 8 Schedules, but now Constitution of India has 448 Articles, 25 Parts and 12 Schedules. So far, 106 amendments have been made in the Indian Constitution.

Single Citizenship

The Indian Constitution provides single citizenship which means that all Indians, irrespective of their resident state, are citizens of India. There is no separate citizenship of different states. Unlike USA, in India a person cannot be a citizen of their state as well as the country, e.g. people born in Kerala or Assam or Haryana are not citizens of their respective states, they can only be a citizen of India. According to the **Citizenship Amendment Act of 2003**, any person who migrated to other countries after 26th January, 1950 will be granted dual citizenship. But, this only applies if they are PIOs, (Person of Indian Origins). These people can enjoy all the privileges of being an Indian citizen apart from the Right to Vote.

Universal Adult Franchise

It guarantees every Indian citizen of the age 18 and above to vote or contest in the elections. This right is provided to all people, irrespective of their caste, colour, creed, race, religion, faith, etc. This system promises political equality in democratic India.

According to this system, resident voters of a constituency have to vote for the same candidates irrespective of any biases on caste or creed. Some seats are also reserved for representation of Scheduled Castes (SCs), Scheduled Tribes (STs) and Other Backward Classes (OBCs). This step was taken to curb communal politics and bring about national harmony.

Fundamental Rights

The Fundamental Rights are enshrined in Part III of the Indian Constitution (Articles 12-35). The Indian Constitution has guaranteed six Fundamental Rights to all its citizens which are

(i) Right to Equality
(ii) Right to Freedom
(iii) Right against Exploitation
(iv) Right to Freedom of Religion
(v) Cultural and Educational Rights
(vi) Right to Constitutional Remedies

These rights are binding and are enforceable in courts of law and guarded by the Judiciary.

Fundamental Duties

Fundamental Duties are specified under Article 51A (Part IV A) of the Indian Constitution. The Indian Constitution lists eleven fundamental duties for the people of the country. The eleven fundamental duties are

(i) To abide by the Constitution and respect its ideals, institutions, the national flag and the national anthem.
(ii) To cherish and follow the noble ideals which inspired our national struggle for freedom.
(iii) To uphold and protect the sovereignty, unity and integrity of India.
(iv) To defend the country and render national service when called upon to do so.
(v) To promote harmony and the spirit of common brotherhood amongst all the people of India transcending religious, linguistic and regional diversities, to renounce practices derogatory (abusive) to the dignity of women.
(vi) To value and preserve the rich heritage of composite culture.
(vii) To protect and improve the natural environment including forests, lakes, rivers and wildlife and to have compassion for living creatures.
(viii) To develop the scientific temper, humanism and the spirit of inquiry and reform.
(ix) To safeguard public property and to **abjure**[4] violence.
(x) To strive towards excellence in all spheres of individual and collective activity, so that the nation constantly rises to higher endeavour and achievement.
(xi) It is the duty of the parents or guardians to make sure their children between the age of 6 and 14 years get enough opportunities for education.

Directive Principles of State Policy

The Directive Principles are included in Part IV of the Constitution under Articles 36 to 51. The governments must keep these Directives Principles of State Policy in mind while making and implementing any law.

4. **Abjure** It means to formally reject a belief, cause or claim.

These directives are vital because they give direction to the state to achieve the following aims for the welfare of the people

- It secures social and economic justice to the people.
- It secures social and economic equality for the people.
- It promotes international peace and serenity.
- It establishes a welfare state.

Welfare State

A welfare state is a form of government in which the state protects and promotes the economic and social well being of its citizens. The main responsibility of the Government of India is to look after its general welfare. It has to provide means of livelihood to all citizens, promote equal distribution of wealth, encourage the areas of agriculture and cottage industries, provide medical assistance to its citizens, work for international co-operation and to demote unemployment.

To achieve such a system of the welfare state, the Indian Constitution has laid down several Directive Principles of State Policy. It has the aim to guide the governments to strive more for the general welfare of the people.

QUiCK Revision

- The Constitution of any country is a comprehensive document, which contains laws and rules by which a country/nation is governed.
- The Constitution was enforced on 26th January, 1950.
- The first meeting of the Constituent Assembly was held on 9th December, 1946.
- The Chairman of the Drafting Committee was Dr BR Ambedkar.
- The Constituent Assembly took 2 years 11 months 18 days to complete its historic task of drafting the Constitution for Independent India.
- The Constitution was made, enacted and adapted by the Constituent Assembly.
- At the time of enforcement, the Constitution has 395 Articles, 22 Parts and 8 Schedules.
- The Preamble is a kind of introduction to the Constitution.
- The Preamble of the Indian Constitution is based on the principles/ ideals of Sovereignty, Socialist State, Secular State, Democratic State, Republic, Justice, Liberty, Equality and Fraternity.
- India is a Sovereign State which implies that India is not under any outside authority.
- Being a secularist country, India does not have an official religion.
- The ideals of Liberty, Equality, Fraternity have been taken from French Revolution.
- The Constitution of India is a legally sanctified document that lists the basic principles of the governance of the state.
- Our Constitution is a written one and is perhaps one of the lengthy and detailed Constitutions of the world.
- The Indian Constitution provides for single citizenship, which means that all Indians, irrespective of their resident state are citizens of India.
- Universal Adult Franchise guarantees every Indian citizen of the age 18 and above to vote and contest election.
- There are six Fundamental Rights, which have been guaranteed by the Constitution.
- There are eleven Fundamental Duties.
- The Constitution provides some very special directives to the Central and State Governments. They must keep these Directives of State Policy in mind while making and implementing any laws.
- The main responsibility of the Government of India is not only to save India from internal/external invasions, but also to look after their general welfare.

Chapter Practice

Section-I

Multiple Choice Questions

1. Cabinet Mission which proposed setting up of Constituent Assembly arrived in India in which year?
(a) 1944 (b) 1945
(c) 1942 (d) 1946

Ans. (d) 1946

2. The people who were granted dual citizenship were the people who migrated to other countries after ....
(a) 26th January, 1950 (b) 15th August, 1947
(c) 26th January, 1949 (d) 15th August, 1975

Ans. (a) 26th, January, 1950

3. What is the minimum age for casting vote in India?
(a) 16 (b) 18
(c) 21 (d) 24

Ans. (b) 18

4. Which of the following is not a fundamental right provided by the Constitution of India?
(a) Right to Equality (b) Right to Vote
(c) Right to Freedom (d) Right against Exploitation

Ans. (b) Right to Vote

5. Complete the given analogy.
Enactment : 26th November, 1949 : :
Enforcement : ?
(a) 26th November, 1946 (b) 26th November, 1950
(c) 26th January, 1949 (d) 26th January, 1950

Ans. (d) 26th January, 1950

6. Replace the underlined word
The first meeting of Constituent Assembly was Presided by <u>KM Munshi</u>.
(a) Sachidanand Sinha (b) Rajendra Prasad
(c) Dr BR Ambedkar (d) Jawaharlal Nehru

Ans. (a) Sachidanand Sinha

7. Complete the following table.

Articles in original constitution	395
Schedules in original constitution	?

(a) 12 (b) 10
(c) 8 (d) 6

Ans. (c) 8

8. Complete the following table.

Permanent Chairman	Dr. Rajendra Prasad
Chairman of Drafting Committee	?

(a) KM Munshi (b) Jawaharlal Nehru
(c) BR Ambedkar (d) Sardar Vallabhbhai Patel

Ans. (c) BR Ambedkar

9. Which of the following principles is/are added by 42nd Constitutional Amendment?
(i) Sovereignty (ii) Socialist State
(iii) Secular State (iv) Liberty

Codes
(a) Only (ii) (b) (ii) and (iii)
(c) (i) and (iv) (d) (i), (ii) and (iii)

Ans. (b) (ii) and (iii)

10. Match the following.

List-I	List-II
A. A nation where people are governed by elected representatives.	1.Democratic state
B. It implies that the people of India elect their government by a system of Universal Adult Franchise.	2.Secular state
C. This principle aims to end poverty, ignorance, disease and inequality from the society.	3.Republic
D. It implies that all religions have equal respect and recognition from the state.	4.Socialist state

Codes

	A	B	C	D		A	B	C	D
(a)	1	2	3	4	(b)	2	3	4	1
(c)	3	1	4	2	(d)	4	3	2	1

Ans. (c)

Section-II

Very Short Questions

1. When was the first meeting of Constituent Assembly held?

Ans. The first meeting of Constituent Assembly was held on 9th December, 1946.

2. When was the Drafting Committee formed? Who was the Chairman of the Drafting Committee?

Ans. The Drafting Committee was formed on 29th August, 1947. The Chairman of the Drafting Committee was Dr BR Ambedkar.

3. How much time was spend on the making of the Constitution?

Ans. 2 years 11 months and 18 days were spend on the making of the Constitution.

4. When was the draft of the Constitution was published for public opinion?

Ans. The draft of the Constitution was published on 21st February, 1948 for public opinion.

5. What important resolution did Congress pass in the 1930 Lahore session?

Ans. The important resolution that Congress passed in the 1930 Lahore session was 'Purna Swaraj'.

6. When was the Constitution of India implemented?

Ans. The Constitution of India was implemented on 26th January, 1950.

7. How many Articles were in the original Constitution of India?

Ans. There were 395 Articles in the original Constitution of India.

8. How many Schedules were in the Constitution when it came into force?

Ans. There were 8 Schedules in the Constitution when it came into force.

9. What does the term 'Preamble' mean?

Ans. Preamble is the introductory part of the Constitution, which throws light on the aims and objectives of the Constitution.

10. What the words 'We, THE PEOPLE OF INDIA' signify?

Ans. The words 'We, THE PEOPLE OF INDIA' in the Preamble signify the ultimate sovereignty of the people of India.

11. Which principle in the Preamble says that India is free to conduct its own affairs both internal and external?

Ans. The principle of sovereignty says that India is free to conduct its own affairs both internal and external.

12. What is the aim of the principle of socialist state?

Ans. The principle of socialist state aims to end poverty, ignorance, disease and inequality from society.

13. Which principle says that India will not uphold any particular religion?

Ans. The principle of secular state says that India will not uphold any particular religion.

14. In the principle of democratic state , who are the source of supreme power?

Ans. In the principle of democratic state, the people are the source of supreme power.

15. What is the meaning of republic?

Ans. Republic is the term used for a nation which is governed by elected representatives not hereditary representation.

16. Which type of justice have been ensured in the Principle of Justice?

Ans. The principle of justice ensures three type of justice i.e. social, economic and political.

17. Why does the preamble lay so much emphasis on justice?

Ans. The preamble lays so much emphasis on justice because Indians had already suffered a lot of injustice from British rulers.

18. The principle of liberty ensures which type of liberty to the Indian citizens?

Ans. The principle of liberty ensures to every citizens of India liberty of thought, expression, belief, faith and worship.

19. Which types of equality have been secured in the principle of equality?

Ans. The principle of equality secures to all citizens of India, the equality of status and opportunity.

20. By which provision, fraternity has been promoted in the Indian Constitution?

Ans. The Indian Constitution promotes fraternity by the system of single citizenship.

21. Name the words added to the Preamble according to the 42nd Amendment.

Ans. The words added to the Preamble according to the 42nd Amendment are Socialist and Secular.

22. What is the significance of the Preamble?

Ans. The Preamble serves as a key to understand the Constitution and to interpret the mind of the makers of the Constitution.

23. What is meant by the term 'Single Citizenship'?

Ans. Single Citizenship means that all Indians irrespective of the state of their domicile are the citizens of India.

24. Give an example of a feature adopted by the framers of our Constitution from the Constitution of another country.

Ans. The rule of law and single citizenship were adopted from the Constitution of UK.

25. According to the Citizenship Amendment Act, 2003, people who moved to foreign states after which date would be allowed dual citizenship?

Ans. According to the Citizenship Amendment Act, 2003, people who moved to foreign states after 26th January, 1950 would be allowed dual citizenship.

26. What do you mean by Person of Indian Origins (PIOs)?

Ans. Person of Indian Origins (PIOs) are those people who have their ancestoral root in India, but they migrated to the foreign nations and aquired the citizenship of that nation.

27. How does citizenship in India differ from that of the USA?

Ans. India has single citizenship, whereas, USA has dual citizenship.

28. Why were joint electorates introduced?

Ans. Joint electorates were introduced to curb communal politics and bring about national harmony.

29. How many Fundamental Rights are there in the Constitution?

Ans. There are six Fundamental Rights in the Constitution.

30. How many fundamental duties are there in the Constitution ?

Ans. There are eleven fundamental duties in the constitution.

31. Which articles deals with the Directive Principles of State Policy?

Ans. Articles 36-51 deals with the DPSP. It is mentioned in Part IV of the Indian Constitution.

Structured Questions

1. Constituent Assembly framed the Constitution. With reference to this, answer the following questions

(i) Explain the composition of the Constituent Assembly.
(ii) What is the historical significance of 26th January?
(iii) Explain the working of Drafting Committee.
(iv) Define the meaning of the Constitution.

Ans. (i) Constituent Assembly was an elected body organised to frame the Constitution of free India. A total of 389 members, formed the Constituent Assembly.
Out of these, 292 members were from British India, 93 from Princely States and 4 from Commissioner's Provinces. The first sitting of the Constituent Assembly was held on 9th December, 1946.

(ii) The date 26th January, 1950 for commencement of the Constitution was selected for its historical significance. 26th January, 1930 was declared as Purna Swaraj or Complete Independence Day and exactly after 20 years on 26th January, 1950 the Indian Constitution was finally enforced. Since then this day is known as the Republic Day of India.

(iii) The Drafting Committee was established to prepare the Draft of Constitution, which was introduced in Constituent Assembly. This Committee was constituted on 29th August, 1947. It had 7 members and Dr BR Ambedkar was its Chairman. After making countless amendments, the draft of Constitution was published on 21st February, 1948. The detailed discussion were held in the Constituent Assembly before enactment of the Constitution.

(iv) The Constitution is a comprehensive document of any country, which contains laws and rules by which a country/nation is governed. It is also known as fundamental law of the land because it is supreme in all the documents of governance. The main objective of the Constitution is to ensure welfare of its people by means of its good governance. It regulates the position and powers of the three organs of the government, the Legislative, the Executive and the Judiciary.

2. With regards to the Preamble, explain the following terms

(i) Fraternity
(ii) Equality
(iii) Liberty
(iv) Sovereignty

Ans. (i) Fraternity means feeling of brotherhood and a sense of belonging to each-other. The Constitution promotes feeling of fraternity by the system of single citizenship. Fraternity is an evolving process. The Preamble declares that fraternity has to assure two things, the dignity of the individual and the unity and integrity of the nation.

(ii) The preamble secures to all citizens of India, equality of status and opportunity. Equality implies to recognise the status of a person as a human being and to give him equal opportunities to grow and develop into the best of himself. It advocates the absence of special privileges to any section of the society and the provision of adequate opportunities for all individuals without any discrimination.

(iii) The preamble secures to all citizens of India, liberty of thought, expression, belief, faith and worship. Everyone should be able to think freely about any subject and express his/her views freely without any fear. Everyone should be free to believe his/her ideologies, to have faith in anyone or anything and to worship his/her God freely. Liberty as elaborated in the Preamble is very essential for successful functioning of the Indian democratic system. Liberty does not mean that an individual is free to do whatever he wants, but he has to enjoy his rights within Constitutional limits.

(iv) Sovereignty means that India is neither a dependent nor a dominion of any other sovereign. There is no authority above it and it is free to conduct its own internal and external affairs.

3. What does the following imply in the Constitution of India ?

(i) Economic justice
(ii) Political justice
(iii) Social justice

Ans. (i) Economic justice denotes the non-discrimination between people on the basis of economic factors. It involves the elimination of inequalities in wealth, income and property. Economic justice ensures that wealth should be distributed in such a manner that it should not accumulate in few hands.

(ii) Political justice implies that all citizens should have equal political rights, equal access to all political offices and equal voice in the government. It allows universal adult franchise, freedom to contest elections and right to form a political party to every citizens of India without any discrimination.

(iii) Social justice denotes the equal treatment to all citizens without any social distinction based on caste, colour, race, religion, sex and so on. It means absence of privileges being extended to any particular section of the society and improvement in the conditions of backward classes (SCs, STs and OBCs) and women. But, it is noteworthy to mention here that the state may make special provisions for the socially backward classes.

4. Explain the following.

(i) Significance of the Constitution.
(ii) Discuss about the changes made in the Preamble.
(iii) Preamble in its original form.
(iv) Explain the term 'Democratic state' as mentioned in the Preamble.

Ans. (i) Significance of the Constitution is

- It aims for social, economic and political justice for all people of the country.
- It ensures freedom of thought and expressions, freedom of faith, freedom of belief and worship.
- It strives for equality of status and opportunity for all individuals irrespective of religious beliefs.
- It promotes a sense of brotherhood among all citizens.
- It aims at the unity of the nation being the hallmark of the efforts of the government.

(ii) The changes made in the preamble was that in 1976, according to the 42nd Constitution Amendment Act, 'Sovereign Democratic Republic' was changed to 'Sovereign Socialist Secular Democratic Republic'. This amendment emphasised on the words Secular and Socialist, to make the intentions of the Constitution clearer.

(iii) Refer to chapter theory page no. 4.

(iv) The word 'Democratic' implies that the people of India elect their government by a system of Universal Adult Franchise popularly known as 'One Man, One Vote.' Every citizen of India who is 18 years of age and above has right to vote and right to be elected.

5. Explain the following feature of the Constitution.

(i) Single citizenship
(ii) Universal Adult Franchise
(iii) Welfare state
(iv) Written and lengthy document

Ans. (i) The Indian Constitution provides single citizenship which means that all Indians, irrespective of their resident state, are citizens of India. There is no separate citizenship of different states. Unlike USA, in India a person cannot be a citizen of their state as well as the country, e.g. people born in Kerala or Assam or Haryana are not citizens of their respective states, they can only be a citizen of India. According to the Citizenship Amendment Act of 2003, any person who migrated to other countries after 26th January, 1950 will be granted dual citizenship. But, this only applies if they are PIOs, (Person of Indian Origins). These people can enjoy all the privileges of being an Indian citizen apart from the Right to Vote.

(ii) Universal Adult Franchise guarantees every Indian citizen of the age 18 and above to vote or contest in the elections. This right is provided to all people, irrespective of their caste, colour, creed, race, religion, faith, etc. This system promises political equality in democratic India.
According to this system, resident voters of a constituency have to vote for the same candidates irrespective of any biases on caste or creed. Some seats are also reserved for representation of Scheduled Castes (SCs), Scheduled Tribes (STs) and Other Backward Classes (OBCs). This step was taken to curb communal politics and bring about national harmony.

(iii) A welfare state is a form of government in which the state protects and promotes the economic and social well being of its citizens. The main responsibility of the Government of India is to look after its general welfare. It has to provide means of livelihood to all citizens, promote equal distribution of wealth, encourage the areas of agriculture and cottage industries, provide medical assistance to its citizens, demote unemployment and work for international co-operation etc.

(iv) Indian Constitution is a written document. It is one of the most lengthy and detailed Constitutions of the world. The framers of the document have written all the relevant information about the working of the Legislature, the Executive and the Judiciary. There is information about Citizenship,

Fundamental Rights, Directive Principles of State Policy, relations between Centre and State, Public Relations, Public Services, etc. A lot of amendments have been made in the original Constitution, over a period of time.

6. Explain the following.
(i) What are the six Fundamental Rights?
(ii) What are Directive Principles of State Policy?
(iii) Write any two Fundamental Duties.
(iv) Which fundamental duty was added later in the Constitution?

Ans. (i) The Indian Constitution has guaranteed six Fundamental Rights to all its citizens which are
(i) Right to Equality
(ii) Right to Freedom
(iii) Right against Exploitation
(iv) Right to Freedom of Religion
(v) Cultural and Educational Rights
(vi) Right to Constitutional Remedies

(ii) The Constitution provides some guidelines to the Central and State Governments to be followed in the governance of the country.
These guidelines are called Directive Principles of State Policy. The governments must keep these Directives Principles of State Policy in mind while making and implementing any law. The directives are included in Part IV of the constitution under Articles 36 to 51. These directives are vital because they give direction to the state to achieve the following aims for the welfare of the people
- It secures social and economic justice to the people.
- It secures social and economic equality for the people.
- It promotes international peace and serenity.
- It establishes a welfare state.

(iii) The two fundamental duties are
(i) To abide by the Constitution and respect its ideals, institutions, the national flag and the national anthem.
(ii) To cherish and follow the noble ideals which inspired our national struggle for freedom.

(iv) The fundamental duty that was added later in the Constitution was that it is the duty of the parents or guardians to make sure their children between the age of six and fourteen years get enough opportunities for education.

Chapter Assessment

Section-I

Multiple Choice Questions

1. When did the Complete Independence Day was observed for the first time?
   (a) 26th January, 1950 (b) 26th November, 1950
   (c) 26th January, 1946 (d) 26th January, 1930
2. Who described Preamble as the 'Political Horoscope of India' ?
   (a) KM Munshi
   (b) Dr. BR Ambedkar
   (c) Sachidanand Sinha
   (d) Dr. Rajendra Prasad
3. The ideals of liberty in Indian Constitution are taken from
   (a) Africa (b) Ireland
   (c) USA (d) France
4. How many Schedules were originally there in the Constitution?
   (a) 8 (b) 12
   (c) 10 (d) 14
5. Which of the following countries do not have the concept of single citizenship?
   (a) India (b) Afghanistan
   (c) USA (d) Brazil

Section-II

Very Short Questions

1. Which is the most important Committee of the Constituent Assembly?
2. State the significance of 26th January.
3. Explain the significance of term 'Democratic' in the Preamble.
4. What is meant by the term 'Justice' as an ideal of the Indian Constitution?
5. Why was the term 'Secular' incorporated in the Preamble?
6. What does the Preamble say about Fraternity in India?
7. What does PIO stand for?
8. Give one reason to explain why the Indian Constitution is so long.
9. What does Universal Adult Franchise entail?
10. Why does India not provide dual citizenship?
11. List any one Fundamental Right.
12. Why are seats reserved for backward classes?

Structured Questions

1. Answer the following with respect to the Constitution
   (i) Composition of the Constitution.
   (ii) Enactment of the Constitution.
   (iii) Significance of the Constitution.
   (iv) Meaning of the Constitution
2. Explain the following
   (i) The principle of 'Socialist State' in the Preamble?
   (ii) Mention what the Preamble says about equality.
   (iii) Original form of Preamble.
   (iv) Changes made in the Preamble.
3. Answer the following questions
   (i) 'India is a welfare state'. Explain.
   (ii) Indian Constitution is a lengthy and detailed Constitution. Explain.
   (iii) Write down any three fundamental duties of Indian citizens.
   (iv) What is Universal Adult Franchise?

CHAPTER 02

Fundamental Rights and Duties

SYLLABUS

Fundamental Rights and Fundamental Duties

Fundamental Rights

Fundamental Rights are the basic resources of social life. They comprise a number of freedoms that allow citizens to live fearlessly and develop their talents. These rights are called fundamental because these freedoms are essential for the progress of an individual.

These rights are enforceable in the courts of law and cannot be altered or abolished by any ordinary legislature. The Fundamental Rights are incorporated in the Indian Constitution in Part-III.

Importance of Fundamental Rights

- They provide the conditions essential for the all-round development of the citizen.
- They protect people from unjust discrimination or exploitation of any kind.
- They are considered essential because they give a sense of security and confidence to the people.
- They allow a check on any unfair arbitrary actions of the State or Union Governments.
- They make the way for international peace and order.

Features of Fundamental Rights

- **Unchangeable** Fundamental Rights provide certain safeguards that cannot be changed by any ordinary legislation. Changes in these rights can only be brought through an amendment in the Constitution. This constitutional change can only happen when a two-third majority of attending and voting members of both Houses of Parliament agree to it. This is done to remove any possibility of **despotism**[1] rules or legislatures.
- **Universal** Fundamental Rights are provided to all citizens irrespective of their caste, creed, colour, sex, faith, religion, property, qualifications, place of residence or education. This ensures equality.
- **Justiciable** These rights are justiciable in nature. This means that citizens can ask or file case for justice in the High Court or Supreme Court if their rights are violated.
- **Not Absolute** These rights can be enjoyed until they do not go against the rights of others. The Parliament has the right to impose certain restrictions on these rights if a larger issue is concerned.

1 **Despotism** Exercise of power in a cruel or oppressive way.

- **Suspension** In the event of a National Emergency under Article 352, these rights can be suspended to safeguard the security and integrity of the country.

Suspensions are placed under following conditions

(i) **War/External Aggression** If the country is in the midst or about to face any disturbances that threaten the unity or security of the country, rights can be suspended. This can happen for both internal and external causes.

(ii) **Conflicting Interests** If at any time, these individual rights conflict with general welfare, public interest, **morality**[2], decency, security or integrity of the nation, they can be **curtailed**[3]. This can only be carried out by the Parliament. Moreover, it is also subject to judicial review by the High Court or Supreme Court.

Classification of Fundamental Rights

There are six basic Fundamental Rights which are

1. Right to Equality (Articles 14 to 18)

The Right to Equality include equality before law, prohibition of discrimination, equality of opportunity, abolition of untouchability and abolition of titles

- **Equality before Law** It falls under Article 14. It basically means that all persons are equal in the eyes of the law. It guarantees equality before law and the equal protection of law within the territory of India.
- **Prohibition of Discrimination** It falls under Article 15 and dictates that the state cannot discriminate against any individual on the basis of caste, colour, creed, sex, religion, place of birth etc. All people have the right to go to shops, public places, hotels, parks, educational institutions, entertainment centers, etc. They can also freely use any public services like roads, buses, trains, metros, etc.
- **Equality of Opportunity** It falls under Article 16. According to this right, equal opportunities are given to all citizens in matters of employment in an office under the Central or State Government. People should be allowed to hold a government job or public office without any discrimination. But the government is allowed to make reservations of posts, seats in favour of Scheduled Castes or Scheduled Tribes. For example, in 1992, the Supreme Court of India allowed 27% reservation for Other Backward Classes (OBCs). 15% for Scheduled Castes and 7.5% for Scheduled Tribes in government service posts.
- **Abolition of Untouchability** It falls under Article 17. It declares that "Untouchability is abolished and its practice in any form is forbidden". Any person or community preventing any other person from entering a public place of worship, public well, public transport system or public toilets, etc can be punishable by law. The Untouchability Offences Act of 1955 (amended in 1976) penalties the act of untouchability with imprisonment of six months and fine of up to ₹ 500.
- **Abolition of Titles** It falls under Article 18. According to this article, the State is prohibited to confer any titles like Raja, Maharaja, Rai Sahib, Khan Bahadur, etc. Citizens of India are also not allowed to accept any titles from foreign states. Titles can only be conferred for military, sports or academic distinctions. For example, Bharat Ratna, Padma Bhushan, Padma Shri, Paramvir Chakra, Vir Chakra, Jeevan Raksha and Arjuna Award.

2. Right to Freedom (Articles 19 to 22)

The Right to Freedom include six basic freedoms, protection in case of conviction for an offence, protection of life and personal liberty and protection against arrest and detention

- **Six Basic Freedoms** Under **Article 19** of the Right to Freedom, every citizen is provided with six basic freedoms. These are
  (i) Freedom of speech and expression
  (ii) Freedom to assemble peacefully and without arms
  (iii) Freedom to form associations or unions
  (iv) Freedom of movement throughout India
  (v) Freedom to reside and settle in any part of India
  (vi) Freedom to practice any occupation or carry out any profession
- **Protection in Case of Conviction for an Offence** Under **Article 20**, any person who is accused or convicted for an offence has three protections.

2 **Morality** It is the system of values and principles of conduct.
3 **Curtailed** It refers to something reduced in extent or quantity.

These are

(i) The person cannot be punished except for a violation of law present at the time of the occurrence of the crime. Also, they cannot be given a greater penalty than what is prescribed by the law in relation to the crime committed.

(ii) The person cannot be punished or prosecuted for the same offence more than once.

(iii) No person accused of any offence shall be compelled to be a witness against himself.

- **Protection of Life and Personal Liberty Article 21** states that no person can be deprived of their life or personal liberty except through a procedure prescribed by law. Personal liberty comprise of the right of the person to like or dislike a thing, choices of food and dress, hobbies, way of living, preference in art and culture, etc.
- **Protection against Arrest and Detention Article 22** protect citizens under the following circumstances

(i) **Ordinary Circumstances** A person arrested under ordinary circumstances has the following rights

- To be informed about the cause of offence.
- To be defended by a lawyer of his choice and have the time to prepare a case.
- Every arrested person must be presented before magistrate within 24 hours from the time of arrest. The person cannot be detained more than this duration without the order of the magistrate.

(ii) **Preventive Detention** It refers to detention of a person without trial in order to prevent them from committing further crimes. Such a person can be detained for three months (now two months according to 44th Amendment of 1978 but not implemented yet) without a trail. The following rights are allowed to them

- Preventive detention is a precautionary measure and by no means confirms the accusation against the detainee.
- Detention beyond three months can only be extended by an Advisory Board consisting of a Judge from the High Court.
- The detainee is to be told all the information about the reason for detention immediately. They are also allowed to make representation against the detention order.

Right to Information and Right to Education

- **Right to Information** [Article 19(i)] It is an implied Fundamental Right as it is implicit in the Right to Freedom of Speech and Expression. The Right to Information (RTI) Act came into force on 12th October, 2005. It give the following rights to the citizens of India
  - To receive information from government and other public authorities.
  - To ask for certified copies of documents and inspect them.
  - To ask for sample of materials.
  - To ask certain questions from the government or other public authorities.
- **Right to Education (Article 21A)** By the 86th Amendment of 2002, Right to Education right was granted to people. It states that, the State shall provide free and compulsory education to all children of the age of 6 to 14 years in such manner as the State may, determine by law. The Act also enjoins on the State to endeavor to provide early childhood care and education to all children until they complete 6 years of age.

Limitations on Right to Freedom

- Right to Freedom can be suspended during Emergency.
- Some legislations like **Essential Services Maintenance Act (ESMA)**[4] and preventive detention impose some restrictions on the Right to Freedom.
- The Parliament has the power to specify the maximum period of preventive detention.

Check Your LEARNING...

1. State one point stating importance of Fundamental Rights?
2. How can we say that the 'Fundamental Rights' are universal?
3. How are Fundamental Rights justiciable?
4. Which article of the Indian Constitution deals with Right to Freedom?

3. Right against Exploitation (Articles 23 and 24)

Right against exploitation include prohibition of forced labour and traffic in human beings and prohibition of employment of under age children

- **Prohibition of Forced Labour and Traffic in Human Beings** Article 23 provides freedom from slavery, beggary or any other forms of forced labour. The State holds the power to introduce compulsory service for such persons in order to stop this practice from happening. But, the State is not allowed to discriminate on any basis. Human trafficking refers to buying or selling of human beings like

4 **Essential Services Maintenance Act** (ESMA) This act was established to ensure delivery of certain services, which if obstructed would affect the normal life of the people.

commodities. Sale of men, women or children of any age is prohibited. This right also bans the use of women for immoral purposes.

- **Prohibition of Employment of Underage Children** Under Article 24, the employment of children under the age of 14 in factories, industries, mines or other such hazardous work places is illegal and punishable. The practice of bonded labour has been declared unlawful.

4. Right to Freedom of Religion

(Articles 25 to 28)

Right to Freedom of Religion include freedom of conscience and free propagation, freedom to manage religious affairs, freedom from payment of taxes and freedom from attending religious instruction

- **Freedom of Conscience and Free Propagation** According to Article 25, all citizens of India have the freedom of conscience and the right to **profess**[5], practise, and **propagate**[6] their religion.
- **Freedom to Manage Religious Affairs** Every religious community has following rights to management, guaranteed by Article 26
  - They can maintain institutions for charitable purposes.
  - They can manage their own affairs in matters of religion.
  - They can own and acquire movable and immovable property.
  - They can administer such property in accordance with law.
- **Freedom from Payment of Taxes** According to Article 27, no person can be morally or forcefully compelled to pay taxes for the propagation of a particular religion. In other words, the taxes can be used for the promotion or maintenance of all religions.
- **Freedom from Attending Religious Instruction** According to Article 28, if any religious institution or body is maintained wholly from State funds, then they are prohibited to profess any religious instructions. But, State-aided or State-recognised institutions are relieved from this rule. However, no person can be absolutely required to take part in such instructions unless they give their consent. In case of minor, the consent of his guardian has to be obtained.

5. Cultural and Educational Rights

(Articles 29 and 30)

India is a vast and **multilingual**[7] state. Each region include people with variety of cultural norms, traditions and identities. It is thus appreciable for the government to grant the following cultural and educational rights to minorities and backward communities

- **Right to Conserve Language, Script and Culture** Under Article 29, minorities and other communities have the right to conserve their unique language, script and culture. They are allowed to enter and make use of any State maintained educational institutions without discrimination based on caste, colour, religion, creed or sex.
- **Right to Establish Educational Institutions** According to Article 30, minorities have the right to establish and administer any educational institutions of their choice. They cannot be discriminated against for admission in State owned or maintained educational institutions. No person can be forcefully kept away from education or made to learn anything that doesn't fit in their own cultural framework.

6. Right to Constitutional Remedies

(Article 32)

The Right to Constitutional Remedies is given to the people to appeal to the Judiciary (Supreme Court) to enforce their other Fundamental Rights. This is done to safeguard the rights of the people and check any arbitrary action of the State. In true form, this is not a right, but a remedy. Dr BR Ambedkar referred to this right as **the heart and soul of the Constitution.**

Under Article 32, when any of the Fundamental Rights is violated, then citizens can directly approach the Supreme Court or the High Court. Both courts have the power to issue writs for the enforcement of the rights.

A 'writ' is a formal written order issued by the Supreme Court and the High Courts to provide legal remedies to individuals who do not obtain adequate protection under ordinary laws. Writs are named in Latin.

5 **Profess** To practice something as a profession.
6 **Propagate** To spread and promote.
7 **Multilingual** In using several languages.

The most important writs are

- **Habeas Corpus** In literary sense, it means, 'To have the body'. This writ issues the order of producing the detainee in court. It also orders the State or officer to tell the detainee, the time and cause of his arrest. If the Supreme Court regard the arrest unnecessary or unlawful, it has the power to release the detainee at once. This safeguards the personal freedom of a citizen.
- **Mandamus** In literary sense, it means, 'we order.' This writ is a command from a higher court to a lower court or administrative officers to perform their duties.
- **Prohibition** This writ is an order issued by a higher court to a subordinate court to stop the proceeding on any case or trial. This writ is issued on the ground of excess of jurisdiction, absence of jurisdiction or for acting in violation of principle of natural justice.
- **Certiorari** This writ is an issue of order from a higher court to a subordinate court to handover the records and information of a particular case. This is different from the prohibition writ in one sense. Writ of Prohibition is issued when proceedings are going on, but writ of Certiorari is issued after the lower court has already issued a conclusion.
- **Quo-Warranto** In literary sense, it means, 'by what order'. The purpose of the writ is to prevent a person from holding an office, which he is not legally entitled to hold. The court demands him to show under what authority he has claimed it. If the court finds his explanation wrong or insatisfactory, it can remove him from office.

Right to Privacy

It was declared as a Fundamental Right by the Supreme Court on 24th August, 2017. It is an element to restrict governmental and private actions that threaten the privacy of individuals. It protects individuals from the inspection of the state in their home, of their reproductive choice, their movements, food habits, etc. However, the state can impose restrictions on this right to protect state's legal interests.

Fundamental Duties

The Fundamental Duties of citizens were added to the Constitution by the 42nd Amendment Act, 1976 upon the recommendations of the Swaran Singh Committee and inserted in Article 51A of Part IVA of the Constitution. Earlier, there were ten Fundamental Duties but now there are eleven Fundamental Duties.

Note : *The eleven Fundamental Duties are already discussed in Chapter 1 : Our Constitution and its Features.*

Importance of Fundamental Duties

- They serve as a warning against the anti-national and anti-social activities like burning the national flag, destroying public properties.
- They warn citizens to do and not to do certain things in the interest of their country.
- They protect and awaken the people to their cultural heritage.
- They control anti-social elements in society.
- They strengthen national harmony by stirring up patriotism.

Evaluation of Fundamental Duties

Fundamental Duties are critised by some of the following arguments

- Some of the Fundamental Duties are already mentioned in the Civil and Criminal laws of the land. So, it seems like a repetition.
- The duties are not legally enforceable.
- Some of the duties are vaguely worded. Words like 'scientific temperament', 'humanism' and 'composite culture' can be interpreted differently.

In spite of the above criticism, Fundamental Duties are of extreme importance. The performance of duties calls for desirable change in every Indian. It aims to develop national character and spirit. The duties call upon Indian citizens to strive for self-excellence and self-improvement. They talk about not only the betterment of the society, but also the betterment of an individual. To maintain a balance between personal liberties and national integrity, a combination of rights and duties is required.

Check Your LEARNING...

1. Write any one of the essential Freedom guaranteed to the citizens under Article 19.
2. Name the Fundamental Rights that aims at the preservation of culture, language and script of the minorities.
3. Name the courts which can issue writs.
4. Write two importance of Fundamental Duties.

QUiCK Revision

- Fundamental Rights are the basic resources of social life that are essential for the all-round development of an individual.
- Fundamental Rights are unchangeable, universal, justiciable, non-absolute and allowed to be suspended.
- Fundamental Rights have certain features that separate them from other non-linear rights.
- There are six Fundamental Rights, namely - Right to Equality, Right to Freedom, Right against Exploitation, Cultural and Educational Rights, Right to Freedom of Religion and Right to Constitutional Remedies.
- Right to Equality includes equality before law, prohibition of discrimination, equality of opportunity, abolition of untouchability and abolition of titles.
- Right to Freedom includes six basic freedoms, protection in case of conviction for an offence, protection of life and personal liberty and protection against arrest and detention.
- Right against Exploitation includes prohibition of slavery, prohibition against human trafficking and prohibition of child labour.
- Right to Freedom of Religion includes freedom of conscience and free propagation, freedom to manage religious affairs, freedom from payment of taxes for religious promotions and no religious instructions in state funded institutions.
- Cultural and Educational Rights include right to conserve language, script and culture and right to establish educational institutions.
- There are five kinds of writs-Habeas Corpus, Mandamus, Prohibition, Certiorari and Quo-Warranto.
- The Fundamental Duties were inserted in Article 51 A of Part IV of the Constitution, by the 42nd Amendment Act, 1976.
- There are eleven Fundamental Duties.
- Even though some critics argue about their importance, Fundamental Duties are vital in keeping the balance of the nation.

Chapter Practice

Section-I

Multiple Choice Questions

1. Fundamental rights are incorporated in which part of the Constitution?
(a) IIIrd (b) IVth
(c) IInd (d) Vth

Ans. (a) IIIrd

2. 'Equal Protection of Law' comes under which Article of Indian Constitution?
(a) 12 (b) 13
(c) 14 (d) 15

Ans. (c) 14

3. Which of the following article deals with Right to Education?
(a) Article 19 (b) Article 20
(c) Article 21 (d) Article 21A

Ans. (d) Article 21 A

4. Which Article is referred by Dr BR Ambedkar as 'the heart and soul of the Constitution'?
(a) Article 19 (b) Article 21
(c) Article 14 (d) Article 32

Ans. (d) Article 32

5. Complete the given analogy.
Prohibition of Forced Labour : Article 23 : : ? : Prohibition of Employment of underage Children
Choose the correct option.
(a) Article 22 (b) Article 24
(c) Article 25 (d) Article 26

Ans. (b) Article 24

6. Complete the given analogy.
To have the body : Habeas Corpus :: We Order : ?
Choose the correct option.
(a) Prohibition (b) Quo-Warranto
(c) Certiorari (d) Mandamus

Ans. (d) Mandamus

7. Replace the underline word.
The Fundamental duties of a citizens were added to the Constitution by the <u>44th Amendment Act, 1972.</u>
Choose the correct option.
(a) 42nd Amendment Act, 1992
(b) 43rd Amendment Act, 1976
(c) 42nd Amendment Act, 1976
(d) 44th Amendment Act, 1972

Ans. (c) 42th Amendment Act, 1976

8. Complete the following table.

Abolition of untouchability	Article 17
?	Article 18

Codes
(a) Equality of Opportunity
(b) Prohibition of Discrimination
(c) Equality before Law
(d) Abolition of Titles

Ans. (d) Abolition of Titles

9. Complete the following table.

Protection of life	Article 21
Protection in case of conviction for an offense	?

Codes
(a) Article 20 (b) Article 19
(c) Article 22 (d) Article 23

Ans. (a) Article 20

10. Which of the following is/are feature/features of Fundamental Rights?
(i) Changeable (ii) Universal
(iii) Not absolute
Codes
(a) (i) and (ii)
(b) (ii) and (iii)
(c) (i) and (iii)
(d) All of the above

Ans. (b) (ii) and (iii)

11. Match the following.

	List I (Fundamental Rights)	List II (Articles)
A.	Right to Conserve Language, Script and Culture	1. Article 30
B.	Right to establish Educational Institutions.	2. Article 27
C.	Right to Constitutional Remedies	3. Article 29
D.	Freedom from Payment of Taxes	4. Article 32

Codes

	A	B	C	D
(a)	3	2	4	1
(b)	3	1	4	2
(c)	2	3	4	1
(d)	1	2	3	4

Ans. (b)

Section-II

Very Short Questions

1. What are Fundamental Rights?

Ans. Fundamental Rights are the basic resources of social life that are essential for the all-round development of an individual.

2. Who can bring changes in the Fundamental Rights?

Ans. The Parliament can bring changes in the Fundamental Rights.

3. Why are Fundamental Rights universal in nature?

Ans. Fundamental Rights are universal in nature because they do not discriminate a citizen on the basis of sex, creed, caste, colour, religion, faith, place of residence or education.

4. What does justiciable mean?

Ans. Justiciable means that citizens can file a suit in the High Court or Supreme Court if their rights are violated.

5. Are Fundamental Rights absolute?

Ans. Fundamental Rights are not absolute. This means that freedom is not unlimited.

6. Name one factor which may lead to suspension of Fundamental Rights.

Ans. War or external aggression may lead to suspension of Fundamental Rights.

7. How many Fundamental Rights are in the Constitution of India?

Ans. There are six Fundamental Rights in the Constitution of India.

8. Which Articles constitute the Right to Equality?

Ans. Articles 14,15,16,17 and 18 constitute the Right to Equality.

9. Article 15 prohibits discrimination on which grounds?

Ans. Article 15 prohibits discrimination on grounds of caste, creed, sex, race, colour or faith.

10. Which Act abolished untouchability?

Ans. Untouchability Offences Act of 1955 abolished untouchability.

11. Which Articles constitute the Right to Freedom?

Ans. Articles 19, 20, 21 and 22 constitute the Right to Freedom.

12. Which Fundamental Rights was added to the list by the 86th Amendment Act, 2002?

Ans. Right to Education (Article 21A) was added by the 86th Amendment Act of 2002. It provide free and compulsory education to all children of the age of 6 to 14 years.

13. Which Fundamental Rights will be violated if a student from an OBC community is disqualified from taking part in examinations?

Ans. Right to Education and Right to Equality will be violated if a student from an OBC community is disqualified from taking part in examinations.

14. Name any one Right given to a person under Preventive Detention.

Ans. Right to make representation against the detention order.

15. Which Articles constitute the Right against Exploitation?

Ans. Articles 23 and 24 constitute the Right against Exploitation.

16. Which Articles constitute the Right to Freedom of Religion?

Ans. Articles 25, 26, 27 and 28 constitute the Right to Freedom of Religion.

17. Which institutions are banned from giving religious instructions?

Ans. Wholly state funded institutions are banned from giving religious instructions.

18. Which Articles constitute Cultural and Educational Rights?

Ans. Articles 29 and 30 constitute Cultural and Educational Rights.

19. What does minority communities can preserve?

Ans. Minority communities can preserve their unique language, culture and script.

20. What are Constitutional Remedies?

Ans. The rights to appeal to Supreme Court for enforcement of other Fundamental Rights are constitutional remedies.

21. What is writ?

Ans. A writ is a formal written order issued by the Supreme Court and the High Courts to provide legal remedies to individuals, who do not obtain adequate protection under ordinary laws.

22. When was the 11th Fundamental Duty added to the Constitution?

Ans. The 11th Fundamental Duty was added in 2002.

23. Name any one reason why Fundamental Duties are important.

Ans. Fundamental Duties are important as they protect and awaken the people to their cultural and heritage.

24. Name any two words present in the Fundamental Duties that are subject to interpretation.

Ans. Scientific temperament and humanism are subject to interpretation.

Structured Questions

1. Discuss Right to Equality with reference to
   (i) Prohibition of Discrimination
   (ii) Abolition of Untouchability
   (iii) Abolition of titles
   (iv) Equality before Law

Ans. (i) Prohibition of Discrimination falls under Article 15 and dictates that the state cannot discriminate against any individual on the basis of caste, colour, creed, sex, religion, place of birth etc. All people have the right to go to shops, public places, hotels, parks, educational institutions, entertainment centers, etc. They can also freely use any public services like roads, buses, trains, metros, etc.

(ii) Abolition of Untouchability falls under Article 17 declares that, "Untouchability is abolished and its practice in any form is forbidden." Any person or community preventing any other person from entering a public place of worship, public well, public transport system or public toilets, etc can be punishable by law. The Untouchability Offences Act of 1955 (amended in 1976) penalties the act of untouchability with imprisonment of six months and fine of up to ₹ 500.

(iii) Abolition of Titles falls under Article 18. According to this article, the State is prohibited to confer any titles like Raja, Maharaja, Rai Sahib, Khan Bahadur, etc. These titles are considered a negation of equal status for all. Citizens of India are also not allowed to accept any titles from foreign states.
Titles can only be conferred for military, sports or academic distinctions. For example, Bharat Ratna, Padma Bhushan, Padma Shri, Paramvir Chakra, Vir Chakra, Jeevan Raksha and Arjuna Award.

(iv) Equality before law basically means that all persons are equal in the eyes of the law. This right falls under Article 14 and gurantees equal protection of law within the territory of India.

2. Discuss Right to Freedom with reference to
   (i) Six basic freedoms
   (ii) Protection of life and personal liberty
   (iii) Protection in case of conviction for an offence
   (iv) Protection against arrest and detention.

Ans. (i) The six basic freedoms are
   (a) Freedom of speech and expression.
   (b) Freedom to assemble peacefully and without arms.
   (c) Freedom to form associations or unions.
   (d) Freedom of movement throughout India.
   (e) Freedom to reside and settle in any part of India.
   (f) Freedom to practice any occupation or carry out any profession.

(ii) Article 21 states that no person can be deprived of their life or personal liberty except through a procedure prescribed by law. Personal liberty comprise of the right of the person to like or dislike a thing, choices of food and dress, hobbies, way of living, preference in art and culture, etc.

(iii) Under Article 20, any person who is accused or convicted for an offence has three protections. These are
   (a) The person cannot be punished except for a violation of law. Also, they cannot be given a greater penalty than what is prescribed by the law in relation to the crime committed.
   (b) The person cannot be punished or prosecuted for the same offence more than once.
   (c) No person accused of any offence shall be compelled to be a witness against himself.

(iv) Protection against arrest and detention can be provided in the following ways
   - **Ordinary Circumstances** A person arrested under ordinary circumstances has the right to be informed about the cause of offence and to be defended by a lawyer of his choice and have the time to prepare a case.
   - **Preventive Detention** It refers to detention of a person without trial in order to prevent them from committing further crimes.

3. In the context of Fundamental Rights, answer the following
   (i) Name the six Fundamental Rights.
   (ii) Why are they called Fundamental Rights?
   (iii) Explain Right to Freedom of Religion.
   (iv) Explain the 'Right against Exploitation'.

Ans. (i) The six Fundamental Rights are
   (a) Right to Equality
   (b) Right to Freedom
   (c) Right against Exploitation
   (d) Right to Freedom of Religion
   (e) Cultural and Educational Rights
   (f) Rights to Constitutional Remedies

(ii) Fundamental rights are called 'fundamental' because these freedoms are essential for the progress of an individual, are enforceable in the courts of law and cannot be altered or abolished by any ordinary legislature.

(iii) Right to Freedom of Religion include the following
   - **Freedom of Conscience and Free Propagation** According to Article 25, all citizens of India have the freedom of conscience and the right to profess, practise, and propagate their religion.
   - **Freedom to Manage Religious Affairs** Every religious community has following rights to management, guaranteed by Article 26
     - They can maintain institutions for charitable purposes.
     - They can manage their own affairs in matters of religion.
     - They can own and acquire movable and immovable property.
     - They can administer such property in accordance with law.

- **Freedom from Payment of Taxes** According to Article 27, no person can be morally or forcefully compelled to pay taxes for the propagation of a particular religion.
- **Freedom from Attending Religious Instruction** According to Article 28, if any religious institution or body is maintained wholly from State funds, then they are prohibited to profess any religious instructions.

(iv) The 'Right against Exploitation' include the following

- **Prohibition of Forced labour and traffic in human beings** Article 23 provides freedom from slavery, beggary or any other forms of forced labour. The State holds the power to introduce compulsory service for such persons in order to stop this practice from happening. But, the State is not allowed to discriminate on any basis. Human trafficking refers to buying or selling of human beings like commodities. Sale of men, women or children of any age is prohibited. This right also bans the use of women for immoral purposes.
- **Prohibition of Employment of Underage Children** Under Article 24, the employment of children under the age of 14 in factories, industries, mines or other such hazardous work places is illegal and punishable. The practice of bonded labour has also been declared unlawful.

4. With reference to the Right to Constitutional Remedies, answer the following questions

(i) Why is this right called the heart and soul of the Constitution?

(ii) Explain Habeas Corpus.

(iii) Explain Certiorari.

(iv) Explain Quo-Warranto.

Ans. (i) The Right to Constitutional Remedies is called the heart and soul of the Constitution by Dr BR Ambedkar as it makes other rights effective. According to this right, when any of the other Fundamental Rights are violated, then citizens can directly approach the Supreme Court or the High Court. Both courts have the power to writs (Habeas Corpus, Mandamus, Prohibition, Quo-Warranto and Certiorari) for the enforcement of the rights.

(ii) In literary sense, Habeas Corpus means, 'to have the body'. This writ issues the order of producing the detainee in court. It also orders the State or officer to tell the detainee, the time and cause of his arrest. If the Supreme Court regard the arrest unnecessary or unlawful, it has the power to release the detainee at once. This safeguards the personal freedom of a citizen.

(iii) Certiorari is an issue of order from a higher court to a subordinate court to handover the records and information of a particular case. This is different from the prohibition writ in one sense. Writ of Prohibition is issued when proceedings are going on, but writ of Certiorari is issued after the lower court has already issued a conclusion.

(iv) Quo-Warranto in literary sense means, 'by what order'. The purpose of this writ is to prevent a person from holding an office, which he is not legally entitled to hold. The court demands him to show under what authority he has claimed it. If the court finds his explanation wrong or insatisfactory, it can remove him from office.

5. With reference to the significance of Fundamental Duties, answer

(i) "Critics doubt whether inclusion of Fundamental Duties serve any purpose." Give reasons.

(ii) Why are Fundamental Duties important?

(iii) What are the eleven Fundamental Duties?

Ans. (i) Critics sometimes debate about whether the inclusion of the Fundamental Duties actually serve any purpose. Reasons for this are

- Some of these duties are already mentioned in the Civil and Criminal laws of the land. So, it seems like a repetition.
- The duties are not legally enforceable.
- Some of the duties are vaguely worded. Words like 'scientific temperament', 'humanism' and 'composite culture' can be interpreted differently.

(ii) Fundamental Duties are important because

- They make the citizens awarable of their social and economic obligations.
- They warn them to do and not to do certain things in the interest of their country.
- To protect and awaken the people to their cultural heritage.
- To control anti-social elements in society.
- To strengthen national harmony by stirring up patriotism.

(iii) The eleven fundamental duties are

(a) To abide by the Constitution and respect its ideals, institutions, the national flag and the national anthem.

(b) To cherish and follow the noble ideals which inspired our national struggle for freedom.

(c) To uphold and protect the sovereignty, unity and integrity of India.

(d) To defend the country and render national service when called upon to do so.

(e) To promote harmony and the spirit of common brotherhood amongst all the people of India transcending religious, linguistic and regional diversities, to renounce practices derogatory (abusive) to the dignity of women.

(f) To value and preserve the rich heritage of composite culture.
(g) To protect and improve the natural environment including forests, lakes, rivers and wildlife and to have compassion for living creatures.
(h) To develop the scientific temper, humanism and the spirit of inquiry and reform.
(i) To safeguard public property and to abjure violence.
(j) To strive towards excellence in all spheres of individual and collective activity, so that the nation constantly rises to higher endeavour and achievement.
(k) It is the duty of the parents or guardians to make sure their children between the age of 6 and 14 years get enough opportunities for education.

Chapter Assessment

Section-I

Multiple Choice Questions

1. Which among the following authorities decides 'how far the Fundamental Rights can apply to the Members of the armed forces in India?
   (a) President of India (b) Parliament
   (c) Armed Forces (d) Supreme Court
2. Supreme Court has made the right to free education as the part of which of the following rights?
   (a) Right to Life
   (b) Right against Exploitation
   (c) Right to Freedom of Speech and Expression
   (d) Cultural and Educational Rights
3. Which of the following is not a correct statement with respect to Freedom of Speech and Expression in India?
   (a) It is enshrined in Part III of the Constitution.
   (b) It is not an absolute right to express one's thoughts freely.
   (c) It can not be curtailed by legislation.
   (d) It can be suspended in emergency.
4. Fundamental duties have been added to the Constitution in accordance with the recommendation of
   (a) Sarkaria Commission
   (b) Mandal Commission
   (c) Swarn Singh Committee
   (d) Kasturirangan Committee

Section-II

Very Short Questions

1. Define Fundamental Rights.
2. Which Rights constitute the Right to Equality?
3. Which Right is exercised if a group of citizens are holding a meeting?
4. Name any two fundamental freedoms.
5. What does the Constitution stipulate regarding the education of minorities in India?
6. What is the writ of Mandamus?
7. Why did the Constitution abolish the old system of conferring titles and honours?
8. What is preventive detention?
9. What does the Constitution say about slavery?
10. Which Fundamental Right is violated when a child of age 12 is employed in a factory?

Structured Questions

1. Answer the following questions based on Fundamental Rights.
   (i) Explain the Right to Equality.
   (ii) Explain about any two freedom guaranteed under the Right to Freedom of Religion.
   (iii) Explain any two writs of Right to Constitutional Remedies.
   (iv) Explain about Right to Life
2. Write short notes on
   (i) Right to Freedom
   (ii) Right against Exploitation
   (iii) Educational Rights
   (iv) Explain the Right of Equality and Opportunity.
3. In the context of Fundamental Duties , answer the following
   (i) Mention any three duties of Indian citizens.
   (ii) What are the importance of Fundamental Duties in our Constitution?
   (iii) Give some arguments about Fundamental Duties.
   (iv) Fundamental Duties were inserted in which part of Constitution and on whose recommendation, they were added and by which Constitutional Amendment?

CHAPTER 03

Directive Principles of State Policy

SYLLABUS

Directive Principles of State Policy (meaning), Difference between Fundamental Rights and Directive Principles

Meaning of Directive Principles of State Policy

The Directive Principles are the guidelines to be followed by the government in the governance of the country. They are called Directive Principles because before making laws, the government has to take them in consideration.

It aims to ensure social, economic and legal justice to every Indian. These principles give a positive assurance to the people for a bright future. These principles are not found in any other Constitution of the world except those of India and Ireland.

Sources of Directive Principles

The framers of the Constitution were inspired by five different sources at the time of drafting of the Constitution, which are

- Constitution of the Irish Republic that contains the Principles of Social Policy for the guidance of legislators.
- The Declaration of the Rights of Men and Citizens of revolutionary France.
- The ideals of Mahatma Gandhi.
- Charter of Human Rights, that was framed by the United Nations.
- The Universal Declaration of Human Rights that was adopted by the United Nations when the Constituent Assembly was deliberating over the Indian Constitution.

Classification of Directive Principles

Directive Principles can be classified into three categories, which are

(i) **Socialist Principles (Articles 38, 39, 41, 42 and 43)** These principles reflect the ideology of socialism.

The aims of these principles are

- to promote the welfare of the people.
- to minimise inequalities in income, status, facilities and opportunities.
- to secure the right to adequate means of livelihood for all citizens.
- the equitable distribution of material resources of the community for the common goods.

- prevention of concentration of wealth and means of production.
- equal pay for equal work for men and women.
- opportunities for healthy development of children.

(ii) **Gandhian Principles (Articles 40, 43, 45, 46, 47 and 48)** These principles are based on Gandhian ideology. These principles represent the programme of reconstruction established by Gandhiji during the national movement. Some provisions such as to promote village panchayats, cottage industries, the education and economic interests of SCs, STs and other weaker sections of the society, reflect the Gandhian Principles.

(iii) **Liberal-Intellectual Principles** Following provisions reflect these principles

- To secure for all citizens a **Uniform Civil Code**[1] (Article 44).
- To organise agriculture and animal husbandry on modern and scientific lines (Article 48).
- To protect and improve the environment and to safeguard forests and wildlife (Article 48 A).
- To protect monuments, places and objects of artistic historic interest which are declared to be of national importance (Article 49).
- To separate the judiciary from the executive in the public services of the State (Article 50).
- To promote international peace and security and maintain just and honourable relations between nations (Article 51).

Implementation of Directive Principles

The implementation of Directive Principles of State Policy can be seen in the following reforms of Union and State Governments

Welfare State

The Directive Principles of State Policy emphasise that the goal of the Indian polity is a Welfare State where the state has a positive duty to ensure its citizens social and economic justice and dignity to the individual. The Union and the State Governments have taken many steps and made many laws over the years to implement this Welfare State vision. Five Year Plans are also directed towards this goal.

Social Equality and Justice

- The Right to Education Act makes it mandatory for every child between the ages 6-14 to be provided with free education in all government and government aided schools. As part of the public-private partnership plan, private schools are required to reserve 25% of their seats for children belonging to economically weaker sections.
- Socially and economically weaker sections of the society are provided special scholarship.
- Scheduled Castes and Scheduled Tribes are provided with reserved seats in jobs and educational institutions.
- Untouchability has been made illegal and punishable by law.
- A major objective of our national policy according to the Five Year Plans is the upliftment of weaker sections of the society.

Economic Welfare

- The land reform programme has been implemented to remove the old **feudal**[2] socio-economic structure of rural India. The government has abolished the Zamindari system and has made the tillers of the soil the owners of their land.
- Nationalisation of major banks, insurance corporations and key industries to ensure that the material resources of the community are used to serve the common good.
- The Minimum Wages Act of 1948 (amended from time- to-time) ensures fair pay and equal pay for equal work.
- With the objective of raising the poorest families in the rural areas above the poverty line, the government launched the Integrated Rural Development Programme (IRDP) in 1978-79. Another such programme is the Jawahar Rozgar Yojana launched by late Prime Minister Rajiv Gandhi.
- Mahatma Gandhi National Rural Employment Guarantee Act (MGNREGA) 2005 was launched that provides assurance of a minimum of 100 days of paid labour for rural people.

1. **Uniform Civil Code** It means that all sections of the society irrespective of their religion will have similar personal laws governed by legal rights and not by religious laws.
2. **Feudal** According to resembling or denoting the system of Feudalism.

- Right to Fair Compensation and Transparency in Land Acquisition, Rehabilitation and Resettlement Bill 2013 was passed in September 2013.
  This Act established a law on land acquisition, as well as the rehabilitation and resettlement of those directly affected by the land acquisition in India.
  It ensures transparency in the process of acquisition of land to set up factories or buildings and fair compensation to those whose land has been taken away.
- The Parliament passed the National Food Security Act in 2013. The law ensures food and nutritional security to all the people by making adequate quantities of quality food accessible. According to the law, India can subsidise foodgrains for 67% of India's 1.2 billion population.
- **Jan Dhan Yojana** was launched on the 15th August, 2014. This scheme provides bank accounts to the poor. Each account will have a life insurance cover of ₹ 30000 adding to the 1 lakh accidental insurance benefit already available under the account. A Rupay enabled debit card can be used to access the account. This scheme aims at bringing thousands into the financial mainstream and freeing them from money lenders and **usurpers**[3]. It also gives them the benefit of insurance cover.
- Pradhan Mantri Fasal Bima Yojana was launched on 13th January, 2016.
- Pradhan Mantri Gramin Awas Yojana was launched to provide financial assistance for construction of *pucca* house to all houseless and those who are living in dilapidated houses.
- Some other schemes are Pradhan Mantri Samaan Nidhi Yojana, Pradhan Mantri Ujjwala Yojana and Ayushman Bharat Yojana.

Political, Legal and Administrative Reforms

- Panchayati Raj has been established in the remote villages to uplift the concept of local self-government.
- Free legal aid is given to those people, who cannot engage lawyers themselves. This has been done to ensure justice to all. Legal Aid and Advisory boards have been set-up in some states.
- 1/3rd of the total number of seats have been reserved for women in the Panchayat and local bodies.

Foreign Policy

- India is strongly against colonialism, **apartheid**[4] and racism. It has helped many countries to win their freedom struggle. It supported South Africa against apartheid.
- India completely follows all international laws. It has stood for settlement of international disputes by mutual understanding. It also tries its best to have honourable and justful relations with all countries, including China and Pakistan.
- India stands for total Nuclear Disarmament by all countries including the 5 big nations of the Nuclear Club. India has been firm against the attempts of some powerful countries for partial disarmament and wants nuclear power to be used for energy and peaceful purposes only.

Importance of Directive Principles

- Directive Principles provide a framework i.e. a social, political and economic programme for a modern socialist democratic state.
- They are responsible for giving guidelines to the government to make laws and draft their policies.
- They provide a sort of permanence in a democracy.
- They allow people to judge a government's performance.
- They direct the government to move towards the goal of having a Welfare State.
- They embody the ideas of liberty, justice, equality and fraternity.
- They enlighten the people and educate them about their expectations from the politicians they vote for.
- They provide direction to the courts in order to safeguard the rights of the citizens.
- They clearly layout the idea of social and economic order.

According to 42nd Amendment Act, 1976, if a law is made to implement Directive Principles, then it will not be declared unconstitutional even if it takes away any of the rights under Articles 14, 19 and 31. If there is any conflict between the Fundamental

3. **Usurpers** Someone who wrongfully takes someone else's place.
4. **Apartheid** A policy or system of segregation or discrimination on grounds of race.

Rights and Directive Principles, then the Directive Principle shall prevail because welfare of the people as a who is more significant than the welfare of an individual.

Criticism for Directive Principles

Some scholars have criticised the Directive Principles on the following basis

- **Non-Enforceable** The Directive Principles are not enforceable by law in any part of the country according to Article 37. This necessarily means that the citizens cannot bring their complaints and grievances to the courts of law if the government fails to implement these directives. But, on moral grounds, the government and the courts are required to take knowledge of these directives.
- **Lack of Resources** Lack of efficient resources is often cited as a reason for non-implementation of Directive Principles. These principles are considered noble and significant goals for the achievement of a welfare state, but cannot always be carried out effectively.
- **Lack of Classification** These principles are vague in nature because they have not been defined clearly. They aren't logically classified or arranged in any manner.
- **Lack of Time Limit** There is no set time limit for implementation of these Directive Principles. The Universal Primary Education is yet to be achieved. Women empowerment is yet to be implemented purposefully.

Difference between Fundamental Rights and Directive Principles

Fundamental Rights	Directive Principles
These are provided in Part III of the Constitution.	These are provided in Part IV of the Constitution.
They are justiciable.	They are not justiciable or enforceable by the law.
They are privileges in existence for the citizens to enjoy.	They are meant for the government to create certain privileges for the citizens.
They restrict the power of the state.	They are only mere directions to the state for the attainment of certain goals.
They aim to establish political democracy.	They aim to establish a Welfare State.
Their scope is limited as they are concerned with individual's rights.	Their scope is much wider because they deal with a wide range of subjects including international peace and security.

Check Your LEARNING...

1. Give any one source of Directive Principles?
2. Which principle advocates to promote International peace?
3. With what purpose Panchayati Raj has been established?
4. What do you mean by apartheid?
5. What do you mean by 'Directive Principles are not enforceable'?

QUiCK Revision

- Directive Principles are the guidelines to be followed by the government in the governance of the country.
- They are called Directive Principles because before making any laws, the government has to take them in consideration.
- The framers of the Constitution were inspired by five different sources at the time of drafting the principles.
- Directive Principles can be classified into 3 categories such as Socialist, Gandhian and Liberal-Intellectual.
- Directive Principles of State Policy emphasise that the goal of the Indian polity is a welfare state where the state has a positive duty to ensure to its citizens social and economic justice and dignity to the individual.
- Directive Principles have been implemented in the fields of social equality and justice, economic welfare, political, legal and administrative reforms and foreign policy.
- There are several reasons why Directive Principles of State Policy are important to the nation and its citizens.
- Some scholars have criticised the Directive Principles due to non-enforceable, lack of resources, lack of classification and lack of time limit.
- Fundamental Rights are provided in Part III of the Constitution whereas Directive Principles are provided in Part IV of the Constitution. Fundamental Rights aim to establish political democracy whereas Directive Principles aim to establish a Welfare State.

Chapter Practice

Section-I

Multiple Choice Questions

1. Which of the following Articles consists of equal pay for equal work for men and women?
(a) Article 38 (b) Article 37
(c) Article 39 (d) Article 45

Ans. (c) Article 39

2. Which of the following Articles in the Constitution state the Gandhian principle?
(a) Articles 40-48 (b) Articles 41-48
(c) Article 42 (d) Articles 40-51

Ans. (a) Articles 40-48

3. Complete the given analogy.
The Land Reforms : Economic Welfare ::
The Right to Education : ?
Choose the correct option.
(a) Welfare State (b) Social Equality and Justice
(c) Political Justice (d) Legal Reforms

Ans. (b) Social Equality and Justice

4. Replace the underlined word.
To separate the Judiciary from the executive in the public services of the state is a <u>Gandhian Principle</u>.
(a) Liberal–Intellectual Principle (b) Socialist Principle
(c) Marxist Principle (d) None of these

Ans. (a) Liberal-Intellectual Principle

5. Complete the following table.

To secure for all citizens a Uniform Civil Code	Article 44
To protect and improve the environment and to safeguard forests and wildlife	?

Choose the correct option.
(a) Article 45 (b) Article 48
(c) Article 48A (d) Article 46

Ans. (c) Article 48A

6. Complete the following table.

Integrated Rural Development Programme [IRDP]	1978-79
Jan Dhan Yojana	?

Choose the correct option.
(a) 2014 (b) 2016 (c) 2015 (d) 2013

Ans. (a) 2014

7. Consider the following statements and choose the correct options.
(i) National Food Security Act was passed in 2013.
(ii) Jan Dhan Yojana was launched in 2014.
(iii) Articles 36 to 51 deals with Directive Principles of State Policy.

Codes
(a) Only (i) (b) Both (i) and (ii)
(c) Both (ii) and (iii) (d) All of these

Ans. (d) All of these

8. Match the following.

	List I (Directive Principles of State Policy)	List II (Articles)
A.	To organise agriculture and animal husbandary on modern and scientific lines.	1. Article 49
B.	To separate the Judiciary from the Executive.	2. Article 48
C.	To promote international peace and security.	3. Article 51
D.	To protect monuments, places and objects of artistic historic interest.	4. Article 50

Codes

	A	B	C	D
(a)	2	3	4	1
(b)	1	2	3	4
(c)	2	4	3	1
(d)	4	3	2	1

Ans. (c)

Section-II

Very Short Questions

1. Name all the categories of Directive Principles.

Ans. Socialist, Gandhian and Liberal-Intellectual principles, are three categories of Directive Principles.

2. What are Five Year Plans dedicated towards?

Ans. Five Year Plans are dedicated towards making India a successful Welfare State.

3. Directive Principles have been implemented in which fields?

Ans. Directive Principles have been implemented in the fields of social equality and justice, economic welfare, political, legal and administrative and reforms foreign policy.

4. What does the Right to Education Act say?

Ans. The Right to Education Act makes it mandatory for every child between the ages 6-14 to be provided with free education in all government and government aided schools.

5. When was the Right to Fair Compensation and Transparency in Land Acquisition, Rehabilitation and Resettlement Bill passed?

Ans. Right to Fair Compensation and Transparency in Land Acquisition, Rehabilitation and Resettlement Bill was passed in September 2013.

6. Which Act was passed in 1948 to ensure equal pay for equal work?

Ans. To ensure equal pay for equal work the Minimum Wages Act was passed in 1948.

7. What is the full form of MGNREGA?

Ans. Mahatma Gandhi National Rural Employment Guarantee Act is the full form of MGNREGA.

8. How much of the foodgrains produced in India can be subsidised, according to the National Food Security Act?

Ans. 67% of the foodgrains produced in India can be subsidised according to National Food Security Act.

9. Name one country India has helped in international political matters.

Ans. India has helped South Africa in international political matters.

10. Give one example to show how Directive Principles have no time limit for enforcement.

Ans. The Universal Primary Education is yet to be achieved is the example to show how Directive Principles have no limit for enforcement.

Structured Questions

1. In reference to Directive Principles, answer the following
   (i) What are Directive Principles?
   (ii) What are the sources of the Directive Principles?
   (iii) Explain the categories of DPSPs.

Ans. (i) The Directive Principles are the guidelines to be followed by the government in the governance of the country. They are called Directive Principles because before making laws, the government has to take them in consideration. Articles 36 to 51 in Part IV of our Constitution deal with the Directive Principles of State Policy. These principles give directions to the state to undertake certain policies and programmes for the welfare of the people. They also give a positive assurance to the people for a bright future.

(ii) The framers of the Constitution were inspired by five different sources at the time of drafting of the Constitution, which are

- Constitution of the Irish Republic that contains the Principles of Social Policy for the guidance of legislators.
- The Declaration of the Rights of Men and Citizens of revolutionary France.
- The ideals of Mahatma Gandhi.
- Charter of Human Rights, that was framed by the United Nations.
- The Universal Declaration of Human Rights that was adopted by the United Nations when the Constituent Assembly was deliberating over the Indian Constitution.

(iii) Directive Principles can be classified into three categories, which are

(a) **Socialist Principles (Articles 38, 39, 41, 42 and 43)** These principles reflect the ideology of socialism. Some aims of these principles are
- to promote the welfare of the people.
- to minimise inequalities in income, status, facilities and opportunities.
- to secure the right to adequate means of livelihood for all citizens.

(b) **Gandhian Principles (Articles 40, 43, 45, 46, 47 and 48)** These principles are based on Gandhian ideology. These principles represent the programme of reconstruction established by Gandhiji during the national movement.

(c) **Liberal-Intellectual Principles** Some provisions that reflect these principles are
- To secure for all citizens a Uniform Civil Code (Article 44).
- To organise agriculture and animal husbandry on modern and scientific lines (Article 48).
- To protect and improve the environment and to safeguard forests and wildlife (Article 48 A).

2. In reference to the implementation of Economic Welfare, answer the following
   (i) Name some programmes launched by the government to ensure employment in rural areas.
   (ii) Implementation on Political and Legal matters.
   (iii) Implementation in Foreign Policy.
   (iv) Implementation of Social Equality and Justice.

Ans. (i) With the objective of raising the poorest families in the rural areas above the poverty line, the government launched the Integrated Rural Development Programme (IRDP) in 1978-79. Another such programme is the Jawahar Rozgar Yojana launched by late Prime Minister Rajiv Gandhi. There is also the Mahatma Gandhi National Rural Employment Gurantee Act (MGNREGA) 2005, that provides assurance of a minimum of 100 days of paid labour for rural people.

(ii) For political and legal matters, the following have been impemented
- Panchayati Raj has been established in the remote villages to uplift the concept of local self-government.
- Free legal aid is given to those people, who cannot engage lawyers themselves. This has been done to ensure justice to all. Legal Aid and Advisory boards have been set-up in some states.

- 1/3rd of the total number of seats have been reserved for women in the Panchayat and local bodies.

(iii) For foreign policy, the following have been implemented

- India is strongly against colonialism, apartheid and racism. It has helped many countries to win their freedom struggle. It supported South Africa against apartheid.
- India completely follows all international laws. It has stood for settlement of international disputes by mutual understanding. It also tries its best to have honourable and justful relations with all countries, including China and Pakistan.

(iv) Directive Principles are implemented for social equality and justice through following provisions

(a) Socially and economically weaker sections of the society are provided special scholarships. Scheduled Castes and Scheduled Tribes are provided with reserved seats in jobs and educational institutions.

(b) Untouchability has been made illegal and punishable by law.

3. Write short notes on

(i) What is the Jan Dhan Yojana?

(ii) Differentiate between Fundamental Rights and Directive Principles.

(iii) Why are Directive Principles important?

(iv) Mentions any two sources of Directive Principles.

Ans. (i) Jan Dhan Yojana was launched on 15th August, 2014. This scheme provides bank accounts to the poor. Each account will have a life insurance cover of ₹ 30000 adding to the 1 lakh accidental insurance benefit already available under the account. A Rupay enabled debit card can be used to access the account. This scheme aims at bringing thousands people into the financial mainstream and freeing them from moneylenders and usurpers. It also gives them the benefit of insurance cover.

(ii) Differences between Fundamental Rights and Directive Principles are

Fundamental Rights	Directive Principles
These are provided in Part III of the Constitution.	These are provided in Part IV of the Constitution.
They are justiciable.	They are not justiciable or enforceable by the law.
They are privileges in existence for the citizens to enjoy.	They are meant for the government to create certain privileges for the citizens.
They restrict the power of the state.	They are only mere directions to the state for the attainment of certain goals.
They aim to establish political democracy.	They aim to establish a Welfare State.
Their scope is limited as they are concerned with individual's rights.	Their scope is much wider because they deal with a wide range of subjects including international peace and security.

(iii) The Directive Principles are important because

- Directive Principles provide a framework i.e. a social, political and economic programme for a modern socialist democratic state.
- They are responsible for giving guidelines to the government to make laws and draft their policies.
- They provide a sort of permanence in a democracy.
- They allow people to judge a government's performance.
- They direct the government to move towards the goal of having a Welfare State.
- They embody the ideas of liberty, justice, equality and fraternity.

(iv) Refer to chapter theory page no. 25.

4. In lieu of the criticism around Directive Principles, explain the below mentioned

(i) Lack of resources

(ii) Lack of classification

(iii) Non-Enforceable

(iv) Lack of time limit.

Ans. (i) Lack of efficient resources is often cited as a reason for non-implementation of Directive Principles. These principles are considered noble and significant goals for the achievement of a welfare state, but cannot always be carried out effectively due to lack of resources.

(ii) Directive Principles are vague in nature because they have not been defined or classified clearly. They aren't logically classified or arranged in any manner. The declaration mixes up relatively unimportant issues with the most vital, economic and social questions.

(iii) Directive Principles are not enforceable by law in any part of the country according to Article 37. This necessarily means that the citizens cannot bring their complaints and grievances to the courts of law if the government fails to implement these directives. But, on moral grounds, the government and the courts are required to keep these Directive Principles into consideration.

(iv) There is no set time limit for implementation of Directive Principles. The Universal Primary Education is yet to be achieved. Women empowerment is yet to be implemented purposefully.

Chapter Assessment

Section-I

Multiple Choice Questions

1. Which Article states about Uniform Civil Code through out the country?
   (a) Article 48 (b) Article 44
   (c) Article 42 (d) Article 49
2. Which Amendment made elementary education for all children a fundamental right? Also choose the article added after that
   (a) 86th Amendment, Article 21A
   (b) 86th Amendement, Article 22
   (c) 80th Amendment, Article 40
   (d) 76th Amendment, Article 30
3. From which country has India borrowed DPSP?
   (a) USA (b) Ireland
   (c) France (d) Japan

Section-II

Very Short Questions

1. What are Directive Principles of State Policy?
2. List one source of the Directive Principles.
3. What principles have been directed to ensure economic quality? Mention any two of them.
4. How can people access their accounts according to the Jan Dhan Yojana?
5. What is the objective of the National Food Security Act, 2013 ?
6. India is strongly against which international issues?
7. Give one reason for the importance of Directive Principles.
8. Give one point of criticism received by Directive Principles.

Structured Questions

1. Write short notes on
   (i) National Food Security Bill
   (ii) Gandhian Principles
   (iii) Liberal-Intellectual Principles
   (iv) Socialist principle
2. Keeping in mind the implementation of Directive Principles, answer the following
   (i) How are socially or economically backward classes being given social equality and justice?
   (ii) How has the land reform policy changed India?
   (iii) How are political, legal and administrative reforms implemented for Welfare State?
   (iv) How DPSP are implemented in Foreign Policy?
3. Answer the following
   (i) "Scholars have often criticised Directive Principles." Give reasons.
   (ii) Differentiate between Fundamental Rights and Directive Principles.
   (iii) Explain 42nd Amendment Act, 1976 in detail.
   (iv) What is 86th Constitutional Amendment?

CHAPTER 04

Elections

SYLLABUS

Meaning, Composition and Functions of Election Commission of India
• Direct and Indirect election
• General election • Mid-term election and By-election

Meaning of Elections

The mechanism or procedure by which people choose their representatives at regular interval is called Election. Democracy is a government of the people, for the people and by the people. The people are the real source of sovereign power in a democracy. If people are not satisfied with the working of the government then they can change the government in the next term of elections. In a democracy, elections are held periodically i.e. after 3 to 5 years.

Need of Elections

Elections are necessary for the following reasons

- In order to choose the desired representatives, elections are necessary.
- The people get a greater choice of selection i.e. for whom to cast their vote.
- During the elections, people can learn and know about the ideologies of different political parties *via* their election manifestos.
- The elections uphold all the 6 fundamental rights given to the people of India. The right to vote can be accessed by any person of or above 18 years old, irrespective of race, creed, caste, religion, sex, etc. Candidates and elected representatives can use freedom of speech, freedom of expression, etc in their electoral journey.
- Elections help candidates to develop their leadership skills.
- The people have right to be able to decide who is going to rule the country or who is to be removed. This stimulates interest in the people about the well-being of the country.
- Any democracy without the rule of free and fair elections will be a **farce**[1]. Elections are needed by democracies to perform in the way which is in the best interest of the people of the country.

Types of Elections

Elections are of two types i.e. direct elections and indirect elections.

Direct Elections

In this type of elections, voters directly cast their votes in favour of their candidates. The members of the Lok Sabha (called MPs) and the members of the State Legislative Assemblies (called MLAs) are elected by direct system of election.

1. **Farce** A situation that is very badly organised or unfair.

The party (or combination of parties) having the largest number of legislators elect their leader from among themselves. This leader in the state is elected as the Chief Minister and in centre as the Prime Minister.

Indirect Elections

In this type of elections, the voter doesn't directly elect the candidate. The voter votes for a middle man, who then votes for the candidate on behalf of the voter. There is no contact between the voter and the candidate to be elected. The President, Vice-President, members of Rajya Sabha and State Legislative Councils are elected in this manner.

The President is elected by an Electoral College, which consists of elected MPs and MLAs. The Vice-President is elected indirectly by the members of the Lok Sabha and Rajya Sabha. Out of 250 Rajya Sabha members, 238 are elected by the elected members of the Legislative Assembly of each state. The remaining 12 are nominated by the President. In case of the Legislative Councils, the members are elected by the members of the Legislative Assembly from amongst people not in the assembly.

System of Elections in India

Three systems of elections are prevalent in India i.e., general elections, by-elections and mid-term elections

(i) **General Elections** The elections for the Lok Sabha and Vidhan Sabha in the states, that happen after every 5 years are called general elections. Elections to some State Legisative Assemblies might happen along with the Parliamentary General Elections.

(ii) **By-Elections** When a seat held by any member of Parliament or the Legislative Assembly of State falls vacant on account of death, resignation of member before completion of term; elections are held to fill up this vacancy. This election is called by-election. The person elected remains member for the unexpired term of the House.

(iii) **Mid-term Elections** When State Legislative Assembly or Lok Sabha is dissolved before the completion of a full 5 years term, elections need to be held. These are called mid-term elections. The new house elected will have a full 5 years term.

Constituencies

To conduct elections, the entire country is divided into fixed electoral areas with specific bodies of registered voters. These areas are called constituencies. Each constituency elects a representative for the State Assembly.

Five or six assembly constituencies grouped together to form a parliamentary constituency. In case of Municipal Election, constituencies are called **Wards.** Efforts are made to keep the size of the constituencies as equal as possible. When a change occurs in the strength of the population, the boundaries of the constituencies are revised. This is called **Delimitation** of the Constituencies.

Under Article 82, the Parliament enacts a Delimitation Act after every census. Following this, a Delimitation Committee is formed. This committee demarcates the boundaries of the constituencies of the Parliamentary constituencies, according to the Delimitation Act. This is done for ensuring that each state will have maximum representation in the Lok Sabha. The number of seats in the Lok Sabha is fixed at 550.

Types of Constituencies

There are three types of constituencies which are

- **Single-Member Constituency** In this type, there is one representative from each constituency. After the conduction of the elections, the candidate who gets the highest number of votes, becomes the one and only representative of that constituency. This system is simple and convenient. It also gives a stable majority in the legislature. Many democratic countries like India and England have single-member constituencies.
- **Multi-Member Constituency** In this type, there are a multiple number of representatives from each constituency. In this system, the voter has as many usable votes as the total number of candidates. If there are 5 candidates contesting the elections, each voter has 5 votes. The first 3 candidates have to secure the highest votes to win. This system is disadvantageous because many groups emerge in the legislature which creates difficulty in establishing stability. Germany, France and Italy had multi-member constituencies. They later moved over to single-member constituencies for ease.

- **Reserved Constituency** It is reserved for both Scheduled Castes and Scheduled Tribes in Parliamentary as well as Assembly elections. General candidates cannot contest in it and the voters have to choose from the candidates that belong to Scheduled Castes or Scheduled Tribes.

Check Your LEARNING...

1. State one point indicating necessity of elections.
2. When is a mid-term election held?
3. What are wards?
4. Why is Delimitation needed?

Election Commission

The Election Commission is an **statutory**[2] body responsible for the management of the elections. Its functions range from technical preparations to the declaration of results. This Commission is formed under Article 324(1) of the Constitution.

From 1950 to 1989, the Election Commission was a single member constitutional body. It was made a multi-member body in 1989.

Composition

The Commission has a Chief Election Commissioner and two other Election Commissioners. They are appointed by the President, upon the recommendations of the selection committee which comprises of Prime Minister, Union Cabinet Minister and Leader of Opposition of the largest opposition party in Lok Sabha. The Regional Election Commissioners in states are also appointed by the President.

Term of Office

In 1994, the Parliament passed an Act as laid down in Article 324 (5) of the Constitution. This Act stated the terms of office and the conditions of the Election Commission as

- The members of the Commission are appointed for a period of 6 years. If any member attains the age of 65 years, he has to vacate the office on the day of reaching this age, even if his term is still in effect.
- The salary of the Chief Election Commissioner and all other such commissioners shall be equal to and not more than a Supreme Court Judge.
- If there is any difference of opinion between the Chief Election Commissioner and the other members, then the conclusion is decided according to a majority vote.

Powers and Functions of Election Commission

The powers of Election Commission under the Representation of the People (Amendment) Act, 1996 are

- **Delimitation of Constituencies** The Election Commission divided the entire area (where elections will be held) into clear cut constituencies. This is done to make elections simple and organised.
- **Preparation of Electoral Rolls** The Election Commission prepares one electoral roll for every constituency. An electoral roll is a voter's list containing the name, father's name, age and sex of the voter.
- **Recognition of Political Parties** The Election Commission grants recognition to political parties. A political party can be recognised as a national party only if it is recognised in four or more states.
- **Allotment of Symbols** The Election Commission allots symbols to the recognised political parties and the candidates for election. The Commission may have reserved symbols and free symbols as well. Independent candidates or non-registered political parties can come and select a symbol of their choice based on first-come, first-serve basis.
- **Examination of Nomination Papers** The Election Commission examines the nomination papers of the candidates and can accept and reject them accordingly. This duty is performed by the Returning Officer who notifies the date, time and place for the formal scrutiny of nomination papers, to all contesting candidates.
- **Appointment of Polling Officers** The Election Commission assigns Polling Officers for every constituency. Each constituency is put under a 'Returning Officer' whose responsibility is to declare a candidate fit for contesting election.
- **Conduct of Elections** The Election Commission is obliged to conduct all the elections to the Parliament and State Assemblies. It is also required to supervise the elections to the office of the President and Vice-President of India.

2. **Statutory** Relating to an act passed by the legislative body.

- **Ensuring Free and Fair Elections** The Election Commission has to prescribe a code of conduct to guide the candidates and all other concerned persons. It ensures that votes are cast without any fear. It keeps a check on political parties which wrongly use their authority.
- **Publication of List of Contesting Candidates** The Election Commission publishes a proper list of contesting candidates, which is made known to everyone.
- **Declaration of Results** The Election Commission runs and supervises the counting of votes and the declaration of results.
- **Other Functions** The Election Commission prescribes a model code of conduct for the political parties and the candidates, which is used to be followed by them. It also advises the President or the Governor of the state about electoral matters, election disputes, disqualification of members, etc.

Independence of the Commission

The Constitution assures that the Election Commission can act as an independent body. For this, the following provisions are made

- The Chief Election Commissioner shall not be removed from his position except in the manner and the basis on which a Judge of Supreme Court can be removed. Other Election Commissioners cannot be removed without the recommendation of the Chief Election Commissioner.
- The conditions of service, salary, allowances and other facilities provided to Chief Election Commissioner and other Election Commissioners cannot be varied after their appointment and during their tenure.
- The President of India and the Governors of States have a legal duty to provide the Election Commission with as much staff as required for the conduction of elections. The Commission has a complete control on the staff on election duty.

Check Your LEARNING...

1. Who appoints the Election Commissioner?
2. Mention any one function of the Election Commission?
3. Who has to perform the function of preparing electoral rolls?
4. Why Election Commission acts as an independent body ?

QUiCK Revision

- Election is a procedure whereby persons are chosen, by voting, to represent the voters for running the government.
- There are two types of elections- direct elections and indirect elections.
- The three system of elections in India are general elections, by-elections and mid-term elections.
- Indian Lok Sabha and State Assemblies are elected for 5 years.
- The entire country is divided into fixed electoral areas with specific bodies of registered voters, called constituencies.
- There are three types of constituencies which are single member constituency, multi-member constituency and reserved constituency.
- The Election Commission is a statutory body that is responsible for the management of the elections.
- The Commission has a Chief Election Commissioner and two other Election Commissioners.
- In 1994, the Parliament passed an Act as laid down in Article 324 Clause 5 of the Constitution. This Act stated the terms of office and the conditions of the Election Commission.
- The Election Commission prepares electoral rolls, delimits constituencies, conducts elections, recognises political parties, allots symbols, ensures free and fair elections, appoints polling officers, examines nomination papers and declares results.
- The Constitution assures that the Election Commission can act as an independent body.

Chapter Practice

Section-I

Multiple Choice Questions

1. Why elections are necessary in democracy?
   (a) To choose the desired representatives.
   (b) People get a greater choice of selection.
   (c) It helps to develop leadership skills.
   (d) All of the above

Ans. (d) All of the above

2. Delimitation Commission comes under which Article of Indian Constitution?
   (a) 80 (b) 81 (c) 84 (d) 82

Ans. (d) 82

3. What is the maximum age up to which an Election Commissioner can hold office?
   (a) 60 years (b) 62 years
   (c) 58 years (d) 65 years

Ans. (d) 65 years

4. Complete the given analogy.
   Delimitation Commission : Article 82 : : ? : Article 324 (1)
   (a) Election Commission (b) Gram Panchayat
   (c) UPSC (d) Finance Commission

Ans. (a) Election Commission

5. Replace the underlined word to correct the sentence
   The Prime Minister is elected by an electoral college which consists of elected MPs and MLAs.
   (a) The Governor (b) The President
   (c) The Vice Presiden (d) The Speaker of Lok Sabha

Ans. (b) The President

6. Complete the following table.

Direct Elections	Member of Parliament [Lok Sabha]
Indirect Elections	?

Codes
(a) MLAs (b) Leader of Gram Panchayat
(c) MLCs (d) None of these

Ans. (c) MLCs (Member of Legislative Councils)

7. Consider the following statements about member of Rajya Sabha and select the correct option.
   (i) There are 250 seats in Rajya Sabha.
   (ii) 230 members are elected by the elected members of Legislative Assembly.
   (iii) Twelve members are elected by President.
   (iv) They have fixed tenure of 6 years.

Codes
(a) Only (i) (b) Both (i) and (ii)
(c) Only (iii) (d) All of these

Ans. (d) All of these

8. Match the following.

List-I	List-II
A. Article 82	1. Delimitation
B. Article 74	2. Council of Ministers to aid and advise the President
C. Article 324	3. Composition of Election Commission
D. Article 324(5)	4. Terms of office and conditions of the Election Commission

Codes

	A	B	C	D
(a)	1	2	3	4
(b)	4	3	2	1
(c)	3	1	4	2
(d)	2	4	1	3

Ans. (a)

Section-II

Very Short Questions

1. What is election?

Ans. Election is a procedure whereby representatives are chosen by voting to represent the voters for running the government.

2. How frequently are elections held in a democracy?

Ans. In a democracy, elections held at the interval of 3 to 5 years.

3. Who are MPs and MLAs?

Ans. The members of the Lok Sabha are called MPs and the members of the State Legislative Assemblies are called MLAs.

4. Name one position in Indian legislature that is filled by indirect elections.

Ans. The post of the President of India is filled by indirect elections.

5. What does the Electoral College do?

Ans. The Electoral College elects the Indian President and Vice President.

6. What are Constituencies?

Ans. For ease in elections, the entire country is divided into fixed electoral areas with specific bodies of registered voters. These areas are called Constituencies.

7. When is a Delimitation Act passed and by whom?

Ans. Delimitation Act is passed after every census, by the Parliament.

8. What is the maximum strength of the Lok Sabha?

Ans. The maximum strength of the Lok Sabha is 550.

9. How many types of constituencies exist?

Ans. Three types of constituencies exist i.e. Single Member Constituency, Multi-member Constituency and Reserved Constituency.

10. Name two countries with single member constituency.

Ans. India and England are two countries with single member constituency.

11. Name two countries that had multi-member constituencies.

Ans. Germany and Italy had multi-member constituencies.

12. The Election Commission is formed under which Article of the Constitution?

Ans. The Election Commission is formed under Article 324(1) of the Indian Constitution.

13. What is the composition of the Election Commission?

Ans. The Election Commission has a Chief Election Commissioner and two other Election Commissioners.

14. What is the tenure of members of Election Commission?

Ans. The members of Election Commission are appointed for 6 years.

15. How much salary is paid to the Chief Election Commissioner?

Ans. The Chief Election Commissioner is paid salary equal to and not more than a Supreme Court Judge.

16. What does an electoral roll have in it?

Ans. An electoral roll contains the name, father's or husband's name, age, sex and address of the voters.

17. What is the responsibility of a Returning Officer?

Ans. Each constituency is put under a 'Returning Officer' whose responsibility is to declare a candidate fit for contesting the election.

18. What is the fixed condition of service for the Election Commission?

Ans. Fixed condition of service means that the salary, allowances and other facilities provided to the commissioners cannot be varied after their appointment and during their tenure.

Structured Questions

1. With reference to the elections, answer the following
   (i) Explain the meaning of elections in brief.
   (ii) Why do democracies need elections?
   (iii) How are elections usually fought in modern societies?
   (iv) Why are elections important?

Ans. (i) The mechanism or procedure by which people choose their representatives at regular interval is called Election. Democracy is a government of the people, for the people and by the people. The people are the real source of sovereign power in a democracy. If people are not satisfied with the working of the government then they can change the government in the next term of elections. In a democracy, elections are held periodically i,e, after 3 to 5 years.

(ii) Elections are one of the most useful and mandatory features of a democratic nation. Without the expansion of elections, a nation would never truly be, of the people, for the people and by the people. In a democracy, people should have the right to choose their representatives either directly or indirectly to run the country. Election is a procedure whereby representatives are chosen, by voting, to represent the voters for running the government. In most cases, there are multiple choices of candidates for one post.

(iii) In modern societies, like ours, elections are almost always fought on party lines. Political parties are formed and the political party (or combination of parties) getting the highest amount of votes gets the opportunity to run the government.

(iv) Elections are important due to following reasons
   (a) People get opportunities to choose the desired candidates.
   (b) The people get a greater choice of selection i.e. for whom to cast their vote.
   (c) Elections let the people to know the ideologies of different political parties through their election manifestos.
   (d) It prepares stage to raise various issues for the well-being of the people.

2. On the basis of the types of elections, answer
   (i) What are direct elections?
   (ii) What are indirect elections?
   (iii) What is the system of elections for the Rajya Sabha and State Legislative Council?

Ans. (i) In direct elections, voters directly cast their votes in favour of their candidates. The members of the Lok Sabha and the State Legislative Assemblies are elected by direct system of election. All citizens above the age of 18 years are eligible to vote for electing their representatives to Lok Sabha, Vidhan Sabha and local bodies.

(ii) In Indirect elections, the voters do not directly elect their candidates. The voters first elect their candidates by direct election. These elected candidates caste their votes on behalf of their people and then the candidate is elected. The President, Vice-President, members of Rajya Sabha and State Legislative Councils are elected in this manner.

(iii) Indirect elections are held for the Rajya Sabha and State Legislative Council. Out of 250 members of the Rajya Sabha, 238 are elected by the elected members of the Legislative Assembly of each state. The remaining 12 are nominated by the President. In case of Legislative Councils, the members are elected by the members of Legislative Assembly of the concerned state.

3. Write short notes on
(i) General elections
(ii) By-elections
(iii) Mid-term elections

Ans. (i) The elections for the Lok Sabha and Vidhan Sabha in the states, that happen after every 5 years are called general elections. Elections to some State Legisative Assemblies might happen along with the Parliamentary General Elections.

(ii) When a seat held by any member of Parliament or the Legislative Assembly of State falls vacant on account of death, resignation of member before completion of term; elections are held to fill up this vacancy. This election is called by-election. The person elected remains member for the unexpired term of the House.

(iii) When State Legislative Assembly or Lok Sabha is dissolved before the completion of a full 5 years term, elections need to be held. These are called mid-term elections. The new house elected will have a full 5 years term.

4. On the basis of the Election Commission, answer
(i) What is the Election Commission?
(ii) What is the composition of the Commission?
(iii) Write any two terms of office that apply to the Commission.
(iv) Write any two functions of Election Commission?

Ans. (i) The Election Commission is a statutory body responsible for the management of the elections. Its functions range from technical preparations to the declaration of results. This Commission is formed under Article 324(1) of the Constitution.

(ii) The Commission has a Chief Election Commissioner and two other Election Commissioners. They are appointed by the President, but at the recommendations of the selection committee.
The Regional Election Commissioners are also appointed by the President.

(iii) Two terms of office that apply to the Election Commission are
(a) The members of the Commission are appointed for a period of 6 years. If any member attains the age of 65 years, he has to vacate the office on the day of reaching this age, even if his term is still in effect.
(b) The salary of the Chief Election Commissioner and all other such Commissioners shall be equal to and not more than a Supreme Court judge. They are also entitled to avail the benefit of pension.

(iv) Two functions of Election Commission are
(a) **Recognition of Political Parties** The Election Commission grants recognition to political parties. A political party can be recognised as a national party only if it is recognied in four or more states.
(b) **Allotment of Symbols** The Election Commission allots symbols to the recognised political parties and the candidates for election. The Commission may have reserved symbols and free symbol as well. Independent candidates or non-registered political parties can come and select a symbol of their choice based on first-come, first-serve basis.

5. On the basis of the system of constituencies, answer the following.
(i) What are constituencies?
(ii) Write three benefits of Delimitation.
(iii) Explain the concept of Delimitation.

Ans. (i) Refer to chapter theory page no. 34.

(ii) Following are the benefits of Delimitation
(a) It ensures proportional representation because the basis of delimitation is population.
(b) It make representatives accountable to their votes.
(c) It ensures broader geographical representation in the Parliament.

(iii) When a change occurs in the strength of the population, the boundaries of the constituencies are revised. This is called Delimitation of the Constituencies. Under Article 82, the Parliament enacts a Delimitation Act after every census. Following this, a Delimitation committee is formed. This committee demarcates the boundaries of the constituencies of the Parliamentary constituencies, according to the Delimitation Act. This is done simply to ensure that each state will have maximum representation in the Lok Sabha.

6. In reference to types of constituencies, answer
(i) What are Single-Member Constituencies?
(ii) What are Reserved Constituencies?
(iii) What are Multi-Member Constituencies?

Ans. (i) In single-member constituencies, there is one representative from each constituency. After the conduction of the elections, the candidate who gets the highest number of votes, becomes the one and only representative of that constituency.
This system is simple and convenient. It also gives a stable majority in the legislature.
Many democratic countries like India and England have single-member constituencies.

(ii) Reserved constituency is a constituency which is especially reserved for weaker section. Such weaker section are— SCs, STs, OBCs and women etc. On these seats persons belonging to concerned reserved category can contest the election. This system of reserved constituencies makes our democracy a real representative democracy.

(iii) In multi-member constituencies, there are a multiple number of representatives from each constituency. In this system, the voter has as many usable votes as the total number of candidates. If there are 5 candidates contesting the elections, each voter has 5 votes. The first 3 candidates have to secure the highest votes to win. This system is disadvantageous because many groups emerge in the legislature which creates difficulty in establishing stability. Germany, France and Italy had multi-member constituencies. They later moved over to single-member constituencies for ease.

7. Write short notes on
   (i) Recognition of political parties
   (ii) Allotment of symbols
   (iii) Declaration of election results
   (iv) Independence of the Election Commission.

Ans. (i) The Election Commission grants recognition to political parties. A political party can be recognised as a national party only if it is recognised in four or more states. Some major political parties recognised by the Election Commission are–Bharatiya Janata Party, Indian National Congress, Nationalist Congress Party, Bahujan Samaj Party, Communist Party of India.

(ii) Refer to chapter theory page no. 35.

(iii) The Election Commission runs and supervises the counting of votes and the declaration of results. At 5 pm on the polling day, after voting is over, the ballot boxes are sealed and placed under security. Counting starts in a day or two. Each party appoints their counting agents. The candidate with highest number of votes in each constituency is declared winner. In case of a tie, the Returning Officer decides winner via a draw.

(iv) The Constitution assures that the Election Commission can act as an independent body. For this, the following provisions are made

(a) The Chief Election Commissioner shall not be removed from his position except in the manner and grounds of that of a Supreme Court Judge. Other Election Commissioners cannot be removed without the recommendation of the Chief Election Commissioner.

(b) Conditions of service, salary, allowances and other facilities provided to the Chief Election Commissioner and other Election Commissioners cannot be varied after their appointment and during their tenure.

Chapter Assessment

Section-I

Multiple Choice Questions

1. How many systems of election are there in India?
   (a) 2 (b) 3 (c) 4 (d) 1
2. Which of the following countries has shifted from multi-member constituencies to single member constituencies?
   (a) Germany (b) Canada
   (c) England (d) India
3. Consider the following statements with reference to the Election commissioner
   (i) The commission has the power to set limits of campaign expenditure per candidate.
   (ii) It has the power to investigate inner-party democracy and regulations of Party finances.

   Which of the given statements is/are correct?
   (a) Only (i) (b) Only (ii)
   (c) Both (i) and (ii) (d) Neither (i) nor (ii)

Section-II

Very Short Questions

1. What are the two types of Elections?
2. What are wards?
3. Who elects the members of the Rajya Sabha?
4. Name any one country that shifted from multi-member constituency to single member constituency.
5. What security of service is provided to the Chief Election Commissioner?
6. Who allot the symbol to political parties?
7. Who is a Returning Officer?
8. How can the Election Commissioner be removed from his office?

Structured Questions

1. On the basis of the types of elections, answer the following.
   (i) How are the elections of President and Vice President of India held?
   (ii) What are the main points of difference between direct and indirect elections?
   (iii) Name any two legislative posts filled by direct elections and any two filled by indirect elections.
   (iv) What is mid-term elections?
2. With reference to power and functions of Election Commission, answer the following.
   (i) Explain the role of Election Commission in fixing the dates of elections and conducting the elections.
   (ii) What is the role of Election Commission in scrutiny of nomination papers?
   (iii) How does the Election Commission ensure free and fair elections?
   (iv) Comment on the independence of Election Commission.

CHAPTER 05

The State Legislatures

SYLLABUS

Meaning The Legislative Assembly and the Legislative Council.
Meaning of Unicameral and Bicameral
Legislature, term, composition, qualification for membership, powers and functions

The State Legislature is the law-making body in each state of India. It has the power to make laws on subjects mentioned in the State List and the Concurrent List of the Constitution.

Meaning of Unicameral and Bicameral Legislatures

Unicameral Legislature A state with only one legislative house (Legislative Assembly) is called a unicameral legislature. Examples *Gujarat, Rajasthan*.

Bicameral Legislature A state with two houses - Legislative Assembly and Legislative Council - is called a bicameral legislature. Examples: Uttar Pradesh, Maharashtra.

There are 6 states where bicameral legislature exists in India, those states are Andhra Pradesh, Bihar, Karnataka, Maharashtra, Telangana and Uttar Pradesh.

Composition of Legislative Assembly

The legislative assembly consists of representatives elected by the people on the basis of universal adult franchise. Its maximum strength is fixed at 500 and minimum strength at 60. It means that its strength varies from 60 to 500 depending upon the population size of the state.

Territorial Constituencies

Each state is divided into electoral areas called constituencies. The number of voters in each constituency is kept roughly equal to ensure fair representation. In other words, the Constitution ensures that there is uniformity of representation between different constituencies in the state.

Readjustment After Census

After each census, the number of assembly seats and constituency boundaries are reviewed. Parliament has enacted the Delimitation Commission Acts in 1952, 1962, 1972 and 2002 for this purpose. The 87th Amendment of 2003 made some changes based on the 2001 census but did not change the total number of seats.

Reservation of Seats for SCs and STs

The reservation of seats for Scheduled Castes (SCs) and Scheduled Tribes (STs) in legislatures was introduced to ensure their fair representation in law-making bodies. Historically, these communities faced social and economic disadvantages which limits their participation in politics. When this system was introduced, it was meant to last only for ten years until 1960. However, the government extended it every decade and the latest extension came with the 104th Amendment Act of 2019 which set the reservation period further until 2030.

Nominated Anglo-Indian Members

The Governor can nominate one member from the Anglo-Indian community if it is not adequately represented in the legislature. This provision was originally for ten years but was extended multiple times, however this provision was deleted by 104th Amendment Act of the Constitution.

Check Your LEARNING...

1. How is the number of seats in the Legislative Assembly determined?
2. When is a mid-term election held?
3. Until which year has the reservation for SCs and STs in state legislatures been extended by the 104th Amendment Act?

Composition of the Legislative Council

Unlike the members of the legislative assembly, the members of the legislative council are indirectly elected. The maximum strength of the council is fixed at one-third of the total strength of the assembly and the minimum strength is fixed at 40. It means that the size of the council depends on the size of the assembly of the concerned state.

Manner of Election of the total number of members of a legislative council:

- 1/3 are elected by the members of local bodies in the state like municipalities, district boards, etc.
- 1/12 are elected by graduates of three years standing and residing within the state.
- 1/12 are elected by teachers of three years standing in the state, not lower in standard than secondary school.
- 1/3 are elected by the members of the legislative assembly of the state from amongst persons who are not members of the assembly.
- The remaining are nominated by the Governor from amongst persons who have a special knowledge or practical experience of literature, science, art, cooperative movement and social service.

Thus, 5/6 of the total number of members of a legislative council are indirectly elected and 1/6 are nominated by the Governor. The members are elected in accordance with the system of proportional representation by means of a single transferable vote.

Qualifications

The Constitution lays down the following qualifications for a person to be chosen a member of the state legislatures and council, which are as follows;

- He must be a citizen of India.
- He must be not less than 30 years of age in the case of the legislative council and not less than 25 years of age in the case of the legislative assembly.
- He must make and subscribe to an oath or affirmation before the person authorised by the Election Commission for this purpose. In his oath or affirmation he swears the follows
- He swears that he will bear true faith and allegiance to the Constitution of India.
- He will uphold the sovereignty and integrity of India.

Term of Two Houses

Duration of Legislative Assembly

The legislative assembly is not a continuing chamber. Its normal term is of five years. However, the Governor is authorised to dissolve the assembly at any time even before the completion of five years which can leads to elections and formation of fresh government into state.

Duration of Council

Legislative Council is a permanent body and is not subject to dissolution but one-third of its members retire on the expiration of every second year and the maximum term of a member is of 6 years. Thus, legislative council is also called continuing chamber. The retiring members are also eligible for re-election and re-nomination any number of times.

Check Your LEARNING...

1. Who nominates members to the Legislative Council and on what basis?
2. What is the term duration of the Legislative Assembly and the Legislative Council?
3. Why is the Legislative Council considered a permanent body, while the Legislative Assembly is not?

Presiding Officers of the State Legislature

Each House of state legislature has its own presiding officer. There is a Speaker and a Deputy Speaker for the legislative assembly and Chairman and a Deputy Chairman for the legislative council. A panel of chairmen for the assembly and a panel of vice-chairmen for the council is also appointed so that houses can work efficiently in the absence of the presiding officers.

Speaker of the Assembly

The Speaker is elected by the assembly itself from amongst its members. Usually, the Speaker remains in office during the life of the assembly. However, he vacates his office earlier in any of the following three cases:

1. If Speaker ceases to be a member of the assembly;
2. If Speaker resigns by writing to the deputy speaker;
3. if Speaker is removed by a resolution passed by a majority of all the then members of the assembly. Such a resolution can be moved only after giving 14 days advance notice to him.

Deputy Speaker of the Assembly

Deputy Speaker of Assembly like the Speaker, the Deputy Speaker is also elected by the assembly itself from amongst its members. He is elected after the election of the Speaker has taken place. Like the Speaker, the Deputy Speaker remains in office usually during the life of the assembly. The Deputy Speaker performs the duties of the Speaker's office when it is vacant or absent.

Chairman of Council

The Chairman is elected by the council itself from amongst its members. As a presiding officer, the powers and functions of the Chairman in the council are similar to those of the Speaker in the assembly. However, the Speaker has one special power which is not enjoyed by the Chairman. The Speaker decides whether a bill is a Money Bill or not and his decision on this question is final.

Deputy Chairman of the Council

The Deputy Chairman performs the duties of the Chairman's office when it is vacant. He also acts as the Chairman when the latter is absent from the sitting of the council. In both the cases, he has all the powers of the Chairman. The Chairman nominates the panel from amongst the members. Any one of them can preside over the council in the absence of the Chairman or the Deputy Chairman.

Powers and Functions of the Legislature

Legislative Powers

- The State Legislature has the authority to enact legislation concerning the State List and the Concurrent List.
- In bicameral states, the Assembly has the more powers where bicameral legislatures exists in terms of passing of bills.
- The Legislative Council can only delay bills but cannot stop them permanently.

Financial Powers

- The State Legislature has the authority to collect taxes on all of the State List's topics and it is also the guardian of the state's money.
- Money Bills can only be introduced in the Legislative Assembly.
- The Legislative Council cannot reject Money Bills and it can only delay them for maximum 14 days.
- The State Government cannot collect money or levy or collect taxes without the agreement of the State Legislature.
- The state budget and all other financial policies and programmes are only operative if the State Legislature has approved them.
- In emergencies declared under Articles 352, 356 or 360 the state's financial authorities become subject to the Union Parliament.
- Any bill to become act requires the assent of the Governor of the state.

Executive Powers

- The Council of Ministers is responsible to the Legislative Assembly.
- The Legislative Assembly can question ministers, pass motions and remove the government through a no-confidence motion.
- The Legislative Council has no control over the government.

- The State Legislative Assembly has control over the State Council of Ministers. In the State Legislative Assembly and the state Chief-Minister is usually the leader of the party in the house.

Constitutional Powers

- Certain constitutional amendments require ratification by state legislatures under Article 368.
- The President must consult the Assembly before introducing a bill to change the state's boundaries or name etc. The advice tendered by the state legislature is not binding on the President.

Electoral Powers

- The Legislative Assembly participates in the election of The President of India and members of the Rajya Sabha (Upper House of Parliament).
- Some members of MLCs (Legislative Council Members) are partly elected by votes of the MLAs (Assembly Members).

Other Functions

- State Legislature members elects and removes the Presiding officers in the house.
- Legislature members reviews reports from bodies like the Auditor-General and State Public Service Commission.

Limitations on the powers of the State Legislature

- Certain bills can only be tabled in a state legislature with the prior approval of the President of India only.
- The Governor can reserve specific bills for the President's Assent after the state legislature has enacted them. They become law only once the President has granted such bills.
- If the Rajya Sabha approves a resolution with a 2/3rd majority of the members present and voting then parliament can make law on that topic not the state legislature.

Check Your LEARNING...

1. On which lists can the State Legislature make laws?
2. How can the Legislative Assembly remove the government if needed?
3. What role does the Legislative Assembly play in the election of the President of India?

QUiCK Revision

- The State Legislature can make laws on matters of the the State List and the Concurrent List of the Constitution.
- A Unicameral Legislature has only one house known as the Legislative Assembly and Bicameral Legislature has two houses.
- The members of the Legislative Assembly are elected through universal adult franchise.
- After each census, the number of seats and constituency boundaries are reviewed by the Delimitation Commission.
- The Governor nominated one Anglo-Indian member in Legislative Assembly but this provision was removed by the 104th Amendment Act.
- The Term of the Legislative Assembly is 5 years while the Council is of 6 years.
- Money Bills can only be introduced in the Legislative Assembly.
- No confidence motion can be initiated in the Legislative Assembly only.
- The members of the Legislative Assembly votes in the elections of the President and Rajya Sabha Members.
- The State Legislature reviews reports of the Auditor-General and State Public Service Commission.
- Certain bills requires the President approval before being introduced in the Legislatures.
- If the Rajya Sabha passes a resolution with a two-thirds majority then parliament can legislate on state subjects.

Chapter Practice

Section-I

Multiple Choice Questions

1. Complete the given analogy
Parliament : Union Legislature :: ________ : State Legislature.
(a) Legislative Assembly (b) Local Government
(c) Rural Government (d) None of these

2. Which of the following states has a Bicameral Legislature?
(a) Gujarat (b) Rajasthan
(c) Maharashtra (d) Punjab

3. Identify the odd one out of the following which is not part of the State Legislatures.
(a) Prime Minister (b) Legislative Council
(c) Legislative Assembly (d) Governor

4. Which of the following statement is correct about feature of a Bicameral Legislature?
(a) It consists of only Legislative Assembly.
(b) It has both Legislative Assembly and Legislative Council.
(c) It exists in all Indian states.
(d) It is decided solely by the Chief Minister.

5. The total number of seats in the Legislative Assembly of a state is determined based on ....
(a) the decision of the Chief Minister
(b) the population size of the state
(c) the recommendation of the Governor
(d) the number of districts in the state

6. Who is responsible for reviewing and adjusting the number of Assembly seats after each census?
(a) Election Commission of India
(b) Governor of the State
(c) Delimitation Commission
(d) Supreme Court of India

7. Which of the following factors is NOT considered while determining the number of seats in a Legislative Assembly?
(a) Population size of the state
(b) Delimitation Commission recommendations
(c) Decision of the Chief Minister
(d) Both (a) and (b)

8. Who can nominate the members of the Anglo-Indians into states?
(a) Governor (b) President
(c) Speaker (d) Deputy Speaker

9. Given below are details of a few Indian citizens.

Person	Age (in years)	Description
A	28	A social worker actively involved in public welfare but not a citizen of India.
B	40	A Doctor who has been activately treating patients since 2005.
C	22	A college student pursuing law.
D	25	A foreign national who recently moved to India.

Select the one who is eligible to become a Member of the Legislative Council (MLC).
(a) A (b) B
(c) C (d) D

10. Which Article of emergency will lead to shifting the charge of state legislature to parliament?
(a) Article 12 (b) Article 32
(c) Article 324 (d) Article 352

11. Which of the following is NOT a qualification to become a member of the State Legislature?
(a) Must be a citizen of India
(b) Must be at least 30 years old for the membership of Legislative Assembly
(c) Must take an oath of allegiance to the Constitution
(d) Must uphold the sovereignty and integrity of India

12. Which statement of the following is true regarding the Legislative Council?
(a) It is a permanent body where 1/3rd of its members retires in every 2 years
(b) It is dissolved every 5 years like the Legislative Assembly
(c) The Governor has the power to dissolve the Council at any time
(d) All members of the Council are directly elected by the voters of the state

13. The Speaker of the Legislative Assembly vacates office in all the following cases except ....
(a) if he resign by writing to the Deputy Speaker
(b) if he is removed by a resolution passed by a majority of assembly members
(c) if he cease to be a member of the assembly
(d) if the Chief Minister ask him to give resign

14. Observe the given picture. In case of a similar unruly situation in the State Legislature and choose the action that may be taken by the Speaker.

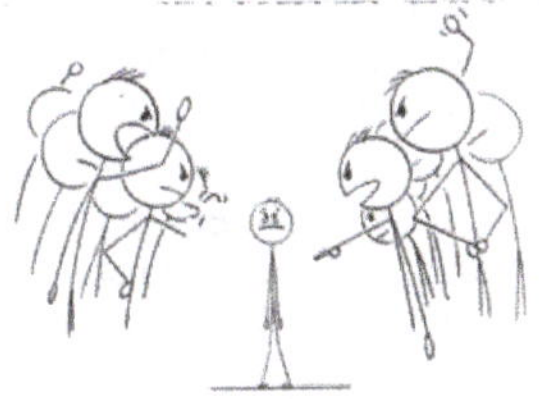

(a) Adjourn the house for lack of quorum.
(b) Dissolve the Council.
(c) Adjourn the house for lack of discipline.
(d) Disqualify the members under Anti-defection law.

15. Identify the powers of the Legislative Assembly.

P : Can make laws on subjects in the State List
Q : Can introduce and pass Money Bills
R : Can't remove the Governor through any motion
S : Appointment of the Deputy Chairman

(a) P and Q (b) Q and R
(c) P and S (d) R and S

Very Short Answer Type Questions

1. Mention any two differences between Unicameral and Bicameral Legislatures.

Ans. The two differences between the Unicameral and Bicameral Legislatures are as follows

- Unicameral legislature consists of only single house commonly called Legislative Assembly while Bicameral Legislature state consists of two houses.
- Unicameral legislature members are elected directly by the people whereas in Bicameral legislature the member of Legislative council are elected indirectly.

2. Imagine you are a member of the Legislative Assembly. Mention any two ways you would ensure fair representation of the people.

Ans. I would ensure that each constituency has an equal number of voters so that every citizen's vote carries the same weight. I would support policies that promote fair elections and equal representation for all regions in the state.

3. What is meant by the term Territorial Constituencies?

Ans. Territorial Constituencies refer to the electoral areas into which a state is divided for the purpose of elections. Each constituency elects one representative to the Legislative Assembly. The number of voters in each constituency is kept roughly equal to ensure fair representation.

4. Whose recommendations leads to readjustment of Seats into states?

Ans. The recommendations of Delimitation commission leads to readjustment of seats into states.

5. Mention those states where Bicameral legislatures exists in India and what is the maximum composition limit on the seats of the state legislative assembly.

Ans. There are six states where Bicameral legislatures exist in India, those states are Uttar Pradesh , Maharashtra , Telangana , Bihar , Karnataka and Andhra Pradesh. The maximum composition limit on the seats of the legislative assembly is fixed at 500.

6. What is the minimum number of seats fixed by the Constitution of India in State Legislative Assembly?

Ans. The minimum number of seats in state assembly is fixed at 60.

7. How does reservations of seats work in adjustment of seats in state legislatures?

Ans. The reservation of seats for Scheduled Castes (SCs) and Scheduled Tribes (STs) in State Legislatures is based on their population ratio in each state. These reserved constituencies are decided in such a way that fair representation is given to these communities.

8. Which Amendment Act led to the continuation of the SC/ST reservation till 2030 in India?

Ans. The 104th Amendment Act of 2019 continued the reservation for SC/ST till 2030 in India.

9. What was the special provision for Anglo-Indian Members in state legislatures before the 2019 amendment?

Ans. The Governor could nominate a member of the Anglo Indian Community if it was not adequately represented in any state legislature. This provision was deleted by the 104th Amendment Act of the 2019.

10. What is the minimum and maximum number of seats fixed by the Constitution of India in state legislatures of India?

Ans. The minimum number of seats for legislative council is fixed at 60 and maximum at the 1/3rd of the Legislative Assembly.

11. Mention any two conditions which are required to become the member of the legislative council in India.

Ans. To become a member of the Legislative Council in India, a person must fulfill the following conditions:

- The person must be at least 30 years old.
- The person must be a citizen of India.

12. What is the maximum term of the state legislative assembly ?

Ans. The maximum term of the state legislative assembly is fixed at 5 years and it can be dissolved earlier.

13. How many members of the Legislative Council retire in every 2 years?

Ans. The 1/3rd members of the Legislative council retire in every 2 years.

14. Who is known as the presiding officer of the legislative assembly?

Ans. Speaker is known as the presiding officer of the legislative assembly.

15. Who presides over the Assembly when Speaker and Deputy Speaker are absent in legislative assembly?

Ans. One of the member from the panel of the chairman preside over the assembly when both Speaker and Deputy Speaker are absent in the house.

16 Mention two conditions when speaker of the assembly ceases to be the member of the assembly.

Ans. The two conditions when speaker of the assembly ceases to be the member of the assembly are as follows

- The speaker ceases to hold the office of speaker if he ceases to be a member of the assembly
- The speaker also cease to hold office if he resigns by writing to the Deputy Speaker also.

17. What is the time limit for the notice which should be given to speaker before moving any motion against him?

Ans. The motion for the removal of speaker can be moved only after the 14 days when an advanced notice is also served to them.

18. Who decided whether a bill is money bill or not?

Ans. The speaker of the legislative assembly decides about a bill is money bill or not.

Structured Questions

1. Legislative Assemblies are the law making bodies in states. With reference to this statement answer the following questions

(i) Why readjustment of the seats are required after each census?

(ii) What is the essence of legislative assemblies in states?

(iii) Explain about the provision of reservations in legislatures in India.

Ans. (i) Readjustment of seats is required after each census to ensure fair representation based on population changes. Since the population of different regions in a state may increase or decrease, the number of seats and their distribution in the Legislative Assembly are adjusted to maintain equal representation among all citizens.

(ii) The Legislative Assembly is the key law-making body at the state level. Its importance lies in the following:

- It ensures that the voices of the people in the state are heard and considered in governance.
- It makes laws on subjects mentioned in the State List and Concurrent List.
- It keeps the State Government accountable by discussing policies, passing budgets and questioning the government on various issues.

(iii) The Indian Constitution provides for the reservation of seats in Legislatures to ensure fair representation of Scheduled Castes (SCs) and Scheduled Tribes (STs) into states. The number of reserved seats in each state is based on the population proportion of SCs and STs. To implement this reservation certain electoral constituencies are marked as reserved where only SC or ST candidates can contest but all voters in the constituency can vote for them in the election.

2. With regards to the Legislative Assembly and Council explain about the following

(i) The post of the Speaker and Deputy Speaker.

(ii) The post of Chairman and Deputy Chairman.

(iii) The Qualifications required for membership of the council.

(iv) Terms of the both houses.

Ans. (i) The Speaker is the presiding officer of the Legislative Assembly who is responsible for maintaining order and conducting proceedings smoothly. The Speaker is elected by the members of the Assembly. The Deputy Speaker assists the Speaker and takes charge in his/her absence. Both ensure fair discussions and decision-making in the Assembly.

(ii) In the Legislative Council, the Chairman is known as the presiding officer as similar to the Speaker in the Assembly. The Deputy Chairman assists and presides over sessions when the Chairman is absent. They both are also responsible for maintaining order and conducting debates in a disciplined manner.

(iii) To become a member of the Legislative Council , a person should fulfill the following conditions

- He /She should be a citizen of India.
- He /She should be at least 30 years old.
- He /She should possess qualifications as prescribed by Parliament or State Legislature.
- He /She should not be holding any office of profit under the government.

(iv) The Legislative Assembly has a term of five years but it can be dissolved earlier by the Governor. The Legislative Council is a permanent body where one-third of its members retires in every two years. Before taking office, all members of both houses must take an oath of office by swearing allegiance to the Constitution of India and pledging to uphold its values.

3. Explain the following.

(i) Legislative Powers of the Assembly

(ii) Executive Powers of the Assembly

(iii) Financial Powers of the Assembly

Ans. (i) The Legislative Assembly has the power to make laws on subjects mentioned in the State List and the Concurrent List.

- In states with a bicameral legislature, the Assembly has the final say in passing a bill even if the Legislative Council rejects or delays it.

- The Legislative Assembly can supersede the decision of the council.

(ii) The Council of Ministers in a state is responsible to the Legislative Assembly.

- The Assembly can question ministers , discuss government policies and pass motions on state administration.
- It also holds the power to remove the government through a no-confidence vote but the Legislative Council does not have control over the government.

(iii) The Legislative Assembly controls state finances and plays a key role in passing the state budget.

- Money Bills can only be introduced in the Assembly and the Legislative Council cannot reject them but can only delay them for 14 days.
- No tax can be imposed or removed without the approval of the Assembly which makes Assembly as the main financial authority in the state.

4. Explain the following

(i) Constitutional Powers of the Legislature

(ii) Electoral Powers of the Legislatures

(iii) Limitations on the powers of the legislatures.

Ans. (i) The Legislative Assembly have some constitutional powers which help them to revive the aim of federalism in country. Certain constitutional amendments by parliament require approval from state legislatures under Article 368 and the President has to consult the State Assembly before introducing a bill that changes the state's boundaries. However, the state legislature's advice is not binding on the President.

(ii) The electoral power of the legislature are as follows

- The Legislative Assembly participates in the election of the President of India.
- MLAs also elect members of the Rajya Sabha (Upper House of Parliament).
- In states with a Legislative Council (Vidhan Parishad) some MLCs (Legislative Council Members) are elected by MLAs.

(iii) The limitations on the powers of the state legislature are as follows

- Certain bills require prior approval from the President before being introduced in the State Legislature.
- The Governor can reserve specific bills for the President's assent even after the State Legislature has passed them. Such bills become law only after the President's approval.

Chapter Assessment

Multiple Choice Questions

1. Who presides over the sessions of the Legislative assembly?
   (a) Speaker (b) Deputy Chairman
   (c) Chairman (d) Governor
2. The house of the state where all members are elected by people directly in the state is known as ....
   (a) Lok Sabha
   (b) Legislative Council
   (c) Legislative Assembly
   (d) None of the Above
3. Who can reserve the bill of legislative assembly for the assent of the President?
   (a) Speaker (b) Chief Minister
   (c) Prime Minister (d) Governor
4. Who can initiate for the transfer of any subject of National Importance from State list to the Union or Concurrent list?
   (a) Lok Sabha
   (b) Rajya Sabha
   (c) Governor
   (d) Legislative Assembly

Very Short Answer Type Questions

1. How many members support is required in Rajya Sabha for the transfer of some specific subject from State list to the Union or Concurrent list?
2. What is the minimum age required to become the member of the Legislative Assembly?
3. What is the maximum term of the Legislative Assembly?
4. Who presides over the house when Speaker is absent in the house in Assembly?

Structured Questions

1. Explain the following:
   (i) Meaning of Unicameral and Bicameral Legislatures.
   (ii) Composition of the Legislative Assembly.
   (iii) Reservation of Seats for SCs and STs.
2. Explain the following:
   (i) Composition of the Legislative Council.
   (ii) Manner of Election of Legislative Council Members.
   (iii) Qualifications to become a Member of the Legislature.
3. Explain the following:
   (i) Term of the Legislative Assembly and Legislative Council.
   (ii) Presiding Officers of the State Legislature.
   (iii) Powers and Functions of the Speaker of the Assembly.

HISTORY

CHAPTER

01

The Harappan Civilisation

SYLLABUS

Sources Great Bath, citadel, seals, bearded man, dancing girl, dockyard, granaries, script. Urban planning, trade, art & craft and its decline.

Civilisation is the process by which a society or place reaches an advanced stage of social and cultural development and organisation. When man began to live in towns, it marked the beginning of the civilisation. From about 3300 BC, bronze age started in which man began to use metals. By about 2500 BC, four bronze age civilisations emerged which were

(i) The Harappan or Indus Valley Civilisation

(ii) The Mesopotamian Civilisation

(iii) The Chinese Civilisation

(iv) The Egyptian Civilisation

Harappan Civilisation

Till the beginning of the 20th century, it was believed that Indian History began with the vedic culture. But this belief was removed with discovery of Indus Valley Civilisation. This civilisation was much extensive than any of its contemporary civilisations, which lived around 3rd millennium BC in different parts of the world. The most of the Indus Valley civilisation settlements were located in valley of Saraswati river system which is extinct today.

The Harappan Civilisation is also known as the **Indus Valley Civilisation**. It is considered to be one of the greatest civilisations of all times.

The earliest excavations in the Indus Valley were done at Harappa in the West Punjab and Mohenjodaro in Sindh. Both these places are located in Pakistan now. The total spread of this civilisation was bigger than Egypt and Mesopotamia. Earliest reference about this civilisation was made by **Charles Masson**. The Harappan culture belongs to the Bronze Age, thus Indus Valley Civilisation is also known as **Bronze Age Civilisation**.

The age of this civilisation according to John Marshall, the Director of Archaeological Survey of India, is around 4000 BC to 2500 BC. But the **radio-dating**[1] process puts the date of this civilisation between 2300 BC to 1700 BC.

1. **Radio-dating** A method of dating rocks and minerals using radioactive isotopes.

Important Sites of the Harappan Civilisation

Harappa

It was the first Indus site to be discovered and also the reason behind the nomenclature of this civilisation. It is situated in Montgomery district of West Punjab in Pakistan, on the left bank of the river Ravi. It was discovered and excavated by **Rai Bahadur Daya Ram Sahni in 1921**. But large-scale excavation was carried on by **Mortimer Wheeler**. The important findings from Harappa are granaries and red stone torso of a naked male figure.

Mohenjodaro

The site of Mohenjodaro was discovered by **RD Banerjee** in 1922. The literal meaning of Mohenjodaro in Sindhi is 'the mound of dead'. It is situated in Larkana district of Sindh in Pakistan on the right bank of the river, Indus. It is considered as one of the capitals of the Indus Valley Civilisation.

Some of the important findings from Mohenjodaro are bronze dancing girl, Great Bath and Pashupati Mahadev seal.

Sources of Harappan Civilisation

The sources of Harappan Civilisation include archaeological remains like buildings, pottery, sculpture, seals, etc.

Some sources of Harappan civilisation are

Citadel

It is a fortified area which include important civic and religious public buildings. In cities of Indus Valley Civilisation, Citadel were occupied by members of the ruling class and the lower town was inhabited by the common people.

The remarkable thing about the arrangement of the houses in the cities is that they followed the grid system. Citadel includes large public buildings like granaries, assembly hall, workshops, etc. The buildings were constructed on the mud-bricks platforms.

Great Bath

It is one of the best-known structures among the ruins of the ancient Indus Valley civilisation at Mohenjodaro in Sindh, Pakistan. Archaeological evidence indicates that the Great Bath was built in the 3rd millennium BC, just sometime after raising of the Citadel mound on which it is located.

The Great Bath was a large **rectangular tank** in a courtyard surrounded by a corridor on all four sides. There were two flights of steps on the North and South leading into tank, which was made watertight by setting bricks on edge and using a mortar of gypsum.

The water for the bath was provided by a well from an adjacent room. Most of the scholars believed that the Great Bath might have been used for religious purposes while some believed that the rooms were provided for changing clothes.

The Great Bath is significant source of information about the life and culture of Indus Valley people as

- It indicates the perfection in the art of building that had reached at that time.
- It indicates the importance attached to ceremonial bathing in sacred tanks, pools and rivers since time immemorial.
- Its design indicates efficient planning in the structural features relating to the water supply and sewage disposal.

Great Bath

Seals

Seals are the greatest artistic creation of the Harappan people. Craftsmanship in cutting and polishing of seals is excellent. Figures of human beings and animals were engraved on seals. The materials used in making the seals include terracotta, agate, steatite, etc. Mostly, the seals are rectangular or square in shape, but some of them are circular in shape.

Of all the seals discovered, the most important one is the **Pashupati seal** found from Mohenjodaro. It depicts a three-faced male god sitting cross-legged on a throne.

He is wearing a buffalo-horned headdress and is surrounded by a tiger, a buffalo, an elephant and a rhinoceros. Two deer/goats are sitting under the throne. He is sitting in a yogic posture and resembles Shiva.

Pashupati Seal

Importance of seals is

- The seals of Indus Valley civilisation serve as an authentic source of information about the culture and civilisation of the Harappan people.
- The information about the social life such as the physical feature, ornaments, hairstyles, clothing, etc were provided by the figures engraved on the seals.
- The seals also explains the religious faith and beliefs of the Harappan people like the seals of Mother Goddess, Pashupati, etc.
- The idea of economic activities like trade and commerce, transport, weight and measures, etc were also provided by the seals.
- The seals reflect the outstanding skill of the artists and the scripts prevalent in those days.
- The seals were used by traders to stamp their goods.

Bearded Man

The stone sculpture of a bearded nobleman or **high priest** has been found from **Mohenjodaro**. It is 17.5 cm tall. The figure is wearing a shawl over the left shoulder with trefoil pattern and eyes are half closed. It bears a close resemblance to a similar figure discovered in the Sumerian sites of Ur and Susa. The head and arms of the figure were carved separately and socketed into holes drilled on the torso. Its features like half closed eyes, thick lips, straight nose, stylised beard and hair, hair taxture, excessive use of lines to create beard and design on garment shows the definite artistic portraiture of the Indus Valley artists. Some scholars believe that this is the statue of a Yogi.

Priest King

Dancing Girl

The **bronze sculpture** of dancing girl was discovered at **Mohenjodaro**. It is perhaps the greatest surviving achievement of the metal work of the Harappan age. It gives an idea that the Harappan people were fond of dancing and singing. The bronze statues were made by the **lost wax technique**[2].

Bronze Dancing Girl

In this sculpture, the female dancing figure is standing as if relaxing after a dance, with her right hand on her hip and her left hand is dangling free.

She is wearing a large number of bangles, probably made of bone or ivory on her left arm together with a couple of pairs on her right arm.

Dockyard

A dockyard has been found from Lothal situated in Gujarat. It was built of burnt bricks and was rectangular in shape. It was connected by channels to the **Gulf of Cambay**. It is 200 m long and 35 m in width. It has a depth of 8 m. It indicates that Lothal was an important trading and manufacturing centre and was used for carrying out overseas trade.

2. **Lost Wax Technique** It is a method of metal casting in which a molten metal is poured into a mould that has been created by means of Wax model.

Script

The earliest specimen of Harappan script was noticed in 1853 by **Alexander Cunningham**. The Harappan script was pictographic and was written from right to left and left to right in the **Boustrophedon style**[3]. The script could not be deciphered yet. The number of signs of Harappan script is known to be between 375 and 400. The script is found on a number of seals, copper tablet and terracotta artefacts and jewellery, etc.

Letters on an Ancient Signboard showing Harappan Script

Check Your LEARNING...

1. What was the shape of the Great Bath?
2. Give any characteristic feature of citadel.
3. What does Pashupati seal depict?
4. Dockyard has been found at which site?
5. Name the script of Indus Valley which is undeciphered.

Boundaries of the Harappan Civilisation

The North-South spread of this civilisation was 1400 kilometers and the West-East spread was 1600 kilometers.

Some of the centres of civilisation in India are Manda, Kalibangan, Banawali, Alamgirpur, Lothal, Ropar and Rangpur.

- **Northernmost site** Manda (J & K)
- **Southernmost site** Daimabad (M.H.)
- **Westernmost site** Sutkagan Dor (Pakistan)
  Easternmost site Alamgirpur (Uttar Pradesh)

Town/Urban Planning of the Harappan Civilisation

The town planning of the Harappan Civilisation was based on **grid pattern** or **chess board pattern**. Entire city complex was divided into two parts, citadel and lower town. The main streets followed a grid pattern running from North to South or from East to West.

The streets and lanes cut each other at right angles dividing the city into a number of rectangular blocks. The street corners were round in shape to allow the carts to pass easily. There were lamp-posts at regular distances for street lights in every street and lane.

Features of Urban Planning

Drainage System

- This was one of the most remarkable features of the Harappan Civilisation.
- The houses were connected to the main drain equipped with manholes. The drains were mostly made of bricks with lime mortar. The mixture of gypsum and lime was used to make the drains water-tight.
- The drains were covered with bricks or stones. There were **cesspits**[4] inside the houses to deposit solid wastes.
- The floors of the kitchen and bathroom were water-tight and had a slight slope towards one corner to allow the water to drain into the narrow drain situated alongside.

Houses

- The houses were plain without much decoration and were made of baked brick and wood.
- The houses or residential buildings were built according to a set plan on a high mound in order to protect them from floods.
- The entrances to the houses were from the narrow lanes.
- An average house comprised a courtyard and four to six living rooms. Every house had doors, windows and ventilators.
- Square and rectangular pillars of burnt brick were used in larger rooms and round pillars were absent.
- The houses can be divided into three main groups, which are dwelling houses, larger buildings and public baths.
- The kitchen was made in a sheltered corner of the courtyard.

Granaries

- Granaries were used to store food. They have been found at several sites i.e. Mohenjodaro, Harappa, Lothal and Kalibangan.

3. **Boustrophedon Style** Written words from right to left and from left to right in alternate lines.
4. **Cesspits** A pit used to collect sewage and waste water.

- At Harappa, there were two rows of six granaries each. The Harappa was located near Ravi River, which suggested that food grains were brought to this place by boat.
- Granary was built on raised platform to protect it from floods and it had ventilation to prevent the stored food or grains from getting degraded.

Economic Life of the Harappan Civilisation

Agriculture and Food

Agriculture was the main occupation of the Indus Valley people. Crops such as wheat, barley, peas and bananas were raised. Rice was also probably grown. There is evidence to show that date palms were grown in the area. People used to plough the land with wooden ploughshares drawn by men and oxen. Besides these, the diet of the people consisted of fruits, vegetables, fish, milk and meat of animals i.e. beef, mutton and poultry.

Domestication of Animals

The Harappan people domesticated animals like oxen, buffaloes, pigs, goats and sheep. Camels were also used as means of transport. Dogs and cats were kept as pets. The humped bull was considered a great asset in the farming community.

Trade and Commerce

- Harappans carried out internal trade with Maharashtra, Saurashtra, South India and external trade with Mesopotamia, Egypt, Greece and Bahrain. The exchanges were done through **barter system**[5].
- The Indus Valley sites like Mohenjodaro, Harappa and Lothal were important centres for **metallurgy**[6], producing tools and weapon as well as kitchenware and other objects for wide distribution.
- Rice seems to have been imported to Punjab from Gujarat.
- Chanhudaro and Balakot were the centres of bangle making.
- Lothal and Chanhudaro were centres for the manufacturing of the beads.
- Various metals, precious stones and other articles were imported.
- **Lapis Lazuli** (a bright blue stone) was imported from Afghanistan, copper from Rajasthan and gold from Karnataka.
- Lothal, Surkotada and Balakot were some of the important trading coastal towns which carried on trade with Mesopotamia and other West Asian sites. Cotton was exported by Lothal and Surkotada for the expending townships of Mohenjodaro, Harappa, Banawali, etc.
- The Mesopotamian records of about 2350 BC onwards refer to the trade relations with Meluha (the ancient name given to the Indus region).
- Two intermediate trading stations called Dilmun and Makan are mentioned by Mesopotamian texts, which lay between Mesopotamia and Meluha.
- The text of Mesopotamian mentioned Meluha as a land of seafares. Besides this, the depictions of ships and boats on seals also indicate this fact.
- Cylindrical seals of Mesopotamia have been found from Mohenjodaro. Indus seals have been discovered from various Mesopotamian cities like Ur and Susa. This shows existence of trade and commerce.

Weights and Measures

A number of weights have been discovered from Indus valley. The people of the Indus Valley used sets of cubical stone weights. They used 16 (now equal to 14 grams) as basic unit. The larger weights were multiples of 16 like 32, 48, 64, 128, etc and smaller weights were fractions of 16.

Transport

Discovery of a number of seals with pictures of ships engraved on them indicate the use of ships as means of transport during the Harappan civilisation. The Harappan people also used boats. The most popular means of transport within the cities were bullock carts which is evident from the terracotta models of carts.

Carts used in those days resemble the modern *Ekka* (horse-cart). Copper or bronze models of bullock carts with seated drivers were found from Harappa and Chanhudaro.

5. **Barter System** It is a system in which goods and services are exchanged between two parties without using money.
6. **Metallurgy** A process which is used to extract metal from ores.

Check Your LEARNING...

1. What were the Northernmost and Southern most limits of Indus Valley Civilisation ?
2. Which types of houses were found at Harappan Civilisation?
3. What do you mean by barter system?
4. Name the animals used as means of transport in Harappan Civilisation.
5. What was the most popular means of transport?

Religion of the Harappan Civilisation

The information and facts regarding the religion of the Indus Valley people are less. However, through archaeological facts, it is known that they practised image worship. A figurine of a female deity (goddess) was discovered, whom the Indus Valley people regarded as the source of all power and creation.

This figurine was more or less resembled 'Shakti' or Mother Goddess. Similarly, a three-faced male-God in a seated figure and carved on a small stone was discovered. This figure resembled **Shiva (Pashupati)** of later Hinduism. Besides these, they held certain animals and trees as sacred and worshipped them such as humped bull, elephant, buffaloes, tiger, bison etc. **Pipal tree** was also worshipped by them. The Indus Valley people had the traditional belief of life after death.

Arts and Crafts of the Harappan Civilisation

The arts of Indus Valley Civilisation, emerged during the second half of the 3rd millennium BC (Bronze Age). The forms of art found from various sites of civilisation include sculptures, pottery, ornaments, etc

- **Sculpture** Stone statues of Bearded man (Priest Man, Priest-King) and Male Torso found in Indus Valley sites are excellent examples of stone sculptures. Bronze casting was practiced in wide scale in almost all major sites of the civilisation.
- **Bronze Casting** Human as well as animal figures are present in the bronze casting. The best examples of bronze casting is sculpture of dancing girl found from Mohenjodaro. Copper dog and bird of Lothal and the bronze figure of a bull from Kalibangan shows that bronze casting was popular at all the centers of Indus Valley Civilisation.
- **Pottery** Indus Valley pottery consists of very fine wheel made wares, very few being handmade. Pottery was found in a large number from the sites of Harappan civilisation. Figures of birds, animals and trees and geometric figure were depicted on the pots. Some of the pottery that are evidences of the artistic skills of the Indus Valley people are large jars with narrow neck and red pots with black decoration.

Harappan Pottery

- **Terracotta Figures** As compared to the stone and bronze statues, the terracotta representations of human form are crude in the Indus Valley. They are more realistic in Gujarat sites and Kalibangan. Deities like bearded man and Mother Goddess, toy carts and animals were common in terracotta figures.
- **Dress** Men of Indus Valley used to wear a dhoti and wore a shawl as an upper garments as shown by the famous figure of the priest from Mohenjodaro. The women wore a type of skirt and use to cover their upper portion with a cloak.

  The discovery of needles and buttons at some sites show that some of the clothes were stiched. Men kept their hair short and beard trimmed. On the other hand, women kept long hair and dressed their hair in a variety of styles.
- **Beads, Cosmetics and Ornaments** Well developed beads industries were present at Chanhudaro. Materials made of ivory and metal for holding and applying cosmetics were found in Indus Valley.

  This prove that women of Harappan civilisation knew the use of face paint and collyrium. Jewellery found at Mohenjodaro and Lothal include necklaces of gold and semi-precious metal, stones, copper bracelets, gold earrings and head ornaments.

Decline of the Harappan Civilisation

Definite reason that led to the decline of Harappan Civilisation is not known. However, some of the based on speculative (based on guessing) causes for the decline of the civilisation are

- **Floods and Climate Change** The sudden subsidence or uplift of the land resulting in floods is believed to be one of the reasons for the decline of Harappan civilisation.

  According to historians, the rainfall in the Indus region declined in the 2nd millennium BC which adversely affected agriculture and stock breeding. It is also believed that expansion of neighbouring desert led to the decrease in soil fertility thereby increasing salinity.
- **Deforestation** The excessive use of wood in Indus Valley to bake bricks, to produce jewellery, to make pottery, stoneware and manufacture furniture and boats could have caused deforestation leading to climatic changes in the area thereby causing the decline of the civilisation.
- **Attack** Some historians like Mortimer Wheeler believed that the invading Aryans destroyed the Indus settlements. The discovery of the skeletons of 13 males and females alongwith one child lying in a room also support this cause.
- **Earthquake** It is also believed by some historians that sudden earthquakes might have altered the course of river Indus, causing immense damage to the cities of the Indus Valley.
- **Increased Aridity** Some historians stated that the Harappan Civilisation declined because of increasing aridity in the area and the drying up of the river Ghaggar. Yamuna and Sutlej used to be of the tributaries of the river Ghaggar. Due to some tectonics disturbances, the Sutlej streams was captured by the river Indus and Yamuna shifted East to join the Ganga. As a result of this change, the river Ghaggar became waterless.

Check Your LEARNING...

1. What was the religion of Indus valley people?
2. Define Torso.
3. Give few examples of Terracotta sculpture.
4. Name the major reasons behind the decline of Harappan civilisation.

QUiCK Revision

- The Harappan civilisation was one of the earliest urban civilisation in India.
- Till the beginning of the 20th century, it was believed that Indian History began with the vedic culture. But this view was shattered with the discovery of Indus Valley civilisation.
- Earliest reference about this civilisation was made by Charles Masson.
- Some of the important cities of the Indus Valley civilisation are Mohenjodaro, Harappa, Lothal, Dholavira, etc.
- The sources available to understand the Harappan civilisation includes seals, ornaments, tools etc.
- The earliest specimen of Harappan script was noticed in 1853 by Alexander Cunningham. The Harappan script was pictographic.
- The Harappan civilisation extend from Punjab in the North-West to Gujarat and some parts of South India. This civilisation was largest (in terms of area) than the other ancient civilisation.
- The town planning of the civilisation was based on 'Grid pattern' or 'chess board pattern'. Some of the features of urban planning were drainage system, houses, granaries, etc.
- Agriculture was the main occupation of the Indus Valley people.
- The Harappan people domesticated animals like oxen, buffaloes, goats, sheep, etc.
- Harappans carried out trade extensively. The exchanges were done through Barter system.
- The most popular means of transport within the cities were bullock carts.
- The religious life of the Harappan people can be identified from the various seals and figurines discovered in the excavations at various sites.
- The Indus Valley people practised image worship. They had also begun the worship of fire.
- Many statues, figurines of men and women made of terracotta, stone and metal were found which indicate that people of the Harappan civilisation were great artists and sculptors.
- Definite reason that led to decline of the Indus Valley civilisation is not known.

Chapter Practice

Section-I

Multiple Choice Questions

1. .... Civilisation is considered to be one of the greatest civilisation of all times.
(a) Greek (b) Mesopotamian
(c) Indus Valley (d) Both (a) and (b)

Ans. (c) Indus Valley

2. Mohenjodaro is located in
(a) Gujarat (b) Sindh
(c) Kalibangan (d) Punjab

Ans. (b) Sindh

3. In which year Harappan site was discovered?
(a) 1919 (b) 1920 (c) 1921 (d) 1922

Ans. (c) 1921

4. The houses in the Harappan cities followed which system?
(a) Row (b) Column
(c) Grid (d) None of these

Ans. (c) Grid

5. .... were made by the 'lost wax technique'.
(a) Granaries (b) Bronze statues
(c) Seals (d) Dockyard

Ans. (b) Bronze statues

6. A dockyard has been found from ....
(a) Harappa (b) Lothal
(c) Ropar (d) Rakhigarhi

Ans. (b) Lothal

7. The North-South spread of Harappan civilisation was how much kilometers?
(a) 1300 km (b) 1400 km
(c) 1600 km (d) 1700 km

Ans. (b) 1400 km

8. Which of the following was the limits of Southernmost site of Harappan Civilisation?
(a) Manda (b) Daimabad
(c) Sutkagan (d) Alamgirpur

Ans. (b) Daimabad

9. Which of the following are characteristics of seals?
(a) Pashupati seal has been found at Mohenjodaro.
(b) It serves as an authentic sources of information.
(c) Some seals were also been found in gold and ivory items.
(d) All of the above

Ans. (d) All of the Above

10. Which of the following was true about the earliest specimen of Harappan script ?
(a) It was noticed in 1953.
(b) The Harappan script was pictographic.
(c) It was written from left to right only.
(d) It was found on doakyard.

Ans. (b) The Harappan script was pictographic.

11. Complete the given analogy.
Mohenjodaro : Indus River :: Harappa : ?
(a) Sutlej (b) Ravi
(c) Jhelum (d) Saraswati

Ans. (b) Ravi

12. Complete the given analogy.
Dockyard : Lothal : : Bearded man : ?
(a) Harappa (b) Mohenjodaro
(c) Rakhigarhi (d) Banawali

Ans. (b) Mohenjodaro

13. Replaced the underlined word and correct the sentence.
The portrait of a bearded nobleman or high priest has been found from <u>Lothal</u>.
(a) Kalibangan (b) Dholavira
(c) Mohenjodaro (d) Harappa

Ans. (c) Mohenjodaro

14. Replaced the underlined word and correct the sentence.
<u>Banawali</u> was an important trading and manufacturing centre and was used for carrying out overseas trade.
(a) Dholavira (b) Harappa
(c) Lothal (d) Rakhigarhi

Ans. (c) Lothal

15. Complete the given table.

Northernmost IVC site	Manda
Easternmost IVC site	?

(a) Sutkagan Dor (b) Alamgirpur
(c) Baluchistan (d) Daimabad

Ans. (b) Alamgirpur

16. Granaries were found at
(i) Mohenjodaro (ii) Harappa
(iii) Lothal (iv) Kalibangan

Codes
(a) Only (i) (b) Only (ii)
(c) Both (ii) and (iii) (d) All of these

Ans. (d) All of these

17. Which of the following is true about the agriculture and food of Indus people?
(i) Agriculture was there main occupation.
(ii) Wheat, barley, peas and banana were raised.
(iii) They used to plough the land.
(iv) Rice was also probably grown by them.

Codes

(a) Only (i) (b) Only (ii)
(c) Both (ii) and (iv) (d) All of these

Ans. (d) All of these

18. The causes of decline of Harappan civilisation was/were
(i) climate changes and floods (ii) deforestation
(iii) earthquake (iv) attack

Codes

(a) Only (i) (b) Both (i) and (ii)
(c) Only (iii) (d) All of these

Ans. (d) All of these

19. Match the following.

List-I	List-II
A. Sculpture	1. Bearded man
B. Bronze casting	2. Earrings
C. Pottery	3. Fine wheel
D. Ornaments	4. Dancing girl

Codes

	A	B	C	D		A	B	C	D
(a)	1	2	3	4	(b)	4	3	2	1
(c)	1	4	3	2	(d)	3	1	4	2

Ans. (c)

20. Match the following

List-I	List-II
A. Metallurgy	1. Surkotada
B. Cotton	2. Mohenjodaro
C. Bangle making	3. Karnataka
D. Gold	4. Balakot

Codes

	A	B	C	D		A	B	C	D
(a)	4	3	2	1	(b)	1	2	3	4
(c)	3	4	1	2	(d)	2	1	4	3

Ans. (d)

Picture Based Question

21. With reference to the given picture, answer the following questions.

(i) Identify the picture given above.
(a) A priest (b) A peasant
(c) A king (d) A common man

Ans. (a) A priest

(ii) Where was the statue of bearded man found?
(a) Mohenjodaro (b) Kalibangan
(c) Lothal (d) Dholavira

Ans. (a) Mohenjodaro

(iii) The statue of bearded man was made of
(a) bronze (b) stone
(c) copper (d) gold

Ans. (b) stone

(iv) Which among the following was an example of Harappan sculpture?
(a) Granary
(b) Great Bath
(c) Seals
(d) Statue of Bearded Man

Ans. (d) Statue of Bearded Man

Passage Based Questions

22. Read the passage and answer the following questions.

The most important among the Indus figures are those representing the mother goddess. In terracotta, we also find a few figurines of bearded males with coiled hair, their posture rigidly upright, legs slightly apart, and the arms parallel to the sides of the body. The repetition of this figure in exactly the same position would suggest that he was a deity. A terracotta mask of a horned deity has also been found. Toy carts with wheels, whistles, rattles, birds and animals, gamesmen and discs were also rendered in terracotta.

(i) Terracotta are more realistic in sites of
(a) Gujarat (b) Kalibangan
(c) Dholavira (d) Both (a) and (b)

Ans. (d) Both (a) and (b)

(ii) .... images were also created, but they were less refined as compared to the stone statues.
(a) Pottery (b) Seals
(c) Terracotta (d) Bronze casting

Ans. (c) Terracotta

(iii) Which among the following is an important terracotta image?
(a) Bearded Man (b) Dancing Girl
(c) Mother Goddess (d) Seals

Ans. (c) Mother Goddess

(iv) Which of the following terracotta toys have also been found at the site?
(a) Wheels (b) Whistles
(c) Birds (d) All of these

Ans. (d) All of these

23. Read the given passage and answer the following questions.

In bronze we find human as well as animal figures. Amongst animal figures in bronze the buffalo with its uplifted head, back and sweeping horns and the goat are of artistic merit. Bronze casting was popular at all the major centres of the Indus Valley civilisation. The copper dog and bird of Lothal and the bronze figure of a bull from Kalibangan are in no way inferior to the human figures of copper and bronze from Harappa and Mohenjodaro. Metalcasting appears to be a continuous tradition. The late Harappan and Chalcolithic sites like Daimabad yielded excellent examples of metal-cast sculptures. They mainly consist of human and animal figures.

(i) The art of bronze casting was practiced on wide scale by the

(a) Greek (b) Mesopotamian
(c) Harappan (d) All of these

Ans. (c) Harappan

(ii) The lost wax technique was used by Harappans for the statue of

(a) stone (b) copper (c) bronze (d) wood

Ans. (c) bronze

(iii) Which of the following is an example of bronze casting?

(a) Harappan Seal (b) Statue of Bearded Man
(c) Both (a) and (b) (d) Statue of Dancing Girl

Ans. (d) Statue of Dancing Girl

(iv) Daimabad is located in which state?

(a) Gujarat (b) Maharashtra (c) Haryana (d) Punjab

Ans. (b) Maharashtra

Section-II

Short Questions

1. What do you understand by the term 'civilisation'?

Ans. Civilisation is the process by which a society or place reaches an advanced stage of social and cultural development and organisation. When man began to live in towns, it marked the beginning of the civilisation.

2. What was the unique feature of bronze age?

Ans. The unique feature of bronze age was the introduction of metal and metal implements. This age saw the earliest written script and witnessed much evolution in society and life.

3. Mention other civilisations contemporary to the Harappan civilisation.

Ans. The given below civilisations contemporary to the Harappan civilisation are

(i) The Mesopotamian civilisation
(ii) The Chinese civilisation
(iii) The Egyptian civilisation

4. Is it correct to call the Indus Valley civilisation a riverine civilisation?

Ans. Yes, it is correct to call the Indus Valley civilisation a riverine civilisation because most of its settlements were located in valley of Saraswati river system which extinct today.

5. Why the Indus Valley civilisation is known as Harappan civilisation?

Ans. The Harappan civilisation is named so because Harappa was the first site to be discovered in this civilisation.

6. What is the literal meaning of Mohenjodaro? Who discovered it?

Ans. The literal meaning of Mohenjodaro in Sindhi is 'the mound of dead'.

It was discovered by RD Banerjee in 1922.

7. Where is Mohenjodaro situated?

Ans. The city of Mohenjodaro is situated in Larkhana district of Sindh in Pakistan, on the right bank of the river, Indus.

8. Mention some important findings from Mohenjodaro.

Ans. Some important findings from Mohenjodaro are Bronze Dancing Girl, Great Bath and Pashupati Mahadev Seal.

9. Who discovered and excavated the site of Harappa?

Ans. The site of Harappa was discovered and excavated by Rai Bahadur Daya Ram Sahni in 1921. But large- scale excavation was carried on by Mortimer Wheeler.

10. What are the various sources which gives a detailed description about the Indus Valley civilisation?

Ans. The various sources which gives a detailed description about the Indus Valley civilisation are the Great Bath, seals, portrait of a bearded man, bronze dancing girl, cemeteries and dockyard.

11. When was the Great Bath built?

Ans. Archaeological evidence indicates that the Great Bath was built in the 3rd Millennium BC, just sometime after raising of the 'citadel' mound on which it is located.

12. What was a citadel?

Ans. A citadel was a fortified area which housed important civic and religious public buildings including granaries and residences of the ruling class.

13. What do we come to know about the Harappans from the seals?

Ans. Seals are the greatest artistic creation of the Harappan people. Thus, we come to know about the excellence of the Harappan people in the field of arts and crafts.

14. What does seals indicate? Which animals were depicted on the seals apart from unicorn?

Ans. Seals indicate dresses, ornaments, religious beliefs, script of Harappan people, etc. It also marked ownership of property, trade contacts and commercial relations. Other animals depicted on seals apart from unicorn are elephant, tiger, rhinoceros, antelope, etc.

15. What were the various art pieces made of bronze belonged in the Indus Valley Civilisation?

Ans. The various art pieces made of bronze belonged to the Indus Valley Civilisation are bronze figures of a buffalo, a humped bull and the famous dancing girl.

16. From where do we get an evidence of a dockyard? What was it made of? What does it indicate?

Ans. A dockyard has been found from Lothal situated in Gujarat.

It was built of burnt bricks and was rectangular in shape. It was connected by channels to the Gulf of Cambay.

It indicates that Lothal was an imporant trading and manufacturing centre and was used for carrying out overseas trade.

17. Explain about the Harappan script. What are the materials on which we get the Harappan script?

Ans. The Harappan script was pictographic and was written from right to left and left to right in the Boustrophedon style. The script could not be deciphered yet. The Harappan script is found on a number of seals, copper and terracotta, artefacts and jewellery etc.

18. Name some important cities of the Indus Valley civilisation.

Ans. The important cities of the Harappan civilisation are Mohenjodaro, Harappa, Lothal, Kalibangan, Dholavira, etc.

19. What are the different sources available to understand the Harappan Civilisation?

Ans. The sources available to understand the Harappan Civilisation are

(i) Harappan seals.

(ii) Sources left by the people such as their houses, pots, ornaments, tools etc.

20. What is the extension of the Harappan Civilisation?

Ans. The Harappan Civilisation extended to the Punjab, Sindh, North-West Frontier Province (now in Pakistan), Baluchistan, Rajasthan, Uttar Pradesh, Gujarat and even some parts of South India.

21. What helps us to understand the features of Harappan Civilisation?

Ans. In order to understand the features of Harappan Civilisation, we have a large number of archaeological sources available. For example, the written source like the Harappan script which has not been deciphered yet, town-planning, drainage system, granaries, art & crafts, etc.

22. What was the importance of Assembly Hall found in Mohenjodaro?

Ans. The importance of the Assembly Hall was that it was used as ruler's court.

23. How can it be proved that the Indus valley people paid great attention to sanitation and health?

Ans. The presence of a systematic drainage system proves that the Indus valley people paid great attention to sanitation and health.

24. How the houses of the Harappan civilisation can be divided?

Ans. The houses of Harappan civilisation can be divided into following three main groups

(i) Dwelling houses (ii) Larger buildings

(iii) Public baths

25. What was the importance of the granaries in the Harappan civilisation?

Ans. The granaries were one of the important features of the Harappan civilisation as they were meant to store food grains.

26. What was the main occupation of the Indus Valley people? What were the main crops of the Harappans?

Ans. Agriculture was the main occupation of the Indus Valley people. The main crops of the Harappans were wheat and barley. Rice was also probably grown. Other crops grown were peas, date palm, mustard etc.

27. Which animals were domesticated by the people of Indus Valley?

Ans. The Harappan people domesticated animals like oxen, buffaloes, pigs, goats and sheep. Camels were used as means of transport. Dogs and cats also were kept as pets.

28. What were the centres of internal and external trade of the Indus valley people?

Ans. Indus Valley people carried out internal trade with Maharashtra, Saurashtra, South India and external trade with Mesopotamia, Egypt, Greece and Bahrain.

29. How was the trade relation of the Harappans with the other contemporary civilisation?

Ans. Traders of Harappans carried on extensive trade in the country as well as with other countries like Egypt, Babylon and Afghanistan. Many seals of Harappa found in Mesopotamia show that trade existed between the two countries.

30. Explain the weights and measures of Harappans. Cubical stone weights.

Ans. The people of the Indus Valley used sets of cubical stone weights. They used 16 (now equal to 14 grams) as basic unit. The larger weights were multiples of 16 like 32, 48, 64, 128 etc and smaller weights were fractions of 16.

31. How do we come to know that the Harappan people were great artists and sculptors?

Ans. During excavation many statues, figurines of men and women in terracotta, stone and metal were found which indicate that people of the Harappan civilisation were great artists and sculptors.

32. Were the Harappans fond of paintings and utensils? Give evidences.

Ans. Yes, the Harappans were fond of utensils and paintings. Archaeologist have found beautifully designed pottery on jars, bowls etc. They also used metal and clay utensils which indicates advanced craftsmanship in daily life.

33. How the Harappans dressed themselves?

Ans. The dress of Harappan men and women consisted of two pieces of cloth. Men use to wear a dhoti and wore a shawl as an upper garments. Women wore a a type of skirt and used to cover their upper portion with a cloak.

34. Mention some religious beliefs of the Harappan people.

Ans. The religious beliefs of Harappan people were as follows

- They worshipped trees like pipal.
- Animals like bull, buffalo and tiger were worshipped by them.
- They believed in magic and charms.

35. What were the various reasons for the decline of the Indus Valley Civilisation?

Ans. Some reasons regarding the decline of such a vast civilisation are

(i) Invasions of Aryans (ii) Climate change
(iii) Deforestation (iv) Earthquake
(v) Floods

Structured Questions

1. Give an account of the Indus Valley civilisation with reference to
(i) Mohenjodaro
(ii) Harappa
(iii) Boundaries of Indus Valley Civilisation

Ans. (i) Mohenjodaro was the chief city of the Indus Valley civilisation. It was discovered by RD Banerjee in 1922. It was situated in the Larkhana district of Sindh in Pakistan on the right bank of the river Indus. It was discovered as a big mound and was called 'mound of the dead'. From the ruins, it was concluded that it was once a well planned city with straight, wide roads and a very highly developed system of drainage and sanitation.

(ii) Harappa is situated on the banks of the river Ravi, in the Montgomery district of West Punjab in Pakistan. It was discovered by Rai Bahadur Daya Ram Sahni in 1921. Large scale excavation was carried on by Mortimer Wheeler and it was concluded that it was also a well planned city like Mohenjodaro.

(iii) Refer to chapter theory page no. 56.

2. With reference to the important findings from Mohenjodaro, explain.
(i) Bronze Dancing Girl
(ii) Pashupati Mahadev Seal
(iii) Great Bath
(iv) Granaries

Ans. (i) Refer to chapter theory page no. 55.

(ii) The most important one is the Pashupati seal found from Mohenjodaro. It depicts a three-faced male god sitting cross legged on a throne. He is wearing a buffalo-horned headaress and is surrounded by a tiger, a buffalo, an elephant and a rhinoceros. Two deer/goats are sitting under the throne. He is sitting in a Yogic posture and resembles Shiva.

(iii) Refer to chapter theory page no. 54.

(iv) Refer to chapter theory page no. 56-57.

3. With reference to the infrastructure of the Indus Valley Civilisation, explain about the following.
(i) Houses
(ii) Drainage System
(iii) Town Planning
(iv) Citadel

Ans. (i) Refer to chapter theory page no. 56.
(ii) Refer to chapter theory page no. 56.
(iii) Refer to chapter theory page no. 56.
(iv) Refer to chapter theory page no. 54.

4. With reference to the social and economic life of the Harappan Civilisation, explain
(i) Ornaments
(ii) Domestication of Animals
(iii) Food and Agriculture
(iv) Transportation

Ans. (i) Refer to chapter theory page no. 58.
(ii) Refer to chapter theory page no. 57.
(iii) Refer to chapter theory page no. 57.
(iv) Refer to chapter theory page no. 57.

5. With reference to the art and sculptures of the Harappan people, describe
   (i) Bronze casting
   (ii) Pottery
   (iii) Stone Sculpture
   (iv) Dress

Ans. (i) Refer to chapter theory page no. 58.
(ii) Refer to chapter theory page no. 58.
(iii) Refer to chapter theory page no. 58.
(iv) Refer to chapter theory page no. 58.

6. Though the definite reason for the decline of Harappan civilisation is unknown, there are some speculative causes. In contact of this, explain.
   (i) The effects of deforestation.
   (ii) Foreign Attack.
   (iii) The effects of floods and climate change.
   (iv) Earthquake.

Ans. (i) Refer to chapter theory page no. 59.
(ii) Refer to chapter theory page no. 59.
(iii) Refer to chapter theory page no. 59.
(iv) Refer to chapter theory page no. 59.

Picture Based Question

1. With reference to the given picture, answer the following questions

   (i) Identify this image and give a brief description about it.
   (ii) Materials used in making seal. Give one example of seal made by Terracotta.
   (iii) Importance of seals.

Ans. (i) Refer to Structured Question 2 (ii).
(ii) The seals were made of steatite, sometime of copper, agate, ivory and terracotta. The figure of Mother Goddess is one of the siginficant terracotta sculpture.
(iii) Refer to chapter theory page no. 55.

Chapter Assessment

Section-I

Multiple Choice Questions

1. Mohenjodaro site was discovered in
   (a) 1919 (b) 1920
   (c) 1921 (d) 1922
2. Dancing girl which was found at Mohenjodaro was made up of which of the following ?
   (a) Bronze (b) Stone
   (c) Copper (d) Wooden
3. Complete the given analogy.
   Chanhudaro : Bangle Making : Lothal : : ?
   (a) Kitchenware
   (b) Rice
   (c) Cotton
   (d) None of the above
4. Replaced the underlined word and correct the statement. The most popular means of transport within the cities were <u>Rhinoceros.</u>
   (a) Camel (b) Bullock cart
   (c) Boat (d) All of these

Section-II

Very Short Questions

1. Why is Indus Valley civilisation also known as the 'Harappan civilisation'?
2. Which is the oldest civilisation in India?
3. Where is the great granary found in Indus Valley civilisation?
4. What does the Terracotta figure of the Mother Goddess symbolise?
5. What type of game the people of the Indus Valley civilisation played?
6. What were the food habits of Indus Valley civilisation?

Structured Questions

1. With reference to the economic life of the Harappan people, discuss about
   (i) Agriculture
   (ii) Harappan seals
   (iii) Trade and commerce
   (iv) Transport

CHAPTER 02

The Vedic Age

SYLLABUS

Sources Names of the four Vedas and importance of epics; Early Vedic Period; Social organisation-Family-Position of the king; Rig Vedic Assemblies-Sabha, Samiti, Vedatha Brief comparative study of position of women in Early and Later Vedic Period. A brief comparison between the economy of Early and Later Vedic Period The four class division, the four ashramas and the education system

After the decline of the Indus Valley Civilisation, another glorious civilisation known as 'Vedic Civilisation' flourished in India. The Vedic culture grew in India around 1500 BC by the advent of the Aryans.

The Advent of Aryans

Arya literally means the man of 'noble character' and the 'free born'. They belonged to the group of people known as Indo-Europeans. They entered into India from the North-West and first settled in Punjab. The Aryans lived in **Saptasindhu** region of India for a long time. It is also known as the land of seven rivers; which were, Indus, Jhelum, Chenab, Ravi, Beas, Sutlej and Saraswati.

Aryans spoke the Indo-European languages from which modern languages like Sanskrit, Persian, Latin, Greek, Celtie and Gothic have developed. It is generally believed that Aryans were not the original **inhabitants**[1] of India.

According to German scholar Max-Muller, the original home of the Aryans was somewhere near the Caspian Sea.

The Aryans who had migrated to India are known as the **Indo-Aryans**. They were the first people who entered India through the North-Western passes.

Sources of Vedic Age

In order to understand about the Vedic age, the sources have been divided into two parts namely

1. Literary Sources

The Vedic text was divided into two broad groups i.e. the early Vedic texts (1500-1000 BC) when the most **hymns**[2] of the Rig Veda were composed and the later Vedic texts (1000 BC - 600 BC) which belongs to Brahmanas, Upanishad and Aranyakas. Vedas became the storehouse of knowledge as they reflect the social, political, economic and religious life of the people. The Vedic literature was written in Sanskrit. It was divided into two parts

(i) **Shruti** It was believed that it was revealed to the sages by God and they passed on that knowledge orally from generation to generation.

(ii) **Smriti** It was composed by the Saints (*Rishis*).

1. **Inhabitant** A person or animal that lives in or occupies a place.
2. **Hymns** A religious song or poem of praise to God.

The Vedic literature can be classified into the following categories

- The Four Vedas
- The Brahmanas
- The Aranyakas
- The Upanishads

The Four Vedas

The word 'Veda' is derived from the Sanskrit word 'vid', which means 'to know'. The Vedas are known as *Nitya* i.e. the eternal. They are collection of hymns, prayers, charms and sacrificial formulae.

The four Vedas are

(i) **The Rig Veda** It is the oldest of all the Vedas and also the earliest text of Indo-Europeans groups of literature. It is the first testament of mankind. It is the collection of hymns to be recited at the time of sacrificial rites and other rituals. It contains 1028 hymns divided into 10 mandalas and 8 ashtakas.

The 3rd mandala is devoted to Gayatri, which contains the famous Gayatri Mantra, the 9th mandala talks about the Vedic God Soma and the 10th mandala contains the Purushasukta hymn referring to the four-fold caste system.

(ii) **The Sama Veda** The word 'sama' means 'sweet song'. Sama Veda is a collection of hymns taken from the Rig Veda and set to tunes for the purpose of singing. It is sung by a type of priest, known as ***Udgatri***. It is regarded as the origin of Indian music.

(iii) **The Yajur Veda** It is a collection of rituals for performing different sacrifices and recited by the priests known as ***Adhrvau***. It contains 40 chapters which throw light on the social and religious life of the Aryans.

(iv) **The Atharva Veda** This Veda contains approximately 730 hymns meant for warding off evils and demons, winning over friends and gain material success. It is a collection of charms, magic and spells. Apart from this, the hymns also deal with *gyan* (knowledge), *karma* (action) and *upasana* (citation). Some hymns also deal with medicines for the treatment of various diseases.

The Brahmanas

The Brahmanas are elaborate prose texts and are also known as **Liturgies**. These are texts on sacrificial rituals. They contain explanations of hymns, their origin and describe their application. They advocate *Karma Marga* for attainment of **salvation**[3].

The Aranyakas

The literal meaning of 'Aranyakas' is 'forest'. They are known as **forest books**. The Aranyakas deal with **mysticism**[4], moral values and philosophical doctrines of the Aryans who were ascetics and hermits living in the forests.

The Upanishads

The word 'Upanishad' literally 'to sit down near someone'. It denotes a student sitting at the feet of his guru to learn. The Upanishads deal with philosophical and metaphysical (spiritual) issues. They were composed between 800-500 BC and they are 108 in numbers. They contain the first clear exposition of belief in the passage of soul from one birth to another.

Allied Vedic Literature

It include Vedangas, Sutras, Upavedas, Darshans, Dharmashastras, Manusmriti, Ashtadhyayi and the epics.

Vedangas

They give insights into the structure, language and meaning of the Vedas, as well as helping to understand other post-Vedic texts and aspects of Hindu and yogic philosophy. The six Vedangas are ***Shiksha, Kalpa, Vyakarana, Nirukta, Chhanda*** and ***Jyotisha***. *Shiksha* deals with pronunciation, *Kalpa* with rituals, *Vyakarana* with grammar, *Nirukta* with etymology, *Chhanda* with metre and *Jyotisha* with astronomy.

Sutras

They are concise, brief and/or memorable expression of a general truth or principle which are handed down the generations as a tradition. It is divided into three groups

(i) ***Grihya Sutra*** It include domestic rituals connected with birth, marriage and funerals.

(ii) ***Srauta Sutra*** It include public sacrifices meant for princes and higher varnas.

(iii) ***Dharma Sutra*** It provides rule of conduct for the various classes of people and the various stages of human life.

3. **Salvation** State of being saved or protected from harm or sin.
4. **Mysticism** It is a religious practice in which people search for truth, knowledge and closeness to God through meditation and prayer.

Upavedas

They are the subsidiary of the Vedas. There are four Upavedas, namely *Dhanurveda* (deals with the art of warfare), the *Gandharvaveda* (deals with music), *Shilpa veda* (deals with architecture) and *Ayurveda* (deals with the science of life). They do not form an integral part of the Vedic literature but each of them enjoys great **sanctity**[5].

Darshans

There are six schools of Indian philosophy known as *Shad-Darshans*. These are *Nyaya*, *Vaishesika*, *Sankhya*, *Yoga*, *Purva* and *Uttara Mimamsa*. They all propagate the virtues of life and are opposed to external rituals.

Dharmashastras

They throw considerable light upon the social and religious conditions of ancient India, family life, gender and caste based distinctions and principles of ancient jurisprudence. The *Dharmashastras* elaborate the duties of common folk, royal officials and kings. *Manusmriti* elaborates the Hindu code of law and gives details about the *Varnas* i.e. the castes and different *Ashramas* of individual life.

Manusmriti

It was an ancient legal 'text' or *Dharmashastra* of Hinduism. It describe the social system prevailed at the time of the Aryans. It was famous for preaching casteist and patriarchal norms that ridiculed the dalits and women by stripping away all the basic rights and leaving them to the mercy of the upper-class individiual.

Ashtadhyayi

It is a Sanskrit treatise on grammar written in the 6th to 5th century BCE by the Indian grammarian **Panini**. This work set the linguistic standards for classical Sanskrit. It sums up in 4,000 sutras and contains the science of phonetics and grammar that had evolved in the Vedic religion.

The Epics

The two great Indian epics are the Ramayana and the Mahabharata.

Ramayana

Sage Valmiki wrote the Ramayana in 3rd century BC. It tells the story of Lord Rama, who was sent to an exile for 14 years along with his brother and wife. He fought battle with the demon king Ravana of Lanka, who had kidnapped his wife Sita. The epic is full of morals and thought provoking lines. The devotion of each and every character in this epic is commendable.

Mahabharata

The epic Mahabharata was composed by the great **sage Ved Vyasa**. Mahabharata is over 100000 lines long in its original poetic form. It illustrates the victory of good over evil through the story of Pandavas who were five brothers. The Pandavas were symbolised as good and their cousins Kauravas were symbolised as evil in human nature.

The Pandavas and their wife Draupadi, were put through various ordeals which were a direct consequence of the **malice**[6] of the Kauravas. Finally, in the end, the Pandavas who were supported by Lord Krishna defeated the Kauravas in an eighteen-day long battle.

The **Bhagavad Gita** is a (700-verse) Hindu scripture that is part of the epic Mahabharata. It is considered to be one of the holy scriptures for Hinduism. The Gita is set in a narrative framework of a dialogue between Pandava prince Arjuna and his guide and charioteer Krishna, the supreme personality of Godhead.

It openly synthesises and inclusively accepts multiple ways of life that harmonise spiritual pursuits through action (*karma*), knowledge (*gyana*), and devotion (*bhakti*). Gita teaches that the soul is immortal.

Importance of the Epics

- The epics are the main sources of information on the political institutions and the social and cultural organisation of the epic period.
- They give information on various Aryan kingdoms, their armies and their weapons like the Kshatriyas were entrusted with the defence of their kingdoms and they believed that the death on the battlefield was the noblest act in the life of a warrior.
- They reveal the high ideals of family life of the Aryans.
- They are considered as the finest literary works of the ancient period and are acclaimed for their literary and philosophical values.

5. **Sanctity** The state of being holy.
6. **Malice** It is the desire to harm someone.

- They are based on established traditions which narrates the deeds of old heroic figures.
- The Bhagavad Gita elaborates the Karma and immortality of the soul.

2. Archaeological Sources of Vedic Age

The available archaeological source that give information about the Vedic Age, include iron artifacts and remains of pottery.

Metal and Tools

The Vedic Aryans became aware of iron around 1000 BC. Evidences of iron tools have been found at Atranjikhera in Uttar Pradesh. Arrowheads and spearheads are found most frequently. Iron artifacts have also been found from Kausambi near Allahabad, Jakhera in Etah district (Uttar Pradesh) and Hallur in Karnataka.

Pottery Remains

The popularity of agriculture led to the development of pottery. The later Vedic Aryans developed the knowledge of pottery. The **Grey Ware (GW)** and **Painted Grey Ware (PGW)** pottery has been discovered at different sites of Punjab and Haryana. It is believed that they to belonged to the Rig Vedic Aryans.

Check Your LEARNING...

1. According to Max Muller, which is the original home of Aryans?
2. Define the term 'Sutras'.
3. What do you mean by the term 'Shad-Darshanas'?
4. When was the iron discovered?

Early Vedic Period

The Early Vedic period is also known as Rig Vedic period because the first Veda named Rig Veda was composed during this time. The period of the Early Vedic period is fixed between 1500 and 1000 BC when Aryans came and settled in India.

Social Organisation During Early Vedic Period

King and Society

The early Vedic Aryans lived in villages. A group of villages was called the **Vishu/Vis**. Many Vishas formed a Jana. The head of the village was called Gramini, the head of the Vis/Vishu was called Vishapati and the head of Jana was called Rajan. Some other officers included the Senani (the commander of the army) and the Purohita (who performed religious ceremonies).

There was very little interference of the king in village life. The king governed the village with the help of ministers. Three important assemblies advised the king that were

(i) **Sabha** It was the assembly of the people. It performed judicial and advisory functions.

(ii) **Samiti** It was the council of the elders.

(iii) **Vidatha** It was the earliest assembly that performed all kind of funcitons like economic, religious, social and military functions.

There was joint family system prevalent in the early Vedic period. The family was the fundamental unity of society and it was patriarchal. The head of the family was its eldest male member and he was known as **Grihapati**.

Class Divisions

The caste system is not mentioned in the Rig Veda, but there were some kinds of class divisions during early Vedic period. The division of the society into different classes was based on their professions. People were allowed to adopt any profession of their choice, but with time the profession became hereditary. This resulted in division of society on the basis of occupation.

The early Aryans, called the local inhabitants as **Dasyus** and did not mix with them during this period. The tribal chiefs and the priests acquired a large share of the booty (stolen goods) and became rich at the cost of their kinsmen. This created division in the tribal society and emergence of three groups i.e. warriors, priests and the people.

The fourth group called the Shudras appeared towards the end of Rig Vedic period, because the word Shudra is mentioned for the first time in the Tenth Mandala of Rig Veda which is usually considered a latest addition.

Position of Women

- During the Rig Vedic or early Vedic period, women were respected and enjoyed equal status as men. Women could participate in various assemblies.
- The daughters were given the freedom to choose their husbands and also the system of widow remarriage was prevalent.

- There were no examples of child marriage and the marriage age in the Rig Veda seems to have been 16 to 17 years.

Education

Education was imparted through Gurukuls in the early Vedic period. The residence of the Guru or the teacher was called Gurukul (family of the guru) and was considered the most sacred institution.

The students had to reside in the Gurukuls, situated in forests or on the outskirts of villages. Most of the education was imparted orally. Physical, spiritual and mental development in pupils was the main object of such education. Vedas, Grammar, Puranas, Mathematics, Ethics, Logic and Military Science were the subjects in the early Vedic period. Two women teachers *Maitreyi* and *Gargi* were prominent and considered gifted. The Gurukul system also continued in the later Vedic period.

Food, Dresses and Amusements

- The diet of Rig Vedic Aryans was both balanced and enriching which included both vegetarian and non-vegetarian dishes.
- Wheat and barley, milk and its products like curd and ghee, vegetables and fruits were the chief articles of food.
- Fish, birds, goats, rams, bulls and horses were slaughtered for their food. Slaughter of the cow was prohibited since it was considered a sacred animal. People also drank intoxicating liquor, 'Soma'.
- The Aryans wore dresses made from cotton, wool and deer skin.
- The garments consisted of three parts i.e. an undergarment called *'Nivi'*, a garment called *'Vasa'* or *'Paridhan'* and a mantle known as *'Adhivasa'*.
- Both men and women wore gold ornaments.
- The women used earrings, necklace, bangles and anklets.
- The main sources of amusements in the early Vedic period were horse races, hunting, singing, dancing, chariot races, gambling, etc.

Religious Belief

- The religious life of the Rig Vedic Aryans was simple. They worshipped and personified the natural forces into many gods such as *Prithvi* (Earth), *Agni* (Fire), *Vayu* (Wind), *Varuna* (Rain) and *Indra* (Thunder).
- Indra was the most important God and was also known as **Purandara** (the destroyer of forts) and God of rain. Agni was second important god after Indra.
- There were also female gods like Aditi and Ushas. However, the male gods were more important than female gods in the patriarchal set-up of the period.
- There were no temples and no idol worship during the early Vedic period. Prayers were offered to the gods in the expectation of rewards. Ghee, milk and grain were given as offerings. Elaborate rituals were followed during the worship.
- Worship was not meant for the spiritual uplift or ending miseries, but it was intended mainly for *praja* (children), *pashu* (cattle), food, wealth, health, etc.
- The magical power of the word was not considered so important as it came to be in later Vedic times.
- Animals like horses, buffaloes, rams, bulls and even cows were also sometimes sacrificed. There was no priestly class for performing the religious rites.
- The theory of reincarnation or rebirth was not completely formed. The Rig Vedic hymns had no consistent theory regarding life after death.

Economy during Early Vedic Period

- **Agriculture** The Rig Vedic economy was primarily rural in nature. People had knowledge of agriculture and practised it to supplement their food requirements. There are references of producing yava (jau or barley), during that period.
- **Cattle Rearing** Cattle rearing was the main occupation and considered as the most important economic activity of the Rig Vedic Aryans. Cows were the principal wealth. They were given to the priests as gifts for performing sacrifices. A wealthy person was known as **gomat** and his wealth was measured in terms of number of cows he owned. Prayers were offered for an increase in the number of cattle. Gopa and Gopati were **epithets**[7] given to the king.
- **Other Activities** Other economic activities included hunting, carpentry, tanning, pottery weaving, chariot making, fishery, etc. Chariot makers had

7. **Epithets** Descriptive phrase expressing a quality characteristic of the person.

an important position. Women were also engaged in crafts like weaving, dying, spinning and knitting. Wool obtained from sheep was the most common raw material.

- **Trade** The products were exchanged through **barter system**. Cow and *Nishka* (gold ornaments) were used as medium of exchange. Towns and cities in turn provided further impetus to trade. No regular system of taxation was there. Bali (tax paid by the members of tribe to the king) and war booty played important part in the economy.

Later Vedic Period

The period between 1000 and 600 BC in which Aryans found new settlements is known as later Vedic period.

Society during Later Vedic Period

The later Vedic period witnessed evolution in its various aspects. Following are the features of the later Vedic society

- The powers of the father in the family increased to great extent. It marked the beginning of the practice of **primogeniture**[8].
- The society was more rigid. Change of occupations was not easy and various professions became **hereditary.**[9]
- The power and prestige of Brahmins increased immensely because of excessive growth of sacrifices and rituals.

Ashrama System

Ashrama system came into existence in later Vedic period which means four stages in the long journey of life of a man. These were

(i) **Brahmacharya Ashrama (from birth to 25 years of age)** It was the first stage in Aryan man's life. The student went to a Gurukul and typically would live with a Guru to acquire knowledge of philosophy, science and logic. Students learned there to live a life of *Dharma* (righteousness, morals, duties).

(ii) **Grihastha Ashrama (the age of 25 to 50 years)** It is the second stage in Aryan man's life. A man was supposed to marry and lead a family life by following a set of customs and traditions. *Grihastha* stage was considered as the most important of all stages in sociological context. Human beings in this stage not only pursued a virtuous life, but they produced food and wealth that sustained people in other stages.

(iii) **Vanaprastha Ashrama (the age of 50 to 75)** It is the third stage in which a person handed over household responsibilities to the next generation, took an advisory role and gradually withdrew from the world. He was expected to lead a life of complete detachment and to utilise his time for the study of Upanishads, Sutras and meditation. It was believed that a person who died while pursuing *Vanprastha Ashrama* attained *moksha.*

(iv) **Sanyasa Ashrama (the age of 75 to 100)** A man had to abandon his complete social life and devote all his time in the service of God to attain salvation or *moksha.* Historically, *Sanyasa* has been a stage of renunciation, *ahimsa* (non-violence), peaceful and simple life and spiritual goals in Indian traditions.

Class Divisions

The four-fold Varna system came to be firmly established during the later Vedic period.
These were

(i) **Brahmins** They learnt the Vedas and performed religious ceremonies and taught the people.

(ii) **Kshatriyas** They were the fighting class. They composed hymns and performed sacrifices and also challenged the supremacy of Brahmanas.

(iii) **Vaishyas** They were engaged in trade, industry, agriculture and animal husbandry. They were debarred from the privileges which were enjoyed by the Brahmanas and Kshatriyas. However, the richer people among the vaishyas were known as *Sresthin* who were highly honoured in the royal court.

(iv) **Shudras** The condition of the Shudras was very miserable. They had to serve the other three castes. They were untouchables. They had no right to approach the sacred fire, i.e. perform sacrifice or to read the sacred texts.

8. **Primogeniture** The right of succession belonging to the first born child.
9. **Hereditary** A descriptive term for conditions capable of being transmitted from one generation to another.

Position of Women

- Position of women declined to some extent in the later Vedic period.
- Women lost the right to the **Upanayana ceremony**[10]. They were not allowed to take part in Sabha and Samiti.
- Birth of a daughter came to be regarded as a source of misery.
- Women were not allowed to own property and widow marriage was not allowed.

Food and Dresses

- Rice became the staple food of the later Vedic Aryans.
- The practice of eating meat declined and slaughtering of cow became crime.
- Drinking of Sura or wine was still favoured.
- Wool and silk was increasingly used for dress in addition to cotton.

Religious Belief

- Varun and Indra were the most important Gods of Rig Vedic age but lost prominence in later Vedic period.
- Prajapati or *Adipurush* became the Supreme God in later Vedic phase.
- Shiva was regarded as the destroyer of the Universe and Vishnu as the preserver and protector.
- Rituals, sacrifices and requirement of supervising priest (Purohita) made religious life complex.
- Few instances of idol worship were reported during later Vedic period.
- Magic and omen entered the socio-religious life.
- At the end of later Vedic period, Upanishadik philosophers made efforts to simplify the religious practices.
- Few Kshatriyas, in later Vedic period, like Janak and Vishswamitra succeeded in knowing the supreme i.e. Brahma.
- In later Vedic period, new doctrines were included by the Brahmanas which were *karma* (action), dharma (duty) and moksha (salvation). There was an emergence in the belief of rebirth.

Economy during Later Vedic Period

- **Agriculture** The Aryans gave up nomadic life and started living a settled life. It was a transition from pastoral economy to a sedentary agrarian economy. The availability of fertile soil made possible the growth of agriculture as Aryans had moved to the Gangetic plains by this period (1000 BC). People were familiar with plough cultivation. A large variety of crops like *vrihi* (rice), wheat, barley, millets, sugarcane, etc were grown. Knowledge of iron technology transformed economic life and brought about far reaching changes in cultivation.
- **Trade** Uses of metal and leather work, carpentry and pottery grew during later Vedic period, which gave rise to trade and enabled exchange of goods in the market. Coins were not used, but *Nishka* and *Satamana* which were gold ornaments during Rig Veda age came to be used for trade and commerce. Beginning of regular taxation system, *Bali* became a compulsory tax.

  In addition to internal trade, foreign trade also became extensive. The later Vedic people were familiar with the sea and therefore, they traded their goods through the maritime route also.

  A class of hereditary merchants (*Vaniya*) also came into existence. They also carried on trade and commerce. The trade also led to the development of markets and the markets led to the development of cities and towns.

10. **Upanayana Ceremony** It marked the acceptance of a student by a guru and individual's initiation into a school during Vedic times.

Comparative Study of the Early Vedic Period (Rig Vedic) and Later Vedic Period

Basis	Early Vedic Period	Later Vedic Period
Social Life	• Family was the basic unit.	• Joint family system prevailed.
	• Women enjoyed equal rights.	• Significant decline in the status of women.
	• Rigidity in the caste system was not prevalent. Four fold division of varnas was made primarily on the basis of occupation.	• The caste system became more rigid; birth became the basis of one's caste; each class has its distinct role; four ashramas developed.
	• Gurukul system of education.	• Gurukul system was further enlarged.
	• Food included milk, barley, rice, fruits, vegetables and meat.	• Consumption of meat reduced.
	• Worship of nature and natural phenomena prevailed. Worship of forefathers and belief in life after death prevailed.	• Religion became more complex.
	• Absence of temples of idols.	• Brahmans introduced many rituals and made their position secure.
	• Hymns were chanted in the open.	• New principles of penance (acknowledge punishment for wrong doing), doctrine of Karma, transmigration and salvation developed.
Economic Life	• In the beginning, the main occupation was domestication of animals and agriculture was secondary.	• Agriculture became the chief occupation and domestication of cattle also continued.
	• Cattle was the important source of wealth.	• Land was the important source of wealth.
	• Many people were engaged in trade and commerce.	• Trade continued in barter and currency mode of exchange was in silver coins.
	• Barter system prevailed and was carried out in terms of bullocks and horses.	• Traders guilds had come up and vaisyas also carried on trade and commerce.
	• Dyeing, embroidery, hunting, carpenting, tanning, pottery, weaving, chariot making, fishery, crafts in gold and iron were important occupations.	• Besides occupations of earlier period, many new occupations like physicians, musicians and many other professions emerged. Metal work, leather work, jewellery making, carpentry and pottery made great improvement.
Religious Life	• Worshipped a number of nature God's such as Varuna, Surya, Indra, Agni and Pushan.	• Worshipped many new Gods such as Brahma, Vishnu, Shiva, Rama, Krishna and Rudra were observed.
	• Female goddess like Aditi and Usha were also worshipped.	• Rituals became more complicated, belief in spells and charms increased.
	• Sacrifices and yajnas were performed.	• Priesthood and animal sacrifice became prominent.

Check Your LEARNING...

1. Name the God of early Vedic period.
2. What do you mean by gomat?
3. Which stage in Ashrama system sustains other stages?
4. Name some crops grown by the people of later Vedic period.
5. What is term used for regular taxation system in later Vedic age?

QUiCK Revision

- After the decline of the Indus Valley Civilisation, another glorious civilisation the Vedic Civilisation flourished in India. The pepole who were responsible for the evolution of this civilisation called themselves Aryas or Aryans.
- It is generally believed that Aryans were not the original inhabitants of India. Many theories have been put forward in favour and against the argument. According to some historians, the original home of Aryans was Central Asia.
- In order to understand about the Vedic age, the sources have been divided into two parts namely literary sources (the four Vedas, the Brahmanas, the Aranyakas, the Upanishads, Allied Vedic literature and Epics) and archaeological sources (metal and tools, pottery remains).
- In early Vedic period, the division of society into different classes were based on their profession. People were allowed to adopt any profession of their choice, but with time it changed.
- The political life was tribal in times of the early Vedic age. Kula (family) was the basic unit. Gramini (head of the village) also played important role during Rig Vedic age.
- The early Aryans, called the local inhabitants as Dasyus and did not mix with them during early Vedic period.
- Position of women was high and respectable. The women enjoyed right to attend religious ceremonies and political assemblies like Sabha and Samiti.
- The religious life of early Vedic age was primarily personification of the forces of nature. Aryans gave the natural events the names of Gods. There was no idol worship and temple worship.
- The Rig Vedic life was pastoral in nature. People were aware of agriculture, but it was not very popular. Yava (barley) was the main crop and cattle rearing was the main occupation.
- The later Vedic period witnessed evolution in its various aspects. The powers of the father in the family increased to great extent. It marked the beginning of the practice of Primogeniture.
- The society was more rigid. Change of occupation was not easy and various professions became hereditary.
- Ashrama system came into existence which means a stage in the long journey of life of a man.
- The four-fold Varna system came to be firmly established. These were Brahmanas, Kshatriyas, Vaisyas and Sudras.
- The Aryans gave up nomadic life during the later Vedic age and started living a settled life. It was a transition from pastoral economy to a sedentary agrarian economy.
- The availability of fertile soil made possible the growth of agriculture as Aryans had moved to the Gangetic plains by this period (1000 BC).
- Knowledge of iron technology transformed economic life and brought about far reaching changes.
- During the later Vedic age, there was a rise of new Gods into prominence – Vishnu, Rudra and Prajapati. Gods like Indra, Varuna and Agni lost their supreme position.
- The sacrifices became more elaborate and complex and gained pre-eminence over prayers.
- The union of tribes led to the rise of large kingdoms, which led to the growth of royal power during the later Vedic age.

Chapter Practice

Section-I

Multiple Choice Questions

1. The Vedic culture grew in India around ......
   (a) 2500 BC (b) 1750 BC
   (c) 1500 BC (d) 1000 BC

Ans. (c) 1500 BC

2. Aryans spoke which of the following language?
   (a) Hindi
   (b) Latin
   (c) Persian
   (d) Indo-European

Ans. (d) Indo-European

3. .... is the oldest Veda.
   (a) Rig Veda (b) Sama Veda
   (c) Yajur Veda (d) Atharva Veda

Ans. (a) Rig Veda

4. Which of the following Veda is collection of charm, magic and spell ?
   (a) Riga Veda
   (b) Sama Veda
   (c) Yajur Veda
   (d) Atharva Veda

Ans. (a) Atharva Veda

5. .... are known as forest book.
   (a) Upanishads (b) Vedas
   (c) Aranyakas (d) Epics

Ans. (c) Aranyakas

6. Identify the appropriate use of iron by Vedic Aryans
   (a) Iron tools were used for cleaning forest
   (b) It was used for weapons
   (c) It was also used for occupational purposes like weaving and spinning
   (d) All of the above

Ans. (d) All of the above

7. Which of the following statement is true about the position of women during early Vedic age ?
   (a) Women were respected and enjoyed equal status as men.
   (b) Women couldn't participate in assemblies.
   (c) Women were not given the freedom to choose their husband.
   (d) System of widow remmariage was not prevalent.

Ans. (a) Women were respected and enjoyed equal status as men.

8. A man had abandon his complete social life and devote all his time in the service of God to attain salvation is called
   (a) Grihastha Ashrama
   (b) Vanoprastha Ashrama
   (c) Sanyasa Ashrama
   (d) Brahmacharya Ashrama

Ans. (c) Sanyasa Ashrama

9. Who became the Supreme God in later Vedic phase?
   (a) Prajapati (b) Varun
   (c) Indra (d) Sun

Ans. (a) Prajapati

10. Complete the given analogy.
    Ramayana : Valmiki :: Mahabharata : ?
    (a) Ved Vyas (b) Pawini
    (c) Tulsidas (d) Kalidas

Ans. (a) Ved Vyas

11. Complete the given analogy.
    Brahmacharya Ashrama : 25 years : : *Grihastha Ashram* : ?
    (a) 25-50 years (b) 50-75 years
    (c) 75-100 years (d) None of these

Ans. (a) 25-50 years

12. Complete the given analogy
    Brahmanas : Vedas religious ceremonies :: Vaisyas : ?
    (a) Fighting (b) Trade
    (c) Serve others (d) All of these

Ans. (b) Trade

13. Replace the underlined word and correct the statement.
    <u>Mahabharata</u> tells the story of Lord Rama, who was sent to an exile of 14 Years along with his brother and wife.
    (a) Bhagavada Gita (b) Ramayana
    (c) Veda (d) Upanishad

Ans. (b) Ramayana

14. Replaced the underlined word and correct the statement.
    During early Vedic period products were exchanged through barter system <u>buffalo</u> and Niksh (gold ornaments) were used as medium of exchange.
    (a) Ox (b) Camel
    (c) Goat (d) Cow

Ans. (d) Cow

15. Complete the given table.

Early Vedic Period	1500-1000 BC
Later Vedic Period	?

(a) 1500 BC - 400 BC (b) 1000 BC - 400 BC
(c) 1000 BC - 600 BC (d) 1000 BC - 800 BC

Ans. (c) 1000 BC - 600 BC

16. Identify the correct statement associated with the remains of pottery
(i) They were made using wheel
(ii) Smooth surface
(iii) Grey to ash grey in colour
(iv) They had nearly 42 designs

Codes
(a) Only (i) (b) Both (i) and (ii)
(c) (i), (ii) and (iii) (d) All of these

Ans. (d) All of these

17. Identify the religious god during early Vedic period
(i) Agni (ii) Indra
(iii) Prithvi (iv) Acliti

Codes
(a) Only (i) (b) Both (i) and (ii)
(c) (i), (ii) and (iii) (d) All of these

Ans. (d) All of these

18. Select the correct option about position of women during later Vedic period
(i) Position declined to some extent
(ii) Lost the right to the Upanayana
(iii) Not allowed to take part in Sabha
(iv) Daughter regarded as a source of misery

Codes
(a) Only (i) (b) Only (ii)
(c) Both (ii) and (iv) (d) All of these

Ans. (d) All of these

19. Match the following.

A. Hymns	1. It is the desire to harm someone
B. Salvation	2. Preservation from harm, ruins or loss
C. Malice	3. A religious song / poems
D. Impetus	4. The force or energy

Codes

	A	B	C	D		A	B	C	D
(a)	4	3	2	1	(b)	3	2	1	4
(c)	1	2	3	4	(d)	2	1	4	3

Ans. (b)

20. Match the following.

A. Brahmacharya Ashrama	1. 25 years
B. Grihastha Ashrama	2. 50-75 years
C. Vanaprastha Ashrama	3. 75-100 years
D. Sanyasa Ashrama	4. 25-50 years

Codes

	A	B	C	D		A	B	C	D
(a)	1	2	3	4	(b)	4	3	2	1
(c)	3	2	1	4	(d)	1	4	2	3

Ans. (d)

Picture Based Question

21. With reference to the given picture, answer the following question.

(i) Identify the picture, from which class of the Vedic age the person belongs to
(a) Kshatriya (b) Brahmana
(c) Vaisya (d) Trader

Ans. (a) Kshatriya

(ii) What was the duty of Kshatriya, mentioned in Vedic age?
(a) To fight with enemies (b) To learn vedas
(c) Engage in trade
(d) Performed religious ceremonies

Ans. (a) to fight with enemies

(iii) Which of the following was not the duty of Kshatriya?
(a) Performing Yajanas (b) Donation of alms
(c) Studying (d) To serve other caste

Ans. (d) To serve other caste

(iv) During the Vedic age who can challenge the supremacy of Brahmana ?
(a) Vaisya (b) God
(c) Kshatriya (d) Tribe

Ans. (c) Kshatriya

Passages Based Questions

22. Read the passage given below and answer the following questions.

Careful studies have shown that the Vedic texts reflect two stages of development in terms of literature as well as social and cultural evolution. The Rig Veda which is the oldest Vedic text reflects one stage of social and cultural development, whereas the other three Vedas reflect another stage. The first stage is known as the Rig Vedic period or Early Vedic period and the later stage is known as the Later Vedic period. The age of the Early Vedic period corresponds with the date of the composition of the Rig Vedic hymns. This date has been fixed between 1500 BC and 1000 BC. The later Vedic period is placed between 1000 BC and 600 BC. Recently, the Rig Veda has been included by the UNESCO in the list of literature signifying World Human Heritage.

(i) Which among the follwoing Vedas was compiled first?
(a) Yajur Veda (b) Sama Veda
(c) Rig Veda (d) Atharva Veda

Ans. (c) Rig Veda

(ii) The famous 'Gayatrimantra' was mentioned in
(a) Rig Veda (b) Sama Veda
(c) Artharva Veda (d) Yajur Veda

Ans. (a) Rig Veda

(iii) The family of the Rig Vedic Aryan was
(a) Matriarchal (b) Patriarchal
(c) Matriliveal (d) None of these

Ans. (b) Partriarchal

(iv) The Riga Veda contains how many hymns?
(a) 1028 (b) 2086 (c) 1875 (d) 731

Ans. (a) 1028

23. Read the passage given below and answer the following questions.

The functions of different gods reflect their needs in the society. Thus, since the Rig Vedic people were engaged in wars with each other they worshipped Indra as a god. He is the most frequently mentioned god in the Rig Veda. He carried the thunderbolt and was also respected as a weather god who brought rains. Maruts the god of storm aided Indra in the wars in the way tribesmen aided their leader in the tribal wars. Agni, the fire god was the god of the home and was considered an intermediary between gods and men. Soma was associated with plants and herbs. Soma was also a plant from which an intoxicating juice was extracted. This juice was drunk at sacrifices. Varuna, another important deity, was the keeper of the cosmic order known as rita.

(i) Which was the most important god of early Vedic age ?
(a) Indra (b) Agni (c) Sun (d) Prithvi

Ans. (a) Indra

(ii) Which of the following god was considered as an intermediary between gods and men?
(a) Agni (fire) (b) Varuna
(c) Indra (d) Soma

Ans. (a) Agni (fire)

(iii) Which of the following god is associated with rain ?
(a) Agni (b) Indra
(c) Rama (d) Parshurama

Ans. (b) Indra

(iv) Why Indra was most important?
(a) Because he was considered as warrior God.
(b) They always blessed people
(c) They forced people to worship
(d) None of the above

Ans. (a) Because he was considered as warrior God.

Section-II

Short Questions

1. What do you understand by the term 'Arya'?

Ans. Arya literally means the man of 'noble character' and the 'free born.' They belonged to the group of people known as Indo-Europeans.

2. What do you understand by the term 'Sapta-Sindhu'?

Ans. Sapta-Sindhu is the land of seven streams. It was Aryans' core region. These seven streams were Indus, Jhelum, Chenab, Ravi, Beas, Sutlej and Saraswati.

3. Which language did the Aryans speak?

Ans. The Aryans spoke the Indo-European languages from which modern languages like Sanskrit, Persian, Latin, Greek, Celtie and Gothic have developed.

4. What is the importance of the Sanskrit language?

Ans. The Sanskrit language served as the mother language for many regional languages and became a unifying force in the sub-continent.

5. What are the different theories about the origin of Aryans?

Ans. Different theories about the origin of Aryans are as follows

- According to some historians, the original home of Aryans was Central Asia.
- Some are of the view that the original home of Aryans was in Southern Russia.

6. How is the common descent of the Aryans indicated?

Ans. The common descent of Aryans is indicated by the fact that Sanskrit, the language of the Indo-Aryans is closely related to many languages of Europe and some languages of Western Asia.

7. Mention the different Vedic literatures.

Ans. The Vedic literature can be classified into the following categories
(i) The Four Vedas (ii) The Brahmanas
(iii) The Aranyakas (iv) The Upanishads

8. Explain the term Veda. Give its importance.

Ans. The word Veda is derived from the Sanskrit word 'Vid', which means 'to know.' The Vedas are known as 'Nitya', i.e. the eternal and are collection of hymns, prayers, charms and sacrificial formulae.

9. What does the Atharva Veda contain?

Ans. The Atharva Veda contains 731 hymns meant for warding off evils and demons, winning over friends and gain material success. Apart from this, the hymns also deal with *gyan* (knowledge), *karma* (action) and *upasana* (invocation).

10. What are Brahmanas? Which path they advocate to attain salvation?

Ans. The Brahmanas are elaborate prose texts and are also known as Liturgies. It contains explanations of hymns, their origin and describe their application.

They advocate *Karma Marga* for attainment of salvation.

11. Why are Aranyakas known as 'forest books'?

Ans. The literal meaning of Aranyakas is 'forest.' They were meant for the ascetics and hermits living in the forest. So, the Aranyakas are known as forest books.

12. What is the importance of Vedas and Upanishads?

Ans. The Vedas and the Upanishads are very important because they became the basis for the present day Hindu religion. They primarily discuss philosophy, meditation and the nature of God.

13. Explain the term Vedangas.

Ans. The Vedangas mean limbs of the Vedas. They are six in numbers. They were written by scholars of the later Vedic period. They interpret the Vedas in simple language and deal with the pronunciation of words, grammar, astronomy as well as rituals.

14. What are *sutras*? How many sutras are there?

Ans. *Sutras* explain the customs and rituals of the later Vedic period, especially with the rituals relating to soma (yajna) sacrifice. There are two sutras i.e. the Dharmasutras and the *Grihya Sutras*.

15. Mention the six schools of philosophy with the name of their founders.

Ans. The six schools of Indian philosophy are known as *Shad-Darshanas*. They are

(i) *Sankhya Shastra* of Kapila
(ii) *Yoga Shastra* of Patanjali
(iii) *Nyaya Shastra* of Gautama
(iv) *Vaisheshika Shastra* of Kanada
(v) *Purva Mimamsa* of Jaimini
(vi) *Uttara Mimamsa* of Vyasa

16. Mention some texts of *Dharmashastras*.

Ans. The *Dharmashastras* contain texts like Manusmriti, the Yajnavalkya Smriti, the Vishnu Smriti and the Narad Smriti.

17. How *Manusmriti* is important for Hindus?

Ans. The most important smriti is the *Manusmriti*, which contains the Hindu code of law and the duties of the four Varnas and thus, it is important for Hindus.

18. Who wrote the book Ashtadhyayi? What is the unique feature of the book?

Ans. Ashtadhyayi is a non-religious book written by Panini. It is a work of Sanskrit grammar.

The unique feature of the book is that it is perhaps the greatest grammar book of those times ever written in any languages.

19. Who wrote the epic of Mahabharata? What does it illustrate?

Ans. The epic Mahabharata was composed by the great sage Ved Vyasa.

It illustrates the victory of good over evil through the story of Pandavas who were five brothers. The Pandavas were embodiment of good and their cousins Kauravas symbolised all that was evil present in human nature.

20. What led to the development of pottery? Mention some features of Painted Grey Ware pottery?

Ans. The popularity of agriculture led to the development of pottery. Some of the features of Painted Grey Ware pottery were as follows

(i) They were made using wheel.
(ii) They had smooth surface.
(iii) They were grey to ash-grey in colour.

21. Mention two important uses of iron in the Vedic period.

Ans. The two important uses of iron are

(i) Iron tools were used for clearing forest and to carry out expansion of agriculture.
(ii) The emergence of iron also paved way for new trades by providing implements like saws, chisels, hammers and nails.

22. Make a list of the different practices prevailed during the early Vedic age.

Ans. Some of the practices which prevailed were inter-varna marriages, widow-remarriage, niyoga (type of surrogacy) and inter-dining among the varnas.

23. Was the society of early Vedic age rigid?

Ans. The social stratification in early Vedic age was not rigid because the Varna could be changed by changing the profession. In Rig Veda people were allowed to adopt any profession of their choice.

24. How education was provided during the Vedic age?

Ans. During Vedic age, education was imparted orally through Gurukuls in Vedic period. The residence of the Guru or teacher was called Gurukuls, situated in the forest or on the outskirt of villages. The students had to reside in the Gurukuls to bring about physical, spiritual and mental development in them. At Gurukuls teachers imparted knowledge not only of religion but also about warfare, statecraft, medicine and astrology.

25. How was the economic life of the early Vedic people?

Ans. The Rig Vedic economic life was pastoral in nature. People were aware of agriculture, but it was not very popular. *Yava* (barley) was the main crop. Cattle rearing was the main occupation and cows were the principal wealth.

26. Mention two features of the religion of early Vedic age.

Ans. Following were the two features of Rig Vedic religious life

(i) Aryans gave the natural events the names of Gods and there was no idol worship and temple worship.

(ii) Rig Vedic religion was characterised by the predominance of male Gods. Very few Goddess find mention in Rig Veda.

27. What was the importance of sacrifice during early Vedic period?

Ans. Sacrifice was the one of the important part of Aryan religion. It incorporated the use of formulae, performance of rituals, active role of priestly class and large scale slaughter of animals.

28. What was the position of king during the early Vedic age?

Ans. The king was mere tribal head and functioned more like a leader. Protection of members of the tribe from attacks was the main function of the king.

29. Mention two features of the society of the later Vedic age.

Ans. The later Vedic period witnessed evolution in its various aspects. Following were the two features of the later Vedic society

(i) The powers of the father in the family increased to great extent.

(ii) The society was more rigid. Change of occupation was not easy and various profession became hereditary.

30. What was the last stage of a human life?

Ans. *Sanyasa* (a renounced life in the forest) was regarded as the last stage of human life where a person had to abandon his complete social life and devote all his time in the service of God to attain salvation.

31. What was the four-fold caste system? Explain any two classes.

Ans. The four-fold Varna system came to be firmly established during the later Vedic age. They are Brahmins, Kshatriyas, Vaishyas and Shudras.

The Brahmins learnt the Vedas and performed religious ceremonies and taught the people.

The Kshatriyas were the fighting class. They composed hymns and performed sacrifices and also challenged the supremacy of Brahmanas.

32. Is it correct to say that the position of women slightly declined during the later Vedic age?

Ans. Yes, the position of women declined during the later Vedic age. Women lost the right to the upanayana ceremony. They were also not allowed to take part in sabha and samiti. Widow marriage was also not allowed.

33. What change took place in the economic life of later Vedic age?

Ans. The Aryans gave up nomadic life and started living settled life in the later Vedic age. It was a transition from pastoral economy to a sedentary agrarian economy. People were familiar with plough cultivation. A large variety of crops like wheat, barley, millets, sugarcane etc. were also grown.

34. Write two features of later Vedic religious life.

Ans. Two features of later Vedic religious life were as follows

(i) There was a rise of new Gods into prominence Vishnu, Rudra and Prajapati. Early Vedic age Gods like Indra, Varuna and Agni lost their supreme position.

(ii) The sacrifices became more elaborate and complex and gained pre-eminence over prayers.

Structured Questions

1. Most important component of the Vedic literature are the Four Vedas. With reference to this explain

(i) The Sama Veda

(ii) The Yajur Veda

(iii) The Rig Veda

(iv) Atharva Veda

Ans. (i) Refer to chapter theory page no. 67.

(ii) Refer to chapter theory page no. 67.

(iii) Refer to chapter theory page no. 67.

(iv) Refer to chapter theory page no. 67.

2. In context of the available archaeological sources about Vedic age, explain.

(i) Pottery

(ii) Features of Painted Grey Ware

(iii) Metal and Tools

Ans. (i) The popularity of agriculture led to the development of pottery. The later Vedic Aryans developed the knowledge of pottery. The Grey Ware (GW) and Painted Grey Ware (PGW) pottery has been discovered at different sites of Punjab and Haryana. It is believed that they to belonged to the Rig Vedic Aryans. These cultures are regarded as Rig Vedic because they belong to the same period and same region which was mentioned in Rig Veda.

(ii) Refer to chapter theory page no. 69.

(iii) Refer to chapter theory page no. 69.

3. With reference to the society of the early Vedic age, explain.
(i) Nature of the society
(ii) Position of women
(iii) Education
(iv) Economy

Ans. (i) The division of the society into different classes was based on their professions. People were allowed to adopt any profession of their choice but with time, the professions became hereditary. This resulted in division of society on the basis of occupation.
(ii) Position of women was high and respectable. The women enjoyed right to attend religious ceremonies and political assemblies like sabha and samiti. Some of the woman like Lopamudra, Apala, Goshala composed Rig Vedic hymns. Monogamy was the usual practice though polygamy was also practiced by many.
(iii) Refer to chapter theory page no. 70.
(iv) Refer to chapter theory page no. 70.

4. In the context of the economy of the early Vedic age/period, explain.
(i) Barter system
(ii) Other economic activities
(iii) Main occupation
(iv) Principal wealth

Ans. (i) Barter system means exchange of goods to fulfill their requirements. Cow and Nishka (gold ornaments) were used as medium of exchange. Towns and cities in turn provided further impetus to trade.
(ii) Other economic activities included hunting, carpentry, tanning, pottery weaving, chariot making, fishery, etc. Chariot makers had an important position. Women were also engaged in crafts like weaving, dying, spinning and knitting. Wool obtained from sheep was the most common raw material.
(iii) Cattle rearing were their main occupation and was considered to be the most important economic activity of the Rig Vedic Aryans. Cows were the principal wealth. Prayers were offered for an increase in cattle. Cows were given to priests as gifts for performing sacrifices.
(iv) During the Early Rig Vedic age cows were the principal wealth. They were given to the priests as the gifts for performing sacrifices.

5. Ashrama system came into existence which means a stage in the long journey of life of a man. Explain
(i) *Brahmacharya Ashrama*
(ii) *Grihastha Ashrama*
(iii) *Vanaprastha Ashrama*

Ans. (i) Refer to chapter theory page no. 71.
(ii) Refer to chapter theory page no. 71.
(iii) Refer to chapter theory page no. 71.

6. With reference to the economy of the later Vedic period, explain
(i) Foreign trade
(ii) Use of iron
(iii) Sedentary agrarian economy

Ans. (i) In addition to internal trade, foreign trade also became extensive during later Vedic period. The Later Vedic people were familiar with the sea and therefore, they traded their goods through the maritime routes also. A class of hereditary merchants (*Vaniya*) also came into existence. They also carried on trade and commerce. The trade also led to the development of markets and the markets led to the development of cities and towns.
(ii) Iron was used in different forms as
- Iron tools were used for clearing forest to carry out expansion of agriculture.
- The use of iron ploughshare enabled deeper ploughing which paved the way for beginning of wet paddy cultivation.
- The emergence of iron also paved way for new trades by providing implements like saws, chisels, hammers and nails.
- Iron was also used in making weapons (swords, armours and shields) which were stronger than the copper and bronze weapons, which were used earlier.

(iii) In later Vedic period, the Aryans gave up nomadic life and started living settled life. It was a transition from pastoral economy to a sedentary agrarian economy. The availability of fertile soil made possible the growth of agriculture as Aryans had moved to the Gangetic plains by this period (1000 BC). People were familiar with plough cultivation. A large variety of crops like wheat, barley, millets, sugarcane, etc were grown.

7. With reference to the features of religious life of the later Vedic period, explain
(i) Name the new God's came into prominence
(ii) Nature of ideas
(iii) Nature of thoughts
(iv) Food and Dresses

Ans. (i) During the later Vedic age, there was a rise of new Gods into prominence like Vishnu, Rudra and Prajapati. Gods like Indra, Varuna and Agni lost their supreme position. Vishnu was regarded as the protector and preserver of the universe and Shiva was regarded as the destroyer.

(ii) Growth of pessimistic ideas came into existence during later Vedic period and this tendency resulted in philosophical speculation, meditation, penance and asceticism.

(iii) Later Vedic period marked the rise of upanishad thoughts i.e. the concept of Brahma, salvation by means of knowledge and realisation, etc. Rituals became more complicated, belief in charms and spells increased. Priesthood and animal sacrifice became prominent.

(iv) Refer to chapter theory page no. 70.

8. Major transformation took place in various areas, from Rig Vedic age to later Vedic age, explain
(i) Religious changes
(ii) Economic changes
(iii) Social changes

Ans. (i) Refer to chapter theory page no. 73.
(ii) Refer to chapter theory page no. 73.
(iii) Refer to chapter theory page no. 73.

Chapter Assessment

Section-I

Multiple Choice Questions

1. The time period of the later Vedic period is
(a) 1000-400 BC (b) 1500-1000 BC
(c) 1000-600 BC (d) 1750-1200 BC

2. Who composed Mahabharata?
(a) Ved Vyasa (b) Valmiki
(c) Panini (d) Tulsidasa

3. Replace the underlined word and correct the statement
The Vedic Aryans became aware of <u>stone</u> around 1000BCE and after that this metal is used in different forms.
(a) Copper (b) Iron (c) Bronze (d) Clay

4. Identify the correct answer associated with the economy of early Vedic age
(i) Cattle earing was the main occupation
(ii) A wealthy person was known as Gomat
(iii) People had knowledge of agriculture
(iv) Chariot makers had an important position
Codes
(a) Only (i) (b) Both (i) and (ii)
(c) Both (ii) and (iii) (d) All of these

Section-II

Very Short Questions

1. Mention any three of the early Aryan settlements.
2. Explain briefly what is Sama Veda.
3. Name the two political institutions prevailed during the Vedic age.
4. Why Vedic culture is known as 'Shruti'?
5. What were the subjects taught in the Gurukul?
6. Mention any one feature of Ayurveda.
7. List two impacts of the Aryan invasion.
8. What was the term used for grain in the Rig Veda?

Structured Questions

1. With reference to the features of economic life of the early Vedic age, explain
(i) Domestication of animal
(ii) Trade
(iii) Agriculture
(iv) Transport

2. Name the Veda and explain which include
(i) Hymn to God Soma
(ii) Recitation by the priest Adhrvau
(iii) Origin of Indian music
(iv) Magic and spell

3. With reference to the origin of Aryans, mention
(i) Probable place of their origin.
(ii) Place of their early settlement in India.
(iii) Area where Aryans settled during the later Vedic Age.

CHAPTER 03

Jainism and Buddhism

SYLLABUS

Sources Angas, Tripitikas and Jatakas (brief mention); Causes for their rise in the 6th century BC; Doctrines–Jainism–Tri-ratnas, karma, equality, moksha
Buddhism–The four Noble truth, The Eight-fold path, Nirvana

The 6th century BC is regarded as an important era in the world history which saw the emergence of thinkers like Confucius in China, Zoroaster (Zarathustra) in Persia and Vardhamana Mahavira and Gautama Buddha in India.

In India, it was the phase when orthodox religious beliefs and practices were challenged and rejected by the new sects. But the two sects Jainism founded by Mahavira and Buddhism founded by Gautama Buddha were emerged as the most influential religious reform movement.

Sources of Jainism

Angas or Agamas are the literary sources that give information about Jainism. They are texts of Jainism based on the discourses of the *Tirthankaras*. These discourses were recorded by the *Gandharas* (disciples) and compiled into 12 parts. The Angas are collectively known as Dwadashangi. The 12 parts of Angas are

(i) **Acharang Sutra** (*Aayarang*) This Anga laid down the guidelines for the conduct and behaviour of hermit life and the description of the atonement (penance) of Lord Mahavira. It serves to be the oldest Anga from linguistic point of view.

(ii) **Sutrakratang Sutra** (*Suyagdang*) This Anga provides detailed description of the theory of non-violence, Jain **metaphysics**[1] and the **refutation**[2] of other religious theories such as Kriyavada, Akriyavada, Ajnanvada and Vinayvada.

(iii) **Sthananga Sutra** (*Thananga*) This Anga defines and categorises the main principles of the Jain religion i.e. it defines Jain metaphysics.

(iv) **Samavayanga Sutra** This Anga defines and categorises the main principles of the Jain religion from a different perspective.

(v) **Vyakhya Prajnapti or Bhagavati Sutra** (*Viyah Pannati*) This is the largest of the other eleven Angas. It explains the precise knowledge of soul, matter and other related subjects. It comprises of 36000 questions and answers in discussion form.

(vi) **Jnata Dharma Kathanga Sutra** (*Nayadhammakahao*) This text is very useful in perceiving the religious preaching of Lord Mahavira as it explains Jain principles through examples and stories.

(vii) **Upasaka Dashanga Sutra** (*Uvasagdasao*) This Anga explains the code of conduct of the ten lay followers (*Shravaks*) of Lord Mahavira.

1. **Metaphysics** It is the branch of philosophy that deals with the first principles of things including abstract concepts such as being, knowing, identity, time and space.
2. **Refutation** A set of facts that prove that something is false.

It is very useful for understanding code and conduct of ordinary people (*Shravaka Dharma*) in the Jain religion.

(viii) **Antah Kradashanga Sutra** *(Anatagaddaso)* This Anga depicts the stories of ten sacred monks attaining salvation by denouncing their *karmas*.

(ix) **Anuttaroupa Patika Dashanga Sutra** *(Anuttarov Vaiya Dasao)*. This Anga depicts the story of ten additional dedicated monks, who accomplished the top-most heaven.

(x) **Prashna Vyakrana Sutra** (*Panha Vagarnai*) This Anga depicts the five great vows, Mahavratas and the five worst sins of Jain religion.

(xi) **Vipaka Sutra** (*Vivagsuyam*) This Anga depicts the ultimate conclusion of good and evil *karmas* through stories.

(xii) **Drastivada Sutra** This Anga consists of 14 Purva texts and also known as Purvas or Purva Anga. Among ang-agams, Purvas were the oldest sacred texts and its knowledge were gradually related to Lord Mahavira's *nirvana* (enlightenment). However, Drastivada is lost and only references are found into other Jain scriptures.

Origin of Jainism

Jainism originated in the 6th century BC. It rejected Vedic religion and avoided its rituals. **Rishabhadeva** was the first *Tirthankara* (saints or spiritual gurus) and Mahavira was the 24th *Tirthankara* (last one) of Jainism.

Life of Vardhamana Mahavira

Vardhamana was born in 599 BC at Kundagrama near Vaishali, in Bihar. His father name was Siddhartha. He was the head of a famous Kshatriya clan, Nyaya. His mother name was Trishala. She was a princess of the Licchavi clan.

Vardhamana was married to Yashoda, a princess. They had a daughter named Priyadarshini. At the age of 30, Vardhamana left his home and family. He became an ascetic (monk). He wandered from place to place in search of truth for 12 years. At the age of 42, he conquered his senses. He was now called Mahavira (great hero) or Jina (conqueror). His followers came to be called Jinas or Jains (those who have conquered their desires).

Vardhamana Mahavira

Preaching of Mahavira

Mahavira taught his religion for the next 30 years in places such as Kosala, Magadha, Vaishali, Mithila and Champa. He gave his first sermon at Mount Vipul in Rajagriha, the capital of Magadha. He died at the age of 72 in 527 BC at a place called Pavapuri near modern Rajgir. At the time of his death, he had about 14,000 followers.

Teachings of Mahavira

The teachings of Mahavira were simple. His teachings were based on three thoughts which are called Triratna or Three jewels. They are

(i) Right faith (*Samyak Vishwas*)

(ii) Right knowledge (*Samyak Gyan*)

(iii) Right conduct or action (*Samyak Karma*)

Doctrines of Jainism

- **The Five Vows** It is believed that the first four vows were established by Parshvanatha (23rd *Tirthankara*) and the fifth vow was added by Mahavira. These five vows are

  (i) ***Ahimsa*** (Not-injury or Non-violence) Not to cause harm to any living being.

  (ii) ***Asateya*** (Not-stealing) Not to take any thing which is not properly given.

  (iii) ***Satya*** (Truth) not telling a lie.

  (iv) ***Aparigraha*** (Non-possession) Complete detachment from people, places and material things.

  (v) ***Brahmacharya*** (Chastity) Practising chastity or to lead a virtuous life.

- **Hard Penance** The preachers of Jainism believe in hard penance, giving all sorts of injuries to their human bodies. To die while starving oneself is regarded a virtue by them.

- **No Belief in God** Lord Mahavira denied the power of the God as the creator and controller of the whole universe. He believed that every object whether living or non-living has a soul and man is responsible for his own fate.
- **No Faith in Yajna, Sacrifice and Ritualism** Jainism was a sort of revolt against the superiority of the Brahmins and their yajnas, sacrifices and useless ritualism. They refused to accept the authority of the Vedas.
- **Worship of 24 Tirthankaras** Instead of respecting the Brahmins and worshiping their Gods, the Jains began to worship their own *Tirthankaras*.
- **Promoted Equality** Jainism opposed the caste system and all sorts of class distinctions. It preached the equality of human beings and universal brotherhood.
- **Attainment of Moksha** The Jains believe that the chief aim of a man is to attain salvation *(moksha)* or freedom from the cycle of birth and rebirth. This salvation can be achieved by following three jewels or ***triratnas*** of right faith, right knowledge and right conduct.
- **Next Life and Karma Theory** The Jains believe in next life and transference of soul. According to them, one acquires new life according to his actions or *karma* of his past lives. If one does good actions during his life he is bound to get a good life next time.
- **Nine Truths** Apart from five vows, Jains should have the knowledge of the nine truths. These nine truths include *Jiva* (living things), *Ajiva* (non-living things), *Punya* (result of good deeds), *Paap* (sin), *Ashrav* (good deeds), *Sanvar* (hindrances in the way of *karma*), *Bandha* (bondage), *Nirjara* (*destruction of karmas*) and *Moksha* (salvation).
- **Immortal Soul** Mahavira believed that the soul is immortal because only the body dies not the soul.

Two Sects of Jainism

After the death of Mahavira during the reign of Chandragupta Maurya, a severe famine led to a great migration of Jain monks from Ganga valley to the Deccan. This migration led to differences in Jainism. These differences between the followers of Jainism came out during the first Jain Council 300 BC, due to which Jains were divided into two sects. The two sects of Jainism are

(i) ***Digambaras* (The Sky Clad)** They were the followers of Bhadrabahu, the last acharya of undivided Jain Sangha and the spiritual teacher of Chandragupta Maurya. Bhadrabahu insisted on the retention of the rule of nudity. *Digambaras* followed Bhadrabahu to the South.

According to *Digambaras*, living without clothes signified detachment from the world pleasures. They were orthodox followers of Mahavira. They kept long fasts and led an austere (strict) life.

(ii) ***Svetambaras* (The White Clad)** They were the followers of Sthulabhadra, a disciple of Bhadrabahu. They remained in North India during famine. Sthulabhadra allowed his followers to wear white garments. They fasted but did not believe in extreme penance and austerity.

Spread of Jainism

Jainism had royal patronage thus it spread to various parts of India. In South India, Jainism was patronised by Rashtrakuta and Chalukya Kings. Later, it became a dominant religion in Karnataka and spread to region of Odisha, Rajasthan and Gujarat.

The causes for the spread of Jainism were

- **Local Language** Mahavira use the language of local people i.e. Prakrit to preach the doctrines of Jainism. This led to spread of Jainism as people found it easier to follow the preachings in local language.
- **Attractive** People found Jainism attractive due to its simplicity, austerity and spirituality. There was no class distinction in this religion and no animal sacrifices were performed.
- **Royal Patronage** Jainism received the royal patronage from many rulers like Chandragupta Maurya, Kharavela, etc which led to the spread of Jainism in different parts of the country.

Impact of Jainism

- **Growth of Language and Literature** Jainism influenced Indian language and literature. Vardhamana Mahavira preached in 'Ardha-Magadhi' language which was the language of the common man. The people knowing 'Magadhi' and 'Sauraseni' could easily follow the preaching's of Mahavira. In due course of time, the Jaina canonical texts were written in Prakrit language. Thus, the vernacular and regional languages were enriched by Jainism. Further, the Jaina texts like 'Anga', 'Upanga', 'Kalpasutra', etc were also written in Sanskrit. Thus, the literature also grew due to the rise of Jainism.
- **Principle of Non-Violence** Mahavira Jaina was the embodiment of peace. His concept of non-violence largely influenced the course of Indian history.

- **Influence on Politics** Jainism also influenced the Indians politics. By following the principle of non-violence the kshatriyas became kind hearted and tolerant. Due to this, their fighting ability suffered. Thus, Jains could not build any political empire of their own.
- **Growth of Trading Community** Jainism contributed a lot for the growth of trading community. At first, Jainism became popular among the traders and merchants. It fostered brotherhood among them which gave rise to guild system in future. The merchants became rich and got a special position in the society.
- **Creation of Healthy Society** Mahavira preached against the caste system. With the end of caste system in society, the grip of the higher caste over the lower cast ended. The lower class people were not to be exploited by the higher caste people. Thus, the bitterness between the two antagonistic sections of the society was removed.
- **Growth of Art and Architecture** Jainism helped a lot in the growth of art and Architecture. The kings patronised Jainism. So many Jaina texts and the images of Jaina *Tirthankara* were found in many parts of India.

  The statue of **Bahubali** (Gomateswara) in Shravanabelgola in Karnataka is the highest Jaina statue ever carved in India. The Jaina images found in Mathura, Bundelkhand, Northern Madhya Pradesh, Odisha and Benaras are important Jaina art remains in India.

  The cave art of Udayagiri in Bhubaneswar, Ellora in Maharashtra are unique examples of Jaina art. The Dilwara Jaina temple at Mount Abu of Rajasthan is a classic example of Jain architecture. Thus, Jainism helped in the growth of art and architecture in India.

Dilwara Jain Temple

- **New Touch of Life** Jainism criticised the Vedic religion and the pre-dominance of Brahminism. Thus, the people turned away their attention from the unnecessary ritualistic practices. They led a very simple and normal life. This influenced the society a lot and shaped its character in future.

Decline of Jainism

The causes for the decline of Jainism were as follows

- **Factionalism[3] in Jainism** Factionalism among the Jains after the death of Mahavira was the cause of the decline of Jainism. Some followers advocated to literally follow the teachings of Mahavira, while others wanted to tone down the severity of Jainism.
- **Spread of Buddhism** Buddhism came as formidable obstacle in the path of the spread of Jainism. Buddhist was simple and intelligible. There was no severity in it like Jainism. Even a householder could follow it. Thus, it led to decline of Jainism.
- **Unintelligible Philosophy** Most of the Jaina philosophy was not understandable to the masses. The concepts of *Jeeva, Ajeeva, Pudgala, Syadbada*, etc could not be understood properly by the people. Many could not accept the view that stone, water, tree or earth had a soul of their own.
- **Lack of Efforts** Jainism did not spread to foreign countries. There was also a decline in the missionary zeal and sincerity of the Jaina mendicants. They were no more exclusive in undertaking the strain of spreading Jainism in villages and towns.
- **Role of Hindu Preachers** Hinduism posed threats to Jainism. Nimbarka, Ramanuja, Sankaracharya, etc came to make the foundation of Hinduism more solid and stronger.

Check Your LEARNING...

1. What does the Sthananga Sutra define?
2. Who was the first Tirthankara of Jainism?
3. At what age, Lord Mahavira conquered his senses.
4. What are the two sects of Jainism?

Sources of Buddhism

Tripitaka

Tripitaka is the traditional term used for the Buddhist scriptures. It means the **Three Baskets**. These scriptures are in Pali language. They are

(i) **Vinaya Pitaka** The first basket is the 'Discipline Basket', which set out the rules and guidelines for living the monastic life of the Sangha.

3. **Factionalism** It is a condition in which an organisation or group split into two or more smaller groups.

It consists of the rules and regulations for the Bhikshus and the Bhikshunis. It also covers guidelines for interaction between the monks, nuns and the society. It also include an account of life and teachings of Buddha and some important aspects, customs and arts of the ancient Indian history.

(ii) **Sutta Pitaka** The second basket is the 'Discourse (speak) Basket' and it contains records of the Buddha's sermons. These discourses of the Budhha present matters of **theology**[4] and moral behaviour for all Buddhists. It also include the discourses of Buddha's disciples like Sariputta and Ananda. An important component of this pitaka is Dhammapada (way of truth).

(iii) **Abhidhamma Pitaka** The third basket is that of the 'Special Teachings'. It is essentially a miscellaneous collection of short writings containing everything from songs and poetry to stories of the Buddha and his previous lives.

The Jatakas

Jatakas come from the Sanskrit word 'Jaatak' meaning 'birth'. The Jatakas are a voluminous body of literature concerning the previous births of Buddha in both human and animal form. Each story has some moral lesson.

They are also part of the Buddhist sacred literature. Though they are written after the Mauryan period, but still they depict the social and economic condition of Buddha's time. They also reflect Buddhist morals, ethics and principles.

Origin of Buddhism

The word 'Buddhism' comes from 'budhi' meaning 'to awaken'. Buddhism has its origins about 2500 years ago when Siddhartha was known as the Buddha and got enlightenment at the age of 35. Buddhism is followed in India as well as in abroad.

Life of Gautama Buddha

Siddhartha (Gautama Buddha) was born in 563 BC in Lumbini near Kapilavastu in Nepal. His father was Suddhodana, a Sakya chief of Kapilavastu. His mother 'Mayadevi' died when Siddhartha was only seven days old. Siddhartha was brought up by his step mother Mahaprajapati Gautami. Siddhartha was brought up in great luxury. He was married at young age to princess Yashodhara and they had a son named Rahul.

When he was about 29, Siddhartha persuaded his charioteer, Channa, to drive him outside the palace grounds and into the neighbouring villages. There, he saw an old man, a sick man, a corpse being carried in a funeral procession and a holy (ascetic) man. These sights are known as 'Four Great Sights'.

These four sights had a profound effect on Gautama. For the first time, he faced the reality of old age, sickness and death. Gautama could not forget these experiences. As a result, he became restless and dissatisfied and decided to leave home to seek religious enlightenment. This event is known as **Mahabhinishkramana** or the **Great renunciation**.

For six years, Siddhartha learnt about meditation with some of the famous teachers of that time, such as **Alara Kalama** and **Uddaka Ramaputta**. Siddhartha tried to learn about the true nature of life and how one can get free from suffering.

Enlightenment of Gautama Buddha

Siddhartha wandered from place to place in search of truth. At Bodhgaya (Bihar) he sat under a **bodhi tree** (peepal tree) and did intense penance after which he got **enlightenment (*nirvana*)** at the age of 35. Since then, he was known as the Buddha or the enlightened one.

Mahabodhi Temple was built at the place where Lord Buddha got enlightenment. Buddha was also called as **Tathagata**, the founder of truth.

After the enlightenment, he started preaching his religion. He delivered his first sermon at Deer Park in Sarnath. This event is called as **Dharmachakra-pravartana** or turning of the wheel of sacred law. In Magadha, he established a Bodh Sangha (Buddhist order). He had large number of followers including the rulers of Magadha, Kosala and Kaushambi. His disciples belonged to all classes of society.

Lord Buddha obtained **Mahaparinirvna** at the age of 80 in 483 BC at Kushinagara, Uttar Pradesh. His disciples took his sacred remains to the eight different places where huge stupas were erected.

The Four Noble Truth and Eight-Fold Path of Buddhism

Buddha's teachings were based on *ahimsa* and love for all living beings. Buddha taught **four noble truths** which are

(i) ***Dukkha*** (Sorrow) World is full of sorrow and miseries.

4. **Theology** The study of the nature of God and religious belief.

(ii) ***Dukkha Samudaya*** The desire is the root cause of our sorrows.

(iii) ***Dukkha Nirodha*** Misery can be avoided by overcoming desire.

(iv) ***Dukkha-Nirodha-Gamini Patipada*** The remedy to the sufferings are the **eight fold path or Ashta *Marga***. It constitute the following

- **Right Thought** To remain away from empty rituals and wordly evils.
- **Right Belief** To give up desire.
- **Right Speech** To speak truth.
- **Right Action** To remain away from theft, luxuries and violence.
- **Right Living** Not to become dishonest.
- **Right Effort** To work for deliverance from signs and for the welfare of others.
- **Right Knowledge** To think about right things.
- **Right Meditation** To concentrate only on right things.

Doctrines of Buddhism

- **Attitude towards God** Buddha did not profess the non-existence of God, unlike Mahavira. Rather, he believed that the entire universe works according to the *Dharma* (universal law).
- **The Karma Theory** Gautama Buddha had faith in the theory of *Karma*. It means that the condition in which a man lives his present life and the deeds, might decide the course of his life in the next birth and he has to face the consequence of his actions.
- **Ahimsa** Buddha like Mahavira attached great importance to *ahimsa* or non-violence. He condemned violence against others in any form.
- **No Faith in Caste System** Buddha believed in equality and universal brotherhood. He believed that distinctions on the basis of caste or class should not exist in the society and invited people from various sections of the society to join Buddhism.
- **Nirvana** Attaining *Nirvana* or enlightenment is the principle of Buddhism for eternal bliss and peace.
- **No Belief in Rituals and Sacrifices** Buddha had no faith in the supremacy of the Vedas or the Brahmins. According to him, rituals, yajnas and sacrifices were meaningless ceremonies and not capable to change the destiny of man.
- **Code of Conduct** The Buddha formulated a code of conduct for his disciples. It consisted of the ten commandements which were

(i) To speak truth
(ii) Not to harm creatures
(iii) Not to use intoxicants
(iv) To abide by Brahmacharya
(v) To avoid music and dancing
(vi) Not to use scented goods
(vii) Not to sleep on cushions
(viii) Not to keep money
(ix) To take meals only at fixed times
(x) Not to own property

Organisation of Buddhism

The organisation for teaching of Buddhism is known as **Sangha**. It was a monastic order established to spread Buddhism. It became powerful institution after sometime. The members of this organisation were called **Bhikshus** (monks) and **Bhikshunis** (nuns). The followers had to undergo training for 10 years. The minimum age to join the Sangha at the time of Buddha was 15 years.

Spread of Buddhism

Buddhism spread in India as well as in abroad. It became popular religion in Tibet, China, Thailand, Sri Lanka, Japan, Myanmar, Indo-China and other countries in central and South-East Asia. The spread of Buddhism led to the construction of a large number of cave temples to provide permanent shelters and places of worship to the monks and nuns. **Chaityas** (halls of worship) are built in these cave temples. The stupas were built to recall the important events or to enshrine the relics of the Buddha.

Viharas is a place where the monks and nuns spend their time during training. In the Viharas the members led a life of Chastity (Brahmacharya), austerity (Strictness), devotion and purity.

Two Sects of Buddhism

The teachings of Buddha were not written down during his lifetime, therefore after his death some his followers gave different interpretations to his teachings. Differences arose on the question of discipline for the monks and nuns as well as on the significance of what Buddha had taught.

Thus, soon after the death of Buddha and within a century of the *parinirvana*, the Buddhist fragmented into several sects. Among them, the following two were most prominent

(i) **Hinayana** The Hinayanist sect consider Gautama Buddha as the sole Buddha who reposes in *nirvana* with the absence of desire and striving. According to this creed, Buddha is not a God but only a human being who had attained perfection and give up *karma*.

They believed that each individual has to work for himself and attain *nirvana* by following the noble eight-fold path. They also did not support idol worship. They used Pali language. Buddhism is found in India, Sri Lanka, Myanmar, Combodia and Laos.

(ii) **Mahayana** Mahayana is a combination of Buddhism and Hinduism. Mahayanists consider Buddha as an incarnation of God who could ensure salvation. According to Mahayanists, Boddhisattvas were those holy Buddhists who had not get *Nirvana* yet like Buddha but were proceeding towards it.

They worship the idols of Buddha and Boddhisattvas. According to Mahayanists, an individual should not be satisfied with his own enlightenment or *Nirvana*, but must work good for his fellow men. Mahayanists are mainly found in China and Japan, Taiwan etc.

Impact of Buddhism

- **Impact on Social and Religious Life** The rise of Buddhism led to the doctrine of ahimsa which became a weapon against the ill practices of the society. Animal protection also became a new culture. Buddhism promoted intellectual tradition and abandoned caste distinction. This gave the opportunity to the weaker sections to play a role in the matters of political and social life. Buddhism also proposed a challenge to Hinduism as with the spread of Buddhism, the yajnas and sacrifices were ended.
- **Impact on Culture** Buddhism spread to other countries also apart from India. This led to establishment of close cultural contacts between different countries.

Decline of Buddhism

- **Decline of Buddhist Sanghas** The important cause of the decline and fall of Buddhism was the Sanghas which became centres of corruption.
- **Revival of Brahmanism** The revival of Brahminical Hinduism also served as a cause for the decline of Buddhism. The rites and rituals of hinduism were simplified and it assimilated the positive aspects of Buddhism.
- **Division among Buddhists** The division of Buddhism into a number of groups like 'Hinayana', 'Mahayana' and other seats led to the decline of Buddhism.
- **Use of Sanskrit Language** Pali and Prakrit were the spoken language of most people of India and became the medium for the spread of the message of Buddhism. But Sanskrit replaced these at the Fourth Buddhist Council during the reign of Kaniska.
- **Image Worship** The Mahayana Buddhists started worshipping Buddha as a God. This image worship was a clear violation of the Buddhist doctrines which opposed the critical rites and rituals of Brahminical hinduism.
- **Loss of Royal Patronage** Buddhism lost the royal patronage which it received during the period of Asoka, Kaniska and Harshavardhana as the Rajput rulers could not follow the policy of *ahimsa*.
- **Muslim Invasion** The Muslim invasion of India almost wiped out Buddhism. Their invasions of India became regular and repeated. The invaders plundered the monasteries and looted their wealth. Many Buddhist monks were killed, some of them were converted to Islam and others fled to Nepal and Tibet and took shelter there.

Causes for the Rise of Jainism and Buddhism

Following were the causes for the rise of Jainism and Buddhism in India during the 6th century BC

- **The Vedic Philosophy** The Vedic philosophy had lost its original purity and in the 6th century BC, it was more a bundle of rituals.

  The rites and ceremonies were elaborated and expensive. The common man developed a great dislike for these rituals. The Vedic religion had become very complex and get limited upto superstitions and rituals. The Vedic mantras were not understandable to the average person in society.

- **Sacrifices** The sacrifices prescribed by the Vedas had assumed a cumbrous shape. They were very complicated and a source of wastage of time, energy and money. It also included animal sacrifice which people started condemning because animals became crucial for the growth in trade to agriculture.
- **Rigid Caste System** The caste system had become rigid and brutal and the earlier notion of caste division according to profession was changed to caste according to birth. There were strict restrictions on food, drinks and marriage of Shudras who were considered untouchables. Interchange of caste was not allowed. A person of the low caste had a miserable life.
- **Supremacy of Brahmins** The supremacy of the Brahmans created unrest. They had lost the old ideals and were no longer leading pure and holy life and full of knowledge.
- **Sanskrit Language** All the religious treatises were written in Sanskrit which was the language of the elite and not the masses. The priestly class was the only segment of the society who could read and understand these texts. Mahavira and the Buddha, on the contrary, explained to the people in simple languages like Pali or Prakrit which were the language of the common man at that time.
- **Political Situation** In the 6th century BC, Magadha was ruled by Bimbisara and later by Ajatashatru. Both these rulers were liberal and tolerant. They were free from Brahmanic influence and condemned certain social evils in their kingdoms. When the opportunity come they patronised both Jainism and Buddhism.
- **Corruption in Religion** The religious practices became corrupt as the priests encouraged the ordinary people to perform yajnas, in order to extract money. These practices were opposed by Kshatriyas. Both Jainism and Buddhism were founded by Kshatriya princes.

Check Your LEARNING...

1. Where was Lord Buddha born?
2. According to Buddha's teachings, what are four noble truths?
3. What does the Sutta Pitaka contain?
4. Name the rulers of Magadha who patronised Jainism and Buddhism.

QUiCK Revision

- In the 6th century BC the founders of two great religions of mankind lived in India. They were Lord Mahavira and Lord Gautama Buddha, the founders of Jainism and Buddhism respectively.
- Agams are texts of Jainism based on the discourses of the *Tirthankaras*. Ang-agams are the oldest religious scriptures and the back bone of Jain literature.
- Jainism originated in the 6th century BC. Vardhamana Mahavira was the founder of Jainism. Rishabhadeva was the first *Tirthankara* (saints or spiritual gurus) and Mahavira was the 24th *Tirthankara* (last one).
- The teachings of Mahavira were simple.
- Jainism didn't accept the authority of Vedas.
- The two sects of Jainism are Digambaras and Svetambaras.
- The doctrines of Jainism include the five vows i.e. *Ahimsa*, *Asateya*, *Satya*, *Aparigraha* and *Brahmacharya*, hard penance, no belief in God, no faith in Yajna, sacrifice and ritualism, etc.
- There are two literary sources of Buddhism known as *Tripitakas* and Jatakas.
- Buddhism is a religion to about 300 million people around the world. The word comes from budhi meaning to awaken. It has its origins about 2500 years ago when Siddhartha, known as the Buddha was himself awakened (enlightened) at the age of 35.
- Buddha's teachings were based on ahimsa and love for all living beings.
- The doctrines of Buddhism include Ahimsa, no faith in caste system, the Karma theory, no belief in rituals and sacrifice, etc.
- There are two sects of Buddhism which are divided into Hinayana and Mahayana.
- The Hinayanist sect considers Gautama Buddha as the sole Buddha, who reposes in *Nirvana* with the absence of desire and striving.
- The Mahayanists considered Gautama Buddha as an incarnation of God who could ensure salvation. They worship idols of Buddha and Boddhisattvas.
- Buddhism was declined due to various factors like corruption in Sanghas, split in Buddhism, Reforms in hinduism and invasor etc.
- The causes for the rise of Jainism and Buddhism are the vedic philosophy, sacrifices, rigid caste system, complex vedic religion, supremacy of Brahmans, sanskrit language and political situation.

Chapter Practice

Section-I

Multiple Choice Questions

1. Who was the founder of Jainism?
(a) Rishabhadeva (b) Mahavira
(c) Parbhvanath (d) Tirthankara

Ans. (b) Mahavira

2. Who was the 24th *Tirthankara*?
(a) Mahavira (b) Gautama Buddha
(c) Rishabhadeva (d) Parbhvanath

Ans. (a) Mahavira

3. Lord Mahavira was died at the age of 72 in ......
(a) Vaishali (b) Rajagriha
(c) Pavapuri (d) Pataliputra

Ans. (c) Pavapuri

4. Which of the following is not the vows of Jainism?
(a) Violence (b) Truth
(c) Non-Possession (d) Chastity

Ans. (a) Violence

5. Which of the following rulers patronised Jainism?
(a) Pallava (b) Chalukya
(c) Rashtrakuta (d) Both (b) and (c)

Ans. (d) Both (b) and (c)

6. Gautama Buddha belonged to ...... dynasty.
(a) Nyaya (b) Ikshavaku
(c) Sakya (d) Maurya

Ans. (c) Sakya

7. Lord Buddha gave his first sermon in ....
(a) Kushinagara (b) Bodhgaya
(c) Sarnath (d) Kapilvastu

Ans. (c) Sarnath

8. At which place the first Buddhist Council was held?
(a) Rajagriha (b) Patliputra (c) Kashmir (d) Vaishali

Ans. (a) Rajagriha

9. Complete the given analogy.
Buddhism : Gautama Buddha : Jainism : ?
(a) Parshvanath (b) Mahavira
(c) Siddartha (d) Rishabhadeva

Ans. (b) Mahavira

10. Complete the given analogy.
Digambaras : Bhadrabahu :: Swetambaras : ?
(a) Sthulabhadra (b) Suddhodana
(c) Uddaka Ramaputra (d) Alara Kalma

Ans. (a) Sthulabhadra

11. Complete the given analogy.
Jainism : Angas : : Buddhism : ?
(a) Vinaya Pitaka (b) Acharang Sutra
(c) Bhagvati Sutra (d) All of these

Ans. (a) Vinaya Pitaka

12. Replaced the underlined word and correct the statement.
<u>Acharang Sutra</u> defines and categorises the main substances of the Jain religion.
(a) Sthananga Sutra
(b) Bhagwati Sutra
(c) Samavayanga Sutra
(d) Vipaka Sutra

Ans. (a) Sthananga Sutra

13. Replace the underlined word and complete the sentence.
Rishabhadeva was the <u>22nd Tirthankara</u> of Jainism.
(a) 1st Tirthankara
(b) 29th Tirthankara
(c) 25th Tirthankara
(d) 24th Tirthankara

Ans. (a) 1st Tirthankara

14. Replace the underlined word and complete the sentence.
Gautama Buddha was born in 563 BC in Lumbini near Kapilvastu, <u>India</u>.
(a) Nepal (b) Sri Lanka
(c) Myanmar (d) China

Ans. (a) Nepal

15. Complete the given table.

Mahavira	599 BC
Gautama Buddha	?

Codes
(a) 483 BC (b) 467 BC
(c) 383 BC (d) 563 BC

Ans. (d) 563 BC

16. The Eight Fold of Jainism
(i) Right thought (ii) Right living
(iii) Right speech (iv) Right belief

Codes
(a) Only (i)
(b) Only (ii)
(c) Both (i) and (ii)
(d) All of the above

Ans. (d) All of the above

17. Which of the following is caused of Jainism and Buddhism?
(i) Sacrifices (ii) Comlex Vedic religion
(iii) Rigid caste system (iv) Political situation
Codes
(a) Only (i) (b) Only (ii)
(c) Both (i) and (ii) (d) All of these

Ans. (d) All of these

18. Which of the following is/are philosophies of Buddhism?
(i) Attitude towards God
(ii) *Ahimsa*
(iii) No faith in caste system
(iv) *Nirvana*
Codes
(a) Only (i) (b) Both (i) and (iii)
(c) (i), (ii) and (iii) (d) All of these

Ans. (d) All of these

19. Consider the following associated with the decline of Buddhism and choose the correct option?
(i) Division amongst Buddhist
(ii) Use of Sanskrit Language
(iii) Image Worship
(iv) Loss of Royal Patronage
Codes
(a) Only (i) (b) Only (ii)
(c) Both (ii) and (iii) (d) All of these

Ans. (d) All of these

20. Match the following

A. Mahavira was born	1. Kundagram
B. Gautama Buddha was died	2. Kushinagra
C. Gautama Buddha 1st sermon	3. Sarnath
D. Mahavira died	4. Pavapuri

Codes

	A	B	C	D		A	B	C	D
(a)	1	2	3	4	(b)	4	3	2	1
(c)	2	4	1	2	(d)	3	2	4	1

Ans. (a)

Passage Based Questions

21. Read the passage given below and answer the questions that follow.

The Buddha belonged to a small gana known as the Sakya gana and was a Kshatriya. When he was a young man, he left the comforts of his home in search of knowledge. He wandered for several years, meeting and holding discussions with other thinkers. He finally decided to find his own path to realisation and meditated for days on end under a peepal tree at Bodhgaya in Bihar. After that, he was known as the Buddha or the wise one. He then went to Sarnath, near Varanasi, where he taught for the first time.

The Buddha taught that life is full of suffering and unhappiness. This is caused because we have cravings and desires (which often cannot be fulfilled). Sometimes, even if we get what we want, we are not satisfied and want even more (or want other things). The Buddha described this as thirst or tanha. He taught that this constant craving could be removed by following moderation in everything. He also taught people to be kind and to respect the lives of others including animals. He believed that the results of our actions (called karma) whether good or bad affect us both in this life and the next.

(i) Which event of Gautama Buddha's life is depicted by the wheel and deer in Indian art?
(a) Great departure (b) Enlightenment
(c) First preaching (d) Nirvana

Ans. (c) First preaching

(ii) Gautama Buddha's mother belonged to which of the following clans?
(a) Maya clan (b) Licchavis clan
(c) Koliyan clan (d) Shakya clan

Ans. (c) Koliyan clan

(iii) At which of the following places Gautama Buddha attained *nirvana* (Enlightenment) ?
(a) Lumbini (b) Gaya
(c) Kushinagar (d) Sarnath

Ans. (b) Gaya

(iv) What is common between the teachings of Gautama Buddha and Mahavira?
(a) Both emphasised upon Ahimsa
(b) Both rejected existence of soul
(c) Both rejected existence of god
(d) All of the above

Ans. (a) Both emphasised upon Ahimsa

22. Read the passage given below and answer the following question.

It was very difficult for most men and women to follow these strict rules. Nevertheless, thousands left their homes to learn and teach this new way of life. Many more remained behind and supported those who became monks and nuns, providing them with food. Jainism was supported mainly by traders. Farmers, who had to kill insects to protect their crops, found it more difficult to follow the rules.

Over hundreds of years, Jainism spread to different parts of North India and to Gujarat, Tamil Nadu and Karnataka. The teachings of Mahavira and his followers were transmitted orally for several centuries. They were written down in the form in which they are presently available at a place called Valabhi, in Gujarat, about 1500 years ago.

(i) ...... is the cause of the spread of Jainism.
(a) Local dialect (b) Appeal to people
(c) Royal Patronage (d) All of these

Ans. (d) All of these

(ii) Which of the following is the ultimate goal of education in Jainism?
(a) Non-violence
(b) Renunciation
(c) *Moksha*
(d) Voluntary promotion of human welfare

Ans. (b) *Moksha*

(iii) Which of the following is not included in *triratna* of Jainism?
(a) Right knowledge (b) Right conduct
(c) Right faith (d) Creator

Ans. (d) Creator

(iv) A collective term used by the Jains for their sacred book is ....
(a) Angas (b) Vinaya Pitaka
(c) Jatakas (d) None of these

Ans. (a) Angas

Section-II

Short Questions

1. Who was Vardhamana Mahavira ?

Ans. Vardhamana was born in 599 BC in a village called Kundagrama near Vaishali in Bihar and he was the 24th Tirthankar of the Jainism.

2. How did Mahavira attain enlightenment?

Ans. At the age of 30, Mahavira left his home and family and became an ascetic (monk). He wandered from place to place in search of truth for 12 years. At the age of 42, he conquered his senses. He attained the greatest spiritual knowledge or Kaivalya under a Sal tree.

3. Where did Mahavira teach his religion?

Ans. Mahavira taught his religion in places such as Kosala, Magadha, Mithila and Champa.

4. When and where did Mahavira died?

Ans. Mahavira died at the age of 72 in 527 BC at a place called Pavapuri near modern Rajgir.

5. What are *triratna* ?

Ans. The teachings of Mahavira are based on three thoughts which are called *triratna* or three jewels. They are
(i) Right faith (ii) Right knowledge
(iii) Right conduct or action

6. Mention two philosophies of Jainism.

Ans. Two philosophies of Jainism are
(i) **Ahimsa** This was the first and important principle of Jainism. It means non-injury to anyone.
(ii) **Hard Penance** The preachers of Jainism believe in hard penance and giving up all sorts of injury to their human bodies.

7. What is the idea of salvation according to Jains?

Ans. The Jains believe that the chief aim of a man is to attain salvation (*moksha*) or freedom from the cycle of birth and rebirth. This salvation can be achieved by following three jewels or *triratnas* of right faith, right knowledge and right conduct.

8. Do Jains believe in next life? What is their view about *karma*?

Ans. Yes, the Jains believe in next life and transference of soul.
According to them, one acquires new life according to his actions or *karma* in his past lives. If one does good actions during his life, he is bound to get a good life next time.

9. What were the two sects of Jainism?

Ans. The two sects of Jainism were
(i) **Digambaras** (The Sky Clad) They were the ardent follower of original form of Jainism.
(ii) **Svetambaras** (The White Clad) They were the followers of Sthulabhadra, who modified original form of Jainism to a newer one with some relaxation in norms.

10. What are Agams?

Ans. Agams are texts of Jainism based on the discourses of the *Tirthankaras*. These discourses were recorded by the *Gandharas* (disciples) and composed into Angas.

11. State the importance of *Drastivada Sutra*.

Ans. The twelfth Ang-agam is called *Drastivada*, which consists of 14 purva texts and also known as Purvas or Purva-agams. Among Ang-agams, Purvas are the oldest sacred texts.

12. What is Buddhism?

Ans. The word 'Buddhism' comes from budhi, which means to awaken. It has its origins about 2500 years ago when Siddhartha was himself awakened (enlightened) at the age of 35 and named as Buddha.

13. Give a brief account of the life of Gautama Buddha.

Ans. Gautama Buddha or Siddhartha was born in 567 BC in Lumbini near Kapilavastu in Nepal. His father was Suddhodana, a Sakya chief of Kapilavastu. His mother, Mayadevi died when Siddhartha was only seven days old. Siddhartha was brought up in great luxury. He married Yasodhara and they had a son named Rahul.

14. What were the four signs Gautama Buddha saw?

Ans. When he was about 29, Gautama persuaded his charioteer Channa to drive him outside the palace grounds and into the neighbouring villages. There Buddha saw an old man, a sick man, a corpse being carried in a funeral procession and a holy man. These four signs had a profound effect on Gautama.

15. Mention two noble truths taught by Gautama Buddha?

Ans. The noble truths taught by Gautama Buddha are

(i) ***Dukkha*** (Sorrow) World is full of sorrow and miseries.

(ii) ***Dukkha Samudaya*** The desire is the root cause of our sorrows.

16. Mention the eight-fold path followed by Buddhists.

Ans. The following constitute the eight-fold path or the Ashtangika Marga

(i) Right thought
(ii) Right living
(iii) Right belief
(iv) Right efforts
(v) Right speech
(vi) Right knowledge
(vii) Right action
(viii) Right meditation

17. What were the philosophies of Buddhism?

Ans. The philosophies of Buddhism were as follows

- Gautama Buddha had faith in the theory of *Karma*.
- Buddha neither accepted nor rejected the existence of God. He condemned violence against others in any form.
- Attaining *Nirvana* or enlightment is the basic principle of Buddhism.

18. Which language was used by Mahayanist and Hinayanist to preach their thoughts?

Ans. The Mahayanists adopted Sanskrit and preached in it, while the Hinayanists still preached in Pali which was the local dialect of the common masses.

19. Name the books which contains the teachings of Buddha.

Ans. The teachings of Buddha have been compiled into three books called *Tripitakas* (Three baskets). The three volumes are *Sutta pitaka*, *Vinaya pitaka* and *Abhidhamma pitaka.*

20. What do you mean by *Tripitaka* ?

Ans. Tripitaka is the traditional term used for the Buddhist scriptures. It means the 'Three Baskets'. These scriptures are in Pali language. They are Vinaya Pitaka, Sutta Pitaka and Abhidhamma Pitaka.

21. Which language was used by Mahavira and Buddha to preach their doctrines?

Ans. Mahavira and the Buddha explained to the people in simple spoken Pali or Prakrit, which was the language of the common man at that time.

Structured Questions

1. With reference to the origin of Jainism mention.

(i) The period of its origin and its five vows.

(ii) Its founder.

(iii) Doctrines of Jainism.

(iv) Sects of Jainism

Ans. (i) Jainism originated in the 6th century BC as an alternate religion to Hinduism

The five vows in Jainism are

(i) ***Ahimsa (Non-violence)*** Not to cause harm to any living being.

(ii) ***Satya*** To speak truth

(iii) ***Asateya*** Not to steal.

(iv) ***Aparigraha*** Not to possess property

(v) ***Brahmacharya*** Practising chastity.

(ii) Vardhamana Mahavira was the founder of Jainism. But the orthodox Jains believe that their religion had been founded long ago by the first *Tirthankara*, Rishabhadeva.

(iii) Refer to chapter theory page no. 83-84.

(iv) Refer to chapter theory page no. 84.

2. There are various literary sources of Jainism and Buddhism, in this context explain

(i) *Vinaya Pitaka* and *Sutta Pitaka*

(ii) The *Abhidhamma Pitaka*

(iii) Jatakas

(iv) Aayarang and Suyagdang

Ans. (i) Refer to chapter theory page no. 85-86.

(ii) Refer to chapter theory page no. 86.

(iii) Refer to chapter theory page no. 86.

(iv) Refer to chapter theory page no. 82.

Picture Based Question

1. With reference to the given picture, answer the following questions

(i) Name the person sitting on the chariot and the charioteer.

(ii) What are the four sights he come across while travelling?

(iii) What impact did the sights created on the person?

Ans. (i) The person was sitting on the chariot was Gautama Buddha and Channa the charioteer.

(ii) While travelling in the neighbouring village, he saw an old man, a sick man, a corpse being carried in a funeral procession and an ascetic. These were the four sights.

(iii) These four sights had a profound effect on Gautama Buddha. For the first time, he faced, the reality of old age, sickness and death. Buddha became restless and dissatisfied therefore, he decided to leave home to find the real truth.

Chapter Assessment

Section-I

Multiple Choice Questions

1. Who was the first *Tirthankara* ?
   (a) Rishabhadeva (b) Parshvanath
   (c) Mahavira (d) Bhadrabahu
2. Jainism preaches ...... vows.
   (a) 2 (b) 3
   (c) 5 (d) 6
3. Complete the analogy.
   Mahavira : Kundagrama :: Buddha : ?
   (a) Sarnath (b) Kushinagara
   (c) Bodhgaya (d) Lumbini
4. Replace the underlined word and correct the sentence.
   The founder of Buddhism, Lord Buddha was born in <u>483 BC</u>.
   (a) 563 BC (b) 583 BC (c) 463 BC (d) 663 BC

Section-II

Short Questions

1. Who were *Tirthankaras*?
2. Write the impacts of Jainism on society.
3. Name the four sights which influence Gautama Buddha.
4. What are *Tripitakas* ?

Structured Questions

1. With reference to the life of Mahavira, explain
   (i) When and where he was born?
   (ii) When did he attain enlightenment?
   (iii) Three Jewels
   (iv) The Five Vows
2. Explain the principles of Buddhism with reference to
   (i) *Karma*
   (ii) *Ahimsa*
   (iii) *Dharma*
3. Explain the doctrines of Jainism with reference to
   (i) Belief in God
   (ii) Salvation
   (iii) *Tirthankaras*
   (iv) Caste System

CHAPTER 04

The Mauryan Empire

SYLLABUS

Sources Arthashastra, Indica, Ashokan Edicts, Sanchi Stupa
Name of the kings in chronological order and administration;
Ashoka Dhamma, Principles and Impact

The Mauryan Empire was the first major empire in the history of India, ruled by Mauryan dynasty from 321 BC to 185 BC. It was founded by Chandragupta Maurya.

Sources about Mauryan Empire

The sources to know about the Mauryan Empire can be divided into two parts i.e. literary sources and archaeological sources.

Literary Sources

Kautilya's Arthashastra

Arthashastra was written in Sanskrit by Chanakya who is also called as Indian Machiavelli. Chanakya (Kautilya) was the chief guide and advisor of Chandragupta Maurya. He was well versed in politics and the affairs of the state. In 1905, **R Shamasastry** discovered the manuscript of Arthashastra. It mainly deals with political and administrative issues. It deals with all topics of internal administration and foreign relations. It is a treatise on statecraft economic policy and military strategy. It contains 6000 *shlokas*. The book is divided into 3 parts, 15 sections or *adhikarnas* which are further divided into 150 chapters. The first part of the book deals with the ruler and council of ruler and the departments of Government, the second part contains civil and criminal law and the third part deals with war and diplomacy.

Megasthenes' Indica

Indica was written in Greek by Megasthenes, who was the Greek ambassador of **Seleucus Nicator** (Macedonian Greek General). Megasthenes spent five years in the court of Chandragupta Maurya. The references of Megasthenes throw light on the political, social, religious and economic condition of Mauryan period. Indica also describes the capital city of Mauryanes, Pataliputra.

Vishakhadatta's Mudrarakshasa

Mudrarakshasa is a drama in Sanskrit. It was written during the Gupta period, but it describes about the victory of Chandragupta over Nandas with the assistance of Kautilya. It also gives a detailed account of the socio-economic condition under the rule of Mauryas.

Other Literature

The Puranas and the Buddhist literature such as Jatakas also provide information on the Mauryas. The Ceylonese Chronicles, Dipavamsa and Mahavamsa throw light on the role of Ashoka in spreading Buddhism in Sri Lanka.

Archaeological Sources

Ashoka Edicts

An edict is a **decree**[1] issued by a king. Ashoka was the first ruler of Mauryan Empire who issued edicts. **James Princep** in 1837 first deciphered the inscriptions of Ashoka edicts which were written in Pali language and in some places Prakrit language was used. The Brahmi script was also used for writing on edicts. Ashokan inscriptions in the North-Western India were found in Kharosthi script.

The edicts of Ashoka deal with Ashoka's Dhamma and also about the instructions given to his officials. These edicts are inscribed on rock and pillars throughout the country. There are total fourteen major rock edicts. The **Rock Edict XIII** gives details about the war he fought against Kalinga.

There were many minor rock edicts like Queen's edict, Barabar cave edict and Kandahar bilingual inscription. There were seven pillar edicts. The Pillar Edict VII gives a summary of Ashok'a efforts to promote the Dhamma within his kingdom. Thus, the Ashokan inscriptions remain valuable sources for the study of Ashoka and the Mauryan Empire.

Sanchi Stupa

A stupa is a large hemispherical **dome**[2], containing a central chamber in which the **relics**[3] of the Buddha were placed. The Sanchi Stupa is one of the best preserved early Stupas in Central India. It is 36.5 m in diameter and rises almost 16.5 m high. It was built by Ashoka in 3rd century BC. The Sanchi Stupa is surrounded by a railing with four carved gateways facing all the four directions.

During the Shunga period, the Sanchi Stupa was enlarged and decorated with railings, staircase and a **harmika**[4] on the top. Around the main Stupa, there is a path for **circumambulation**[5]. The railings and gates of the Sanchi Stupa are richly sculptured with different motifs and designs.

An interesting feature of the Sanchi Stupa is that Lord Buddha has been symbolically represented in the form of tree, inanimate figures, footprints, wheels, thrones, etc rather than by his own image. The gateways of Sanchi Stupa contain ornamented depiction of incidents from the life of the Buddha and his previous incarnations as Bodhisattvas described in the Jataka tales.

Sanchi Stupa

Check Your LEARNING...

1. Who was Kautilya?
2. Who firstly deciphered Ashoka's inscriptions?
3. Who wrote Mudrarakshasa?
4. Where is Sanchi Stupa located?

History of Mauryan Empire

The Mauryan Empire started with the rule of Chandragupta Maurya who succeeded to the throne of Magadha in 321 BC. Before 321 BC, Magadha was ruled by Nanda dynasty.

Chanakya helped Chandragupta Maurya to defeat the existing Nanda King Dhananada and made Chandragupta the King of Magadha. Chandragupta Maurya made alliance with chiefs of Punjab and Himalayan territories. He also controlled Greek invasions. This way he unified a large part of India under his centralised government.

Names of the kings of Mauryan Empire were

- Chandragupta Maurya (321-297 BC)
- Bindusara (297-273 BC)
- Ashoka (268-232 BC)
- Dasaratha Maurya (232-224 BC)

Chandragupta Maurya (321-297 BC)

Chandragupta Maurya succeeded to the throne at the age of 25. He succeeded in bringing the most part of the Indian subcontinent together. After the death of Alexander, the Greek ruler who had conquered many states of North-Western part of India, Chandragupta Maurya had taken over these states.

1 **Decree** An official order issued by a legal authority.
2 **Dome** A rounded vault forming the roof or a building of structure or typically with a circular base.
3 **Relics** A part of a deceased holy person's body of belongings kept as an object of reverence.
4 **Harmika** A small platform with a railing located at the very top of a Stupa.
5 **Circumambulation** The act of moving around a sacred object or idol.

In 305 BC, India was attacked by Seleucus Nicator but he was defeated by Chandragupta Maurya. As a result, a treaty was signed between them according to which Chandragupta got Kandhar, Kabul, Herat and Bahuchistari from Seleucus. He also got married with Helen, the daughter of Seleucus. After this victory, Chandragupta appointed Pushyagupta as the Governor of his North-Western province.

Chandragupta's empire extended from Kabul and Kandhar in the North-Western to Mysore in the South and from Saurashtra in the West to Bengal in the East. During his reign, the Mauryan court received two new ambassadors **Deimachus** and **Dionysius** of Greece and Egypt respectively. According to Jain tradition after ruling for 24 years, Chandragupta renounced the world and handed over the kingdom to his son, Bindusara.

Bindusara (297-273 BC)

In 297 BC, Bindusara succeeded to the throne. He was known to the Greeks as **Amitrochates** (*Amitraghata* in Sanskrit, meaning the destroyer of enemy). Bindusara campaigned in the Deccan and extended Mauryan control in the Peninsula as far as South Mysore. He conquered the land between the two seas, the Arabian Sea and the Bay of Bengal. He maintained friendly relations with the rulers of Greece.

During his reign, a revolt took place in Taxila which was ended by his second son Ashoka who was the Governor of Taxila. Bindusara died in 273 BC.

Ashoka (268-232 BC)

Bindusara's death led to a struggle for succession among his sons. It lasted for four years and in 268 BC, Ashoka emerged successful and became the king. Before becoming the king, Ashoka was Governor of Taxila and Ujjain. He was a fierce military leader who expanded his kingdom in the Ganges-Yamuna valley. He continued his victorious campaigns in Southern and Eastern India for 8 years. Ashoka took the title of **Devanamapriya** (The beloved of the Gods) and **Priyadarshi** (The beautiful one).

Kalinga War

In 261 BC, Ashoka fought Kalinga War which had far reaching consequences for him and his empire. It was fought with independent feudal kingdom located on East Coast of the kingdom. The Rock Edict XIII of Ashoka explains about this war.

The main possible reason that led Ashoka to conquer Kalinga was its strategic locations, as it controlled the land and sea routes to South India and South-East Asia.

The Kalinga War filled Ashoka's heart with grief and regret. The mass violence that was committed in Kalinga developed hatred in Ashoka's heart regarding violence. **Dig Vijaya** (victory in all directions) was replaced by **Dhamma Vijaya** (conquest through *dharma*) which was a common code of conduct that dealt with ideas like kindness, charity, non-violence, etc.

Extent of Ashoka's Empire

The Ashokan inscriptions signify that the Mauryan Empire under Ashoka extended from North-Western mountains of Hindukush to the Southern river Pennar of Mysore. Tamralipti (Tamluk), an important port on the Bengal coast which connected Burma and Sri Lanka, was an important part of the Mauryan Empire. Kabul, Herat and Kandahar were also included in Mauryan Empire.

Ashoka shared a conducive relation with the Khotan's Empire of Central Asia and with the Kingdoms of Southern India namely the Chola, Chera and Pandayas. The Mauryan reign under Ashoka had a sub-continent of **pan-Indian**[6] character.

Ashoka's Dhamma

The term 'Dhamma' corresponds to the Sanskrit word 'Dharma' or 'Dharman' which is usually used in the sense of a custom or a law. According to the Buddhist tradition, the term stands for Buddha's doctrines or teachings. However, Ashoka used the term in a broader and much different way than its conventional sense. His edicts are the testimony of his idea of Dhamma. In his edicts, Dhamma is described not as a religion or religious system but as a 'moral law', 'code of conduct' or an 'ethical order' which is common for all religions.

Principles of Ashoka's Dhamma

- Service to father and mother, practice of *ahimsa*, love of truth, reverence to teachers and good treatment of relatives.
- Respect for elders and love for children.
- Prohibition of animal sacrifices and festive gatherings. Avoiding expensive and meaningless ceremonies or rituals.

6 **Pan-Indian** It means relating to the whole of India, or to all its ethnic, religious or linguistic groups.

- Efficient organisation of administration in the direction of social welfare and maintenance of constant contact with people through the system of **Dhammayatras**[7].
- Humane treatment to servants by masters and to prisoners by government officials.
- Consideration and non-violence to animals and courtesy to relations and liberality to Brahmins.
- Tolerance among all the religious sects and appropriate treatment of ascetics.

Propagation or Spread of Dhamma

- To record the doctrines of the Dhamma permanently, Ashoka inscribed them on rocks and pillars. The language of common man, Pali was used to spread the message to all corners of his empire.
- Ashoka also appointed a special class of officers called *Dhamma Mahamattas* for propagating Dhamma and for promoting its practice throughout the kingdom.
- He sent his emissaries to the independent kingdoms of Southern India and to Hellenistic kingdoms to propagate his ideas.
- As an integral part of Dhamma, he tried to promote the welfare of men and animals by digging wells, planting trees, establishing hospitals, etc.
- To facilitate medical treatment, he planted medicinal herbs not only within his kingdom, but also outside its limit as well for the benefit of the inhabitants of those countries, which shows his greatness as a ruler and as a man.
- He ordered the construction of 84,000 stupas to keep the relics of Buddha and gave donations to Buddhist Viharas.
- He commenced the 3rd Buddhist council in 250 BC in Pataliputra.
- He sent his own son, Mahendra and daughter, Sanghamitra to Sri Lanka to propagate Buddhism.

Impact of Dhamma

The policy of Dhamma marked the end of wars and conquest in India and there came a change in the policy of the State. This allowed the kings of Mauryan Empire to concentrate on the economic and social life of the ordinary people. Thus, this ensured all round development and economic prosperity in the following manner

- **Moral Values** People started to lead a moral life.
- **Religious Unity** People gave support to the policy of religious tolerances propagated by their Emperor.
- **Public Welfare** With the end of continuous wars and conquest, the officials paid more attention to the schemes and welfare measures assigned for the common public, which ultimately led to the prosperity of the nation.
- **End of Crimes** The policy of *ahimsa* impacted the people morally, thereby decreasing crimes like theft and various illegal activities.

Later Mauryan Kings

The later Mauryan kings were weak successors such as Dasharatha, Kunal and Samprati. The oppression by the officers made Mauryan rule unpopular and people were forced to revolt. There were factions and quarrel among Mauryan ministers. **Brihadratha** was the last ruler of the Mauryan dynasty. He was killed by his Senapati (commander-in-chief) Pushyamitra Shunga who founded the Shunga dynasty.

Mauryan Administration

The Mauryan administration system was efficient and monarchical. Chandragupta Maurya laid the foundation of an elaborate system of administration. He set up a sound and efficient system of administration with the help of the great diplomat and based on the principles as laid down in Chanakya's book 'Arthashastra'.

Central Administration

- The king was the centre of administrative structure and he used to select ministers and high officials. He had the supreme executive, legislative and judicial power and functions in the government.
- The king had the sovereign power of law making and also the power and right to **supersede**[8] usage and equity. The king was the ultimate authority of the bureaucracy. The king also controlled the revenue system.
- The king was assisted by *mantriparishad* (Council of Ministers). The *mantriparishad* include Yuvaraj (the crown prince), Purohita (the chief priest of the state), Senapati (the commander in chief), Amatya (Civil Servants), Samaharta (taxation expert) and Sannidhata (supreme treasurer).

7 **Dhammayatra** This refers to the procession of a large group of Buddhist monks walking on foot to different areas to spread virtues.
8 **Supersede** To take the place or position.

- The Prime minister was the head of the *mantriparishad* and for each department a separate minister was appointed. *Adhyaksha* or superintendent headed each of these departments.
- The other important officers include incharge of agriculture, Superintendents of mines, ports and weights and measures, Accountant General and Controller of Commerce.

Provincial Administration

- The entire Mauryan empire was divided into two parts
  - (i) The kingdom under the direct rule of the king
  - (ii) The vassal states
- The Mauryan territory that was directly ruled by the king was divided into a number of provinces. The vast empire of Chandragupta Maurya was divided in four provinces Magadha, Avanti, Gandhara and the Southern province. Ashoka had five provinces whose capitals were Taxila, Ujjain, Tosali, Suvarnagiri and Pataliputra.
- Each province (headed by *Kumaras*) was sub-divided into number of districts called **Janapadas**, headed by *Sthanika* and each district was again sub-divided into number of units.
- The village was at the lowest unit headed by *Gramika.*
- The Maurya emperor directly ruled the Central and Eastern part of the empire, whereas the other areas were ruled by the provincial Governors (*Mahamatras*). They were responsible for the day-to-day administration of the provinces. They were expected to consult important matter with the Central administration.
- There were also officers like Pradeshikas (Provincial administrator), Rajuka (modern day Tehsildar or revenue officer) and Yukta (treasurer).

Military Administration

- The king was the supreme commander of the army and head of the military administration of Mauryan Empire.
- The war office of Mauryas were managed by a board of 30 members. They were also divided into six committees, each of the committees had five members to look after navy, transport, supply, infantry, cavalry, the war chariots and war elephants.
- According to Roman writer, Pliny, the Mauryan army consisted of 6,00,000 infantry, 30,000 cavalry and 9,000 war elephants.
- The Mauryan kings had constructed forts at strategic locations for security and safety of the empire.

Judicial Administration

- The Mauryan king was the head of the judicial department. It was his duty to ensure justice to the people and redress their grievances.
- Kautilya refers to the existence of two kinds of courts
  - (i) ***Dharmasthiyas*** They deal with civil matters.
  - (ii) ***Kantakasodhanas*** They dealt criminal cases.
- There were special courts in the cities and villages presided over by the *Pradeshika*, *Mahamatras* and *Rajukas*. The *Pradeshika* were the principal police officers, whose duty was to investigate the crimes committed in the region within their jurisdiction. Police headquarters were found in all principal centres.
- According to Megasthenes, death penalty was the ultimate hard punishment for the serious offenders of law.

Municipal Administration

The cities (capitals) had their own administrative system. *Nagaradhyaksha* was the head of the city. There were the Municipal Boards for cities. Megasthenes had given an account of the municipal administration of Pataliputra.

It had Municipal Board of 30 members divided into six committees. Each of these committees had five members to manage the administration of the city. The six committees had the following duties

- To take care of the foreigners.
- To register the birth and death of the citizens of Pataliputra.
- To look after trade and commerce.
- To supervise different manufacturers.
- To collect excise duties and custom duties.

Espionage System

There was a well-knitted **espionage**[9] system in the Mauryan administration. The detectives were known as *Gudhapurushas*. According to the Arthashastra, there were two kinds of spies, *Sansthana* (stationary) and *Sanchari* (wandering).

9 **Espionage** The practice of spying or of using spies, typically by governments to obtain political and military information.

These spies informed the king about all the details of the **bureaucracy**[10]. The agents included householders, merchants, disciples, ascetics, poisoners, poisonous girls which were called '*Vishkanyas*'. The ambassadors who were appointed in the foreign countries were also sort of spies.

Revenue System

Land revenue was the chief source of income of Mauryan Empire. Two types of taxes namely *Bali* and *Bhaga* were there. Toll tax, tax on liquor, gambling houses, etc were some other taxes. *Samnharta*, the chief of the Revenue Department, was incharge of the collection of all revenues in the empire.

The revenues came from land tax, irrigation tax, customs, shop tax, ferry tax, forests, mines and pastures land tax, license fee from craftsmen and fines collected in the law courts. The land revenue was normally fixed as 1/6th of the produce. The main items of expenditure of the state were related to king and his household, army, government servants, public works, poor relief, religion, etc.

Check Your LEARNING...

1. Name the two new ambassadors who came to the Mauryan court during the reign of Chandragupta.
2. Which rock edict of Ashoka explains about Kalinga war.
3. Into how many provinces Mauryan empire was divided during the reign of Ashoka?
4. What was the main source of income during Mauryan Empire?

QUiCK Revision

- The Mauryan Empire was the first major empire in the history of India, ruled by Maurya dynasty from 321 BC to 185 BC.
- The sources to know about the Mauryan empire can be divided into two parts i.e. literary sources and archaeological sources.
- With the help of Chanakya, Chandragupta overthrew the last Nanda ruler Dhananada and became the king. Chanakya became the Chief Minister in his court.
- In 297 BC, Chandragupta was succeeded by his son Bindusara, known to the Greeks as Amitrochates (Sanskrit, Amitraghata, the destroyer of enemy). Bindusara campaigned in the Deccan, extending Mauryan control in the peninsula as far as South Mysore.
- Bindusara's death in 273 BC led to a struggle for succession among his sons. It lasted for four years and in 268 BC Ashoka successfully became the king. Before becoming the King, he was viceroy of Ujjain.
- The conquest of Kalinga marked a turning point in Ashoka's life and reign. Horrified at the slaughter of the defenders of Kalinga, Ashoka decided to renounce warfare. He sent peace missions to his Asian neighbours as far away as Burma and Sumatra.
- The Mauryan Empire under Ashoka extended from Hindukush mountain in the North-West to Pennar river of Mysore in South. Ashoka also influenced many foreign empires and maintained amicable relation with them.
- The term 'Dhamma' corresponds to the Sanskrit word 'Dharma' or 'Dharman' which is usually used in the sense of a custom or a law. According to the Buddhist tradition, the term stands for Buddha's doctrines or teachings.
- For the purpose of permanently recording the doctrines of the Dhamma, Ashoka inscribed them on rocks and pillars. He also appointed a special class of officers called Dhamma-Mahamattas for propagating Dhamma.
- The policy of Dhamma marked the end of wars and conquest with change in the policy of state, which ensured all round development and economic prosperity of the state.
- The later Mauryan Kings were Dasharatha, Kunal and Samprati. Brihadratha was the last ruler of the Mauryan dynasty. He was killed by his Senapati (commader-in-chief) Pushyamitra Shunga who founded the Shunga dynasty.
- The Mauryan administration system was efficient and monarchical. The king of the Mauryan government was the head of the Mauryan empire administration.
- The entire empire was divided into two parts i.e. the kingdom under the direct rule of the king and the vassal states.
- The king was the supreme commander of the army and head of the Military administration of Mauryan Empire.
- The Mauryan king was the head of the judicial department. It was his duty to ensure justice to the people and redress their grievances
- There were the Municipal boards. Megasthenes had given an account of the municipal administration of Pataliputra.
- There was a well-knitted espionage system in the Mauryan administration. The detectives were known as Gudhapurushas.
- The revenues came from land, irrigation, customs, shop tax, ferry tax, forests, mines and pastures, license fee from craftsmen and fines collected in the law courts.

10 **Bureaucracy** A system of government in which most of the important decisions are taken by state officials rather than by elected representatives.

Chapter Practice

Section-I

Multiple Choice Questions

1. Arthashastra was written by
   (a) Dhanananda (b) Kautilya
   (c) Bimbisara (d) Pushyamitra

Ans. (b) Kautilya

2. The author of Arthashastra was a contemporary of
   (a) Ashoka
   (b) Chandragupta Maurya
   (c) Samudragupta
   (d) Chandragupta Vikramaditya

Ans. (b) Chandragupta Maurya

3. Who was the founder of the Mauryan dynasty?
   (a) Bimbisara
   (b) Chandragupta Maurya
   (c) Ashoka
   (d) Bindusara

Ans. (b) Chandragupta Maurya

4. Name the Greek ambassador at the Mauryan court.
   (a) Alexander (b) Megasthenes
   (c) Plato (d) Aristotle

Ans. (b) Megasthenes

5. The inscriptions of Ashoka and the Brahmi script were deciphered by
   (a) James Princep (b) R Ramasastry
   (c) Megasthense (d) Max Muller

Ans. (a) James Princep

6. The Sanchi Stupa was built by
   (a) Ashoka (b) Chandragupta II
   (c) Samudragupta (d) Kanishka

Ans. (a) Ashoka

7. Which Mauryan king holds the title of Amitraghata?
   (a) Bimbisara
   (b) Chandragupta Maurya
   (c) Bindusara
   (d) Ashoka

Ans. (c) Bindusara

8. Which event brought about a profound change in Ashoka's administrative policy?
   (a) The third Buddhist council
   (b) The Kalinga War
   (c) His embracing of Buddhism
   (d) His sending missionary to Ceylon

Ans. (b) The Kalinga War

9. Which of the following ancient Indian Kings had appointed Dhamma Mahamattas?
   (a) Chandragupta (b) Bindusara
   (c) Ashoka (d) Kanishka

Ans. (c) Ashoka

10. ……… usurped power from the Mauryas after killing the last Mauryan ruler Brihadratha.
    (a) Pushyamitra Shunga (b) Agnimitra
    (c) Vasumitra (d) Jyesthamitra

Ans. (a) Pushyamitra Shunga

11. The Mauryan administration was highly
    (a) decentralised (b) bureaucratic
    (c) centralised (d) despotic

Ans. (c) centralised

12. The one most important feature of the Mauryan administration was
    (a) wide powers enjoyed by the provincial governors.
    (b) the presence of a 'council of ministers'.
    (c) the presence of vast and numerous powers of the bureaucracy.
    (d) an extensive network of spy-system.

Ans. (c) the presence of vast and numerous powers of the bureaucracy.

13. Complete the given analogy.
    Chandragupta Maurya : (321 - 297 BC) : :
    Bindusara : ?
    (a) 297-273 BC (b) 268 : 232 BC
    (c) 232-185 BC (d) 185-72 AD

Ans. (a) 297-273 BC

14. Complete the given analogy.
    Kaling War : 261 BC :: Third Buddhist Council : ?
    (a) 483 BC (b) 250 BC (c) 386 BC (d) 72 AD

Ans. (b) 250 BC

15. Replace the underlined word and correct the statement.
    The <u>Senapati</u> of the Mauryan Government was the head of the Mauryan empire administration.
    (a) King (b) Tehsildar (c) Purohita (d) Amatya

Ans. (a) King

16. Replace the underlined word and correct the statement.
    <u>Amatya</u>, the chief of the revenue department was incharge of the collection of the revenues of the empire.
    (a) Samaharta (b) Yuvaraja
    (c) Senapati (d) Sannidhata

Ans. (a) Samaharta

17. Complete the given table.

Devanamapiya	Ashoka
Amitraghata	?

(a) Chandragupta Maurya (b) Bindusara
(c) Dasharatha (d) Brihadratha

Ans. (b) Bindusara

18. Identify the true statement about Mauryan dynasty
(i) It was founded by Chandragupta Maurya in 321 BC.
(ii) Chandragupta overthrown Mahapadmananda.
(iii) Chandragupta succeeded by Bindusara.
(iv) Brihadratha was the last ruler of Mauryan dynasty.

Codes
(a) Only (i) (b) Only (ii)
(c) Both (i) and (ii) (d) All of these

Ans. (d) All of these

19. Which statement is associated with Ashoka?
(i) Ashoka invaded Kalinga in 261 BC.
(ii) Mahendra and Sanghmitra were the children of Ashoka.
(iii) The 3rd Buddhist Council was held during the reign of Ashoka.
(iv) Ashoka was succeeded by Bindusara.

Codes
(a) Only (i) (b) Both (i) and (ii)
(c) (i), (ii) and (iii) (d) All of these

Ans. (c)

20. Match the following.

List-I	List-II
A. Kalinga war	1. 297 BC
B. 3rd Buddhist Council	2. 250 BC
C. Bindusara became king	3. 261 BC
D. Mauryan dynasty founded	4. 321 BC

Codes

	A	B	C	D		A	B	C	D
(a)	1	2	3	4	(b)	4	3	2	1
(c)	3	2	1	4	(d)	2	4	3	2

Ans. (c)

21. Match the following.

List-I	List-II
A. Samaharta	1. Civil servants
B. Amatya	2. Taxation expert
C. Purohita	3. Supreme Treasure
D. Sannidhata	4. Chief priest

Codes

	A	B	C	D		A	B	C	D
(a)	4	3	2	1	(b)	1	2	3	4
(c)	3	4	1	2	(d)	2	1	4	3

Ans. (d)

Passage Based Questions

22. Read the following passage given below and answer the questions.

When historians began reconstructing early Indian history in the 19th century, the emergence of the Mauryan Empire was regarded as a major landmark. India was then under colonial rule, and was part of the British empire.

19th and early 20th century Indian historians found the possibility that there was an empire in early India both challenging and exciting.

Also, some of the archaeological finds associated with the Mauryas, including stone sculpture, were considered to be examples of the spectacular art typical of empires. Many of these historians found the message on Ashokan inscriptions very different from that of most other rulers, suggesting that Ashoka was more powerful and industrious, as also more humble than later rulers who adopted grandiose titles. So it is not surprising that nationalist leaders in the 20th century regarded him as an inspiring figure.

(i) The time period of Mauryan dynasty was
(a) 321 BC to 185 BC (b) 433 BC to 32 BC
(c) 185 BC to 321 AD (d) 343BC to 167 BC

Ans. (a) 321 BC to 185 BC

(ii) Which among the following is the sources of Mauryan dynasty?
(a) Indica
(b) Kautilya's Arthshastra
(c) Ashoka's rock edicts
(d) All of the above

Ans. (d) All of the above

(iii) Who among the following was not a part of the Mauryan dynasty?
(a) Ajatsatru (b) Bindusara
(c) Chandragupta Maurya (d) Brihadratha

Ans. (a) Ajatsatru

(iv) Who was the Greek ambassador in the court of Chandragupta Maurya?
(a) Megasthenes (b) Seleucus
(c) Porus (d) Alexander

Ans. (a) Megasthenes

23. Read the passage given below and answer the following question.

Some of the most momentous developments in Indian epigraphy took place in the 1830s. This was when James Princep, an officer in the mint of the East India Company, deciphered Brahmi and Kharosthi, two scripts used in the earliest inscriptions and coins. He found that most of these mentioned a king referred to as Piyadassi - meaning "pleasant to behold", there were a few inscriptions which also referred to the king as Ashoka, one of the most famous rulers known from Buddhist texts.

This gave a new direction to investigations into early Indian political history as European and Indian scholars used inscriptions and texts composed in a variety of languages to reconstruct the lineages of major dynasties that had ruled the sub-continent. As a result, the broad contours of political history were in place by the early decades of the 20th century. Subsequently, scholars began to shift their focus to the context of political history, investigating whether there were connections between political changes and economic and social developments.

(i) The capital of Mauryan kingdom was located in
(a) Vaishali (b) Ujjain
(c) Pataliputra (d) Rajagriha

Ans. (c) Pataliputra

(ii) Who amongst the following also had the name 'Devanamapiyadassi'?
(a) King Ashoka (b) Chandragupta Maurya
(c) Gautama Buddha (d) Kanishka

Ans. (a) King Ashoka

(iii) In which Rock Edict Ashoka mentions about the casualities of Kalinga War and declares the renunciation of war?
(a) Maski Edict (b) Rock Edict XIII
(c) Rock Edict XI (d) Rock Edict X

Ans. (b) Rock Edict XIII

(iv) Which among the following is/are the feature of Dhamma?
(a) Respect elders
(b) Generosity towards Brahmanas
(c) Treating slaves and servants kindly
(d) All of the above

Ans. (d) All of the above

Section-II

Short Questions

1. Who was Chanakya?

Ans. Chanakya, also known as Kautilya was a pious, learned and determined Brahman. He managed to terminate the existing Magadha King Dhanananda and made Chandragupta the King.

2. What is the subject matter of Kautilya's Arthshastra?

Ans. The Kautilya's Arthshastra deals with all topics of internal administration and foreign relations. It also refers to economic system.

3. Mention the three parts of the Arthshastra.

Ans. Arthshastra is divided into 15 sections or Adhikarnas which are further divided into 150 chapters into three parts
(i) The first part deals with the ruler and council of ruler and the departments of Government.
(ii) The second part contains civil and criminal law.
(iii) The third part deals with war and diplomacy.

4. What do we come to know from Indica?

Ans. The references of Megasthenes' Indica throw light on the political, social, religious and economic condition of Mauryan period. The capital city of Pataliputra and its administration and military organisation was particularly mentioned.

5. What are the other literature which throws light on the history of the Mauryan Empire?

Ans. The Puranas and the Buddhist literature such as Jatakas, apart from other sources provided information on the Mauryas. The Ceylonese Chronicles, Dipavamsa and Mahavamsa throw light on the role of Ashoka in spreading Buddhism in Sri Lanka.

6. In which languages and script, were the edicts of Ashoka written?

Ans. The edicts of Ashoka were written in Pali language and in some places Prakrit was used. The Brahmi script was also used for writing on edicts. Ashoka inscriptions in the North-Western India were found in Kharosthi script.

7. What does the edicts of Ashoka deals with?

Ans. The edicts of Ashoka deal with Ashoka's Dhamma and also about the instructions given to his officials. The Rock Edict XIII gives details about the war he fought against Kalinga.

8. What are Stupas?

Ans. Stupas are large hemispherical domes which contain a central chamber, in which the relics of the Buddha were placed.

9. Mention two features of Sanchi Stupa.

Ans. The features of Sanchi Stupa are
(i) In the Sanchi Stupa, Lord Buddha has been symbolically represented by footprints, wheels, thrones, etc. rather than by his own image.
(ii) The gateways of Sanchi stupas contain ornamented depiction of incidents from the life of the Buddha and his previous incarnations as Bodhisattvas described in the Jataka tales.

10. Who ruled Magadha before the Mauryan dynasty?

Ans. Before the Mauryan dynasty, Magadha was ruled by the Nanda dynasty. Dhanananda was the last Nanda ruler.

11. Who founded the Mauryan Empire?

Ans. Chandragupta founded the Mauryan Empire by overthrewing the last Nanda ruler, Dhanananda with the help of Chanakya.

12. Who was Seleucus Nicator?

Ans. Seleucus Nicator was Alexander's general who gained control of most Asiatic provinces of the Macedonian Empire.

13. How did the tussle between Chandragupta Maurya and Seleucus Nicator come to an end?

Ans. The tussle between Chandragupta Maurya and Seleucus Nicator come to an end in 303 BC. Both entered into a marriage alliance and established relations.

14 Name the land which was conquered by Bindusara.

Ans. Bindusara is believed to have conquered the land between the two seas, the Arabian Sea and the Bay of Bengal.

15. Give a brief characteristic of Ashoka.

Ans. Before becoming the King, Ashoka was viceroy of Ujjain. He was a fierce military leader who expanded his kingdom in the Ganges-Jamuna valley. He continued his victorious campaigns in Southern and Eastern India for eight years. In 261 BC, he conquered Kalinga (now known as Odisha), a region on the East coast of India.

16. Why did Kalinga war mark a turning point in Ashoka's life?

Ans. The conquest of Kalinga marked a turning point in Ashoka's life and reign. The Kalinga War filled Ashoka's heart with grief and regret. The mass violence that was committed in Kalinga, developed hatred in Ashoka's heart regarding violence.

17. Give a brief account of the Ashokan edicts.

Ans. There are total fourteen major rock edicts. A number of major pillar edicts were erected in important cities. Some edicts were minor rock edicts while some were minor pillar edicts. The Pillar Edict VII gives a summary of Ashoka's efforts to promote the Dhamma within his kingdom.

18. Explain the term Dhamma.

Ans. The term 'Dhamma' corresponds to the Sanskrit word 'Dharma' or 'Dharman' which is usually used in the sense of a custom or a law. According to the Buddhist tradition, the term stands for Buddha's doctrines or teachings.

19. Explain two main features of Dhamma mentioned in edicts.

Ans. The two main features of Ashoka's Dhamma are

(i) Service to father and mother, practice of ahimsa, love of truth, reverence to teachers and good treatment of relatives.

(ii) Prohibition of animal sacrifices and festive gatherings and avoiding expensive and meaningless ceremonies and rituals.

20. What were the different steps taken by Ashoka to propagate Dhamma?

Ans. The different steps taken by Ashoka to propagate Dhamma were

- for the purpose of permanently recording the doctrines of the Dhamma, Ashoka inscribed them on rocks and pillars.
- He also appointed a special class of officers called Dhamma-Mahamattas for propagating Dhamma and for promoting its practice throughout the kingdom.

21. Name the Mauryan kings who succeeded after Ashoka in the Maurya dynasty.

Ans. The later Mauryan Kings were Dasharatha, Kunal, Samprati. Brihadratha was the last ruler of the Mauryan dynasty.

22. Mention the territories conquered by Mauryan Empire during Ashoka's reign.

Ans. The Mauryan Empire under Ashoka extended from Hindukush mountain in the North-West to the Pennar river of Mysore in the South. Ashoka captured Tamralipti (Tamluk) on the Bengal coast and it was an important part of the Mauryan Empire.

23. How was the Mauryan administration?

Ans. The Mauryan administration system was efficient and monarchical. The king of the Mauryan government was the head of the Mauryan empire administration. The administration of Mauryan Empire was decentralised and the administrative powers were divided into convenient administrative units.

24. What was the importance of the king in the central administration in the Mauryan Empire?

Ans. The king was the centre of administrative structure and king used to select ministers and high officials. He had the supreme executive, legislative, judicial power and functions in the government. The king had the sovereign power of law making into empire.

25. How did the Mauryan Empire get divided?

Ans. The Mauryan Empire get divided into two parts i.e. the kingdom under the direct rule of the king and the vassal states.

26. How was the Mauryan territory ruled?

Ans. The Mauryan territory was directly ruled by the king and was divided into a number of provinces. Each province (headed by Kumaras) was subdivided into number of districts called Janapadas which were headed by *Sthanika* and each district was again subdivided into number of units like modern block. The village was at the lowest unit headed by *Gramika*. The vassal states enjoyed a great deal of autonomy.

27. What was the role of the provincial governors?

Ans. The Mauryan Emperor directly ruled the Central and Eastern part of the empire, whereas the other areas were ruled by the provincial Governors (Mahamatras). They were responsible for the day-to-day administration of the provinces. They were expected to consult important matter with the central administration.

28. Mention the officers at the provincial level.

Ans. The officers at the provincial level were as follows

(i) Pradeshikas (Provincial administrator)

(ii) Rajuka (Looked after rural administration and justice)
(iii) Tehsildar (Revenue officer)
(iv) Yukta (Treasurer)

29. How was the military administration of Mauryan Empire?

Ans. The king was the supreme commander of the army and head of the military administration in Mauryan Empire. The war office of Mauryas were managed by a board of 30 members. They were also divided into six committees where each of the committees had five members to look after navy, transport and supply, infantry, cavalry, the war chariots and war elephants.

30. Who was the head of the judicial administration? What are the two courts referred by Kautilya?

Ans. The Mauryan king was the head of the judicial administration. It was his duty to ensure justice to the people and redress their grievances. Kautilya refers to the existence of two kinds of courts. They were
(i) Dharmasthiyas (dealing with civil matters)
(ii) Kantakasodhanas (dealing criminal cases)

31. Who were Pradeshikas?

Ans. The Pradeshikas were the principal police officers, whose duty was to investigate the crimes committed in the region within their jurisdiction. These Police headquarters were found in all principal centres.

32. What were the two kind of spies according to the Arthashastra?

Ans. According to the Arthashastra, there were two kinds of spies
(i) Sansthana (stationary) (ii) Sanchari (wandering)

33. What were the duties of spies?

Ans. The main duty of the spies was to inform the king about all the details of the bureaucracy.

34. What were the sources for revenue in Mauryan Empire?

Ans. The Mauryan Empire's revenue mainly came from land tax which was normally fixed at 1/6th of the produce. Other sources included trade tax, irrigation tax, mining revenue etc.

Structured Questions

1. With reference to the literary sources of the Mauryan Empire, explain
(i) Content of Arthashastra
(ii) Other literary sources
(iii) Description about Indica
(iv) Content of Mudrarakshasa

Ans. (i) Arthashastra is a book written by Chanakya in Sanskrit. It mainly deals with political and administrative issues covering internal administration and foreign relations. It is also a treaty on statecraft economic policy and military strategy. It contains 6000 *shlokas*. Arthashastra is divided into 15 sections containing 150 chapters.

(ii) There are various other literary sources which provides information on the Mauryas such as the Puranas and the Buddhist literature.
The Ceylonese chronicles, Dipavamsa and Mahavamsa throw light on the role of Ashoka in spreading of the Buddhism in Sri Lanka.

(iii) Indica is a book written by a Greek ambassador Megasthenes, who was sent to the court of Chandragupta Maurya by Seleucus Nicator. This book gives detail about Mauryan administration and the references of Megasthenes throws light on the political, social, religious and economic condition of Mauryan period. The capital city of Pataliputra and its administration and military organisation are particularly mentioned in his book.

(iv) Mudrarakshasa is a drama, written by Vishakhadatta in Sanskrit. It was written during Gupta period, but it described the victory of Chandragupta over Nanda with assistence of Kautilya. It also described social economy and cultural condition of Mauryan.

2. In context of the archaeological sources of Mauryan Empire, explain
(i) Define edicts. Who was the first ruler to issue edict? Mention the language of inscription and the script used.
(ii) Importance of edicts
(iii) Classification of edicts

Ans. (i) Edict is a decree (order) issued by a king. Ashoka was the first ruler to issue edicts.
The inscriptions of Ashoka was written in Pali language and in some places Prakrit was also used. The Brahmi script was used for writing on edicts and the Ashokan inscriptions in the North-Western India were found in Kharosthi script.

(ii) The Ashoka inscriptions or edicts remain valuable sources for the study of Ashoka and the Mauryan Empire such as the Rock Edict XIII gives details about the war he fought against Kalinga. The North-Western inscription of Ashoka deals with the Ashoka's Dhamma and the instructions given to his officials. The Pillar Edict VII gives a summary of his efforts to promote Dhamma within his kingdom.

(iii) Throughout the country, the edicts were divided into two parts i.e. Rock edicts and Pillar edicts
(a) Rock Edicts were of two types
- Major rock edicts which were fourteen in numbers i.e. I to XIV and two separate ones found in Orissa.
- Minor rock edicts like the Queen's edict, Barabar cave edict and Kandahar bilingual inscriptions.

(b) Pillar Edicts were seven in numbers and describes various administrative actions taken for public welfare. These pillars are found in various parts of South India like Sanchi, Rampurva, Lumbini, Nandangarh and Lion Capital of Sarnath.

3. In reference to Kalinga War and Dhamma, answer the following
   (i) Give a brief description of the war
   (ii) State the possible reason of the war
   (iii) Impact of the war on Ashoka's life and reign.

Ans. (i) Refer to chapter theory page no. 97.
(ii) The main reasons that led Ashoka to conquer Kalinga were
(a) It was the only kingdom which was not under Mauryan control. It was controlled by the independent feudal kingdom.
(b) It was important from military view point, as it controlled the land and sea routes to South India and South-East Asia.
(iii) The main impacts of Kalinga war on Ashoka's life and reign were
- The Kalinga War filled Ashoka's heart with grief and regret.
- The mass violence that was committed in Kalinga developed hatred in Ashoka's heart regarding violence.
- Dig Vijaya (victory in all directions) was replaced by Dhamma Vijaya (conquest through dharma) which was a common code of conduct that dealt with ideas like kindness, charity, non-violence, etc.
- Ashoka started to propagate Dhamma. In his edicts, Dhamma is described not as a religion or religious system but as a 'moral law', 'code of conduct' or an 'ethical order' which is common for all religions.

4. Ashoka adopted the policy of Dhamma after the Kalinga War. With reference to this, explain.
   (i) Describe Dhamma.
   (ii) Three features of Dhamma
   (iii) Propagation of Dhamma
   (iv) Impact of Dhamma

Ans. (i) Refer to the chapter theory page no. 97.
(ii) Refer to the chapter theory page no. 97-98.
(iii) Refer to the chapter theory page no. 98.
(iv) Refer to the chapter theory page no. 98.

5. Chandragupta Maurya laid the foundation of an elaborate system of administration. In context of this explain
   (i) Central Administration
   (ii) Military Administration
   (iii) Judicial Administration

Ans. (i) Refer to the chapter theory page no. 98-99.
(ii) Refer to the chapter theory page no. 99.
(iii) Refer to the chapter theory page no. 99.

6. The Mauryan administration was decentralised and the administrative powers were divided into convenient administrative units, with reference to this explain
   (i) Municipal Administration
   (ii) Duties of the Municipal Committees
   (iii) Provincial Administration
   (iv) Revenue System

Ans. (i) Refer to the chapter theory page no. 99.
(ii) The duties of the Municipal Committees were
- To take care of foreigners.
- To register the birth and death of the citizens of the empire.
- To look after trade and commerce.
- To supervise different manufacturers.
- To collect excise duties and custom duties.

(iii) Refer to the chapter theory page no. 99.
(iv) Refer to the chapter theory page no. 100

Picture Based Question

1. With reference to the given picture, answer the following questions

   (i) Identify the monument given in picture. Give a brief description about it.
   (ii) Explain the decoration of the monument.
   (iii) How Lord Buddha has been symbolically represented in the monument?

Ans. (i) The monument shown in the given picture is Sanchi Stupa. Sanchi Stupa is a large hemispherical dome, containing a central chamber in which the relics of the Lord Buddha were placed. The Sanchi Stupa is one of the best preserved early Stupas in Central India. It was built by Ashoka. The great Stupa is 36.5 metres in diameter and rises almost 16.5 metres high.
(ii) During the Shunga period the Sanchi Stupa was enlarged and faced with stones and decorated with railings, staircase and a harmika on top. Around the main Stupa, there is a path for circumambulation. This path is enclosed by a railing with gates at each of the four directions. The railings and gates of the Sanchi Stupa are richly sculptured with different motifs and designs.
(iii) Interesting characteristic about Sanchi Stupa is that Lord Buddha has been symbolically represented by footprints, wheels, thrones, etc rather than by his own image. The gateways of Sanchi Stupas contain ornamented depiction of incidents from the Life of Buddha and his previous incarnations as Bodhisattvas were described in the Jataka tales. The Buddha has been shown symbolically in the form of a tree or through other inanimate figures.

Chapter Assessment

Section-I

Multiple Choice Questions

1. Who was the founder of Mauryan Dynasty?
   (a) Kautilya (b) Chandragupta
   (c) Ashoka (d) Bindusara
2. 'Indica' was compiled by
   (a) Chanakya (b) Megasthenes
   (c) Seleucus Nicator (d) Porus
3. Who fought Kalinga War?
   (a) Ashoka (b) Bindusara
   (c) Chandragupta (d) Dhanananda
4. Replace the underlined word to correct the sentence.
   After the Kalinga War in 261 BC <u>Bindusara</u> devoted his life to social welfare.
   (a) Ashoka
   (b) Chandragupta
   (c) Seleucus Nicator
   (d) Chandragupta II
5. Identify the later Mauryan king.
   (a) Dasharatha (b) Kunal
   (c) Samprati
   (d) Brihadratha
   Codes
   (a) Only 1 (b) Only 4
   (c) Both 2 and 4 (d) All of these

Section-II

Short Questions

1. Who was Kautilya?
2. Who was the last Nanda ruler?
3. What do you mean by Ashoka's Dhamma?
4. Why did Ashoka embrace Buddhism?
5. Mention the principles of Ashoka's Dhamma.
6. Name any three rulers of the Mauryan dynasty. Who succeeded the Mauryan dynasty?
7. What does Megasthenes tell us about the city administration?

Structured Questions

1. Discuss the political history under the reign of
   (i) Chandragupta Maurya
   (ii) Bindusara
   (iii) Ashoka
2. With reference to the Mauryan administration, explain
   (i) Status of King
   (ii) Council of Ministers
   (iii) Division of Provinces
   (iv) Spy system

CHAPTER

05

The Sangam Age

SYLLABUS

Sources Tirukkural and Megaliths; Society – Position of Women
Economy – Agriculture and Trade

The Sangam age is the classical period in the history of Tamil Nadu, Kerala and other parts of South India which flourished during 3rd century BC to 3rd century AD. The word 'Sangam' is the Tamil form of the Sanskrit word 'Sangha' which means a group of persons or an association. The Sangam Age refers to the period when a large number of Tamil literature was composed by a body of Tamil poets in three literary gatherings known as Sangam.

The three Sangams of the Sangam age were

(i) The seat of the **first Sangam** (*Iarai sangam*) was Madurai. It was attended by Gods and legendary sages. All the works of the first Sangam have perished.

(ii) The seat of the **second Sangam** (*Idai sangam*) was Kapadapuram, another capital of the Pandyas. It was attended by several poets and produced a large mass of literature, but only Tolkappiyam (the early Tamil Grammar) has survived.

(iii) The seat of the **third Sangam** (*Kadai sangam*) was Madurai. It has also produced vast literature, but only a fraction of it has survived.

Sources of the Sangam Age

The sources of the Sangam age can be classified into two groups i.e. literary sources which include the Sangam literature and the archaeological sources which include megaliths, and inscriptions to support the literary evidence.

Tirukkural

It is a classic of couplets or Kurals (1330 rhyming Tamil couplets) or **aphorisms**[1]. It is a part of the 18 minor works (Pathinenkilkanakku) of the Sangam literature. It was written by a poet sant **Tiruvalluvar** (2nd century BC-5th century AD). The Tirukkural explains various aspects of life and is one of the most important works in the Tamil language.

Tirukkural is a collection of 1330 Tamil couplets and 133 chapters. It is organised into three main sections i.e. Aram (righteousness), Porul (wealth) and Inbam or Kamam (pleasure). Each chapter has a specific subject ranging from 'ploughing a piece of land' to 'ruling a country'.

It preaches simplicity and truth throughout its verses. Each chapter contains 10 couplets. Aram discuss about ethical living in private life while Porul deals with public affairs.

Poems

- **Ettuthogai** It comprises eight works namely Natrinai, Kurunthokai, Akananuru, Ainkurunuru, Kalithokai, Purananuru, Pathitrupathu and Paripadal. It comprises of approxi. 2370 poems written by different poets.
- **Pathupattu** It has ten long poetic works starting from Thirumurugatruppadai and ending with Malaipadukadam. Like Ettuthogai, these works also deal with Aram and Porul.

1. **Aphorism** A short phrase that expresses something that is true in a clever way.

Tolkappiyam

It was written by Tolkappiyar. It is considered as the earliest work on Tamil literary work. It is a work on Tamil grammar, but it also provides insights on the political and socio-economic conditions of that time. It lays down rules for different kinds of poetic compositions. It contains 1610 poems under three parts, Ezhuthu (orthography), Sol (etymology) and Porul (subject matter). Each division was sub-divided into nine more sub-divisions.

Megaliths

A megalith is a large stone that has been used to construct a prehistoric structure or monument, either alone or together with other stones. During Sangam age, megaliths were used to mark burial sites or memmorials.

Some megaliths can be seen on the surface while some are underground. In some megaliths, more than one skeleton have been found. This indicated that people of the same family were buried in the same place but at different time periods.

Things like pitchers, baskets, ornaments, tools, weapons of iron and stone, etc are found in burials which indicated life of the people during the Sangam Age. It also indicates about their belief of life after death. Some megaliths have been found in the districts of Kanchipuram, Vellore, Thiruvannamalai, Cuddalore, Tiruchirappalli and Pudukottai in Tamil Nadu.

Tamil Kingdoms

The area lying to the South of river Krishna and Tungabhadra river is called South India. The Sangam literature describe three South Indian kingdoms. These three kingdoms were always at war with one another.

Their wars and heroic deeds form the themes of Sangam literature. According to this, Cheras had finally asserted their supremacy over Cholas and Pandyas.

Cheras

The Cheras had their rule over major parts of modern Kerala/Malabar areas. Their capital was Vanji or Karur and their important seaports were Tondi and Musiri. The **insignia**[2] of Cheras is the **bow and arrow**. The Pugalur inscription of the 1st century AD has reference to three generations of Chera rulers.

The important ruler of Cheras was **Cheran Senguttuvan** who belonged to 2nd century AD. His military achievements have been chronicled in Silappathikaram (epic) which was composed by his brother **Ilango Adigal.** It has details about his expedition to the Himalayas where he defeated many North Indian rulers. He crossed the river Ganga and defeated his enemies. Senguttuvan introduced the Pattini cult or the worship of Kannagi as the ideal wife, in Tamil Nadu. He was the first to send embassy to China from South India.

Cholas

The Chola kingdom in the Sangam period extended from Northern Tamil Nadu to Southern Andhra Pradesh. Their first capital was Uraiyur. The insignia of Cholas was **tiger**. **King Karikala** was a famous king of the Sangam Cholas. Pattinappalai portrays the life and military conquests of King Karikala.

Many Sangam poems mention the Battle of Venni where he defeated the confederacy of Cheras, Pandyas and 11 minor chieftains. He also built dam called Kallanai near river Kaveri to provide water for reclaimed land from forest for cultivation.

Karikala fortified the port-city of Kaveripoompattinam and made it as his second capital where merchants from foreign countries visited frequently. He was also fond of literature and patronised the Tamil poets.

Pandyas

The Pandyas ruled over the present day Southern Tamil Nadu. The Pandya king were known as Maran, Valudhi and Chezhiyan. Their insignia was the 'carp' (fish).

Their capital was Madurai and their chief port was Korkai. Maduraikkanji was written by Mangudi Maruthanar which describes the socio-economic condition of the flourishing seaport of Karkai.

The Pandyan kings earned fame for their patronage to Tamil Sangam and their capital Madurai remained the capital of Tamil languages literature.

King Nedunchelliyans was a famous Pandya ruler. He was also known as 'Aryappadai Kadantha Nedunchelliyan'. He ordered the execution of

2. **Insignia** An official sign or symbol.

Kovalan (the hero of Silappatikaram) by mistake due to which Kovalan's wife Kannagi burnt and destroyed Madurai.

Thalaiyalanganathu Nedunchezhiyan was another famous Pandya ruler, who defeated the combined force of Chera, Chola and other local chieftains at Tholaiyalanganam.

Local Chieftains of Sangam Age

A number of local chieftains ruled in different parts of Tamil Nadu apart from the three Tamil kingdoms i.e. Chera, Chola and Pandya. They were known as **Velirs.** The most famous among the Velirs were called Seven Patrons or Kadaiyelu Vallalgal. They were Pari, Ori, Malayan, Elini, Pegan, Aay and Nalli.

Tamil poets like Kabilar, Avvaiyar, Nallathanar and Perunchithiranar received patronage from the local chieftains. In turn, these poets hailed them for their generosity. They also helped to resolve any disputes between the rulers.

The local chieftains made generous donations to the poets, bards and their consorts. They had also played a significant role in the political, social and cultural domains during the Sangam age.

Check Your LEARNING...

1. Which city was the seat of third Sangam?
2. What are the narrative and didactic acts of the Sangam literature?
3. Name the three main sections of Tirukkural.
4. What are the things found in megaliths?

Society of Sangam Age

Social Class

In the Sangam age, the Tamil people had a common language and culture but they lived in five different natural landscapes. Tolkappiyam text refers to the five-fold division of lands and the people living in these five divisions had their respective chief occupations as well as Gods for worship.

Caste System

There were caste divisions in the Sangam Age. The Tamil Sangam society was divided on basis of high born or low born that differentiated Brahmins and their patrons from common men. The Tolkappiyam text refers to the existence of four-fold caste system and social inequalities in the Sangam society. The four castes were **Arasar** (ruling class), **Anthanars, Vellalar** and **Vaishyars.**

Position of Women

- Women enjoyed a respectable position but their status was not equal to men in the society.
- Education was provided to women as there were women poets like Avvaiyar, Nachchellaiyar and Kakkaipadiniyar who flourished and contributed to Tamil literature.
- Love marriage was a common practice and women were allowed to choose their life partners. But, life of widows was miserable.
- The practice of Sati was prevalent in the higher level of society.
- The worship of Kannagi (the Chaste Lady) was prevalent.

Food

- Rice was the staple food during the Sangam period. Apart from it, meat, fish, vegetables, milk and milk products were the chief articles of food.
- The food-habits among the people varied according to their economic status. The rich had their feasts every day, while the poor took simple food.
- Chewing betel leaves was most common among the people. Offering betel leaves to guests had become a social formality.

Dress and Ornaments

- The Sangam Tamils paid more attention to their dress. It varied according to their status. The rich wore silk and fine cotton garments. The middle class people generally wore two pieces of clothes made of cotton.
- Women paid much attention to their hairstyle. They used flowers like Jasmine to decorate themselves. Both men and women used perfumes made of Sandalwood and flowers.
- The Sangam literature refers to a variety of ornaments worn by both men and women. They were made of gold, silver, pearls and precious stones. Poor people used ornaments which were made of shells and beads.

Entertainment and Marriage

The people of Sangam age used different means of entertainment during their leisure time as

- Music and dance were a good part of the spare time of men and women.

- Cock fighting, goat fighting and gambling were popular.
- Wrestling was another form of entertainment enjoyed by youth.
- The children played numerous games for entertainment.

According to texts like the Tolkappiyam and the Kalaviyal, the Aryans introduced the rituals and ceremonies of marriage. They refer to eight forms of marriage mentioned in the Sanskrit Dharmashastras and included them in the framework of Tamil scheme.

Administration during Sangam Age

The head of the administration was the king. The king was assisted by ministers and officials.

- The empire was divided into provinces which were also known as *mandalams*. Each *mandalam* was divided into a number of *kottams* or *valandus* which was sub-divided into *nadu*. Each *nadu* was further divided into villages (*Urs*) which form the last unit of administration.
- The close relatives of the king were appointed as viceroys who received orders from the king.
- The main source of income of the government was land revenue. Generally, one-sixth of the land yield was collected as tax. Other sources of income include taxes on mines forests, ports and salt pans, house tax, professional tax, etc.

Economy of Sangam Age

Agriculture

- Agriculture was the chief occupation. The main crops were rice, cotton, sugarcane, ragi, different varieties of fruits, etc.
- The Sangam literature mentions rural activities in poems like cultivation of ragi and sugarcane, harvesting and drying of grain and the making of sugar from sugarcane.

Trade

- Both the internal and foreign trade was extensively carried on throughout the period and most of the trade was carried by barter system.
- The port city of **Puhar** became an important place of foreign trade as big ships entered this port containing precious goods. Other significant ports of commercial activity were Tondi, Musiri, Korkai, Arikkamedu and Marakkanam.
- The periplus (sailing around or voyage) of Red sea described the navigation and trade of Roman Empire with India. It mentioned the ports of Naura (Cannanore), Tyndis (Ponnani) and Muziris (Cranganore) as of leading importance on the West coast. The pearls from the coast were sent to Uraiyur and exported.
- In bigger towns, established markets called angadi were present while at other places, goods were cerried by hawkers to the houses of the people.
- Many gold and silver coins that were issued by the Roman Emperors like Augustus, Tiberius and Nero have been found in all parts of Tamil Nadu indicating flourishing trade.
- Major exports of the Sangam age were cotton fabrics and spices like pepper, ginger, cardamom, cinnamon and turmeric along with ivory products, pearls and precious stones.
- Major imports for the traders were horses, gold and sweet wine.

Check Your LEARNING...

1. What role was played by Brahmans in Sangam society?
2. Name the staple food during Sangam period.
3. Name any two ports of sangam age which were important for commercial activities.
4. What was the other name of the famous Pandyan king 'Neduncheliyans'.

QUiCK Revision

- The Sangam age is the classical period in the history of Tamil Nadu, Kerala and other parts of South India during 3rd century BC to 3rd century AD.
- The sources of the Sangam age can be classified into two groups i.e. literary sources which include the Sangam literature and the archaeological sources which include megaliths, hero stone and inscriptions to support the literary evidence.
- Tirukkural is a classic of couplets or Kurals (1330 rhyming Tamil couplets) or aphorisms. It was written by Thiruvalluvar. It explains various aspects of life and is one of the most important works in the Tamil language.
- The poems of Sangam literature are Ettuthogai which comprises eight works and Pathupattu that has ten long poetic works.
- Tolkappiyam was written by Tolkappiyar. It is considered as the earliest work on Tamil literary work. Though, it is a work on Tamil grammar, but it also provides insights on the political and socio-economic conditions of the time.
- The archaeological sources that inform about the Sangam Age are megaliths. A megalith is large stone that has been used to construct a prehistoric structure or monument, either alone or together with stones.
- The area lying to the South of river Krishna and Tungabhadra river is called South India. During the Sangam Age, it was ruled by three dynasties i.e. the Cheras, Cholas and Pandyas.
- The three major epics of the Sangam literature are Silappatikaram, written by Ilango Adigal, Manimekalai, written by the Tamil Buddhist poet Seethalai Saathanar and Civaka Cintamani, a Jain religious text.
- In the Sangam age, the Tamil people had a common language and culture. But, they lived in five different natural landscapes.
- Tolkappiyam refers to the five-fold division of lands and the people living in these five divisions had their respective chief occupations as well as Gods for worship.
- The Tolkappiyam refers to the existence of caste system such as the Arasar (ruling class), Anthanars, Vellalar and Vaishyars.
- The Sangam social structure rested on traditional caste systems and occupations. The literature speak of farmers, shepherds, hunters, fishermen, blacksmiths, weavers, carpenters, merchants, shippers and priests.
- The Brahmins of Sangam society were ideal priests. They acted as the chief advisor to the kings as scholars and philosophers.
- A lot of information is available in the Sangam literature to understand the position of women during the Sangam age. Women enjoyed respectable position, but their status was not equal to men. There were women poets like Avvaiyar, Nachchellaiyar and Kakkaipadiniyar who flourished and contributed to Tamil literature.
- The food habits among the people varied according to their economic status. Rice was the staple food during Sangam period.
- The Sangam Tamils paid more attention to their dress. It varied according to their status.
- The Sangam literature refers to a variety of ornaments worn by both men and women.
- Agriculture was the chief occupation where rice was main crop.
- Both internal and foreign trade was extensively carried on throughout the period and most of the trade was carried on by barter system.

Chapter Practice

Section-I

Multiple Choice Questions

1. Which of the following ancient Tamil kingdoms came to be known for Sangam literature?
   (a) Chera (b) Chola
   (c) Pandya (d) All of these

Ans. (d) All of these

2. It is believed that the .... Sangam was attended by Gods and legendary sages.
   (a) first (b) second (c) third (d) fourth

Ans. (a) first

3. Tirukkural was written by
   (a) Tolkappiyar (b) Tiruvalluvar
   (c) Ethuthogai (d) Pathupattu

Ans. (b) Tiruvalluvar

4. The megaliths has been found in which of the following districts of Tamil Nadu?
   (a) Kanchipuram (b) Vellore
   (c) Pudukottai (d) All of these

Ans. (d) All of these

5. The 'bow and arrow' was the flag symbol of
   (a) Chera (b) Chola (c) Pandya (d) All of these

Ans. (a) Chera

6. What was the capital of Chola?
   (a) Vanji (b) Madurai
   (c) Kanchipuram (d) Puhar (Tanjore)

Ans. (d) Puhar (Tanjore)

7. The chief diety of Mullai (Pastal) was
   (a) Murugan (b) Mayon (c) Indira (d) Korravai

Ans. (b) Mayon

8. What was the main crop during the Sangam age?
   (a) Rice (b) Wheat
   (c) Cotton (d) Sugarcame

Ans. (a) Rice

9. Major imports for the traders during Sangam age were
   (a) horses (b) gold
   (c) sweet wine (d) All of these

Ans. (d) All of these

10. Complete the given analogy.
    Chola : Uraiyur : : Pandya : ?
    (a) Vanji (b) Madurai
    (c) Kanyakumari (d) Vellore

Ans. (b) Madurai

11. Complete the given analogy.
    Chera : Bow and Arrow :: Chola : ?
    (a) Tiger (b) Fish
    (c) Eagle (d) Sword

Ans. (a) Tiger

12. Replace the underlined word to correct the sentence.
    The poems of Sangam literature are Ethuthogain which comprieses <u>seven</u> works and Pathupattu that has ten long poetic works.
    (a) eight (b) six (c) five (d) nine

Ans. (a) eight

13. Replace the underlined word and correct the sentence
    The port city of <u>Madurai</u> became an important place of foreign trade, as big ships entered this port containing precious goods.
    (a) Tondi (b) Puhar
    (c) Karkai (d) Marakkanam

Ans. (b) Puhar

14. Replace the underlined word and correct the sentence
    The Pugalur inscription of the <u>3rd century</u> AD has reference to three generations of Chera rulers.
    (a) 1st century (b) 2nd century
    (c) 4th century (d) 300 BC

Ans. (a) 1st century

15. Complete the given table.

Chera	Senguttuvan
Chola	?

   (a) Ilango Adigal (b) Karikala
   (c) Neduncheliyans (d) None of these

Ans. (b) Karikala

16. Which of the following Sangam ports were situated on the Western coast?
    (i) Korkai (ii) Puhar
    (iii) Tondi (iv) Musiri
    Select the correct answer from the code given below.
    (a) Only (iii) and (iv) (b) Only (ii) and (iii)
    (c) Only (i) and (ii) (d) Only (iv) and (i)

Ans. (a) Only (iii) and (iv)

17. Identify the true statement about the position of woman during Sangam age.
    (i) Their status was not equal to men in society.
    (ii) There were women poets like Avvaiyar and Nachchellaiyar.

(iii) Women were allowed to choose their life partner.
(iv) Life of widow was miserable.

Codes

(a) Only (i) (b) Both (i) and (iii)
(c) (i), (ii) and (iii) (d) All of these

Ans. (d) All of these

18. Consider the following statement associated with the economy of Sangam age and choose the correct option.

(i) Agriculture was the chief occupation.
(ii) Major exports of Sangam age were cotton and spices, etc.
(iii) People were engaged in spinning and weaving.
(iv) Puhar was the important port city.

Codes

(a) Only (i) (b) Both (i) and (iii)
(c) (i), (ii) and (iii) (d) All of these

Ans. (d) All of these

19. Match the following.

List I	List II
A. Senguttuvan	1. Kadaiyelu
B. Karikala	2. Pandya
C. Neduncheliyans	3. Chola
D. Local Chieftains	4. Chera

Codes

	A	B	C	D		A	B	C	D
(a)	1	2	3	4	(b)	4	3	2	1
(c)	2	4	1	3	(d)	3	1	4	2

Ans. (b)

20. Match the following.

List I	List II
A. Thiruvalluvar	1. Silappadikaram
B. Tolkappiyar	2. Maduraikkanji
C. Ilango Adigal	3. Tirukkural
D. Mangudi Maruthanar	4. Tolkappiyam

Codes

	A	B	C	D		A	B	C	D
(a)	4	3	2	1	(b)	3	4	1	2
(c)	1	2	3	4	(d)	2	4	3	1

Ans. (b)

21. Match the following.

List I (People)	List II (Chief deity)
A. Mullai	1. Korravai
B. Marutam	2. Varunan
C. Neithal	3. Indira
D. Palai	4. Mayon

Codes

	A	B	C	D		A	B	C	D
(a)	4	3	2	1	(b)	1	2	3	4
(c)	3	1	4	2	(d)	2	4	1	3

Ans. (a)

Passage Based Questions

22. Read the passage given below and answer the following questions.

The body of Tamil classical literature composed between 300 BC to 300 AD is known as Tamil Sangam literature. Sangam literature reverberate the existence of the spirited and highly developed literary culture in time honoured Tamilakarn. Tamil Sangam period poems commemorate the traditional practice of erecting megalithic tombs which can open up the hidden fabric of social life.

The Sangam literature reverberate the Sangam Tamil society with its distinguishable heritage and culture, its emotional and material topics such as love, war, governance, trade and bereavement. Of the Eight Sangam Anthologies, Purananuru and Pathitrupathu are implicated with the social life such as the life of the kings (Chera, Chola and Pandya), chieftains (Velirs), wars, patriotism, valour and heroism, the magnificence of kings, the wisdom of bards and poets (also poetesses), ethics and philosophy 'Arrupadai' a form of Sangam literature speaks about the community of poets including various sects known as Paanar, Porunar, Koothar, Viraliyar, Kcdiyar, Akavunar and Pulavar.

(i) What is the meaning of Sangam?
(a) Assembly (b) Dynasty (c) Tamilakam (d) Warrior

Ans. (a) Assembly

(ii) Tolkappiyam in Sangam age is the greatest work of .... literature.
(a) Telugu (b) Sanskrit (c) Malayalam (d) Tamil

Ans. (d) Tamil

(iii) The Sangam age areas were lying on the South of the river
(a) Krishna (b) Cauveri (Kaveri)
(c) Godavari (d) Bhima

Ans. (a) Krishna

(iv) To which part of ancient and medieval India is the Sangam literature related to?
(a) North India (b) North-East India
(c) South India (d) East India

Ans. (c) South India

23. Read the passage given below and answer the following questions.

The Pandyan kingdom was an ancient Tamil state in South India of unknown antiquity. Pandyas were one of the three ancient Tamil kingdoms (Chela, Chera) who ruled the Tamil country from pre-historic times until end of the 15th century. They ruled initially from Korkai, a sea port on the Southern most tip of the Indian peninsula, and in later times moved to Madurai.

The early Pandyan dynasty of the Sangam literature went into obscurity during the invasion of the Kalabhras.

The dynasty revived under Kadungon in the early 6th century, pushed the Kalabhras out of the Tamil country and ruled from Madurai. They again went into decline with the rise of the Cholas in the 9th century and were in constant conflict with them. Pandyas allied themselves with the Sinhalese and the Cheras in harassing the Chola empire until they found an opportunity for reviving their fortunes during the late 13th century.

(i) Madurai was the capital of ....
(a) Pandya (b) Chola (c) Chera (d) Chalukya

Ans. (a) Pandya

(ii) Who among the following was the famous Pandya ruler?
(a) Karikala (b) Rejendra Chola
(c) Senguttuvan (d) Aryappadai Kadantha

Ans. (d) Aryappadai Kadantha

(iii) Who described the Pandyas seaport Korkai in his book Maduraikkanji?
(a) Mangudi Maruthanar (b) Karikala
(c) Thiruvalluvar (d) Tolkappiyam

Ans. (a) Mangudi Maruthanar

(iv) What was the insignia of Pandya?
(a) Carp (fish) (b) Lion
(c) Bow and arrow (d) Tiger

Ans. (a) Carp (fish)

Section-II

Short Questions

1. Define the term Sangam.

Ans. The word 'Sangam' is the Tamil form of the Sanskrit word 'Sangha', which means a group of persons or an association.

2. Mention the three seats of the Sangam.

Ans. The seat of the first Sangam was Madurai, the seat of the second Sangam was Kapadapuram and the seat of the third Sangam was the present Madurai.

3. What is the content of the Sangam literature?

Ans. The content of Sangam literature includes Tolkappiyam, Ettuthogai, Pathupattu, Pathinenkilkanakku and the two epics i.e. Silappathikaram and Manimegalai.

4. Give a brief account of Tirukkural.

Ans. Tirukkural is a collection of 1330 Tamil couplets organised into 133 chapters. Each chapter has a specific subject ranging from 'ploughing a piece of land' to 'ruling a country'. It preaches simplicity and truth throughout its verses. The 1330 couplets are arranged into three main sections i.e. *Aram* (righteousness), *Porul* (wealth) and Inbam or *Kamam* (pleasure) and 133 chapters.

5. What are the different poems of Sangam literature?

Ans. The poems of Sangam literature are

- **Ettuthogai** It comprises eight works namely Natrinai, Kurunthokai, Aganauru, Ainkurunuru, Kalithogai, Purananuru, Pathittupathu and Paripadal. It comprises of 2282 poems written by different poets.
- **Pathupattu** It has ten long poetic works starting from Thirumurugatruppadai and ending with Malaipadukadam. Like Ettuthogai, these works also deals with Akam and Puram.

6. How many poems are there in Tolkappiyam?

Ans. Tolkappiyam contains 1610 poems under three parts. Each division was sub-divided into nine more sub-divisions.

7. What is megalith?

Ans. A megalith is a large stone that has been used to construct a prehistoric structure or monument, either alone or together with other stones. During Sangam age megaliths were used to mark burial sites or memmorials.

8. Where did we find megaliths?

Ans. Megaliths have been found in the districts of Kanchipuram, Vellore, Thiruvannamalai, Cuddalore, Tiruchirappalli and Pudukottai in Tamil Nadu.

9. Which area was ruled by the kingdoms of South India?

Ans. The area lying to the South of river Krishna and Tungabhadra is called South India. During the Sangam age, it was ruled by three dynasties i.e. the Cheras, Cholas and Pandyas.

10. Who was Senguttuvan?

Ans. Senguttuvan was an important ruler of Cheras. His military achievements have been chronicled in epic Silappatikaram with details about his expedition to the Himalayas where he defeated many North Indian rulers. Senguttuvan introduced the Pattini cult or the worship of Kannagi as the ideal wife in Tamil Nadu. He was the first to send embassy to China from South India.

11. What are the different sources which indicate about the King Karikala?

Ans. Pattinappalai portrays the life and military conquests of King Karikala. Karikala was the famous ruler of Chola dynasty. Many Sangam poems mention the Battle of Venni where he defeated the confederacy of Cheras, Pandyas and 11 minor chieftains. He also built irrigation tanks near river Kaveri to provide water for reclaimed land from forest for cultivation.

12. How was the society of Sangam age?

Ans. In the Sangam Age, the Tamil people had a common language and culture. But, they lived in five different natural landscapes. The Sangam social structure rested on traditional caste systems and occupations.

13. How was the position of women in the Sangam age?

Ans. The following points highlight the position of women during the Sangam age

- Women were provided education as there were women poets like Avvaiyar, Nachchellaiyar, and Kakkaipadiniyar, who flourished and contributed to Tamil literature.

- Love marriage was a common practice and women were allowed to choose their life partners. But, life of widows were miserable.

14. What were the food habits of the Sangam age people?

Ans. Rice was the staple food of the people of the Sangam age. The food-habits varied among the people according to their economic status.

15. Was there any presence of class difference in the dress habit of Sangam age people?

Ans. The Sangam Tamils paid more attention to their dress. It varied according to their status. The rich wore silk and fine cotton garments and the middle class people generally wore two pieces of clothes made of cotton.

16. Why the cotton and silk clothes were important items of trade ?

Ans. The cotton and silk clothes were important items of trade because a high expertise was attained in spinning and weaving of cotton and silk clothes. These were in great demand in the Western world, especially for the cotton clothes woven at Uraiyur.

17. What were the major items of export and import during Sangam age?

Ans. Major exports of Sangam age were cotton fabrics and spices like pepper, ginger, cardamom, cinnamon and turmeric along with ivory products, pearls and precious stones. Major items of import were horses, gold and sweet wine.

Structured Questions

1. There are various sources to understand about the Sangam age, in context of the above, explain.
(i) Poems
(ii) Tolkappiyam
(iii) Megaliths

Ans. (i) Refer to chapter theory page no. 108.
(ii) Refer to chapter theory page no. 109.
(iii) Refer to chapter theory page no. 109.

2. With reference to the three dynasties of Sangam age, answer the following.
(i) Name of the kingdoms with their important rulers.
(ii) Name their capital city and seaport.
(iii) Importance of literature.

Ans. (i) The three important dynasties which flourished during Sangam age are Chola, Chera and Pandya Karikala was the most important ruler of early Chola kingdom and their emblem was tiger. Senguttavan was the most important Chera ruler and their emblem was bow and arrow. Neduncheliyan was the important ruler of Pandya kingdom and their emblem was carp (fish).

(ii) The following were the capital and port cities of the three kingdoms The capital of Chola was firstly Uraiyur and later on shifted to Puhar (Tanjore). Karkai was their important seaport. The capital of Chera was Vanji and their important seaports were Tondi and Musiri. The capital of Pandya was Madurai and their import seaport was Kaveripoompattinam (Puhar).

(iii) The literature flourished immensely during the Sangam age and received high degree of patronage from the kings. Karaikala was very fond of literature and generous towards poets and also patronised Tamil poets. The Pandyan kings earned name and fame for their patronage to Tamil Sangam and their capital Madurai remained the capital of the Tamil language and literature.

3. With reference to the society of Sangam age , explain the following.
(i) Caste System
(ii) Food, Dress and Ornaments
(iii) Entertainment

Ans. (i) Refer to chapter theory page no. 110.
(ii) Refer to chapter theory page no. 110.
(iii) Refer to chapter theory page no. 110-111.

4. The economy during the Sangam Age was simple and self-sufficient. In context to this, answer the following.
(i) Occupation
(ii) Ports
(iii) Export and import

Ans. (i) Agriculture was the chief occupation where rice was the most common crop. Beside agriculture, other occupations like handicraft included weaving metal works and carpentry, ship building and making of ornaments using beads, stones and ivory. A high expertise was attained in spinning and weaving of cotton and silk clothes and dyeing was a widespread support industry to weaving.

(ii) The port city of Puhar was an important place of foreign trade, as big ships entered this port containing precious goods. Other significant ports of commercial activity were Tondi, Musiri, Karkai, Arikkamedu and Marakkanam.

(iii) Both internal and foreign trade were extensively carried on throughout the period and most of the trade was carried on by barter system. Many gold and silver coins of Rome have been found in all parts of Tamil Nadu indicating flourishing trade.
Major exports of the Sangam age were cotton fabrics and spices like pepper , ginger, cardamom, cinnamon and turmeric, along with ivory products, pearls and precious stones. Major imports for the traders were horses, gold and sweet wine.

Picture Based Question

1. With reference to the given picture, answer the following questions.

(i) Identify the picture of the poet. Which Tamil text was written by him? Give a brief description about it.

(ii) Why it is said the most important work in Tamil language ?

(iii) Explain division of couplets in it.

Ans. (i) Tiruvalluvar is the poet shown in the picture above. He had written the Tamil text Tirukkural (Thirukkural).

It is a classic of couplets or Kurals or aphorisms. It is a part of the 18 minor works of Sangam literature.

(ii) Tirukkural is one of the most important work in the Tamil language. It expounds on various aspects of life and preaches simplicity and truth throughout its verses. It includes various chapters having specific subject ranging from 'ploughing a piece of land' to 'ruling a country'.

(iii) Tirukkural is a collection of 1330 Tamil couplets organised into 133 chapters. The 1330 couplets are arranged into three main sections i.e. Aram (righteousness), Porul (wealth) and Inbam or Kamam (pleasure) and 133 chapters. Each chapter contains 10 couplets. Aram and Inbam discuss about ethical living in private life, Porul deals with public affairs.

Chapter Assessment

Section-I

Multiple Choice Questions

1. In Sangam literature 'Tolkappiyam' is a text of
   (a) Tamil literature (b) Tamil grammer
   (c) Tamil poetry (d) Tamil polity
2. King Karikala was a famour king of the
   (a) Cheras
   (b) Cholas
   (c) Pandyas
   (d) None of the above
3. Which of the following was the capital of Pandyas?
   (a) Puhar (b) Uraiyur
   (c) Madurai (d) Vanji
4. Replace the underlined word and correct the sentence.
   The Tolkappiyam texts refers to the existence of four fold caste system, among these Vellalar was the ruling class.
   (a) Anthanars (b) Arasar
   (c) Vaishyar (d) All of these

Section-II

Short Questions

1. What is Sangam literature?
2. What is the importance of the Megaliths?
3. Why is Tolkappiyam important?
4. Name any two important ports of Sangam age.
5. What was the staple food of Sangam Age?
6. Name the important source of income of Sangam Age.

Structured Questions

1. With reference to the features of the Sangam age, explain
   (i) Division of society (ii) Trade relation
   (iii) Food habit
   (iv) Position of Women
2. With reference to the archaeological sources, explain
   (i) Hero stone (ii) Megalith
   (iii) Ashokan edicts

CHAPTER 06

The Age of the Guptas

SYLLABUS

Sources Account of Fa-Hien; Allahabad Pillar Inscription. • Names of the kings in chronological orders, Administration; Contribution to the fields of Education (Nalanda University), Science (Aryabhatta) Sushruta (Medicine) and Culture (Works of Kalidasa, Deogarh temple)

The Gupta Empire rose in Magadha around 4th century AD. The Gupta dynasty ruled for more than 200 years from 320 to 540 AD. The Gupta period is popularly known as the **Golden Age of India** because of the numerous achievements in the fields of arts, literature, education and science. During this period, the lifestyle and culture of the Gupta Empire is known through the availability of various ancient scriptures, coins, inscriptions and texts, etc belonging to the Gupta era.

Sources of Gupta Age

The sources of the Gupta Age can be categorised into literary and archaeological sources.

Literary Sources

One of the main literary sources about Gupta period is the **account of Fa-Hien**. Fa-Hien was the first Chinese pilgrim, who travelled India during the age of Chandragupta II. He travelled during c 399-412. His travelogues give a fine impression about Chandragupta's Empire. The various aspects of his empire, i.e. political, religious, social and economic, were clearly reflected in his writings.

His accounts give the following description

- Fa-Hien noted the peacefulness of India, where multiple religions like Vaishnavism, Shaivism, Buddhism and Jainism co-existed harmoniously.
- He stated that the death penalty was not imposed in North India, but most crime was punished by fines and only serious revolt by the **amputation**[1] of one hand.
- Besides agriculture, there were other professions like carpentry, spinning, weaving, goldsmith etc.
- According to Fa-Hien, the Shudras were kept outside the town and entered the town by making a noise with a stick. They were butchers, hunters and fishermen.
- Fa-Hien states that the income of the government was mainly based on the revenue taxes, which were one-sixth of the total production. The roads were kept safe for travellers.
- He stated that the coin sculptures and paintings depicted the Hindu Gods and Goddesses.

1. **Amputation** It is the removal of a limb by trauma, medical illness, or surgery.

- He gave an account of Pataliputra city that had many charitable institutions including a hospital funded by wealthy citizens and the huge palace of Ashoka.
- He also gave an account of Magadha which was a prosperous empire having large towns and wealthy population.

Archaeological Source

The main archaeological source about the Gupta age is the **Allahabad Pillar Inscription** (Pragya Prashasti). It is particularly notable for containing later inscriptions attributed to the Gupta Emperor, Samudragupta (4th century CE).

Harisena, the *Mahadandnayaka* (Commander-in-Chief)/Chief Judicial Officer) and the court poet composed the contents that are inscribed on Allahabad pillar. It records the name and achievements of the real founder of the Gupta Empire, Samudragupta. Besides, it also provides the list of kings and tribal republics conquered by Samudragupta.

The first part of the pillar inscription describes Samudragupta as the one who resolved the eternal conflict between poetry and **propriety**[2] or learning and wealth. The next part gives a list of the conquests of Samudragupta during his Deccan expedition.

Allahabad Iron Pillar

Check Your LEARNING...

1. When did Gupta Empire rise?
2. About how many years did Gupta Dynasty rule?
3. Who was Fa-Hien?
4. Who composed Pragya Prashasti during the Gupta Period?

Names of the Kings in the Chronological Order

The Gupta Empire was founded by **Sri Gupta**. He was succeeded by Ghatotkacha. Not much information is available about the rule of these two Maharajas. Thereafter, following significant rulers from Gupta dynasty ruled during this period. Here are the details about the kings that ruled in Gupta Dynasty.

Chandragupta I (320-330 AD)

He was the son and successor of Ghatotkacha. Chandragupta was a powerful Gupta ruler, who had waged many battles to attain his title of *Maharajadhiraja* (king of kings). He also extended his empire through matrimonial alliance by marrying a Lichchavi princess Kumardevi. He is considered as the real founder of the Gupta Empire.

Samudragupta (330-380 AD)

He was the son and successor of Chandragupta I. He is also known as **Napoleon of India**. He was the greatest among the rulers of Gupta dynasty. His greatest achievement was political unification of India.

The Allahabad pillar inscription gave following information about Samudragupta

- The inscription mentioned that Samudragupta defeated nine rulers of Aryavarta and made their kingdoms as a part of his empire.
- Samudragupta conquered neighbouring states of Assam, Coastal Bengal, Nepal and a number of gana sanghas (organisation of the kings) in the North-West. They paid tribute to him and followed his orders.
- The inscription describe about Samudragupta's expedition of South India (*Dakshnipatha*), whose twelve rulers surrendered to him after being defeated.
- He had close contacts with the kingdom of Ceylon and South-East Asian colonies.
- The Shakas and Kushanas principalities on the West surrendered to him and paid tribute to the Gupta Emperor.

Samudragupta also performed Ashwamedha sacrifices after his military victories. This is known by the gold and silver coins issued by him commemorating him as the **Restorer of Ashwamedha**.

2. **Propriety** Conformity to conventionally accepted standards of behaviour or morals.

He was called by different names, one of them was **Kaviraja** because of his ability to compose verses. Certain coins show him with a Veena. He was a follower of Vaishnavism and had respect towards all other faiths. He also patronised the great Buddhist scholar Vasubandhu.

Chandragupta II (380-415 AD)

He was the son and successsor of Samudragupta. He extended the boundaries of his empire by conquest and matrimonial alliances. His capital city was Pataliputra. Chandragupta II conquered the Western Malwa and Gujarat by defeating the Shaka rulers, who had ruled for about 4 centuries in the region. This earned him the title of ***Sakari*** and ***Vikramaditya***.

After this victory, Chandragupta II gained control over the Arabian sea gaining access to the sea ports under his reign, which enabled the Gupta Empire to control trade with the Western countries.

Chandragupta II entered into matrimonial alliances as a part of his foreign policy. He married Kuberanaga of the Naga family as they supported him in expanding his empire. His daughters's marriage to Vakataka ruler helped him to establish his political influence in the Deccan.

In Chandragupta II's reign, the Chinese pilgrim Fa-Hien visited India, whose accounts inform about flourishing Buddhist religion in his reign. However, the Gangetic valley was a land of Brahmanism.

Chandragupta II was the first Gupta ruler to issue silver coins. He is renowned for his patronage to art, literature, architecture and administration. His court is believed to have been adorned with ***Navratna*** (nine gems) including Kalidasa, Amarasimha and Varahamihira.

Kumaragupta (415-455 AD)

He succeeded Chandragupta II. Huns (a Barbarian tribe of Central Asia) invaded India for the first time during his reign. He laid the foundation of Nalanda University which later grew to become an international centre of learning. He assumed the titles of Mahendraditya and Shakraditya.

Skandagupta (455-467 AD)

He was last great ruler of Gupta dynasty. He saved the empire from second invasion of Huns, but these invasions weakened the empire.

The Later Guptas

After the death of Skandagupta, there were other rulers of the Gupta dynasty like Purugupta, Narasimhagupta and Budhagupta. They were not able to save the empire from Hun invasions. With the rise of Malwa and continuous Hun invasions, the Gupta dynasty got totally disappeared.

Check Your LEARNING...

1. By whom Gupta Empire was found?
2. Who is known as 'Kaviraja'?
3. Who was the first Gupta ruler to issue silver coin?
4. Who was the last ruler of Gupta dynasty?

Gupta Administration

The Gupta Empire had a strong and organised system of administration. Following were the main characteristics of Gupta Administration

Central Administration

- Gupta Empire was a monarchical government which means all powers were centred in the kings. The element of divinity was attached to the kings and they were looked as Gods and Gods' representatives.
- The kings adopted high-sounding titles such as *Maharajadhiraja*, *Paramabhattaraka*, *Chakravarti*, *Paramesvara*, etc.
- The king was assisted by a Council of Ministers. The Minister's office was almost hereditary.
- The supreme judicial power was invested in the king, but the *Mahadandnayaka* carried out the judicial functions.
- The central secretariat also worked under the supervision of the king and the king was the source of all honours and titles.
- All land in the country was the property of the king. He had the sole right to build infrastructure, impose or recover taxes and give justice. The Gupta kings created two new classes *Sandhivigrahika* (Minister of War and Peace) and *Kumaramatyas* (Offices of the Crown Prince).
- Civil and criminal crimes were demarcated in Gupta Empire.

Provincial Administration

- The empire was divided into a number of provinces, which were called *Bhuktis*. Each *Bhukti* was further divided into *Vishaya*. A *Bhukti* was placed under *Uparaka* and *Vishaya* under *Vishayapati*.
- The village level disputes were solved by the village headmen called *Gramapati* or *Gramadhyaksha* and this was the smallest administration unit.
- There were various towns (*janapadas*) which were administered by a committee of five members. They were head by an officer called *Purapala*.
- Chiefs of the **guilds**[3] were called 'Nagarseths', who represented the guild in the urban trading circles.
- The *Sarthavaha* represented the trading communities. The terms *Nivartana*, *Kulyavapa* and *Dronavapa* were used for land measurements.
- The *Araghatta* or *Ghati Yantras* were the instruments of irrigation, which became more popular in Gupta era.

Society

- During the Gupta period, the Caste system or Varna system had become rigid and the Brahmins occupied the top position in the society. Rulers and other wealthy people gave enormous gifts to the Brahmins.
- The practice of untouchability had begun during Gupta period. The Chinese traveller Fa-Hien mentions that 'Chandalas' were separated from the society.

Trade and Commerce

Trade with Romans flourished during Gupta period. Ujjain had become a major commercial centre. The organisation of traders and artisans turned into guilds. The presence of these guilds have been testified on various inscriptions like Indore Copper plate inscription has mention of a guild of oilmen (*teli*).

Contribution of Gupta Empire

During the Gupta period, India reached a high level of civilisation and culture due to its contribution in the fields of education, science, literature and art and architecture. Gupta period is also known as a period of Hindu Renaissance.

Education

Education played an important role in the Gupta period. Primary education could be procured by the people. Formal and higher education was procured by staying in *agraharas* or monasteries. Women could obtain education, unlike in other parts of the world. Cities like Pataliputra, Ayodhya, Valabhi, Ujjain and Nasik were significant educational centers of those times.

Nalanda University situated near Rajgriha in Bihar, was probably the highest centre of Buddhist learning during Gupta period.

Nalanda University

The site of Nalanda is located in Bihar, about 55 miles South-East of Patna. It was a Buddhist centre of learning from 427 to 1197 CE. It has been called one of the first great universities in recorded history.

The University was founded in the 5th century BC. In the 7th century AD, it was visited by the Chinese scholar Xuanzang. Historical studies indicate that the University of Nalanda was established during the reign of the Gupta Emperor Kumaragupta.

The complex was built with red bricks and its ruins occupy an area of 14 hectares. The university attracted scholars and students from as far away as China, Greece and Persia. Panini, Jivaka, Prasenjit and Chanakya were the students of Nalanda University.

The library of Nalanda, known as *Dharma Gunj* (Mountain of Truth) or *Dharmaganja* (Treasury of Truth), was the most renowned **repository**[4] of Buddhist knowledge in the world at the time. The library had three main buildings as high as nine storeys tall. Ratnasagara (Sea of Jewels), Ratnodadhi (Ocean of Jewel) and Ratnaranjaka (Delighter of Jewels).

In this university, courses were drawn from every field of learning such as, Buddhist and Hindu, sacred and secular, foreign and native. The subjects were science, astronomy, medicine, logic, Samkhya, Yoga- shastra, the Veda and the scriptures of Buddhism.

3. **Guild** A medieval association of craftsmen or merchants, often having considerable power.
4. **Repository** A central location in which data is stored and managed.

Initially, this was a Buddhist monastery, but later became a university, Nalanda was ruined by Turkish Muslim invaders under **Muhammad-bin Bakhtiyar Khilji** in 1193, who was a general of Muhammad Ghori.

Nalanda University

Literature

Sanskrit literature flourished under the reign of Guptas. The classical Sanskrit literature include epics, poetry, drama, lyrics and prose. One of the greatest poet during Gupta period was Kalidasa, poet and playwright in the court of Chandragupta Vikramaditya.

Works of Kalidasa

Mahakavi Kalidasa was a great Indian poet in the 4th century CE. Kalidasa's works provide reliable information about the government, society and religion of the Gupta period and also contain the traces of political history.

His dramatic works include *Abhijnanashakuntalam* (love story of King Dushyanta and Shakuntala), *Vikramorvasiyam* (Urvashi won by Valour) and *Malavikagnimitram* (love story of Malavika and Agnimitra) which was written to commemorate the marriage of Chandragupta Vikramaditya daughter's, Prabhavati with Rudrasena.

His poetic works include *Raghuvansham* (Dynasty of Raghu), *Kumarasambhavam* (Birth of the War God) and the *Meghaduta* (the Cloud Messenger).

Science

The Gupta period witnessed a brilliant activity in the sphere of mathematics, astronomy, astrology and medicine. Metallurgy or science of metals had also made a wonderful progress during the Gupta period.

Aryabhatta was a great mathematician and astronomer. He wrote the book **Aryabhattiyam** in 499 AD. It deals with mathematics and astronomy. He also wrote **Surya Siddhanta** in which he explained the exact causes of solar and lunar eclipses.

He was the first to declare that the earth was spherical in shape and that it rotates on its own axis. However, these views were rejected by later astronomers like Varahamihira and Brahmagupta. Aryabhatta had conceptualised the decimal system and use of zero. He also gave the value of Pi.

Sushruta was an ancient Indian physician who is known as the 'Father of Surgery'. His work greatly influenced medicine during the Gupta Empire.

His book, the Sushruta Samhita, was an important medical text studied by doctors in the Gupta Empire Sushruta made groundbreaking contributions to surgery, including the development of techniques like plastic surgery and cataract surgery. He also introduced the use of surgical instruments and stressed the importance of cleanliness during surgeries.

During the Gupta period, Sushruta's teachings became a major influence on medical practices and his methods were passed down, shaping the future of medicine in India.

Varahamihira composed **Pancha Siddhantika**, the five astronomical systems. He was also a great author on astrology. His work **Brihadsamhita** is a great work in Sanskrit literature.

Brahmagupta was an astronomer and mathematician. He described the law of gravitation centuries before Newton. In the field of medicine, the great physicians during Gupta period were Charaka, Sushruta and Dhanwantri. They wrote treatises on Ayurvedic science of medicine, prevention, treatment and cure.

Art and Architecture

In the history of Indian art and architecture, the Gupta period occupies an important place. Both the Nagara and Dravidian styles of art evolved during this period. An important example of art and architecture during Gupta period is the Vishnu Temple at Deogarh.

The Vishnu Temple at Deogarh

This temple was built in the beginning of the 6th century AD. It is located near Jhansi in Uttar Pradesh. This temple was first described in detail by Alexander Cunningham in his tour of 1874-77. It is also known as **Dashavatara Temple** or ***Sagar Marh*** due to presence of ten incarnations of Vishnu depicted on the temple and nearby rock-cut well.

It was built on a platform with a height of 1.5 m. It was completely made of stone and bricks. It is the first North Indian temple with Shikhara (tower).

The walls of the temple were decorated with the scences depicting Ramayana and Lord Krishna's life. The interior of temple have four verandahs. An important feature of this temple is the sculpture of Lord Vishnu in which he is shown asleep on the coil of the giant serpent *Sheshnaga*.

Dashavatara Temple

Check Your LEARNING...

1. Name two new classes created by Gupta kings.
2. What were chiefs of guilds called?
3. Why did the society become more rigid?
4. Who became a major commercial centre during Gupta period?

QUiCK Revision

- The Gupta Empire rose in Magadha around AD 4th century and covered greater part of the Northern India (though smaller than the Mauryan Empire). It is worth noting, the Gupta dynasty ruled for more than about 200 years.
- The Gupta Period is popularly known as the 'Golden Age of India'. The lifestyle and culture of the Gupta Empire is known to us through the availability of various ancient scriptures, coins, inscriptions and texts etc. belonging to the Gupta era.
- The literary sources help us to understand about Guptas through Account of Fa-Hien.
- The archaeological source which help us to understand about the Gupta age is Allahabad pillar inscription.
- The Gupta Empire was founded by Sri Gupta. He was the succeeded by Ghatotkacha. Not much information is available about the rule of these two Maharajas.
- Chandragupta I was the son and successor of Ghatotkacha. He waged many battles to attain his title of *Maharajadhiraja* (king of kings).
- Samudragupta is also known as 'Indian Napoleon'. He was the greatest among the rulers of Gupta dynasty.
- Chandragupta II extended the Gupta Empire by conquest and matrimonial alliances. He is also known as '*Vikramaditya*'.
- Chandragupta II was succeded by Kumaragupta who laid the foundation of Nalanda University.
- Skandagupta was last great ruler of Gupta dynasty.
- After the death of Skandagupta, there were other ruler of the Gupta dynasty like Purugupta, Narasimhagupta and Budhagupta. They were not able to save the empire from Hun invasions.
- There was an efficient administration established in the Gupta Empire. It was a monarchical government which means all powers were centred in the kings.
- The empire was divided into a number of provinces, which were called *'Bhuktis'*. Each *Bhukti* was further divided into *Vishaya*.
- During the Gupta period, the Caste system or Varna system had become rigid and the Brahmins occupied the top position in the society.
- During the Gupta period, India reached a high level of civilisation and culture due to its contribution in the fields of education, science, literature, art and architecture.

Chapter Practice

Section-I

Multiple Choice Questions

1. Which among the following was/were the sources of Gupta Empire?
   (a) Account of Fa-Hien
   (b) Literary works of Kalidasa
   (c) Allahabad Pillar Inscription
   (d) All of the above

Ans. (d) All of the above

2. Fa-Hien was the first Chinese pilgrim, who travelled India during the reign of ....
   (a) Sri Gupta (b) Chandragupta I
   (c) Samudragupta (d) Chandragupta II

Ans. (d) Chandragupta II

3. Who composed the content of Allahabad Pillar associated with Chandragupta II?
   (a) Harisena (b) Aryabhatta
   (c) Amarasimha (d) Varahamihira

Ans. (a) Harisena

4. .... was the last great ruler of Gupta dynasty.
   (a) Sri Gupta (b) Kumaragupta
   (c) Chandragupta I (d) Skandagupta

Ans. (d) Skandagupta

5. .... was the founder of Nalanda University.
   (a) Sri Gupta (b) Samudragupta
   (c) Skandagupta (d) Kumaragupta

Ans. (d) Kumaragupta

6. Raghuvansham was authored by
   (a) Kalidasa (b) Tulsidasa
   (c) Banabhatta (d) Harisena

Ans. (a) Kalidasa

7. Who was the greatest mathematician and astronomer during Gupta Empire?
   (a) Brahmagupta (b) Varahamihira
   (c) Aryabhatta (d) Banabhatta

Ans. (c) Aryabhatta

8. ...... styles of art were evolved during Gupta Period.
   (a) Nagara (b) Dravidian
   (c) Both (a) and (b) (d) None of these

Ans. (c) Both (a) and (b)

9. The 'Dashavatara Temple' is located in
   (a) Madhya Pradesh (b) Uttar Pradesh
   (c) Bihar (d) Karnataka

Ans. (b) Uttar Pradesh

10. Complete the given analogy.
    Samudragupta : Chandragupta II : Kumara : gupta I : : ?
    (a) Sri Gupta (b) Brahmagupta
    (c) Skandagupta (d) Chandragupta I

Ans. (c) Skandagupta

11. Complete the given analogy.
    Allahabad Pillar Inscription : Samudragupta : : Mehrauli (Delhi) Inscription : ?
    (a) Chandragupta II (b) Skandagupta
    (c) Kumaragupta (d) All of these

Ans. (a) Chandragupta II

12. Replace the underlined word to correct the statement.
    During the Gupta Period the district level disputes were solved by the headman called Gramapati.
    (a) Village (b) Bhukti
    (c) Vishaya (d) All of these

Ans. (a) Village

13. Replace the underlined word to correct the statement.
    During the Gupta Period, the Caste system or Varna system had become rigid and the Ministers occupied the top position in the society.
    (a) Brahmanas (b) Traders
    (c) Council of Minister (d) Soldiers

Ans. (a) Brahmanas

14. Replace the underlined word to correct statement.
    The Guptas were followers of Buddhism.
    (a) Hinduism (b) Jainism
    (c) Shaivism (d) All of these

Ans. (a) Hinduism

15. Identify the correct statement associated with Gupta Empire
    (i) Dynasty ruled more than 200 years.
    (ii) Gupta Period is known as 'Golden Age of India'.
    (iii) The coins sculpture and paintings depicted the Hindu God and Goddesses.
    (iv) The library of Nalanda, known as Dharma Gunj.

    Codes
    (a) Only (i)
    (b) Both (i) and (ii)
    (c) (i), (ii) and (iii)
    (d) All of the above

Ans. (d) All of the above

16. Identify the correct statements associated with Samudragupta.
(i) Greatest among the rulers of Gupta dynasty.
(ii) He conquered Nepal, Assam and Bengal.
(iii) He performed 'Ashvamedha'.
(iv) He also called as Kaviraja.

Codes
(a) Only (i)
(b) Both (i) and (ii)
(c) (i), (ii) and (iii)
(d) All of these

Ans. (d) All of these

17. Consider the following statements about revival of Hinduism during Gupta period and select the correct option.
(i) This period is also called the Hindu Renaissance.
(ii) The Gupta kings were Brahmanical Hindus.
(iii) 'Vishnu Smriti' was compiled during this period.
(iv) In this period, Bhagwad Gita became the source of inspiration.

Codes
(a) Only (i)
(b) Both (i) and (iii)
(c) (i), (ii) and (iii)
(d) All of these

Ans. (d) All of these

18. Which is not correct about Chandragupta II ?
(i) He was called as Napoleon of India.
(ii) He conquered the Western Malwa and Gujarat by defeating the Saka rulers.
(iii) His court said to have been adorned with Navratna.
(iv) Kalidasa was contemporary of Chandragupta II.

Codes
(a) Only (i)
(b) Both (i) and (ii)
(c) (i), (ii) and (iii)
(d) All of these

Ans. (a) Only (i)

19. Match the following.

List I	List II
A. Chandragupta I	1. (320-330 AD)
B. Samudragupta	2. (330-380 AD)
C. Chandragupta II	3. (380-415 AD)
D. Kumaragupta	4. (415-455 AD)

Codes

	A	B	C	D
(a)	1	2	3	4
(b)	4	3	2	1
(c)	2	4	1	3
(d)	3	1	4	2

Ans. (a)

20. Match the following.

List I	List II
A. Maharajadhiraj	1. Chandragupta I
B. Napoleon of India	2. Samudragupta
C. Vikramaditya	3. Chandragupta II
D. Save Empire from Hun Invasion	4. Skandagupta

Codes

	A	B	C	D
(a)	4	3	2	1
(b)	1	4	3	2
(c)	1	2	3	4
(d)	3	1	4	2

Ans. (c)

Passage Based Questions

21. Read the passage given below and answer the following questions.

Chandragupta II, as he was now able to target his other enemies better. His greatest military achievement was his victory over the Shaka kings who were ruling in Western India for the last three hundred years. This conquest made Gupta empire reach up to the Western coast. An iron pillar inscription at Mehrauli in Delhi indicates that his empire included even North-Western India and Bengal. He took the title of Vikramaditya i.e. the one who is as powerful as the sun.

Chandragupta II is remembered for his patronage of art and literature. He is credited with maintaining nine luminaries (navaratna) in his court. The great Sanskrit poet and playwright Kalidasa was the most notable of them all. The Chinese Buddhist pilgrim Fa Hien (AD 404-411) visited India during his reign. He has left an account of the life of people in India in the fifth century AD.

(i) Who among the following took the title of 'Vikramaditya'?
(a) Chandragupta I
(b) Samudragupta
(c) Chandragupta II
(d) Skandagupta

Ans. (c) Chandragupta II

(ii) Identify the contemporary scholar of Chandragupta II.
(a) Harisena
(b) Asvaghosha
(c) Kalidasa
(d) Chanakya

Ans. (c) Kalidasa

(iii) The Iron Pillar of Delhi is associated with
(a) Sri Gupta
(b) Samudragupta
(c) Kumaragupta
(d) Chandragupta II

Ans. (d) Chandragupta II

(iv) Which among the following was not written by Kalidasa ?
(a) Kadambari
(b) Malavikagnimitram
(c) Abhigyanashakuntalam
(d) Raghuvansham

Ans. (a) Kadambari

22. Read the passage given below and answer the questions that follow.

Most prashastis also mention the ancestors of the ruler. This one mentions Samudragupta's great grandfather, grandfather, father and mother. His mother, Kumaradevi, belonged to the Lichchhavi gana, while his father, Chandragupta was the first ruler of the Gupta dynasty to adopt the grand title of Maharaj-adhiraja, a title that Samudragupta also used. His great grandfather and grandfather are mentioned simply as maha-rajas. It seems as if the family gradually rose to importance. Samudragupta in turn figures in the genealogies (lists of ancestors) of later rulers of the dynasty, such as his son, Chandragupta II. We know about him from inscriptions and coins. He led an expedition to Western India, where he overcame the last of the Shakas. According to later belief, his court was full of learned people.

(i) Which among the following ruler is known as 'Napoleon of India'?
(a) Samudragupta (b) Skandagupta
(c) Kumaragupta (d) Chandragupta II

Ans. (a) Samudragupta

(ii) Harisena was the court poet of
(a) Srigupta (b) Harshavardhana
(c) Chandragupta I (d) Samudragupta

Ans. (d) Samudragupta

(iii) Samudragupta was succeeded by
(a) Skandagupta
(b) Kumaragupta
(c) Chandragupta II
(d) Srigupta

Ans. (c) Chandragupta II

(iv) Kumaradevi was married to whom?
(a) Sri Gupta (b) Ghatotkacha
(c) Chandragupta I (d) Skandagupta

Ans. (c) Chandragupta I

Section-II

Short Questions

1. Mention the time period of the Gupta age.

Ans. The Gupta Empire rose in Magadha around 4th century AD and covered greater part of the Northern India. The Gupta dynasty ruled for more than about 200 years from 320 to 540 AD.

2. Which period is known as the Golden age and why?

Ans. The Gupta period is known as the Golden age because of the high level of culture and civilisation along with unrestrained flow of arts, literature, education and science.

3. How do we come to know about the lifestyle and culture of the Gupta Empire?

Ans. The lifestyle and culture of the Gupta Empire is known to us through the availability of various ancient scriptures, coins, inscriptions and texts, etc belonging to the Gupta era.

4. Mention some relevant facts given by Fa-Hien about India during the age of Gupta.

Ans. Fa-Hien noted India as a peace country with rare crimes. He also stated that the death penalty was not imposed in North India, but most crime was punished by fines. According to Fa-Hien, the Shudras were kept outside the town and entered the town by making a noise with a stick. They were butchers, hunters and fishermen.

5. Who was Harisena?

Ans. Harisena was the *Mahadandnayaka* (Commander-in-Chief) and the court poet of Samudragupta. He wrote the contents of Allahabad Pillar about Samudragupta.

6. Who was Chandragupta I? What is his importance?

Ans. Chandragupta I was a powerful Gupta ruler, who had waged many battles and attained the title of *Maharajadhiraja* (king of kings). He is considered as the founder of the Gupta era (began with his accession).

7. What was the greatest achievement of Samudragupta?

Ans. Samudragupta's greatest achievement was political unification of India. For this, he is assumed as a greatest ruler of Gupta dynasty and known as Napoleon of India.

8. Give a brief account about Chandragupta II of Gupta Dynasty?

Ans. Chandragupta extended the limits of his empire by conquest and matrimonial alliances. Chandragupta II conquered the Western Malwa and Gujarat by defeating the Shaka rulers. This earned him the title of Sakari and Vikramaditya.

9. Who saved the Gupta Empire from the Hun invasion?

Ans. Skandagupta who was last great ruler of Gupta dynasty saved the empire from Hun invasion coming from Central Asia. But these invasions weakened the empire.

10. Explain about the central administration of Gupta Empire.

Ans. In Central administration, the Minister's office was almost hereditary. The supreme judicial power was invested in the king, but the *Mahadandnayaka* carried out the judicial functions. The Gupta Kings created two new classes *Sandhivigrahika* (Minister of War and Peace) and *Kumaramatyas* (Offices of the Crown Prince).

11. What were the different instruments used for irrigation?

Ans. The *Araghatta* or *Ghati Yantras* were the instruments of irrigation, which became more popular in Gupta era.

12. How was the Indian society during the time of Gupta Empire?

Ans. During the Gupta period, the Caste system or Varna system had become rigid and the Brahmins occupied the top position in the society. Rulers and other wealthy people gave enormous gifts to the Brahmins. The practice of untouchability had begun during Gupta period.

13. What was the condition of the trade and commerce during the Gupta rule?

Ans. Trade with Romans flourished during Gupta period. Ujjain had become a major commercial centre. The organisation of traders and artisans were formed. These organisations had considerable power and were known as guilds. The presence of these guilds have been testified on various inscriptions like Indore Copper plate inscription has mention of a guild oilmen (*teli*).

14. Who founded the Nalanda University?

Ans. Kumaragupta, who succeeded Chandragupta II was the founder of Nalanda University which later grew to become an international centre of learning.

15. Where is Nalanda University situated?

Ans. The site of Nalanda is located in the Indian State of Bihar, about 55 miles South-East of Patna, and was a Buddhist centre of learning from 427 to 1197 CE. It has been called 'one of the first great universities in recorded history.'

16. Give two special features of the Nalanda University.

Ans. Two special features of the Nalanda University are

- It attracted scholars and students from as far away as China, Greece and Persia.
- The library of Nalanda, known as *Dharma Gunj*' (Mountain of Truth) or *Dharmagaja* (Treasury of Truth), was the most renowned repository of Buddhist knowledge in the world at the time.

17. Who destroyed the Nalanda University?

Ans. Nalanda was destroyed by Turkish Muslim invaders under Muhammad-bin Bakhtiyar Khilji in 1913, who was a general of Muhammad Ghori.

18. Why the Vishnu Temple at Deogarh is known as the Dashavatara temple?

Ans. Vishnu Temple at Deogarh is also known as 'Dashavatara temple' or '*Sagar Marh*' due to presence of ten incarnations of Vishnu depicted on the temple and nearby rock-cut well.

Structured Questions

1. In context of the literary sources of the Gupta Empire, explain the following.
   (i) Fa-Hien views on religion.
   (ii) Fa-Hien views about death penalty and Shudras
   (iii) Fa-Hien views about towns and cities.
   (iv) Fa-Hien views about income of Gupta Empire.

Ans. (i) Fa-Hien noted the peacefulness of India, where multiple religions like Vaishnavism, Shaivism, Buddhism and Jainism co-existed harmoniously. He stated that the coin sculptures and paintings depicted the Hindu Gods and Goddesses.

(ii) Fa-Hien stated that the death penalty was not imposed in North India, but most crime was punished by fines and only serious revolt by the amputation of one hand. According to him, the Shudras were kept outside the town and entered the town by making a noise with a stick. They were butchers, hunters and fishermen.

(iii) Fa-Hien gave an account of towns and cities of India. For example, he stated about Pataliputra city that it had many charitable institutions including a hospital funded by wealthy citizens and the huge palace of Ashoka. He also gave an account of Magadha which was a prosperous empire having large towns and wealthy population.

(iv) Fa-Hien states that the income of the government was mainly based on the revenue taxes, which were one-sixth of the total production. The roads were kept safe for travellers.

2. Besides literary sources, there are archaeological sources also which help to understand about the Gupta Age. Describe
   (i) Allahabad Pillar Inscription
   (ii) Dashavatara Temple
   (iii) Features of Dashavatara Temple
   (iv) Nalanda University

Ans. (i) Refer to chapter theory page no. 119.

(ii) Refer to chapter theory page no. 123.

(iii) The features of Dashavatara Temple are

- The walls of the temple were decorated with the scences depicting Ramayana and Lord Krishna's life.
- The interior of temple have four verandahs.
- An important feature of this temple is the sculpture of Lord Vishnu in which he is shown asleep on the coil of the giant serpernt *Sheshnaga*.

(iv) Refer to chapter theory page no. 121-122.

3. Samudragupta is also known as 'Indian Napoleon'. With reference to this explain
   (i) Who was Samudgragupta?
   (ii) Why did he perform Ashwamedha sacrifices?
   (iii) Why Samudragupta was called as Kaviraja?
   (iv) What do we get to know about him from the Allahabad Pillar Inscription?

Ans. (i) Samudragupta (330-380 AD) was the son and successor of Chandragupta I. He was the greatest among the rulers of Gupta dynasty. His greatest achievement was political unification of India. He had close contacts with the kingdom of Ceylon and South-East Asian colonies.

(ii) Samudragupta performed Ashwamedha sacrifices after his military victories as he was a follower of Brahmanism and believed in the sacrifices of the Vedic religion. This is known by the coins issued by him commemorating him as the 'restorer of ashwamedha'.

(iii) Samudragupta was called 'Kaviraja' because of his ability to compose verses. Certain coins show him with a Veena. Samudragupta was not only a brave warrior and conqueror, but also a great ruler, a musician and a poet.

(iv) The Allahabad pillar inscription gave following information about Samudragupta

- The inscription mentioned that Samudragupta defeated nine rulers of Aryavarta and made their kingdoms as a part of his empire.
- Samudragupta conquered neighbouring states of Assam, Coastal Bengal, Nepal and a number of gana sanghas (organisation of the kings) in the North-West. They paid tribute to him and followed his orders.
- The inscription describe about Samudragupta's expedition of South India (*Dakshnipatha*), whose twelve rulers surrendered to him after being defeated.

4. There was an efficient administration established in the Gupta Empire. With reference to this explain

(i) Who are Gods and Gods' representators and why?

(ii) Who assisted king and name the two new classes?

(iii) Provincial Administration

(iv) Central Administration.

Ans. (i) In Gupta Empire, kings were regarded as Gods and Gods' representatives.

(ii) The king was assisted by a Council of Ministers in his administration.

The Gupta kings created two new classes *Sandhivigrahika* (Minister of War and Peace) and *Kumaramatyas* (Offices of the Crown Prince).

(iii) Refer to chapter theory page no. 121.

(iv) Refer to chapter theory page no. 120.

Picture Based Question

1. With reference to the given picture, answer the following questions.

(i) Identify the given image. Who composed the content that are inscribed on this pillar?

(ii) To which period the pillar belong? Mention the historical importance of the pillar.

(iii) What description can be found about Samudragupta on this pillar?

Ans. (i) The given image shows Allahabad Iron Pillar which is particularly notable for containing later inscriptions attributed to the Gupta Emperor, Samudragupta.

Harisena, the *Mahadandnayaka* (Commander-in-Chief) and the court poet composed the content that are inscribed on this pillar.

(ii) Allahabad Iron Pillar belongs to Gupta age.

The historical importance of the pillar is

- The name and fame of the real founder of the Gupta Empire Samudragupta is recorded on it.
- Beside this it also provides the list of kings and tribal republics conquered by Samudragupta.

(iii) Allahabad Pillar Inscription give an exhaustive account of the political career of Samudragupta and the kingdoms conquered by him. The first part of the pillar inscription describes Samudragupta as one who resolved the eternal conflict between poetry and propriety or learning and wealth. The next part gives a list of the conquests of Samudragupta during his Deccan expedition.

Chapter Assessment

Section-I

Multiple Choice Questions

1. Who was the founder of Gupta Empire?
   (a) Chandragupta I (b) Sri Gupta
   (c) Samudragupta (d) Ghatotkacha
2. 'Raghuvansham' was written by
   (a) Banbhatta (b) Vishnu Sharma
   (c) Tulsidasa (d) Kalidasa
3. Complete the given analogy.
   Srigupta : Chandragupta I :: Samundragupta : ?
   (a) Chandragupta II (b) Kumaragupta
   (c) Skandagupta (d) Srigupta
4. Replace the underlined word with the correct sentence.
   Nalanda University was founded by Kumaragupta and it was burnt by muslim invader Allauddin Khilji.
   (a) Qutb-ud-din Aibak (b) Bakhtiyar Khilji
   (c) Firoz Shah Tughlaq (d) Muhammad Ghori

Section-II

Short Questions

1. Which Gupta king can be regarded as the real founder of the dynasty?
2. Name a few important sciences which made progress during the rule of Gupta.
3. What is the importance of the Allahabad Pillar Inscription?
4. Who is known as the 'Napoleon of India'?
5. Mention two features of Gupta sculpture.
6. Name any two titles adopted by Gupta rulers.

Structured Questions

1. With reference to the Golden Age, answer the following questions
   (i) Importance of Sanskrit
   (ii) Progress in the field of medicine
   (iii) Progress in the field of painting
2. In the context of political history of Gupta, explain
   (i) Achievements of Samudragupta
   (ii) Later Gupta rulers
   (iii) Result of Hun invasions
3. With reference to the Nalanda University, explain
   (i) Its library
   (ii) Courses taught
   (iii) Its importance
   (iv) Scholars

CHAPTER

07

Chola Dynasty

SYLLABUS

Sources Inscriptions; Brihadeshwara Temple.
Names of the kings in chronological order and Administration;
Chola Art

Cholas (846-1279 AD) became prominent in the 9th century and established an empire comprising the major portion of South India. They successfully united South India under their rule and through their naval strength, they extended their influence in the South-East Asian countries such as Srivijaya (Indonesia). They dominated the political affairs of Sri Lanka for over two centuries through repeated invasions. They also had continuing trade contacts with the Arabs in the West and with the Chinese Empire in the East.

Sources of Chola Dynasty

Inscriptions

The inscription gives us useful information about the administration of the Chola rulers. The idea of including the main achievements of his reign in the inscriptions was developed by **Rajaraja I**.

The inscriptions of the Cholas are in the form of copper-plate grants, stone inscriptions and inscription inscribed on the walls of the temple. Some of the inscriptions are

- Thiruvananthapuram inscriptions give information about the reign of Rajendra III.
- The Uttaramerur inscriptions give information about the **Kudavolai system**[1], village administration, taxation and land revenue.
- The copper-plate grants known as *Anbil* plates, the Kanyakumari stone inscription, Karanthai plates and Thiruvalangadu copper plates give useful information about the Cholas. These plates are written in ***Sanskrit*** and ***Tamil***.
- The Tanjore Peruvudaiyar temple inscriptions give information about the existence of Shaivism.
- The inscriptions of contemporary rulers like Cheras, Pandyas, Rashtrakutas and Gangas give information about the Cholas' records of land grants villages, plots of farmland or other privileges given by the kings to private individual or institutions.
- Some important inscriptions give a full account of the different stages that intervened between the issues of a royal order. Society, religion, art and crafts can be known from the inscriptions.

The language and script of the Chola inscriptions varied with the time and place of the records. The Sanskrit language employed the Grantha script, closely allied to Tamil in its evolution.

1. **Kudavolai System** In this system, one representative is elected from each ward and every village had 30 wards.

Monuments

Monuments are the most interesting and instructive source of history. These monuments include mostly temples and sculptured halls and towers. These monuments depict the art and architecture religious beliefs and socio-economic condition of the Cholas.

The Brihadeshwara temple of Tanjore, the Gangaikonda Cholapuram temple, Airavatesvara temple of Darasuram and the Kampaheswarar temple in Thirubhuvanam are some of the important monuments of the Cholas.

The Brihadeshwara Temple

The Brihadeshwara Temple is famous Chola temple built at Thanjavur (Tanjore). It is also called the **Rajarajeshwara Temple** after the name of king Rajaraja I who built it in honour of Lord Shiva. The temple was completed in 1010 AD. This temple is one of the best specimen of Dravidian style of architecture and has been declared as world heritage site by UNESCO.

The main features of the temple are

- It is composed of many interconnected structures such as the Nandi pavilion, a pillared portico and a large hall.
- Its **vimana**[2] is 66m high.
- The inner walls of the temple have extensive paintings and sculpture.
- The tower of the temple rises to a height of 57 m, like a pyramid, in 13 successive storeys.
- Its top has a single block of stone, 25 feet high and weigh about 80 tonnes. The structural idea of constructing a **Gopuram**[3] was first conceived by the Chola kings.
- The temple stands in the middle of a rectangular enclosure entered from the East through a gateway which is now ruined.
- The double plastered walls of the temple are elevated on a moulded basement with lions. The storeys those on the central niches depict *Dakshinamurti* (South), *Vishnu* (West) and *Brahma* (North).
- A massive linga on the central pedestal is enshrined within the temple. A stone altar (stone table) carved with a lotus on the top has the *Navagrahas* carved onto the sides.
- Another small structure in the South-West corner of the temple include a Ganesha image. A large Nandi sculpture is constructed in front (East) of the principal temple.

The Brihadeshwar Temple

Names of the Kings in Chronological Order

The Cholas and their contributions have significant place in the history of South India. The early Cholas ruled during the Sangam period. **Karikala** was the greatest king among the early Chola kings.

The later Chola Empire was founded by **Vijayalaya** who was the subordinate commander of the Pallava king. He made Tanjore his capital. He was succeeded by his son **Aditya-I**.

Aditya was succeeded by Parantaka I who conquered Madurai and defeated the Pandya and the rulers of Sri Lanka. The power of Chola had reached the height of its glory during 11th century. Rajaraja I and Rajendra Chola were the prominent rulers of this dynasty between 10th and 11th century.

Rajaraja I (985–1014 AD)

Rajaraja I was son of Parantaka II and Vanavan Mahadevi. He was the most powerful king of the Chola dynasty. His main contributions to the extension of Chola Empire and its culture were

- Rajaraja I defeated the Chera army at Thiruvananthapuram. He also defeated Bhaskar Ravi, the Raja of Kollam.
- He defeated Mahinda V, the King of Ceylon (Sri Lanka) and occupied Anuradhapuram and the Northern part of Ceylon. He made Polonnaruva city as a new capital.

2. **Vimana** It is the structure over the garbhagriha or inner sanctum in the Hindu temple of South India.
3. **Gopuram** A fine gateway to the enclosed walls of the temple.

- He got the title **Mummudi Cholan** after the conquest of three Southern kingdoms Cheras, Pandyas and Ceylon.
- He conquered Kalinga and the present day Maldives Island. He also conquered the Eastern Chalukya kingdom of Vengi and put his own nominee on the throne.
- He knew the importance of controlling the sea, so he carried out raids in the Eastern Chalukyas. The money that was earned from overseas trade had made the coast of the present day Sri-Lanka, Kerala and the Maldives Island quite rich.
- He was an efficient administrator, a great patron of arts and literature. Under his reign, the Cholas became a paramount powerin Southern India and his achievements are inscribed on the walls of Brihadeshwara temple.
- He introduced land survey system and encouraged local self-government throughout his empire.
- He encouraged Buddhism and supported Shaivism. He gave permission for the construction of Buddha Shrine at Nagapattinam and donated anaimangalam village to the Buddhist monastery.

Rajendra Chola I (1014–1044 AD)

Rajendra I was a great administrator and warrior who continued the policies of his father. He shifted his capital from Tanjore to Gangaikonda Cholapuram. His main contributions to the extension of Chola Empire and its culture were

- He captured the whole of Ceylon and consolidated Chola domination over Ceylon.
- He sent a fleet (ship) across Bay of Bengal and conquered Pegu (in Burma) as well as Andaman and Nicobar Islands.
- Rajendra I defeated the Bengal king Mahipala I and brought water from Ganges to Tanjore. This water was put into Cholagangam, a large irrigation tank, near Gangaikonda Cholapuram. In appreciation of this victory, king Rajendra I was given the title **Gangaikondan**.
- The most heroic campaign of Rajendra I was fought in South-East Asia. Here, the merchants of Srivijaya (Indonesia) were creating problems for the Indian merchants. On request of the merchants, Rajendra Chola sent out a huge navy and defeated Srivijaya King. Thereby, he secured the Indian trade in Southern China and South-East Asia.
- He conquered Malaya region in South-East Asia and earned the title **Kadaram Kondan**.
- During his rule, Rajendra I constructed many temples dedicated to Lord Shiva and Vishnu.

Decline of Cholas

Rajadhiraja Chola (1044-1052 AD) was the successor of Rajendra Chola I and the last important ruler of the Chola dynasty. He was killed in the Battle of Koppam (1052 AD). With this, the disintegration of Chola dynasty started as there were weak successors.

Rajendra Chola III was the last ruler of Chola dynasty. He was defeated by Pandya ruler Jatavarman Sundara in 1269 AD who annexed a major part of Chola kingdom.

Check Your LEARNING...

1. What type of information was given by Uttaramerur inscription?
2. Name the language that employed Grantha Script.
3. What were the titles given to Rajaraja I?
4. By whom invasion Chola Kingdom was destroyed?

Chola Administration

The Chola kings followed a highly coherent system of administration with a large measure of local autonomy. The Cholas had three major administrative divisions called 'Central Government', 'Provincial Government' and 'Local Government'.

The king was the head of the administration. The Chola kings and Queens were considered as representatives of God. Their idols were kept in temples. The Chola kingship was hereditary and they followed the concept of **primogeniture**[4]. The apparent heir was called *Yuvaraja*.

The Chola monarchs enjoyed enormous powers and privileges. The Chola kings took up titles which marked their achievements. Kings were assisted by ministers and officials in their administration.

4. **Primogeniture** The state of being the first born child.

Central Administration

- The Central administration was under the headship of the king.
- Council of Ministers and officials took active part in running the administration of Central Government.
- The higher officials were called *Peruntaram* and the lower officials were called *Siruntaram*.
- The officers were paid by giving them assignments in revenue bearing lands.
- The Central administration looked after the matters like external defence, internal law and order cultural progress and promotion of general prosperity of the empire.

Provincial Administration

- The empire was divided into 9 provinces or *mandalams*. The head of the province was called 'Viceroy'.
- Each *mandalam* was divided into number of *Kottams* or *Valanadus*. Each *Kottam* was sub-divided into *Nadu* (districts).
- Each *Nadu* was further divided into *Urs* (villages) which form part of the last unit of the administration.
- All of the territorial divisions had their respected assemblies comprising notable persons.

Local Administration

There were general assemblies in the Chola Empire which included most of the local residents. They were of three categories.

(i) ***Ur*** It consisted of the tax paying residents of an ordinary village. It was the assembly of local members.

(ii) ***Sabha*** It was restricted to the Brahmins of the villages where all land belonged to Brahmins.

(iii) **Nagaram** It was found more commonly in trade centres. It was an assembly of merchants.

The life and work of the villages were discussed in these assemblies or councils. They were considered a source of popular strength as they united the people in the villages.

These assemblies enjoyed full power in the management of local affairs and the villagers who owned land were chosen for the council by vote. The village assemblies run its administration effectively. They gathered taxes, regulated water supply and administered charity institution like schools and temples.

The working of these assemblies differed according to local conditions. The *Ur* was open to all male adults of the village but the older members took a more prominent part. The *Sabha* had the same system and in addition had the power to constitute smaller committees of any size from among its members.

Revenue Administration

- The land revenue was the main source of income of the Chola Government. Proper land survey was made. Lands were classified as taxable land and non-taxable land.
- Generally 1/6th of the land yield was collected as tax either in cash or in kind or both.
- Besides land revenue, there were some other sources of income-like customs and tolls. Taxes on mines, ports, forests and salt pans were collected. Professional tax and house tax were also collected.
- The officials collected taxes on land from village councils while fraction of the revenue was set-aside for the king. The rest of the revenue was used on public works like building roads, tanks, paying the salary of navy and army, etc.

Military Administration

- The Cholas had a well-organised army and navy. The Chola army consisted of elephant, cavalry and infantry.
- The army of Cholas had three organs. They were Nayak, Senapati and Mahandnayak.
- Personal bodyguards called *Vilaikkaras* were kept by most of the Kings.
- Cantonments called *Kadagam* were established for the soldiers. They had a strong navy through which they controlled the Malabar and Coromandel Coast and the entire Bay of Bengal.

Other Aspects of Chola Kingdom

Society

In the Chola society, the practice to untouchability prevailed. The poor lived in slums and the Brahmins were prosperous. The society was based on ***Varnasrama***. Professionals like carpenters, weavers, blacksmiths, masons and goldsmiths also lived there.

Slavery also existed where several grades among the slaves were there. Greater social freedom prevailed among the upper classes.

Marco Polo and some inscriptions state that the status and freedom of women were high as they were appointed as officers. Child marriage and right to property among women of higher caste prevailed and sati was practiced by the women of royal family.

Valangai and Idangai caste groups were also there. The group which stood on the right hand side of the king was called Valangai group. The group that stood on the left hand side of the king was known as Idangai group. There were disputes among these groups.

Education

The temple was a place of worship and a centre of education. The schools were housed in the courtyard and priest of the temples was the teacher. The student learned their lessons in Sanskrit (religious teachings) and in Tamil, which was the widely spoken language.

Chola Kings gave importance for the development of education. There were Veda Padasalas, Buddha Viharas and Jain Pallis. During the reign of Rajendra I, two colleges were established at Chidambaram and Tribhuvanam. Scholarships were also given to students.

Religion

Chola kings were **Shaivites**. They worshipped Lord Shiva. They built many Shiva temples. Parantaka I, Rajaraja I, Rajendra King Gandraditya and his queen Sembiyan Mahadevi contributed more for the development of Shaivism and Bhakti literature.

Chola Kings were also tolerant towards other religions. Vishnu worship was also prevalent there. Chola rulers also supported the spread of Vaishnavism.

Literature

The Chola rule is also considered as the golden age of Tamil literature. Many great Tamil poets namely, Kalladanar, Kamban, Pugalandhi, Ottakoothar, Sekkilar, Avvaiyar and Thirutakkadevar lived during the period of Chola period.

Kamban wrote the Tamil Ramayan. The works of Tamil literature were collected in 11 volumes in 12th century, known as *Tirumurais* and considered sacred and valued as the 5th Veda.

Buddhamitra and Rawankashi wrote treaties on grammar. Literary styles like epics, parani, kovai, ula, kalambakam, pillaitamil and new works on grammar were famous during that period.

Writing meikeerthis, narration of historical incidents and singing songs on religious hero's, were new literary trends of that time. Many inscriptions of Chola Kings were written in both Sanskrit and Tamil.

Chola Art

Chola ruler built many temples, palaces, cities, etc. Their temples were built in Dravidian style. Earlier Chola temple were small while the later Chola temples were grand and larger.

Stone and metal (bronze) sculptures are found in Chola temples. They depict the socio-religious ideas of the Chola period.

The Nataraja sculpture made of bronze is world famous not only for its beauty but also for its spiritual meaning. Scenes from Ramayanam, Mahabharatam, Puranas and lives of the 63 Nayanmars are sculptured in narrative panels on the walls of temples.

Check Your LEARNING...

1. Who was the head of a province in Chola empire?
2. Name the three categories of local administration ?
3. Name any two educational centres where education was imported during Cholas Kingdom.
4. Mention the work of Tamil literature that is valued as 5th Veda.

QUiCK Revision

- In the 9th century CE, Cholas established the greatest empire in South India.
- Some important inscriptions give a full account of the different stages that intervened between the issues of a royal order. We also learn much about society, religion, art and crafts from the inscriptions.
- The language and script of the Chola inscriptions varied with the time and place of the records. The language most commonly employed was Tamil and some Sanskrit records are known.
- Monuments are the most interesting and instructive source of history. These monuments include mostly temples and sculptured halls and towers.
- The Brihadeshwara temple is famous Chola temple built at Thanjavur (Tanjore) and also known as Rajarajeshwara temple after the name of King Rajaraja I.
- Rajaraja I was son of Parantaka II and Vanavan Mahadevi. He was the most powerful king of the Chola dynasty. He introduced land survey system. He encouraged local self-government throughout his empire.
- Rajaraja I was succeeded by his son Rajendra I. He was a great administrator and warrior. He followed his father's policies.
- Rajadhiraj Chola was the last important ruler of the Chola dynasty. He was killed in the Battle of Koppam (1052 AD).
- The king was the head of the administration. The Chola Kings and queens were considered as representatives of God.
- The Central Government was under the headship of the king. Council of Ministers and officials took active part in running the administration of Central Government.
- The empire was divided into 9 provinces or *mandalams*. The head of the province was called Viceroy. Each *mandalam* was divided into number of *Kottams* or *Valanadus*. Each *Kottam* was sub-divided into *Nadu*. Each *Nadu* was further divided into *Urs* (villages).
- The land revenue was the main source of income of the Chola government.
- The Cholas had an efficient army and navy.
- In the Chola society, the practice of untouchability prevailed and poor lived in slums and Brahmins were prosperous the society was based as *Varnasrama*. Valangai and Idangai caste groups were also there. There were disputes among these groups.
- Chola Kings were Shaivites. They worshipped Lord Shiva. They built many Shiva temples. Chola kings were also tolerant towards other religions.
- Stone and metal (bronze) sculptures are found in plenty in Chola temples that depict the socio-religious ideas of the Chola period.

Chapter Practice

Section-I

Multiple Choice Questions

1. Which of the following is/are the archaeological source(s) of Chola dynasty ?
(a) Inscription (b) Monuments
(c) Brihadeshwara temple (d) All of these

Ans. (d) All of these

2. Thiruvananthapuram inscription speak about the reign of
(a) Aditya I (b) Rajendra III
(c) Rajaraja I (d) Rajendra I

Ans. (b) Rajendra III

3. The Brihadeshwara temple is dedicated to Lord
(a) Vishnu (b) Shiva
(c) Indra (d) Krishna

Ans. (b) Shiva

3. In which year Brihadeshwara temple was completed?
(a) 9th Century (b) 1010 AD
(c) 11th Century (d) 1044 AD

Ans. (b) 1010 AD

4. What is the meaning of Gopuram?
(a) Wall painting
(b) The gateway of temple
(c) The main shrine
(d) The style of temple

Ans. (b) The gateway of temple

5. Who laid the foundation of Chola dynasty?
(a) Vijayalaya (b) Rajaraja I
(c) Parantaka I (d) Rajendra Chola

Ans. (a) Vijayalaya

6. Who was considered as the most powerful king of Chola dynasty?
(a) Rajaraja I (b) Aditya Chola
(c) Parantaka (d) Vijayalaya

Ans. (a) Rajaraja I

7. Who was called 'Gangaikonda' ?
(a) Vijalaya (b) Rajaraja
(c) Rajendra I (d) Kulottunga

Ans. (c) Rajendra I

8. Under the Cholas, land-revenue was collected through the
(a) Senapati (b) Gram Sabha (Assembly)
(c) Government officials (d) All of these

Ans. (c) Government officials

9. Which was widely used language during Chola period?
(a) Tamil (b) Sanskrit
(c) Both (a) and (b) (d) Pali

Ans. (c) Both (a) and (b)

10. Who wrote Tamil Ramayana?
(a) Kamban (b) Sekkilar
(c) Pugalandhi (d) Kalladanar

Ans. (a) Kamban

11. The Nataraja sculpture was made of
(a) Copper (b) Bronze
(c) Gold (d) Silver

Ans. (b) Bronze

12. Complete the given analogy
Vijayalaya : Aditya Chola :: Rajaraja I : ?
(a) Rajendra I (b) Rajadhiraja
(c) Virarajendra
(d) Kulottunga I

Ans. (a) Rajendra I

13. Complete the given analogy.
Brihadeshwara Temple: Rajaraja I :: Gangaikonda Cholapuram Temple : ?
(a) Rajendra I (b) Adiya Chola
(c) Parantak I (d) Rajaraja I

Ans. (a) Rajendra I

14. Replace the underlined word to correct the statement.
Rajendra I defeated Mahipala (Pala empire) of <u>Sri Lanka</u>.
(a) Bengal (b) Madurai
(c) Southern China (d) Tanjore

Ans. (a) Bengal

15. Replace the underlined word to correct the statement.
Land revenue was the main source of income for the Chola empire and it was usually <u>one-third</u> of the produce.
(a) one-sixth (b) one-tenth
(c) one-fourth (d) one-eighth

Ans. (a) one-sixth

16. Replaced the underlined word to correct the statement.
<u>Pandya</u> society witnessed a division of caste into 'Idangai' and 'Valangai'.
(a) Chola (b) Chera
(c) Pallava (d) Chalukya

Ans. (a) Chola

17. Complete the given table.

Rajaraja I	985-1014 AD
Rajendra I	?

(a) 1044-1052 AD (b) 1014-1044 AD
(c) 1010-1052 AD (d) 1152-1279 AD

Ans. (b) 1014-1044 AD

18. Consider the following statements and choose the correct option.
(i) Rajaraja I defeated Cheras in the battle of Kandalur Salai.
(ii) Brihadeshwara temple at Tanjore was built in 1010 AD.
(iii) The Cholas maintained a large army.
(iv) There were two types of villages at the local in the Chola empire.

Codes
(a) Only (i) (b) Both (i) and (ii)
(c) (i), (ii) and (iii) (d) All of these

Ans. (d) All of these

19. Which among the following is not correct about the religion of Chola Dynasty?
(i) Chola rulers worshiped Lord Shiva.
(ii) Lord Vishnu was the greatest god.
(iii) Chola Kings were tolerant towards other religion.
(iv) They built many Lord Shiva temples.

Codes
(a) Only (i) (b) Only (ii)
(c) (i), (ii) and (iii) (d) All of these

Ans. (b) Only (ii)

20. Consider the Chola Administration and choose the correct option.
(i) The king was at the top of the administration.
(ii) The Chola inscriptions describe the king as a great warrior and conqueror.
(iii) The Chola Empire was divided into *mandalams.*
(iv) The royal princes or officers were in charge of *mandalam.*

Codes
(a) Only (i) (b) Both (i) and (ii)
(c) (i), (ii) and (iii) (d) All of these

Ans. (d) All of these

21. Which is not true about political history of Chola Empire?
(i) Thousands of inscriptions found in the temples.
(ii) The Cholas are believed to have overthrown the Pandya in South India.
(iii) During the Rajendra I reign, the whole of Sri Lanka was made part of the Chola Empire.
(iv) Rajadhiraja was killed in the Battlefield of Koppam.

Codes
(a) Only (i) (b) Only (ii)
(c) (i), (ii) and (iii) (d) All of these

Ans. (b) Only (ii)

22. Match the following.

	List-I		List-II
A.	Brihadeshwara Temple	1.	Thirubhuvanam
B.	Gangaikonda Cholapuram Temple	2.	Kumbakonam
C.	Airavatesvara Temple	3.	Gangaikonda
D.	Kampaheswarar Temple	4.	Tanjore

Codes

	A	B	C	D
(a)	1	2	3	4
(b)	4	3	2	1
(c)	2	1	4	3
(d)	3	4	1	2

Ans. (b)

Passage Based Questions

23. Read the passage given below and answer the following questions.

Vijayalaya, who belonged to the ancient chiefly family of the Cholas from Uraiyur, captured the delta from the Muttaraiyar in the middle of the 9th century. He built the town of Thanjavur and a temple for goddess Nishumbhasudini there. The successors of Vijayalaya conquered neighbouring regions and the kingdom grew in size and power. The Pandyan and the Pallava territories to the South and North were made part of this kingdom. Rajaraja I, considered the most powerful Chola ruler, expanded control over most of these areas. He also reorganised the administration of the empire.

(i) Vijayalaya was the founder of ....
(a) Chola dynasty
(b) Pallava dynasty
(c) Chalukya dynasty
(d) Chera dynasty

Ans. (c) Chola dynasty

(ii) Who was the king of Chola dynasty during 985 to 1014 AD?
(a) Vijayalaya (b) Rajendra Chola
(c) Rajaraja I (d) Rajadhiraja I

Ans. (c) Rajaraja I

(iii) Rajaraja I was the devotee of ....
(a) Lord Shiva (b) Vishnu
(c) Buddha (d) Indra

Ans. (a) Lord Shiva

(iv) Who succeeded Rajaraja I ?
(a) Rajendra I (b) Parantaka I
(c) Kulottunga (d) Virarajendra

Ans. (a) Rajendra I

24. Read the passage given below and answer the following questions that follow.

Chola temples often became the nuclei of settlements which grew around them. These were centres of craft production. Temples were also endowed with land by rulers as well as by others. The produce of this land went into maintaining all the specialists who worked at the temple and very often lived near it - priests, garland makers, cooks, sweepers, musicians, dancers, etc. In other words, temples were not only places of worship: they were the hub of economic, social and cultural life as well. Amongst the crafts associated with temples, the making of bronze images was the most distinctive. Chola bronze images are considered amongst the finest in the world. While most images were of deities, sometimes images were made of devotees as well.

(i) Which among the following temples were built during Chola period?
(a) Brihadeshwara Temple
(b) Airavatesvara Temple
(c) Gangaikonda Cholapuram Temple
(d) All of the above

Ans. (d) All of the above

(ii) Why temples were important?
(a) Because it provided education
(b) Because it supported social life
(c) Because temples provided basic needs to the people
(d) All of the above

Ans. (d) All of the above

(iii) Which temple is also known as called as Rajarajeshwara Temple?
(a) Mahabaleshwar Temple
(b) Brihadeshwara Temple
(c) Gangaikonda Cholapuram Temple
(d) Meenakshi Temple

Ans. (b) Brihadeshwara Temple

(iv) Most of the Chola empire temple built in
(a) Dravidian style
(b) Nagara style
(c) Vesara style
(d) All of the above

Ans. (a) Dravidian style

Section-II

Short Questions

1. Mention the time period of the Chola rulers.

Ans. Cholas rose to prominence during the middle of the 9th century CE and established the greatest empire in South India. The later Chola kings ruled from 850 to 1279 AD for nearly 430 years.

2. Mention some inscriptions which gives information about Chola.

Ans. Some inscriptions which give information about the Cholas are

- Thiruvananthapuram inscriptions give information about the reign of Rajendra III.
- The Uttaramerur inscriptions give information about the Kudavolai system, village administration, taxation and land revenue.

3. What is the importance of monuments? Name some temples belonging to the Chola dynasty.

Ans. Monuments are the most interesting and instructive source of history. These monuments include mostly temples and sculptured halls and towers.

The Brihadeshwara temple of Tanjore, the Gangaikonda Cholapuram temple, Airavatesvara temple of Dharasuram and the Kampaheswarar temple in Thirubhuvanam are some of the important temples of the Chola dynasty.

4. Who was Rajaraja I?

Ans. Rajaraja I was son of Parantaka II and Vanavan Mahadevi. He was the most powerful king of the Chola dynasty. He defeated the Chera army at Thiruvananthapuram. He also defeated Bhaskar Ravi the Raja of Kollam.

5. Who succeeded Rajaraja I?

Ans. Rajaraja I was succeeded by his son Rajendra I. He was a great administrator and warrior. He captured the whole of Ceylon and consolidated Chola domination over Ceylon.

6. Give a brief account of the achievements of Rajendra I.

Ans. Rajendra I defeated the Bengal king Mahipala I and brought water from Ganges to Tanjore. This water was put into Cholagangam, a large irrigation tank, near Gangaikonda Cholapuram. In appreciation of this victory, king Rajendra I was given the title Gangaikondan. He conquered Malaya region in South-East Asia and earned the title 'Kadaram Kondan'.

7. Who was killed in the Battle of Koppam?

Ans. Rajadhiraja was killed in the Battle of Koppam (1052 AD). He was the last important ruler of the Chola dynasty. With his defeat, the disintegration of Chola dynasty started as there were weak successors.

8. How was the Chola Administration?

Ans. The Chola Kings followed a highly coherent system of administration. Tanjore was the capital of the Cholas. The Cholas had three major administrative divisions called 'Central Government', 'Provincial Government' and 'Local Government' which come under the control of king.

9. What was the concept of kingship followed by the Cholas?

Ans. The king was the head of the administration. The Chola Kings and queens were considered as representatives of God. Their idols were kept in temples.

The Chola kingship was hereditary and they followed the concept of primogeniture. The Chola Kings enjoyed enormous powers and privileges. They took up titles which marked their achievements. The kings were assisted by ministers and officials in their administration.

10. How was the provincial administration of the Chola kingdom?

Ans. According to the provincial administration of Chola kingdom, the empire was divided into 9 provinces or '*mandalams*. The head of the province was called 'Viceroy'. Each mandalam was divided into number of *Kottams* or *Valanadus*. Each *Kottam* was sub-divided into *Nadu*. Each *Nadu* was further divided into *Urs* (villages) which form part of the last unit of the administration.

11. How much strong was Chola kingdom in the field of military?

Ans. The Cholas had a well-organised army and navy. The Chola army consisted of elephant, cavalry and infantry. The army of Cholas had three organs. They were Nayak, Senapati and Mahandnayak.

12. What were the three categories of the local residents of the local self-government of Chola kingdom?

Ans. The three categories of the local residents of the local self- government of Chola kingdom were

(i) ***Ur*** It was consisted of the tax paying residents of an ordinary village. It was the assembly of local members.

(ii) ***Sabha*** It was restricted to the Brahmins of the villages where all land belonged to Brahmins.

(iii) ***Nagaram*** It was found more commonly in trade centres. It was an assembly of merchants.

13. Describe in brief the working of the local assemblies.

Ans. The working of local assemblies differed according to local conditions. The *Ur* was open to all male adults of the village but the older members took a more prominent part. The *Sabha* had the same system and in addition it had the power to constitute smaller committees of any size from among its members.

14. What was the social condition of the people in the Chola kingdom?

Ans. In Chola society, the untouchability and sati system was practiced. Poors were lived in slums and Brahmans were prosperous. The society was based on *Varnasrama*. Child marriage and slavery also existed.

15. Who were Valangai and Idangai groups?

Ans. The group which stood on the right hand side of the king was called Valangai group. The group that stood on the left hand side of the king was known as Idangai group.

16. Did Chola Kings give importance to the education?

Ans. Chola Kings gave importance for the development of education. There were Veda Padasalas, Buddha Viharas and Jain Pallis.

During the reign of Rajendra I, two colleges were established at Rajaraja Chaturvedi Mangalam and Tribhuvanam. Scholarships were also given to students.

17. Comment on the religious life of the Chola kings.

Ans. Chola Kings were Shaivites. They worshipped Lord Shiva and had built many Shiva temples. Parantaka I, Rajaraja I, Rajendra, King Gandraditya and his Queen Sembiyan Mahadevi contributed more for the development of Shaivism and Bhakti literature.

18. How was the condition of Tamil literature during the Chola period?

Ans. The Chola rule is considered as the golden age of Tamil literature. Many great Tamil poets namely, Kalladanar, Kamba, Pugalandhi, Ottakoothar, Sekkilar, Avvaiyar and Thirutakkadevar lived during the Chola period. Literary styles like epics, parani, kovai, ula, kalambakam, pillaitamil and new works on grammar were famous during that period. Writing meikeer this, narration of historical incidents, singing songs on religious hero's, were new literary trends of that time.

Structured Questions

1. There are various Archaeological sources to know about the Cholas. In context of this explain

(i) Inscriptions

(ii) Monuments

(iii) Brihadeshwara temple

Ans. (i) Refer to chapter theory page no. 130.

(ii) Refer to chapter theory page no. 131.

(iii) Refer to chapter theory page no. 131.

2. With reference to the political history of Chola Empire, explain the following

(i) Revival of Cholas

(ii) Rajaraja's conquest

(iii) Conquest of Rajendra

Ans. (i) The greatness of the Chola rule was revived by the Chola King Vijayalaya who was the subordinate commander of the Pallava king. He soon captured Tanjore from the Muttaraiyar chief and made it the capital of his kingdom. He was succeeded by his son Aditya I who was later succeeded by Parantaka I, father of Rajaraja I.

(ii) Rajaraja I succeeded the throne after his father Parantaka II his father. He was the most powerful king of Chola dynasty. The conquest of Rajaraja I was

(a) He defeated the Chera army at Thiruvananthapuram. He also defeated Bhaskar Ravi the Raja of Kollam.

(b) He defeated Mahinda V, the king of Ceylon and occupied Anuradhapuram and Northern part of Ceylon.

(c) He got the title 'Mummudi Cholan' after the conquest of three Southern kingdoms Cheras, Pandyas and Ceylon. He also conquered Kalinga and Maldives Islands.

(iii) Rajendra succeeded his father Rajaraja I and continued his fathers policies. He was a great warrior. The conquest of Rajendra I was

- He defeated the Bengal king Mahipala I and brought water from Gangas to Tanjore. In appreciation to this, he was given the title 'Gangaikondan'.
- The most heroic campaign of Rajendra was fought in South-East Asia where he defeated Srivijaya and secured the Indian trade in Southern China and South-East Asia.
- He defeated the Chera, Pandya and Kalinga king and also fought with the Chalukya king Jayasimeha II.

3. The Chola Kings followed highly coherent system of administration with a large measure of local autonomy. In context of above explain

(i) Central Administration
(ii) Provincial Administration
(iii) Local Administration
(iv) Revenue Administration

Ans. (i) Refer to chapter theory page no. 133.
(ii) Refer to chapter theory page no. 133.
(iii) Refer to chapter theory page no. 133.
(iv) Refer to chapter theory page no. 133.

4. With reference to the socio-religious and cultural aspects of the Cholas, explain

(i) Society
(ii) Education
(iii) Religion
(iv) Literature

Ans. (i) Refer to chapter theory page no. 133-134.
(ii) Refer to chapter theory page no. 134.
(iii) Refer to chapter theory page no. 134.
(iv) Refer to chapter theory page no. 134.

Picture Based Questions

1. With reference to the given picture, answer the following questions.

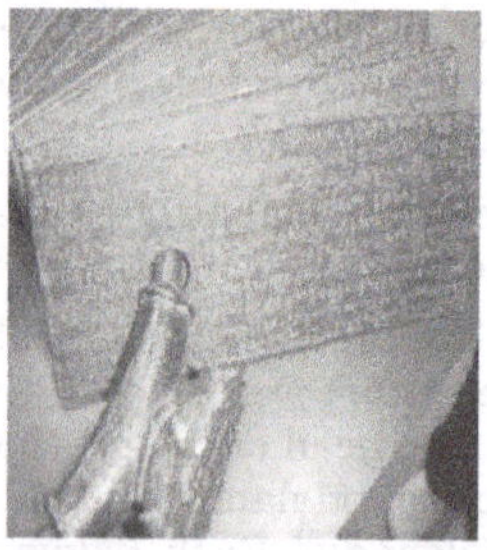

(i) What do you know about Chola from these inscriptions?
(ii) In which language these inscriptions are written? Explain.
(iii) Which inscriptions give us information about the village administration? State the various forms of Chola inscriptions.

Ans. (i) The inscription gives us useful information about the administration of the Chola rulers. Records of land grants villages, plot of farmland or other privileges given by the kings to private individuals or institutions like temples are also inscribed on copper-plates.

(ii) The language and script of the Chola inscription varied with the time and place of the records. The language most commonly employed was Tamil and some Sanskrit records are known. The Sanskrit language employed the Granth script closely associated with Tamil, in its evolution.

(iii) The Uttaramerur inscriptions give informations about the Kudavolai system, village administration, taxation and land revenue. The inscriptions of the Cholas are in the following forms

- Copper-plate grants
- Stone inscriptions
- Inscriptions Inscribed on the walls.
- Inscriptions on Pillars of the temple.

Chapter Assessment

Section-I

Multiple Choice Questions

1. The Chola empire of South India emerged in ....
   (a) 9th century (b) 10th century
   (c) 3rd century (d) 12th century
2. Which inscription talk about the existence of Shaivism?
   (a) Kanyakumari stone inscription
   (b) Karanthai plates
   (c) Thiruvalangadu copper plates
   (d) None of the above
3. Brihadeshwara temple is located in
   (a) Kanyakumari (b) Tanjore
   (c) Coimbatore (d) Madurai
4. Replace the underlined word and correct the sentence.
   Vijayalaya made <u>Madurai</u> his capital.
   (a) Tanjore (b) Vanji
   (c) Uampi (d) Thirubhuvanam

Section-II

Short Questions

1. Name any two archaeological sources to understand about the Chola kingdom.
2. Name some temples constructed during the Chola period.
3. What do you mean by Gopuram and Shikhara?
4. Which Chola King got the title of 'Gangaikonda'?
5. What was the nature of the Chola administration?
6. What was the function of the Council of Ministers?
7. What were the names of provinces and districts under the Cholas?
8. What was the condition of the society during the Chola period?

Structured Questions

1. With reference to the Chola polity, discuss
   (i) Role of the king
   (ii) Central administration
   (iii) Military
   (iv) Local Administration
2. With reference to the various sources about the Chola, explain
   (i) Importance of iiterature
   (ii) Importance of Inscriptions
   (iii) Importance of the monuments
   (iv) Religion
3. Rajaraja I was one of the important rulers of the Chola kingdom. With reference to this, explain
   (i) His military achievements
   (ii) Steps taken by him for merchants
   (iii) Different titles

CHAPTER 08

Delhi Sultanate

SYLLABUS

Sources Inscriptions, Qutub Minar. Name of the dynasties in chronological order
Alauddin Khilji –Market Regulations, Deccan Expedition, Measures against nobility, Military reforms, Revenue reforms. Muhammad Bin Tughlaq – Transfer of capital, Token currency, Taxation in Doab, Plan of Conquests.

The period between 1206 AD and 1526 AD in the Indian history is known as the period of Delhi Sultanate. It was called so because the rulers of the various dynasties that ruled from Delhi as their capital were called the Sultans. During this period, rulers belonging to five different dynasties, the Slaves, the Khiljis, the Tughlaqs, the Sayyids and the Lodhi's, ruled over India.

Sources of Delhi Sultanate

The source of Delhi Sultanate in India can be classified into literary sources and archaeological sources.

Literary Sources

The literary works of Persian and Arab people are the most important sources of history of the medieval period (the Sultanate period). These Persian and Arabic works can be divided into three broad categories such as the **chronicles**[1], the travel stories and the modern works. The literary sources which give information about Delhi Sultanate are

Tarikh-i-Firozshahi

It was written by **Zia-ud-din Barani** who was a political thinker and a historian. His work started with Balban and came down to the sixth year of the reign of Firoz Shah Tughlaq. Barani has clearly written about political and socio-economic condition of the people during medieval India.

Prithviraj Raso

It is an epic poem composed by a court poet, **Chand Bardai**, on the life of a Chauhan king Prithviraj III, who ruled Ajmer and Delhi between 1165 AD and 1192 AD. Chand Bardai claimed to be contemporary of Prithviraj Chauhan.

The Prithviraj Raso is a semi-historical and semi-legendary account that depicts the bravery of Prithviraj Chauhan. It also depicts the struggle between Ghori and the Rajputs and the political, military and the socio-economic structure of the Rajputs. The legend represents the historical events for dramatic effects. Its historicity is considered unreliable by historians.

Archaeological Sources

Following are the archaeological sources which give information about the Delhi Sultanate period

Inscriptions

Indian Islamic inscriptions date from the last decade of the 12th century AD when Muhammad Ghori conquered Delhi and established his kingdom there.

1. **Chronicles** A factual written account of important or historical events in the order of their occurrence.

A number of inscriptions are found in and around Delhi and Uttar Pradesh. They provide information of the land grants made by rulers and chief and battles of rulers, etc.

Certain movable objects like arms, seals, signets, vases, utensils, forts and tombs account for majority of inscriptions.

The language of the records of the early period of the Delhi Sultanate is Arabic. Majority of epigraphically records are in Persian in view of the fact that Persian had been the state or official language right from the beginning of the Muslim rule.

Apart from Arabic, Persian and Urdu inscriptions, there are bilingual inscriptions, i.e. Arabic with regional languages like Gujarati, Marathi, Bengali, Tamil and Malayalam and Persian with the provincial languages like Kannada, Telugu, Oriya, Tamil, Gujarati and Marathi. Some of the inscriptions are written in Sanskrit also.

Monuments

Monuments are important sources for the construction of the history of medieval India. The main characteristic features of the architectural style brought in by Turks on the dome, minarets, arches and supported roof.

The Turks used geometrical and floral designs and combined them with panels of inscriptions containing verses from the Holy Quran, for the purpose of decoration. Some of the important monuments build during the Sultanate period are Qutub Minar, Tomb of Iltutmish, Sultan Garhi, Alai Darwaza, Hauz Khas and Jamait Khana Mosque, etc.

Qutub Minar

Qutub Minar

Qutb ud din Aibak, the Governor of Delhi dedicated Qutub Minar to the Sufi Saint, **Qutbuddin Bakhtiar Kaki**. Aibak started the construction of the Qutub Minar in 1199 AD, which was completed after his death by his successor **Iltutmish**.

The special features of Qutub Minar are

- Originally, Qutub Minar had only four storeys. The fifth storey and some changes were added in 14th century by Firoz Shah Tughlaq.
- It is made of red sandstone, grey quartzite and marble. It is the tallest minaret in India, standing at a height of 238 feet.
- It comprises several superposed **flanged**[2] and cylindrical **shafts**[3], separated by projecting balconies. Each tower has a balcony.
- The walls of the minaret are covered with Indian floral motifs and verses from the Quran.
- The minar is a circular tower of about 13.8 m in diameter and width of about 3 m. It has a circular stairway leading to the top.

Check Your LEARNING...

1. What was the period of Delhi Sultanate?
2. Who is the writer of Tarikh-i-Firozshahi?
3. Name some important monuments of Sultanate period.
4. Write two features of Qutub Minar.

Political History of Delhi Sultanate

The real founder of the Muslim Empire in India was Shihab ad-Din Muhammad Ghori or Muhammad of Ghor.

In 1206 AD the sudden death of Muhammad Ghori led to conflict among his three slaves Tajaldin Yalduz, Nariruddin Qabach and Qutb-ud-din Aibak.

Dynasties of Delhi Sultanate

The Slave Dynasty (AD 1206-1290)

All the Muslim rulers that ascended the throne of Delhi after the death of Muhammad Ghori in 1206 AD till 1290 AD were either slaves or the descendants of these slave rulers. That is why, the rulers belonging to this dynasty are generally known as the 'Slave Rulers' or the Mamluk Sultans and the dynasty is called the Slave dynasty.

2. **Flanged** Projecting flat rim, collar, or rib on an object, serving to strengthen or attach to maintain position on a rail.
3. **Shafts** A long, narrow part or section forming the handle of a tool or club, the body of a spear or arrow or similar.

Some important rulers of this dynasty were

Qutb-ud-din Aibak (1206-1210 AD)

Mohammad Ghori was succeeded by Qutb-ud-din Aibak, a Turkish slave in 1206 AD. He was the founder of Delhi Sultanate with its capital at Lahore. He earned the title of **Lakh-baksh** (Giver of Lakhs) for liberal distribution of money and his generosity. He laid the foundation of Qutub Minar in Delhi and built two mosques, one in Ajmer and the other one in Delhi.

Administration under Qutb-ud-din Aibak

Aibak did not pursue the policy of extension of his kingdom. He remained busy in defending independent position. The affairs in North-West and Bengal in the East were his primary concerns. In his four years' rule, he followed a policy of war and diplomacy. He ruled the country as a military jafir which lacked the elements of stability.

Shamsuddin Iltutmish (1211-1236 AD)

Shamsuddin Iltutmish was a slave and son-in-law of Qutb-ud-din Aibak. He occupied the throne of Delhi in 1211 AD after removing Aram Bakhsh (son of Aibak). He was a very capable ruler and is regarded as the 'real founder of the Delhi Sultanate'.

He made Delhi as the capital in place of Lahore. He saved Delhi Sultanate from the Mongol leader Genghis Khan, by refusing shelter to Khwarazm Shah, whom Genghis was chasing. He introduced the silver coin *tanka* and the copper coin *jital*.

He organised the ***Iqta* system**[4] and introduced reforms in civil administration and army, which was now centrally paid and recruited. He set up an official nobility of slaves known as **Turkan-i-Chahalgani/Chalisa** (group of 40) to break the power of nobles who were reluctant to accept him as a king because of his slave origin. He patronised Minhaj-us-Siraj, author of 'Tabaqat-i- Nasiri'. He nominated his daughter Razia as his successor.

Razia Sultan (1236-1240 AD)

She was the **first and only Muslim lady** who ever ruled India. She was the daughter of Iltutmish. She put an end to the turmoil created by Ruknuddin (brother) and restored law and order.

Altunia, Governor of Bhatinda refused to accept partial control of Razia. Thus, Razia accompanied by Yakut (an Abyssian slave) marched against Altunia. Altunia got Yakut murdered and imprisoned Razia. Subsequently, Razia married Altunia. In 1240 AD, Razia became the victim of a conspiracy and was killed near Kaithal (Haryana).

Balban (1266-1287 AD)

Ghiyas-ud-din Balban, leader of Chalisa ascended the throne in 1266 AD after killing Mahmud (youngest son of Iltutmish). He served as a General and Minister previously for 20 years (1246-1266 AD).

He adopted the policy of **Blood and Iron** to establish a centralised army and to subdue rebel forces. He disbanded Turkan-i-Chahalgani or Chalisa.

The Khilji Dynasty (AD 1290-1320)

After the Slave dynasty, Khilji dynasty ruled over Delhi. The Khiljis were actually Turks who had settled in the Khilji region of Afghanistan for a long time, and had adopted Afghan manners and customs. Therefore, their coming to the throne of Delhi is called Khilji **revulsion**[5]. Some important rulers of this dynasty were

Jalal-ud-din Khilji (1290-1296 AD)

Jalal-ud-din Khilji founded Khilji dynasty and came to the throne after killing Kaikubad. The Turkish Amirs (nobles) misconceived him as an Afghan and were against him. The public also wanted the Sultan to belong from a royal family.

Alauddin Khilji (1296-1316)

Alauddin Khilji was a nephew and son-in-law of Jalal-ud-din Khilji. He killed Jalal-ud-din and succeeded the throne in 1296 AD. He was the first Turkish Sultan of Delhi who separated religion from politics. He proclaimed **'Kingship knows no Kinship'**. He is considered to be the most powerful ruler of this dynasty.

Alauddin annexed Gujarat (1298 AD), Ranthambhore (1301 AD), Mewar (1303 AD), Malwa (1305 AD) and Jalor (1311 AD).

The most important experiment undertaken by the Alauddin was the attempt to control the markets. Alauddin sought to control the prices of almost all commodities such as foodgrains, horse, cattle slaves and costly imported clothes, etc.

Market Regulations

- Alauddin Khilji introduced strict market control to ensure price stability.

4. **Iqta System** A unique type of land distribution and administrative system evolved during the reign of Iltutmish.
5. **Revulsion** A feeling of disgust and hatred.

- He set fixed prices for essential goods like grains and cloth.
- He established government-controlled markets to avoid price manipulation by traders.
- A special department, the Shahna-i-Mandi has been created to oversee market regulations.
- The use of liquor and intoxicants was prohibited.

Deccan Expedition

- Alauddin Khilji launched military expeditions into the Deccan to expand his empire.
- The objective was to conquer the Southern kingdoms and secure resources.
- He annexed the Deccan region with his army led by **Malik Kafur**.
- During the annexation, his army defeated Ram Chandra, Pratap Rudradeva, Vir Ballal III and Vir Pandya. These kingdoms were not conquered but had to pay tribute to the king.
- Malik Kafur attacked Devagiri twice which was ruled by Ramchandra Deva.
- He successfully defeated the **Yadavas of Devagiri**, the **Kakatiyas of Warangal** and the **Hoysalas**.

Measures Against Nobility

- Alauddin Khilji took steps to curb the power of the nobility.
- He implemented the **Iqtadari system** to weaken local nobles and centralise power.
- Nobles were restricted from building personal armies and fortresses.
- The practice of giving large jagirs (land grants) to nobles was reduced.
- He created a system of surveillance to monitor nobles and prevent rebellion.

Alleged disloyalty resulted in harsh punishment or execution of nobles.

Military Reforms

- He introduced the first permanent standing army of India.
- He abolished the *Iqtas* on royal troopers and the payment of their salaries in cash.
- He introduced *Dagh* (branding of horses) and *Chehra* (branding of soldiers).
- He himself approved all recruitments to the army.
- A Department of Intelligence was created to monitor military activity.
- Soldiers were paid in cash.

Revenue Reforms

- Alauddin Khilji introduced land revenue reforms to increase state income.
- He set fixed tax rates, ensuring a steady flow of revenue.
- He established **Diwan-i-Mustakhraj** which was responsible for the recovery of arrears and taxes.
- Abolition of small Iqtas and land measurement (Paimaish).

The Tughlaq Dynasty (1320-1414 AD)

The Khilji dynasty was succeeded by the Tughlaq dynasty. It was founded by Ghiyas-ud-din Tughlaq in 1320 AD. Some of the important rulers of the Tughlaq dynasty were

Muhammad bin Tughluq (1325-1351 AD)

Mohammad bin Tughluq or Prince Jauna, son of Ghiyas-ud-din Tughlaq ascended the throne in 1325 AD. He was an excellent warrior. He had complete command over astronomy, mathematics, medicine and had great interest in religion and philosophy.

He was also a great patron of Persian literature and lover of fine-arts, music and calligraphy. He tried to introduce many administrative reforms.

Some of the reforms and expeditions under Muhammad bin Tughluq were

- **Taxation in the Doab** (1326 AD) Muhammad bin Tughluq increased taxation in the Doab regions of Ganga and Yamuna as he wanted to raise a strong army for conquest. According to Ziauddin Barani, the Muslim political thinker of Delhi sultan, the taxation was raised by ten to twenty times more.

  The taxation was increased at the time when there had been famine, so the peasants instead of paying taxes abandoned their lands and adopted highway robbery. The tax collectors continued to collect taxes by oppression which resulted in widespread revolts.

  However, the Sultan took efficient step to fight the famine, such as he gave loans to peasants, ordered free distribution of grains and improved irrigation facilities but it does not brought any good result for agriculture.
- **Transfer of Capital** (1327 AD) Muhammad bin Tughluq tranferred the capital from Delhi to Devagiri, near Modern Aurangabad and renamed it

Daulatabad. The reasons expected for shifting the capital were

(i) Firstly, for expected and consolidation of South India and make Daulatabad the centre of Muslim culture.

(ii) Secondly, the desire to keep the capital at a safe distance from Mongol invasion.

(iii) Thirdly, the desire of wealth of the South and Delhi was in the grip of severe famine.

Therefore, he ordered the people of Delhi, including the nobles to shift to Daulatabad. Soon after few years, he decided to abandon Daulatabad and shift to Delhi due to administrative inconvenience for North India.

- **Introduction of Token Currency (1329 AD)** Muhammad-bin-Tughluq issued currency made of copper and bronze in place of gold and silver and kept its value at par also. This experiment failed because fake coins generated on a large scale caused disorder in trade and commerce. The token currency was withdrawn by the Sultan completely, as it began to be devalued greatly in the market.

Plan of Conquests

Tughluq sought to extend his influence across the Indian subcontinent and beyond with a vision that reached into regions such as Central Asia and the Deccan.

One of his primary objectives was to strengthen and expand his military capabilities to secure his rule and bring stability to the Sultanate. To achieve this, he pursued multiple military campaigns against neighbouring kingdoms.

His first major conquest was the attempt to invade the Deccan region, which, although initially successful, ended in failure due to logistical difficulties and lack of adequate support. Muhammad bin Tughluq also tried to extend his control over Bengal, Assam and other parts of Eastern India but these efforts faced significant resistance and ultimately proved to be unsuccessful.

Deccan Expedition Plan

In 1327, Muhammad bin Tughluq launched an expedition to extend his empire in Southern India and bring the rebellious Deccan Sultanates under control. His initial success in capturing the city of Devagiri (now Daulatabad) was seen as a significant achievement. However, the campaign proved to be a big failure as the logistical challenges of maintaining control over such a distant region led to a strained supply system. The failure to effectively govern this vast territory led to unrest and the Sultan was forced to abandon his hold on the Deccan.

Bengal Expedition Plan

In 1336, Muhammad bin Tughluq sent a large military force to assert Delhi's authority over Bengal, which had become increasingly independent under local rulers. Tughluq's forces initially made some headway but the region's difficult terrain and strong local resistance made it challenging to maintain control. Eventually, the Sultan was forced to withdraw and Bengal remained independent. These failed campaigns highlight Tughluq's overambitious expedition strategies which often stretched his resources too thin and led to prolonged instability within his empire.

- **Proposed Khurasan Expedition (1329 AD)** The unstable political conditions in Central Asia and Muhammad bin Tughluq's vision of universal conquest encouraged him to undertake the expedition of conquering these territories. The Sultan raised a large army for this purpose and paid it one year salary in advance. In the meantime, situation changed and sultan realised the uselessness of the scheme and disbanded the army.
- **Qarachil Expedition (1330 AD)** Qarachil was located at the foot of the Himalayas, probably in the region now called, Kumaon. According to Ferishta (a Persian scholar), the primary objective of the Sultan was not the conquest of this state but that of China through this state.

Firoz Shah Tughlaq (1351-1388 AD)

Firoz Shah Tughlaq was a cousin of Muhammad bin Tughluq. After Muhammad bin Tughluq's death, the nobles and the theologians of the court selected Firoz Shah as the next Sultan. He established *Diwan-i-Khairat* (department for poor and needy people) and *Diwan-i-Bandagan* (department of slaves). He was a patron of scholars like Ziauddin Barani and also built schools. He made Iqtadari system hereditary. He constructed canals for irrigation, roads, gardens, mosques and manufacturing centres or *Karkhanas* took place during his reign.

He establish the four new towns that were Firuzabad, Fatehabad, Jaunpur and Hissar. He imposed *Jizya* (pilgrim tax) on Hindus. Timur (a Mongol chief) took advantage of Sultan's neglect to safeguard North-West Frontier and invaded it in 1398 AD.

Administration of Delhi Sultanate

Central Administration

In central administration of Delhi Sultanate, the Sultan was the supreme executive, legislative, judicial and military authority. A number of ministers assisted him in administration.

Wazir was an important figure in the administration who acted as Prime Minister. The work of the official was supervised by the *Wazir*. However, the final decisions were always taken by the Sultan. The nobles formed an extremely powerful group as they held positions of military commanders and provincial governors.

Provincial Administration

During Delhi Sultanate, the empire was divided into provinces called *Iqtas*. Each province was controlled by officials called *muqtis*. The provinces were further divided into shiqs and parganas or districts in order to facilitate local administration.

The lowest administrative unit was the village which included officials like the *muqaddam* (the village headman), the *patwari* (the record keeper) and the *mushrif* (the village accountant). There was a panchayat in each village to settle local disputes.

Military Administration

Ariz-i-mumalik was the minister in charge of the army. He had to recruit, equip and pay the army. The commander-in-chief of the army was the Sultan.

Judicial Administration

There were two departments in judicial administration of Delhi Sultanate which were *Diwan-i-Risalat* and *Diwan-i-Insha*. The *Diwan-i-Risalat* was presided by the Chief *Sadar* (a leading *qazi*) and it dealt with the religious matters. The *Diwan-i-Insha* dealt with the state correspondence. The *qazi* was the head of the department of justice and gave advise to the Sultan on civil and religious matters.

Revenue Administration

Iqta system was followed in Delhi Sultanate which was the practice of giving grants of revenue from a territory. Those who were given iqtas were called *iqtadars*. They maintain themselves, their families and some soldiers, from this grant. Many of these *iqtadars* functioned as independent rulers of the territories when the central authority became weak.

Check Your LEARNING...

1. Write the name of two rulers of Slave dynasty.
2. To which dynasty did Razia Sultan belong?
3. Who proclaimed 'kingship knows no kinship'?
4. Who was the successor to Mohammad bin Tughluq?

QUiCK Revision

- The defeat of Prithviraj Chauhan in the second battle of Tarain in 1192 by Shahab-ud-din Muhammad Ghori started an era of Muslim rule in India.
- The literary works of Persian and Arab people are the most important sources of history of the medieval period (the Sultanate period).
- Prithviraj Raso is an epic poem composed by a court poet, Chand Bardai, on the life of a Chauhan king Prithviraj III, who ruled Ajmer and Delhi between 1165 and 1192.
- Some archaeological sources which throw light on Delhi Sultanate are inscription, monuments and Qutab Minar.
- A number of inscriptions are found in and around Delhi and Uttar Pradesh.
- Monuments are important sources for the construction of the history of medieval India.
- Qutb ud-Din Aibak, the Governor of Delhi and subsequently, the first Sultan of the Delhi Sultanate who ruled between 1206-1210 AD, dedicated Qutub Minar to the Sufi Saint, Qutbuddin Bakhtiyar Kaki. Aibak started the construction of the Qutub Minar in 1199, which was completed after his death by his successor Iltutmish.
- The real founder of the Muslim Empire in India was Shihab ad Din Muhammad Ghori or Muhammad of Ghor.
- The conflict between Prithviraj and Muhammad Ghori started for the fort of Tarabhinda (Bhatinda) which led to the First Battle of Tarain in 1191 AD. Muhammad was defeated in the battle.
- Mahammad Ghori was succeeded by Qutb-ud-din Aibak, a Turkish slave in 1206 AD. He was the founder of Delhi Sultanate with its capital at Lahore.
- Shamsuddin Iltutmish was a slave and son-in-law of Qutb-ud-din Aibak. He occupied the throne of Delhi in 1211 AD after removing Aram Bakhsh (son of Aibak).
- Shamsuddin Iltutmish set up an official nobility of slaves known as Turkan-i-Chahalgani/Chalisa (group of 40) to break the power of nobles who were reluctant to accept him as a king because of his slave origin.
- Razia Sultan was the 'first and only Muslim lady who ever ruled India' but she was not acceptable to the nobles and theologians who considered it below their dignity to be ruled by a woman.
- Ghiyas-ud-din Balban, leader of Chalisa ascended the throne in 1266 AD after killing Mahmud (youngest son of Iltutmish). He served as a General and Minister previously for 20 years (1246-1266 AD). He adopted the policy of 'Blood and Iron' to establish a centralised army and to subdue rebel forces.
- The Khiljis were, wrongly believed to be Afghans. They were actually Turks. Therefore, their coming to the throne of Delhi is called 'Khilji revulsion'.
- Alauddin Khilji was a nephew and son-in-law of Jalaluddin Khilji. He killed him and succeeded the throne in 1296 AD. He was the first turkish Sultan of Delhi who separated region from politics. He proclamed 'Kingship knows no Kinship'.
- Alauddin annexed Gujarat (1298 AD), Ranthambhore (1301 AD), Mewar (1303 AD), Malwa (1305 AD) and Jalor (1311 AD). The most important experiment undertaken by the Alauddin was the attempt to control the markets.
- Alauddin Khilji made some reforms in various departments– Market reforms, military reforms and revenue reforms.
- Firoz Shah Tughlaq was a cousin of Muhammad bin Tughluq. After his death the nobles and the theologians of the court selected Firoz Shah as the next Sultan.
- Firoz Shah established *Diwan-i-Khairat* (department for poor and needy people) and Diwan-i-Bandagan (department of slaves).
- In Central Administration of Delhi Sultanate, the Sultan was the Supreme executive, Legislative, judicial and military authority.
- During Delhi Sultanate, the empire was divided into provinces called *Iqtas*.

Chapter Practice

Section-I

Multiple Choice Questions

1. The first dynasty of Delhi sultanate was
   (a) Khilji dynasty (b) Slave dynasty
   (c) Tughlaq dynasty (d) Lodhi dynasty

Ans. (b) Slave dynasty

2. Who was the writer of Tarikh-i-Firozshahi?
   (a) Al-Biruni (b) Abul Fazl
   (c) Ziauddin Barani (d) Chand-Bar dai

Ans. (c) Ziauddin Barani

3. Who was the slave of Muhammad Ghori?
   (a) Qutb ud-Din Aibak
   (b) Iltutmish
   (c) Alauddin Khilji
   (d) Sikandar Lodhi

Ans. (a) Qutb ud din Aibak

4. Which of the following monuments was/were built during Delhi sultanate ?
   (a) Qutub Minar (b) Alai Darwaza
   (c) Hauz Khas (d) All of these

Ans. (d) All of these

5. Qutb ud-Din Aibak was succeeded by
   (a) Iltutmish (b) Razia Sultan
   (c) Aram Shah (d) Balban

Ans. (a) Iltutmish

6. Qutub Minar is located in.......... .
   (a) Delhi (b) Lucknow (c) Agra (d) Ajmer

Ans. (a) Delhi

7. What is the total approximate height of Qutub Minar?
   (a) 150 feet (b) 238 feet
   (c) 368 feet (d) 248 feet

Ans. (b) 238 feet

8. Who saved Delhi Sultanate from Genghis Khan?
   (a) Firoz Shah Tughlaq (b) Muhammad bin Tughluq
   (c) Iltutmish (d) Alauddin Khilji

Ans. (c) Iltutmish

9. .... established Turkan-i-Chahalgani / Chalisa.
   (a) Qutbud din Aibak (b) Iltutmish
   (c) Alauddin Khilji (d) Firoz Shah Tughlaq

Ans. (b) Iltutmish

10. Who adopted the policy of 'Blood and Iron' ?
    (a) Balban (b) Sikandar Lodhi
    (c) Firoz Shah Tughlaq (d) Razia Sultan

Ans. (a) Balban

11. Complete the given analogy.
    Qutb-ud-din Aibak : 1206 - 10AD : : Iltutmish : ?
    (a) 1211 - 36 AD
    (b) 1236 - 40 AD
    (c) 1290 - 96 AD
    (d) 1296 - 1316 AD

Ans. (a) 1211 - 36 AD

12. Replaced the underlined word to correct the statement.
    Muhammad bin Tughluq ascended the throne in 1296 AD .
    (a) 1325 AD (b) 1316 AD
    (c) 1290 AD (d) 1305 AD

Ans. (a) 1325 AD

13. Replaced the underlined word to correct the sentence.
    Firoz Shah Tughlaq transferred the capital from Delhi to Devagiri.
    (a) Muhammad bin Tughluq
    (b) Ghiyas-ud-din Tughlaq
    (c) Sikandar Lodhi
    (d) Balban

Ans. (a) Muhammad bin Tughluq

14. Complete the given table.

Slave Dynasty	1206-1290 AD
Tughlaq Dynasty	?

    (a) 1290-1320 AD
    (b) 1320-1414 AD
    (c) 1440-1451 AD
    (d) 1451-1526 AD

Ans. (b) 1320-1414 AD

15. Consider the following statements about Alauddin Khilji and choose the correct option.
    (i) Alauddin maintained a huge permanent standing army.
    (ii) Alauddin inscribed the title Sikandar-i-saini on his coins.
    (iii) Alauddin was the first Sultan to pay his soldiers in cash.
    (iv) Alauddin created separate department for revenue as Diwan-i- Mustkharaj.

    Codes
    (a) Only (i)
    (b) Both (i) and (ii)
    (c) (i), (ii) and (iii)
    (d) All of the above

Ans. (d) All of the above

16. Consider the following statements and choose the correct option.
(i) Ghiyas-ud-din died accidently in 1325 AD.
(ii) Firoz Shah Tughlaq started the imposition of Jaziy.
(iii) Ibn Battuta, a Morocan traveller visited during the reign of Muhammad bin Tughlaq.
(iv) Razia Sultan married Altuniya (Governor of Bhatinda).

Codes
(a) Only (i) (b) Only (ii)
(c) (i), (ii) and (iii) (d) All of these

Ans. (d) All of these

17. Consider the following statements about Ghiyas-ud-din Balban and choose the correct option.
(i) Balban was greatest in slave dynasty.
(ii) He abolished Chahalghani .
(iii) He established defence department known as Diwan-i-Ariz.
(iv) Balban introduced Persian customs and traditions.

Codes
(a) Only (i) (b) Only (ii)
(c) (i), (ii) and (iii) (d) All of these

Ans. (d) All of these

18. Match the following.

List-I	List-II
A. Slave Dynasty	1. 1290-1320 AD
B. Khilji Dynasty	2. 1414-1451 AD
C. Tughlaq Dynasty	3. 1206-1290 AD
D. Sayyid Dynasty	4. 1320-1414 AD

Codes

	A	B	C	D
(a)	1	2	3	4
(b)	4	3	2	1
(c)	3	1	4	2
(d)	2	4	1	3

Ans. (c)

19. Match the following.

List-I	List-II
A. Qutb-ud-din Aibak	1. 1296-1316 AD
B. Razia Sultan	2. 1236-1240 AD
C. Alauddin Khilji	3. 1206-1210 AD
D. Muhammad bin Tughluq	4. 1325-1351 AD

Codes

	A	B	C	D
(a)	4	3	2	1
(b)	3	2	1	4
(c)	1	2	3	4
(d)	2	4	1	3

Ans. (b)

Picture Based Question

(i) Identify the picture.
(a) Qutub Minar (b) Allahabad Pillar Inscription
(c) Mehrauli pillar (d) None of these

Ans. (a) Qutub Minar

(ii) Who laid the foundation of Qutub Minar?
(a) Muhammad Ghori (b) Ghiyas-ud-din Tughlaq
(c) Iltutmish (d) Qutb-ud-din Aibak

Ans. (d) Qutb-ud-din Aibak

(iii) The Qutub Minar was dedicated to
(a) Qutb-ud-din Bakhtiar Kaki
(b) Baba Fakruddin
(c) Nur Qutub Alam
(d) None of the above

Ans. (a) Qutb-ud-din Bakhtiar Kaki

(iv) The Qutub Minar was repaired by
(a) Sikandar Lodhi
(b) Firoz Shah Tughlaq
(c) Muhammad bin Tughluq
(d) Aram Shah

Ans. (b) Firoz Shah Tughlaq

Passage Based Questions

20. Read the passage given below and answer the questions that follow.

The Delhi Sultanate basically refers to the Muslim rulers who ruled India through Delhi. This basically came into existence after Mohammad Ghori captured Delhi after defeating Prithviraj. After Prithviraj was captured, the Delhi Sultanate went into the hands of one of Ghori's generals known as Qutb ud-Din Aibak.

During the end of the 12th century, he established a series of rulers and this dynasty was called as the slave dynasty since the rulers had been military slaves. Read more about the history of the Delhi sultanate in India.

The extent of Delhi Sultanate was till Bengal in the East and Deccan in the South. Even such a big sultanate faced constant threats from the North-West and was also under pressure from internal politics within independent nobles. There was instability and unrest in the kingdom as there five dynasties that rose and fell which includes

Slave dynasty, Khilji dynasty, Tughlaq dynasty, Sayyid dynasty and Lodhi dynasty.

(i) The time period of Delhi Sultanate was ....

(a) 1106-1626 AD (b) 1206-1526 AD
(c) 1026-1526 AD (d) 985-1757 AD

Ans. (b) 1206-1526 AD

(ii) Who was the founder of Slave dynasty ?

(a) Qutb-ud-din Aibak (b) Iltutmish
(c) Firoz Shah Tughlaq (d) Sikandar Lodhi

Ans. (a) Qutb-ud-din Aibak

(iii) The first muslim women ruler Razia Sultan belonged to

(a) Tughlaq Dynasty (b) Slave Dynasty
(c) Khilji Dynasty (d) Sayyid Dynasty

Ans. (b) Slave Dynasty

(iv) Who was called as Lakh-baksh?

(a) Feroz Shah Tughlaq (b) Qutb-ud-din Aibak
(c) Sikandar Lodhi (d) Alauddin Khilji

Ans. (b) Qutb-ud-din Aibak

21. Read the passage given below and answer the questions that follow.

The consolidation of a kingdom as vast as the Delhi Sultanate needed reliable Governors and administrators. Rather than appointing aristocrats and landed chieftains as Governors, the early Delhi Sultans, especially Iltutmish, favoured their special slaves purchased for military service, called Bandagan in Persian. They were trained man, some of them were most important political offices in the kingdom. Since they were totally dependent upon their master, the Sultan could trust and rely upon them. The Khaljis and Tughlaqs continued to use bandagan and also raised people of humble birth, who were often their clients, to high political positions. They were appointed as generals and governors. However, this also introduced an element of political instability.

(i) Special slaves purchased for military service by the early Delhi Sultanate were called ....

(a) Ghulams (b) Bandagan
(c) Bonded labour (d) All of these

Ans. (b) Bandagan

(ii) Who was the founder of Khilji Dynasty?

(a) Jalal-ud-din Khilji (b) Alauddin Khilji
(c) Mubarak Shah (d) Qasim Khan

Ans. (a) Jalal-ud-din Khilji

(iii) Who introduced market control policy?

(a) Iltutmish (b) Alauddin Khilji
(c) Feroz Shah Tughlaq (d) Bahlol Lodhi

Ans. (b) Alauddin Khilji

(iv) Who was the founder of Tughlaq Dynasty?

(a) Ghiyas-ud-din Tughlaq (b) Firoz Shah Tughlaq
(c) Mohammad bin Tughluq (d) Iltutmish

Ans. (a) Ghiyas-ud-din Tughlaq

Section-II

Short Questions

1. What are the literary sources to understand about the Sultanate period?

Ans. The literary works of Persian and Arab people are the most important sources of history of the medieval period (the Sultanate period). These Persian and Arabic works can be divided into three broad categories such as-the chronicles, the travel stories and the modern works.

2. Give an account of Tarikh-i-Firozshahi in brief.

Ans. Tarikh-i-Firozshahi was written by Ziauddin Barani who was a political thinker and a historian. It covers the data from the reign of Ghiyas-ud-din Balban to the sixth year of the reign of Firoz Tughlaq.

3. Which language has been used in the inscriptions of Delhi Sultanate?

Ans. The language of the records of the early period of the Delhi Sultanate is Arabic. Apart from Arabic, Persian and Urdu inscriptions, there are bilingual inscriptions i.e. Arabic with regional languages like Gujarati, Marathi, Bengali, Tamil and Malayalam and Persian with the provincial languages like Kannada, Telugu, Oriya, Tamil, Gujarati and Marathi. Some of the inscriptions were also written in Sanskrit.

4. Mention some reasons for the success of Turks in India.

Ans. Reasons for the success of Turks in India were

- Rajputs lacked unity and organisation; divided by rivalries.
- There was no Central Government.
- Kingdoms were small and scattered.
- Turks were better organised and took advantage of the lack of mutual co-operation among the Rajputs.

5. What kind of architecture style was brought by the Turkish conquerors of India?

Ans. The Turkish conquerors of India introduced Persian–influenced Islamic architecture. They also popularised the use of red sandstone and intricate carvings, blending Persian, Islamic and Indian styles to create domes, minarets, arches and other monuments.

6. Mention some of the important monuments built during the Sultanate period.

Ans. Some of the important monuments built during the Sultanate period are Qutub Minar, Tomb of Iltutmish, Sultan Garhi, Alai Darwaza, Hauz Khas and Jamait Khana Mosque, etc.

7. Which period in the Indian history is known as the 'Period of the Sultanate of Delhi'?

Ans. The period between 1206 and 1526 AD in the Indian history is known as the 'Period of the Sultanate of Delhi'. During this period, rulers belonging to five different dynasties-the Slaves, the Khiljis, the Tughlaqs, the Sayyids and the Lodhis ruled over India.

8. Why the first dynasty of the Delhi Sultanate was known as the Slave dynasty?

Ans. All the Muslim rulers that ascended the throne of Delhi after the death of Muhammad Ghori in 1206 AD till 1290 AD were either themselves slaves or the descendants of these slave rulers. That is why, the rulers belonging to this dynasty are generally are known as the 'Slave Rulers' or the Mamluk Sultans and the dynasty is called the Slave dynasty.

9. What was unique about Razia Sultan?

Ans. Razia Sultan was the 'first and only Muslim lady who ever ruled India'. She was an able and brave ruler. She dressed like a man and herself led the armies in the battle field.

10. When did Balban ascended the throne and what policy he adopted?

Ans. Balban ascended the throne in 1266 AD after killing Mahmud (youngest son of Iltutmish). He adopted the policy of 'Blood and Iron' to establish a centralised army and to subdue the rebel forces.

11. Who founded the Khilji Dynasty?

Ans. Jalal-ud-din Khilji founded Khilji dynasty and came to the throne after killing Kaikubad. By following mild and generous policies, he won the hearts of the people.

12. What was unique about Alauddin Khilji?

Ans. Alauddin Khilji was the first Turkish Sultan of Delhi who separated religion from politics. He proclaimed 'Kingship knows no Kinship'.

13. Mention some expeditions of Alauddin Khilji.

Ans. Alauddin annexed Gujarat (1298 AD), Ranthambhore (1301 AD), Mewar (1303 AD), Malwa (1305 AD), Jalor (1311 AD). In Deccan, Alauddin's army led by Malik Kafur defeated Ram Chandra, Pratap Rudradeva, Vir Ballal III and Vir Pandya.

14. What was the new department introduced by Alauddin Khilji?

Ans. Alauddin Khilji created a new department *viz* *Diwan-i-Mustakhraj* to enquire into the revenue arrears and to collect them.

15. What were the five ambitious projects of Muhammad bin Tughluq?

Ans. Five ambitious projects for which he has become particulary debatable were

(i) Taxation in the Doab (1326 AD)
(ii) Transfer of Capital (1327 AD)
(iii) Introduction of Token Currency (1329 AD)
(iv) Proposed Khurasan Expedition (1329 AD)
(v) Qarachi expedition (1330 AD)

16. Name two departments created by Firoz Shah Tughlaq.

Ans. Departments established by Firoz Shah Tughlaq were *Diwan-i-Khairat* (department for poor and needy people) and *Diwan-i-Bandagan* (department of slaves).

Structured Questions

1. There are various literary and archaeological sources to understand about the rule of Delhi Sultanate during medieval India. In context of the above explain

(i) Tarik-i-Firozshahi
(ii) Prithviraj Raso
(iii) Monuments

Ans. (i) Refer to chapter theory page no. 142.
(ii) Refer to chapter theory page no. 142.
(iii) Refer to chapter theory page no. 143.

2. Muhammad Ghori's conquest became the nucleus of a new political entity with the establishment of Turkish Empire in India. With reference to this, write short note on

(i) Razia Sultan
(ii) Qutb-ud-din Aibak
(iii) Shamsuddin Iltutmish
(iv) Balban

Ans. (i) Razia Sultan was the first and only Muslim lady who ever ruled India. She was the daughter of Iltutmish. She put an end to the turmoil created by Ruknuddin (brother) and restored law and order. She was popular among the people but she was not acceptable to the nobles and theologians who considered it below their dignity to be ruled by a woman.

(ii) Qutbud-Din Aibak was a Turkish slave who succeeded Mohammad Ghori in 1206 AD. He was the founder of Delhi Sultanate with its capital at Lahore. He earned the title of Lakh-baksh (Giver of Lakhs) for liberal distribution of money and his generosity. He laid the foundation of Qutub Minar in Delhi and built two mosques, one in Ajmer and the other one in Delhi.

(iii) Shamsuddin Iltutmish was a slave and son-in-law of Qutb-ud-din Aibak. He occupied the throne of Delhi in 1211 AD after removing Aram Bakhsh (son of Aibak). He was a very capable ruler and is regarded as the 'real founder of the Delhi Sultanate'.

(iv) Ghiyas-ud-din Balban ascended the throne in 1266 AD after killing Mahmud (youngest son of Iltutmish). He served as a General and Minister previously for 20 years (1246-1266 AD). He adopted the policy of Blood and Iron to establish a centralised army and to subdue rebel forces. He disbanded Turkan-i-Chahalgani or Chalisa.

3. With reference to the reign of Alauddin Khilji, explain

(i) Market regulations
(ii) Revenue reforms
(iii) Military reforms

Ans. (i) Refer to chapter theory page no. 144-145.
(ii) Refer to chapter theory page no. 145.
(iii) Refer to chapter theory page no. 145.

4. Muhammad bin Tughluq was a visionary king and tried to introduce many administrative reforms, but had to face severe criticism. In context of his reforms, explain.
   (i) Policy of Taxation in the Doab
   (ii) Introduction of Token Currency
   (iii) Transfer of Capital
   (iv) Qarachil Expedition

Ans. (i) Refer to chapter theory page no. 145.
(ii) Refer to chapter theory page no. 146.
(iii) Refer to chapter theory page no. 145-146.
(iv) Refer to chapter theory page no. 146.

5. With the reference of the Delhi Sultanate Administration. Explain
   (i) Central Administration
   (ii) Provincial Administration
   (iii) Judicial Administration
   (iv) Revenue Administration

Ans. (i) In central administration of Delhi Sultanate, the Sultan was the supreme executive, legislative, judicial and military authority. A number of ministers assisted him in administration. Wazir was an important figure in the administration who acted as Prime Minister. The work of the official was supervised by the Wazir.

(ii) During Delhi Sultanate, the empire was divided into provinces called Iqtas. Each province was controlled by officials called muqtis. The provinces were further divided into shiqs and parganas or districts in order to facilitate local administration.

(iii) There were two departments in judicial administration of Delhi Sultanate which were *Diwan-i-Risalat* and *Diwan-i-Insha*. The *Diwan-i-Risalat* was presided by the Chief *Sadar* (a leading *qazi*) and it dealt with the religious matters. The *Diwan-i-Insha* dealt with the state correspondence.

(iv) *Iqta* system was followed in Delhi Sultanate which was the practice of giving grants of revenue from a territory. Those who were given iqtas were called *iqtadars*. They maintain themselves, their families and some soldiers, from this grant.

Chapter Assessment

Section-I

Multiple Choice Questions

1. Qutb-ud-Din Aibak was the slave of ....
   (a) Muhammad Ghori (b) Muhammad Ghazini
   (c) Mir Qasim (d) Chengiz Khan
2. In which year Khilji Dynasty was founded
   (a) 1206 (b) 1290 (c) 1305 (d) 1320
3. Malik Kafur was the commander of
   (a) Qutb-ud-Din Aibak (b) Alauddin Khilji
   (c) Firoz Shah Tughlaq (d) Sikandar Lodhi
4. Complete the given analogy
   Slave Dynasty : 1206-1290 : : Khilji Dynasty :
   (a) 1290-1320 (b) 1320-1440
   (c) 1440-1451 (d) 1451-1526

Section-II

Short Questions

1. What do you understand by the term Delhi Sultanate?
2. Which language was developed during the period of Delhi Sultanate?
3. Which battle led to the advent of the rule of Muslims in India?
4. Why Tarikh-i-Firozshahi is regarded as an important source of History?
5. How did the Khilji dynasty emerge?
6. Name two reforms of Alauddin Khilji.
7. Who was the *Wazir*?

Structured Questions

1. With reference to the administration of the Delhi Sultanate, explain
   (i) Role of Sultan
   (ii) Various departments
   (iii) Role of *Wazir*
2. With reference to the structure of the society during the Delhi sultanate, explain
   (i) Condition of women
   (ii) Condition of Hindus
   (iii) Imposition of Jizya
   (iv) Taxation in Doab
3. Muhammad bin Tughluq was one of the important ruler of the Tughlaq dynasty. With reference to this, explain
   (i) Two ambitious projects
   (ii) Revolt during his reign
   (iii) Transfer of capital
   (iv) His death

CHAPTER 09

The Mughal Empire

SYLLABUS

The Mughal Empire Sources : Ain-i-Akbari, Taj Mahal, Jama Masjid and Red Fort.
Names of the Kings in chronological order.
Babur–The three battles waged to consolidate his empire. Akbar–Rajput policy, steps towards integration, social and educational reforms, mansabdari system.

The Mughal Emperors were Central Asian Turco-Mongols belonging to the Timurid dynasty, who claimed direct descent from **Genghis Khan** (founder of the Mongol Empire) through his son Chagatai Khan and **Timur** (Turco-Mongol conqueror who founded the Timurid Empire).

Sources of the Mughal Empire

There are various types of sources of Mughal history such as autobiographies, court chronicles, historical works and the accounts of the foreign travellers.

Literary Sources

One of the most important literary sources of the Mughal dynasty is **Ain-i-Akbari**. The Ain-i-Akbari is a 16th century, detailed document recording the administration of Emperor Akbar's Empire. It was written by his *Wazir* Abu'l Fazl ibn Mubarak who was also one of the nine jewels of Akbar's court.

The Ain-i-Akbari is written in Persian. It is divided into five books, which are

(i) First book deals with the imperial household.

(ii) Second book deals with the servants of the emperor, the military and civil services.

(iii) Third book deals with the imperial administration, containing the regulations for the judicial and executive departments.

(iv) Fourth book provide information about Hindu philosophy, science, social customs and literature.

(v) Fifth book contains sayings of Akbar, an account of the ancestry and biography of the author.

Archaeological Sources

Monuments

Mughal buildings have a uniform pattern of structure and character, including large round domes, slender minarets at the corners, massive halls, large vaulted gateways and delicate ornamentation.

Several monuments were built during Mughal Empire. The most important monuments which are also great source of information about Mughal Empire are

Taj Mahal

The Taj Mahal was built by Shah Jahan, in memory of his beloved wife, Mumtaz Mahal. The work started in 1631 and was finished in 1653. **Ustad Isa Khan** was the master architect of this monument. It had taken about 22 years to complete the whole project. It is situated on the bank of Yamuna river in Agra.

The special features of the Taj Mahal are

- It is made of pure white marble with its special shine and fine texture. The marble has been obtained from Makrana in Rajasthan.
- The central dome rises to a height of 56 metres and has the appearance of an inverted Lotus. There are four smaller domes at the four corners of the building.
- The main structure is surrounded by gardens, fountains and pools.
- The mausoleum is built on a 6.6 metres high plinth. The lower portion is square in design and rises to a height of 32 metres. The graves of Shah Jahan and Mumtaz are in lower chamber underground.
- The interior octagonal chambers are connected to one another by diagonal passages. This pattern is similar to the one followed in Humayun's tomb in Delhi.
- The interior and the exterior of the main building are decorated with screens, calligraphy and inlay work.
- At each of the four corners of the main structure, there is a minaret.
- Due to its splendid beauty and magnificence, it is considered to be one of the seven wonders of the world.
- The Taj Mahal was declared as World Heritage Site by UNESCO in 1983 and also included in Seven Wonders of the world in 2007.

Taj Mahal

Jama Masjid

The Jama Masjid in Delhi was built by Mughal Emperor Shah Jahan during 1650-1656. The main architect was **Ustad Khalil**. It is the largest Mosque in India and has the capacity to accommodate thousands of people at a time. Its main architectural features are

- There are three gateways to the Jama Masjid mosque i.e. on the South, East and North sides.
- The central dome is the largest and highest, made of white marble, decorated with stripes of black colour. On the North and South sides, there are two elegant tapering minaret.
- The chief feature of this building is its symmetry and harmony.
- The face of its spacious prayer hall consists of eleven arches of which the central arch rises till above the roof level.

Red Fort

The Red Fort or *Lal Qila* was built by Shah Jahan when he decided to transfer his capital to Delhi. He began its construction in 1639 and completed it in 1648. Since the Independence of India, every year the Prime Minister of India unfurls the National flag from the ramparts of the Red Fort on the Independence Day.

Its main features are

- It was built by red sandstone and marble on the bank of the Yamuna. Originally, it was known as ***Qila-e-Mubarak***.
- The fort is in the form of a parallelogram measuring 930 metres by 495 metres.
- It is surrounded by a strongly fortified wall.
- The Lahori and Delhi Gates were used by the Public and the Khizrabad Gate was for the emperor.
- Some of the prominent buildings in this fort are *Diwan-i-Aam*, the *Diwan-i-Khas* and the *Rang Mahal*. These buildings are decorated with pure white marble and inlaid with precious stones. Later on Aurangzeb built the Moti Masjid in the Red Fort.

Check Your LEARNING...

1. Name the author of Ain-i-Akbari.
2. What materials were used to make Taj Mahal?
3. Who was the architect of Jama Masjid?
4. What was the original name of Red Fort?

Major Rulers of the Mughal Empire

The major rulers of the Mughal Empire were

- Babur
- Akbar
- Aurangzeb
- Shah Jahan

Babur (1526-1530)

Babur was the founder of Mughal Empire in India. He was the son of Umar Shaikh Mirza, the ruler of Farghana (Uzbekistan). He was related to Timur from his father's side and Genghis Khan to his mother's side. His original name was **Zahir-ud-din Muhammad**.

Babur succeeded to the throne of Farghana at a very early age of 11 years. He wanted to occupy the capital of Timur Samarkard. He captured it twice but was unable to retain it. Babur established himself in Kabul (Afghanistan) in 1504 and then directed his intention towards India.

Daulat Khan, the most significant noble of Punjab, who was dissatisfied with Ibrahim Lodhi, invited Babur to capture India. Babur defeated Ibrahim Lodhi in the First Battle of Panipat in 1526 and established Mughal rule in India.

The three battles waged to consolidate Babur's Empire

Battle of Panipat

The First Battle of Panipat (1526) was fought between Babur and Ibrahim Lodi. Babur, who had come from Central Asia, aimed to establish his rule in Northern India. In this battle, Babur's army defeated Ibrahim Lodi. This battle marked the end of the Delhi Sultanate and the beginning of the Mughal Empire in India.

Battle of Khanwa

The Battle of Khanwa (1527) was fought between Babur and the Rajput ruler of Mewar, Rana Sanga. Sanga had formed a large coalition of Rajput chiefs to challenge Babur's control over Northern India. In this battle, Rana Sanga was defeated. This defeat of Rana Sanga strengthened Babur's position in India and ensured the continuation of Mughal rule over the Northern territories.

Battle of Ghaghra

The Battle of Ghaghra (1529) was fought between Babur and combined forces of Afghan and Rajput soldiers led by Mahmud Lodi, the younger brother of Ibrahim Lodi. The battle took place near the Ghaghra River in present-day Bihar. Babur's forces won a decisive victory and this victory solidified Babur's control over the Eastern region of India.

Babur was succeeded by his son Humayun who was further succeeded by his son Akbar.

Akbar (1556-1605)

Akbar was the greatest of all the Mughal rulers of India He was crowned at Kalanaur at the age of 13 years. Bairam Khan, the tutor of the Prince, became the *Wakil* of the kingdom with the title of *Khan-i-Khana* and rallied the Mughal forces.

Wars fought and campaigns led by Akbar were

- Akbar's first conflict was with Hemu, a general of Adil Shah. On receipt of the news of the capture of Agra and Delhi, Bairam Khan marched to meet Hemu. The two armies met at Panipat in 1556 which is called **Second Battle of Panipat**. Hemu fought bravely in this battle but was defeated and Akbar re-occupied Delhi and Agra.
- Akbar's other campaigns were against *Durgawa of Garh-Katanga* (Gond and Rajput principalties) followed by Chittor.
- Akbar's Deccan campaign began with the siege of Ahmednagar (defended by Chand Bibi). Ahmednagar soon revive itself under the leadership of Malik Amber.
- In 1562, Akbar' made his first pilgrimage to the mausoleum of the Sufi Saint, Sheikh Moin-ud-din Chishti, at Ajmer. On the way, he received Raja Bharmal of Ajmer who made his submission without fighting.
- In 1572, Akbar faced a rebellion in Gujarat, which was crushed by him and to mark this victory, he built the **Buland Darwaza** at Fatehpur Sikri.
- Akbar conquered Gujarat (1572-1573) and Bengal (1574-1576).
- In 1576, the famous **Battle of Haldighati** was fought between Maharana Pratap (ruler of Mewar) and the Mughal army led by Raja Man Singh. Maharana Pratap escaped from the battle when he was heavily wounded.
- In 1591, Akbar sent four missions to the rulers of Khandesh, Ahmednagar, Bijapur and Golconda, calling upon them to recognise his partial control and pay him tribute. Khandesh ruler offered his submission. Ahmednagar was captured in 1600.
- By 1595, Akbar's armies had conquered Kashmir, Sindh, Odisha, Central India and Qandhar.
- Akbar's last campaign was against Asirgarh, resulting in the annexation of Khandesh (1601).

Akbar died in 1605 after which Jahangir (1605-1627) succeeded the throne. After Jahangir, Shah Jahan (1627-1658) succeeded the throne.

Rajput Policy of Akbar

The Rajput Policy of Akbar is praised by many historians. According to this policy, he married the daughter of Raja Bharmal, thus maintaining friendly relations with them. He followed the policy of religious tolerence and gave the Rajputs noble positions in the Mughal government and thus ended the centuries old hatred between Muslim rulers and the Rajputs. But still the Ranas of Mewar resisted Muslim rule.

Integration of the People by Akbar

Akbar took a number of steps to promote greater understanding between the Hindus and the Muslims. Through these steps he created an atmosphere in which liberal views could grow and finally cultural and emotional integration of the people could develop.

Some of these steps were

- To strengthen the liberal principles, Akbar enrolled a number of Hindus into the nobility. While most of these were Rajput Rajas, many of whom entered into a matrimonial alliances with Akbar, *mansabs* (position or rank) were given to others on the basis of their competence.
- Akbar abolished *Jizya* tax, which the non-Muslims were required to pay. He also abolished the pilgrim tax on bathing holy places such as Prayag and Benaras. Further, he abolished the practice of forcibly converting prisoners of war to Islam.

- In 1575, Akbar built **Ibadat Khana** or Hall of Prayer at Fatehpur Sikhri. At this hall, he used to call selected theologians of all religions, mystics and intellectuals and discuss religious and spiritual matters with them.
- In 1579, Akbar issued a 'Declaration' or *mazhar* which made him the supreme or final authority in religious matters and replaced the power of ulema by the power of Emperor.
- In 1582, Akbar promoted a new religion called ***Din-i-Ilahi***. It was based on the principle of oneness of God.The new religion stressed on virtues like courage, loyalty and justice. It also demanded loyalty to the Emperor. The basic purpose of forming *Din-i-Ilahi* was *Sulh-i-Kul* or universal harmony which governed all public policies of Akbar.
- Akbar set up a big translation department for translating works in Sanskrit, Arabic and Greek into Persian. Some of the books which were translated in Persian are Quran, Bible, the Mahabharata, the Gita and the Ramayana.

Educational and Social Reforms of Akbar

- The Education system in Mughal period during Akbar was in advance of his age and made an attempt to raise the intellectual level of the people.
- Akbar emphasised over the study of secular subjects such as mathematics, logic, history and astronomy apart from the study of religious scriptures.
- During Mughal period female education also existed.
- Akbar prohibited the practice of 'sati' and legalised the remarriages of widows.
- Akbar did not encourage child marriages.
- The minimum age for the marriage of girls was raised to 14 years, while the age of the marriage of boys was raised to 16 years. Consent of both bride and bridegroom was necessary before marriage.
- Akbar abolished all inland customs and taxes on trades and professions.

Contribution of Mughal Emperors to Education

Mughal Emperors were the patrons of education and there was considerable development in this area by them. In the fact one of the duties of the public works department, **Shuhra-i-am** was to build schools and colleges.

Jahangir passed a law, whereby if a rich man was to die without an hier, his assests would be used by the State to help in the development and maintenance of educational institutes. Shah Jahan also took some significant educational initiatives like providing scholarships to assist students.

Later Mughals

After Aurangzeb the power of succession started among his three sons, Muazzam, Azam and Kam Baksh. Muazzam ascended the Mughal throne with the title of Bahadur Shah. He pursued **pacifism**[1] policy. Therefore, he was also called **Shahi Bekhabar**.

After Muazzam many emperors followed, but all of them proved to be weak successors. The invasions of Nadir Shah (1739) and Ahmed Shah Abdali (1761) destroyed the Mughal Empire to a large extent.

In 1764 in the Battle of Buxar, the Mughal Emperor Shah Alam II was defeated by the English East India Company. **Bahadur Shah Zafar** was the last Mughal king who was confined by the British to the Red Fort. During the Revolt of 1857, he was proclaimed the emperor by the rebellions. However, he was deported to Rangoon (Myanmar) following the 1857 rebellion.

Check Your LEARNING...

1. When did Babur got the title of 'Ghazi'?
2. Who shifted the capital from Agra to Delhi?
3. What was 'Din-i-ilahi'?
4. Among whom, the battle of Khanwa was fought?

Administration of the Mughal Empire

The Mughal Empire did not try to intervene in the local societies during most of its existence, but rather balanced and pacified them through new administrative system.

Central Administration

The head of the Mughal administration was the emperor. He appointed a number of officers in different departments of the government for the transactions of the multitudinal affairs. These were

- The office of *Wazir* or *Wakil* enjoyed great power in civil and military affairs.
- The *Dewan* was the head of exchequer and the sole incharge of revenue and finance.
- *Mir Bakshi* was the officer responsible for military pay and accounts. He was also responsible for the recruiting soldiers of the army and for maintaining list of *Mansabdars* and other high officials.

1. **Pacifism** It is the opposition and resistance to war, militarism or violence.

Provincial Administration

For the purpose of smooth administration and revenue collection, the Mughal Empire was divided into several provinces known as ***Subas***. Akbar divided his empire into 12 *Subas* which rose to fifteen towards the end of his reign. Successively, they rose to 17 at the time of Jahangir's reign, 19 in the reign of Shah Jahan and 21 in the reign of Aurangzeb.

Local Administration

The *Subas* were divided into *Sarkars* and the *Sarkars* were sub-divided into *Parganas* at the village level. A village was the lowest administrative unit in the Mughal system of administration.

Judicial Administration

The Mughal rulers possessed a great sense of justice and tried to establish an efficient system of judicial administration. The king was at the apex of the judicial administration. The courts of *Sadr-us-Sadur* and *Qazi-ul-Qzat* were next to the king's court. *Sadr-us-Sadur* decided the religious cases and the *Qazi-ul-Qzat* decided all other cases.

Military Administration

The ***Mir Bakhshi*** was incharge of the military department. He managed the recruitment of the soldiers, branding of the horses and the elephants, supplies to the army and training of the soldiers. He also deputed *Mansabdars* for the security of the palace and changed them every day.

The *Mir-i-Atish* or *Daroga-i-Topkhana* was the incharge of the artillery of the emperor.

Mansabdari System

Mansabdari system was made up of the Mughal officers known as *mansabdars*. These officers were given specific rank or *mansab* either in bureaucracy, military hierarchy or the nobility. The lowest rank was 10 and the highest was 5000.

These ranks had two divisions

(i) ***Zat*** It indicated the status or rank of a person and how much he is to be paid.

(ii) ***Sawar*** It stands for the designated number of horse with horseman, he had to maintain. For example, for every 10 cavalrymen, 20 horses were to be kept.

The person holding ranks below 500 **zat** were called *mansabdars*, those holding more than 500, but below 2,500 were called ***amirs*** and those holding ranks of 2,500 and above were called *amir-i-umda* or *amir-i-azam* or *omrahs*.

The *mansab* was not hereditary and it automatically lapsed after the death or dismissal of the *mansabdar*. The son of a *mansabdar*, if he was granted a *mansab*, had to begin afresh.

Another important feature of the *mansabdari* system was the law of escheat or *zabti*. According to it, when a *mansabdar* died, all his property was confiscated by the emperor.

Land Revenue System

There was no Mughal land revenue system before Akbar and his predecessors continued with the existing land revenue system.

A proper land revenue system was founded by Akbar, and Todar Mal drew up schemes for effective tax collection. A uniform system of measurement was established for calculating the land tax.

Check Your LEARNING...

1. Name some books that were translated into Persian language during Akbar's reign?
2. Mughal Emperor Akbar divided his empire into how many subas?
3. In the mansabdari system, what was 'zat'?
4. What was the law of zabti in mansabdar?

QUiCK Revision

- The Mughal Empire began with the Babur's victory in the First Battle of Panipat (1526) over Ibrahim Lodhi, who was the last ruler of the Delhi Sultanate.
- One of the most important literary sources of the Mughal dynasty is Ain-i-Akbari. The Ain-i-Akbari is a 16th century, detailed document recording the administration of Emperor Akbar's Empire, written by his *Wazir* who was also one of the nine jewels of Akbar's court, Abu'l-Fazl ibn Mubarak.
- Mughal buildings have a uniform pattern of structure and character, including large bulbous domes, slender minarets at the corners, massive halls, large vaulted gateways and delicate ornamentation.
- The Taj Mahal was built by Shah Jahan, in the memory of his beloved wife, Mumtaz Mahal. The work started in 1631 and was finished in 1653.
- The Jama Masjid in Delhi was built by Mughal Emperor Shah Jahan during 1650-1656. The main architect was Ustak Khalil.
- The Red Fort or *Lal Qila* was built by Shah Jahan when he decided to transfer his capital to Delhi. He began its construction in 1639 and completed it in 1648.
- The Mughal Emperors were a branch of the Timurid dynasty mainly corresponding to the modern countries of India, Pakistan and Bangladesh from the early 16th century to the early 18th century.
- Babur was the founder of Mughal Empire in India. He was the son of Umar Shaikh Mirza, the ruler of Farghana (Uzbekistan).
- Akbar was crowned at Kalanaur at the age of 13 years. The Rajput Policy of Akbar is praised by many historians. He married the daughter of Raja Bharmal, thus maintaining friendly relations with them.
- After the death of Akbar in 1605, his son Salim sat on the throne by the name of Nuruddin Jahangir. Jahangir was instrumental in restoration of the Mohammedan faith and Hijra Chronology (on coins).
- The head of the Mughal administration was the emperor. He appointed a number of officers in different department like *wazir*, *Dewan*, *Mir Bakshi*, *Khan-i-Saman*, *Qazi*, and *Sadr-us-Sadr* etc.
- For the purpose of smooth administration and revenue collection, the empire was divided into several provinces known as *Subas*.
- The *Subas* were divided into *Sarkars* and the *Sarkars* were sub-divided into *Parganas* at the village level.
- The Mughal rulers possessed a great sense of justice and tried to establish an efficient system of judicial administration.
- The *Mir Bakhshi* was incharge of the military department. He managed the recruitment of the soldiers, branding of the horses and the elephants, supplies to the army and training of the soldiers.
- Mansabdari system was made up of the Mughal officers known as *mansabdars*. These officers were given specific rank or *mansab* either in bureaucracy, military hierarchy or the nobility. The lowest rank was 10 and the highest was 5000 and these ranks had two divisions.
- Akbar made corrections and precisions in the existing system by standardisation of measurement of land, ascertaining the produce per *Bigha* (half acre) of land, fixation of status share in that product and fixing rate of Assessment or *Dahsala or zabti* system.

Chapter Practice

Section-I

Multiple Choice Questions

1. The book Ain-i-Akbari was written in which language?
   (a) Persian (b) Urdu
   (c) Arabic (d) Hindi

Ans. (a) Persian

2. Which of the followng part of the book Ain-i-Akbari deals with Hindu philosophy, science, social customs and literature ?
   (a) First book (b) Second book
   (c) Third book (d) Fourth book

Ans. (d) Fourth book

3. The Taj Mahal was built by Shah Jahan in the memory of
   (a) Harku bai (b)Jodha Bai
   (c) Mumtaz Mahal (d) Noorjahan

Ans. (c) Mumtaz Mahal

4. Who built the Red Fort?
   (a) Babur (b) Akbar
   (c) Shah Jahan (d) Humayun

Ans. (c) Shah Jahan

5. Who was the first ruler of Mughal Empire?
   (a) Akbar (b) Babur
   (c) Shah Jahan (d) Jahangir

Ans. (b) Babur

6. In which year Battle of Ghagra was fought?
   (a) 1526 (b) 1527
   (c) 1529 (d) 1530

Ans. (c) 1529

7. Tuzuk-i-Baburi was written by
   (a) Babur (b) Jahangir
   (c) Humayun (d) Aurangzeb

Ans. (a) Babur

8. Akbar was crowned at the age of
   (a) 12 (b) 13
   (c) 14 (d) 15

Ans. (b) 13

9. Second Battle of Panipat was fought between
   (a) Akbar and Hemu
   (b) Maharana Pratap and Akbar
   (c) Aurangzeb and Hemu
   (d) Babur and Ibrahim Lodhi

Ans. (a) Akbar and Hemu

10. The Battle of Haldighati was fought between Maharana Pratap and Akbar in
    (a) 1526 (b) 1556 (c) 1572 (d) 1576

Ans. (d) 1576

11. Who built 'Ibadat Khana' in 1575?
    (a) Jahangir (b) Humayun
    (c) Akbar (d) Aurangzeb

Ans. (c) Akbar

12. Who introduced *Din-I-Ilahi*?
    (a) Babur (b) Akbar
    (c) Shah Jahan (d) Bahadur Shah Zafar

Ans. (b) Akbar

13. Complete the given analogy.
    Babur: Humayun :: Akbar: ?
    (a) Jahangir (b) Aurangzeb
    (c) Shah Jahan (d) Bahadur Shah Zafar

Ans. (a) Jahangir

14. Complete the given analogy.
    Ist Battle of Panipat : 1526 :: Battle of Khanwa : ?
    (a) 1527 (b) 1528 (c) 1529 (d) 1530

Ans. (a) 1527

15. Complete the given analogy.
    Ibadat Khana: 1575 : : *Din-i-Ilahi* : ?
    (a) 1572 (b) 1576 (c) 1582 (d) 1585

Ans. (c) 1582

16. Replace the underlined word to correct the statement.
    <u>Aurangzeb</u> abolished all inland customs and taxes on trades and professions.
    (a) Akbar (b) Humayun
    (c) Jahangir (d) Sher Shah Suri

Ans. (a) Akbar

17. Replace the underlined word to correct the statement.
    In 1575, <u>Babur</u> built Ibadat Khana.
    (a) Akbar (b) Humayun
    (c) Shah Jahan (d) Aurangzeb

Ans. (a) Akbar

18. Consider the following statements associated with Akbar and choose the correct option.
    (i) Persian language became widespread in the Mughal Empire by the time of Akbar's reign.
    (ii) Akbar patronised Tansen of Gwalior.

(iii) During Akbar's reign, the Humayun's tomb was built.

(iv) To strengthen the liberal principles, Akbar enrolled a number of Hindus into the nobility.

Codes

(a) Only (i) (b) Both (i) and (ii)
(c) (i), (ii) and (iii) (d) All of these

Ans. (d) All of these

19. Consider the following statements and choose the correct option.

(i) Humayun succeeded Babur in 1530.

(ii) Akbar introduced the *mansabdari* system.

(iii) Jharoka Darshan was introduced by Akbar.

(iv) Akbar promoted a new religion called 'Din-i-Ilahi'.

Codes

(a) Only (i) (b) Both (i) and (ii)
(c) (i), (ii) and (iii) (d) All of these

Ans. (d) All of these

20. Match the following.

List-I	List-II
A. First Battle of Panipat	1. 1528
B. Second Battle of Panipat	2. 1576
C. Battle of Haldighati	3. 1556
D. Battle of Chanderi	4. 1526

Codes

	A	B	C	D
(a)	4	3	2	1
(b)	1	2	3	4
(c)	3	1	4	2
(d)	2	4	1	3

Ans. (a)

21. Match the following.

List-I	List-II
A. Raja Man Singh	1. Advisor of Akbar and main Commander
B. Raja Todarmal	2. Musician
C. Birbal	3. Finance Minister
D. Tansen	4. Mansabdar

Codes

	A	B	C	D
(a)	1	2	3	4
(b)	4	3	2	1
(c)	4	3	1	2
(d)	2	1	4	3

Ans. (c)

Picture Based Question

22. Look at the picture given below and answer the following questions.

(i) Identify the picture.

(a) Taj Mahal (b) Jama Masjid
(c) Red Fort (d) Agra Fort

Ans. (c) Red Fort

(ii) This monument was built by ....

(a) Akbar (b) Humayun
(c) Shah Jahan (d) Jahangir

Ans. (c) Shah Jahan

(iii) The monument was completed in

(a) 1526 (b) 1639
(c) 1648 (d) 1668

Ans. (c) 1648

(iv) This Fort is located at which place?

(a) Delhi (b) Lucknow
(c) Agra (d) Jaipur

Ans. (a) Delhi

Passage Based Questions

23. Read the passage given below and answer the following questions.

The Akbar Nama is divided into three books of which the first two are chronicles. The third book is the Ain-i-Akbari. The first volume contains the history of mankind from Adam to one celestial cycle of Akbar's life (30 years). The second volume closes in the fortysixth regnal year (1601) of Akbar. The very next year Abu'l Fazl fell victim to a conspiracy hatched by Prince Salim and was murdered by his accomplice, Bir Singh Bundela. The Akbar Nama was written to provide a detailed description of Akbar's reign in the traditional diachronic sense of recording politically significant events across time, as well as in the more novel sense of giving a synchronic picture of all aspects of Akbar's empire - geographic, social, administrative and cultural- without reference to chronology.

(i) Akbar Nama was written by which of the following?

(a) Abu'l Fazl
(b) Nizamuddin Ahmad
(c) Aurangzeb
(d) Shah Jahan

Ans. (a) Abu'l Fazl

(ii) The reign of Akbar was

(a) 1526-1530 (b) 1530-1556
(c) 1556-1605 (d) 1658-1707

Ans. (c) 1556-1605

(iii) .... was succeeded by Akbar.

(a) Babur (b) Jahangir
(c) Humayun (d) Shah Jahan

Ans. (c) Humayun

(iv) In which year Ibadat Khana was built by Akbar?

(a) 1575 (b) 1580
(c) 1585 (d) 1590

Ans. (d) 1575

24. Read the passage given below and answer the following questions.

The name Mughal derives from Mongol. Though today the term evokes the grandeur of an empire, it was not the name the rulers of the dynasty choose for themselves. They referred to themselves as Timurids, as descendants of the Turkish ruler Timur on the paternal side. Babur, the first Mughal ruler, was related to Genghiz Khan from his mother's side. He spoke Turkish and referred derisively to the Mongols as barbaric hordes.

The empire was carved out of a number of regional states of India through conquests and political alliances between the Mughals and local chieftains. The founder of the empire, Zahiruddin Babur, was driven from his Central Asian homeland, Farghana, by the warring Uzbeks.

(i) Who was the founder Mughal Empire?
(a) Babur (b) Genghiz Khan (c) Jahangir (d) Akbar

Ans. (a) Babur

(ii) Who was Genghiz Khan?
(a) Founder of Mongol Empire
(b) Turkish invaders
(c) Arab invaders
(d) Founder of Mughal Empire

Ans. (a) Founder of Mongol Empire

(iii) The first Battle of Panipat was fought between Babur and ....
(a) Bahlol Lodhi (b) Sikander Lodhi
(c) Ibrahim Lodhi (d) Feroz Shah Tughlaq

Ans. (c) Ibrahim Lodhi

(iv) In which year Mughal Empire was founded ?
(a) 1526 (b) 1536 (c) 1530 (d) 1550

Ans. (a) 1526

Section-II

Short Questions

1. Who wrote Ain-i-Akbari?

Ans. Ain-i-Akbari was written by Abu'l-Fazl ibn Mubarak. He was the *Wazir* of Akbar and one of the nine jewels of Akbar's court.

2. What is the subject matter of the Fourth book of Ain-i-Akbari?

Ans. The Fourth book of Ain-i-Akbari provided information about Hindu philosophy, science, social customs and literature.

3. How far the monuments made its significance during the Mughal period?

Ans. Monuments made its significance in the Mughal period by marking revival of Islamic architecture in Northern India. Mughal buildings have a uniform pattern of structure and character, including large round domes, slender minarets at the corners, massive halls, large vaulted gateways and delicate ornamentation.

4. When did the Mughal architecture flourish?

Ans. Mughal architecture and building style flourished in Northern and Central India under the patronage of the Mughal Emperors from the mid-16th to the late 17th century.

5. Mention two features of Taj Mahal.

Ans. The special features of the Taj Mahal are

- It is made of pure white marble with its special lustre and fine texture. The marble was obtained from Makrana in Rajasthan.
- The main structure is surrounded by gardens, fountains and pools.

6. How did the Mughal Empire establish in India?

Ans. The Mughal Empire established in India with the Babur's victory over Ibrahim Lodhi (the last ruler of the Delhi Sultanate) in the First Battle of Panipat (1526).

7. Who wrote *Tuzuk-i-Baburi* and in which language? What does it depicts?

Ans. *Tuzuk-i-Baburi* was written by Babur himself in Turkish language.

It describes the flora and fauna of India and provides detailed record of his entire career.

8. What is the importance of Bairam Khan in the life of Akbar?

Ans. Akbar was under the protection of Bairam Khan when he became the Mughal Emperor. Bairam Khan, the tutor of the Prince, became the *Wakil* of the kingdom with the title of *Khan-i-Khana* and rallied the Mughal forces.

9. Give an account of the Second Battle of Panipat?

Ans. The Second Battle of Panipat was fought between Mughal Emperor Akbar and Hemu, a general of Adil Shah (Adil Shahi dynasty). Hemu fought bravely, but was defeated in this battle and Akbar reoccupied Delhi and Agra.

10. What was the importance of the Gujarat campaign of Akbar?

Ans. The importance of Gujarat campaign of Akbar was that he crushed the rebellion in Gujarat in 1572 and built the Buland Darwaza at Fatehpur Sikri.

11. How did Akbar get his first victory in Rajasthan?

Ans. Akbar's first victory in Rajasthan was won without bloodshed. In 1562, he made his first pilgrimage to the mausoleum of the Sufi Saint, Sheikh Moin-ud-Din Chishti, at Ajmer. On the way, he received Raja Bharmal of Ajmer who made his submission without fighting.

12. How was the Deccan campaign of Akbar?

Ans. In 1591, Akbar sent four missions to the rulers of Khandesh, Ahmednagar, Bijapur and Golconda, calling upon them to recognise his partial control and pay him tribute. Khandesh ruler offered his submission. By 1595, Akbar's armies had conquered Kashmir, Sindh, Odisha, Central India and Qandhar. Ahmednagar was captured in 1600.

13. What was the Rajput policy of Akbar?

Ans. The Rajput Policy of Akbar is praised by many historians. According to this policy, he married the daughter of Raja Bharmal, thus maintaining friendly relations with them. But still the Ranas of Mewar remained defiant to Muslim rule. Rana Pratap was defeated by the Mughal army in 1576.

14. Who fought in the First Battle of Panipat and what was it's outcome?

Ans. The First Battle of Panipat was fought between Babur and Ibrahim Lodi. Babur won the battle, marking the beginning of the Mughal Empire in India.

15. What was the significance of the Second Battle of Panipat 1556?

Ans. The Second Battle of Panipat was fought between Akbar and Hemu. It restored Mughal power in Northern India after Hemu's defeat, solidifying Akbar's rule.

16. Who became the Mughal ruler after the death of Aurangzeb?

Ans. Muazzam became the Mughal ruler with the title of Bahadur Shah Zafar after the death of Aurangzeb. Aurangzeb died in 1707.

17. Give a brief account of the last Mughal ruler.

Ans. The last Mughal ruler was Bahadur Shah Zafar who was confined by the British to the Red Fort. During the Revolt of 1857, he was proclaimed the emperor by the rebellions. However, he was deported to Rangoon following the 1857 rebellion.

18. What was the role of Mughal Emperor in the central administration?

Ans. The role of Mughal Emperor in the central administration was that he was the head of the Mughal administration. He appointed a number of officers in different departments of the government for the transactions of the multitudinal affairs.

19. Mention the numbers of *Subas* in the provincial administration of the Mughal Empire.

Ans. For the purpose of smooth administration and revenue collection, the Mughal Empire was divided into several provinces known as *Subas*. Akbar divided his empire into twelve *Subas* which rose to fifteen towards the end of his reign. Successively they rose to seventeen in the reign of Jahangir's, nineteen in the reign of Shah Jahan and twenty-one in the reign of Aurangzeb.

20. What was the importance of *Daroga-i-Dak Chowki*?

Ans. *Daroga-i-Dak Chowki* was an important officer of the provinces for conducting intelligence and postal system.

21. What were the sub-divisions of *Subas*?

Ans. The *Subas* were divided into *Sarkars* and the *Sarkars* were sub-divided into *Parganas* at the village level.

22. Who was *Shiqdar*? Which officers assisted him?

Ans. *Shiqdar* was incharge of the general administration, who had to maintain law and order of a *Pargana*.

Shiqdar was assisted by an *Amil* (Revenue Collector), an *Amin* (Revenue Assessor), a *Potadar* (Treasurer), *Qanungo* (Record Keeper of Land) and few *Bitikchis* (Writers or Clerks).

23. What was the lowest administrative unit in the Mughal system of administration? Who headed it?

Ans. A village was the lowest administrative unit in the Mughal system of administration.

The village head was known as *Muqaddam*. He was assisted by the *Patwari*, who took care of village revenue records.

24. Who was *Mir Bakshi*? What was his role in the administrative structure of Mughals Empire?

Ans. The *Mir Bakhshi* was incharge of the military department.

He managed the recruitment of the soldiers, branding of the horses and the elephants, supplies to the army and training of the soldiers.

25. Who was *Mir-i-Atish*?

Ans. The *Mir-i-Atish* or *Daroga-i-Topkhana* was the incharge of the artillery of the emperor. It was an important office and was mostly assigned to a Turk or a Persian.

26. What do you understand by the *mansabdari* system?

Ans. *Mansabdari* system was made up of the Mughal officers known as *mansabdars*. These officers were given specific rank or *mansab* either in bureaucracy, military hierarchy or the nobility. The lowest rank was 10 and the highest was 5000.

27. Who held *mansabs*?

Ans. The *mansabdars* formed the ruling group in the Mughal Empire. Almost the whole nobility, the bureaucracy as well as the military hierarchy, held *mansabs*.

28. What was the mode of payment of the *mansabs*?

Ans. The *mansabdars* of the Mughal Empire received their pay either in cash or in the form of assignments of areas of land or jagir from which they were entitled to collect the land revenue and all other taxes sanctioned by the emperor.

29. What were the two ranks under *mansabdari* system?

Ans. The Mughal *mansab* was dual, represented by two members, one designated *zat* (personal rank) and the other *sawar* (cavalry rank). The chief use of *zat* was to place the holders in an appropriate position in the official hierarchy.

30. What were the different categories of *mansabdars*?

Ans. The person holding ranks below 500 zat were called *mansabdars*, those holding more than 500, but below 2,500 were called amirs and those holding ranks of 2,500 and above were called *amir-i-umda* or *amir-i-azam* or omrahs.

31. What was the system of the law of escheat?

Ans. Escheat or *zabti* was an important law of the *mansabdari* system. According to it, when a *mansabdar* died, all his property was confiscated by the emperor.

32. State the corrections and precision made in the land revenue system by Akbar.

Ans. The corrections and precision in the land revenue system made by Akbar were

- Standardisation of measurement of land.
- Ascertaining the produce per *Bigha* (half Acre) of Land.
- Fixation of status share in that produce.
- Fixing rate of Assessment or *Dahsala or Zabti* system.

Structured Questions

1. There is no scarcity of material sources of Mughal history, in context of the above explain

(i) Ain-i-Akbari
(ii) Red Fort
(iii) Jama Masjid
(iv) Taj Mahal

Ans. (i) Refer to chapter theory page no. 154.

(ii) Refer to chapter theory page no. 155.

(iii) Refer to chapter theory page no. 155.

(iv) Refer to chapter theory page no. 154-155.

2. With referrence to the Mughal Dynasty and advent of Babur, Explain,

(i) Background of Mughal Dynasty.
(ii) Background of Babur before invading India.
(iii) Babur's role in the political history of India.
(iv) First Battle of Panipat.

Ans. (i) The Mughal dynasty was of Central Asian Turco Mongols (now part of modern day Uzbekistan), belonging to the Timurid dynasty, who claimed direct descent from both Genghiz Khan (founder of Mongol Empire) and Timur (Turco-Mongol conqueror who founded the Timurid Empire).

(ii) Zahiruddin Muhammad was the original name of Babur. He was the son of Umar Shaikh Mirza, the ruler of Farghana(Uzbekistan). Babur was related to Timur from his father's side and Genghiz Khan to his mothers side.

He succeeded to the throne of Farghana at a very early age of 11 years. Babur wanted to occupy the capital of Timur, Samarkand but was unable to retain it after capturing it twice. So, he established himself in Kabul (Afghanistan) in 1504 and then directed his intention towards India.

(iii) Babur was the founder of Mughal Empire in India. He defeated Ibrahim Lodhi in the First Battle of Panipat in 1526 and established Mughal rule in India. He defeated Rana Sanga of Mewar in the Battle of Khanwa in 1527 near Agra and secured his position in the Delhi and Agra region and also assumed the title of 'Ghazi'. Babur also defeated the Afghans in the battle of Ghagra in Bihar. Babur, himself wrote *Tuzuk- i-Baburi* in Turkish language which provides detailed record of his entire career.

(iv) The First Battle of Panipat was fought between Babur and Ibrahim Lodhi in 1526. Ibrahim Lodhi was defeated by Babur. It marked the beginning of the Mughal Empire. This was one of the earliest battle involving gunpowder firearms and field artillery.

3. Akbar is considered to be one of the greatest ruler of Indian history, with reference to this explain

(i) Akbar's accession to the throne
(ii) Rajput policy of Akbar
(iii) Expeditions of Akbar

Ans. (i) Akbar succeeded to the throne after the death of Humayun. Akbar was crowned at an early age of 13 years, under the protection of Bairam Khan in 1556-1560. Bairam Khan, tutor of the prince, became the *Wakil* of the kingdom with the title of *Khan-i-Khana* and rallied the Mughal forces.

(ii) Refer to chapter theory page no. 158.

(iii) The expeditions of Akbar were

- Akbar's first conflict was with Hemu, a General of Adil Shah in the second Battle of Panipat, under the leadership of Bairam Khan. Hemu was defeated and Akbar reoccupied Delhi and Agra.
- Akbar's other campaign were against Durgawa of Garha-Katanga (Gond and Rajput principalities) followed by Chittor.
- Akbar conquered Gujarat (1572-1573) and Bengal (1574-1576).
- In 1591, Akbar sent four missions to the rulers of Khandesh, Bijapur, Ahmednagar and Golconda, calling upon them to recognise his partial control and pay him tribute. Ahmednagar was captured in 1600 and the ruler of Khandesh offered his submission.
- By 1595 , Akbar's armies had conquered Kashmir, Sindh, Odisha, Central India and Qandhar.
- Akbar's last campaign was against Asirgarh, resulting in the annexation of Khandesh in 1601.

4. With reference to the Mughal rule, answer the following

(i) Steps of Akbar towards integration of the people.
(ii) Social and educational reforms of Akbar.
(iii) Mansabdari system

Ans. (i) Refer to chapter theory page no. 156 and 157.

(ii) Refer to chapter theory page no. 157.

(iii) The steps taken by Aurangzeb that affected the Mughal Empire were

- Many oppressive land revenues and taxes were abolished by him. He also abolished octroi tax and inland transit duty taxes.
- Rituals like Jharokha darshan and weighing the emperor on his birthday were stopped. He also discontinued the celebration *Nauroz* (Persian new year) and inscribing the *Kalma* (Quranic verses) on the coins. He had re-introduced *Jaziya* and Pilgrim tax.
- His Deccan policy ruined the treasury of the Mughal Empire.

5. The Mughal Empire balanced and pacified the local societies through new administrative system in context of the above. Explain?

(i) Central Administration
(ii) Provincial Administration
(iii) Local Administration

Ans. (i) Refer to chapter theory page no. 157.

(ii) Refer to chapter theory page no. 158.

(iii) Refer to chapter theory page no. 158.

6. With reference to the administration of the Mughal Empire, explain the following

(i) Judicial Administration
(ii) Land Revenue System
(iii) *Mansabdari* System

Ans. (i) Refer to chapter theory page no. 158.

(ii) Refer to chapter theory page no. 159.

(iii) Refer to chapter theory page no. 158.

Picture Based Question

1. With reference to the given picture, answer the following questions.

(i) Who built this monument? Where is it located?
(ii) Why was the monument erected?
(iii) Write four features of this building.

Ans. (i) Taj Mahal was built by Shah Jahan in memory of his beloved wife Mumtaz Mahal.

It is built on the bank of the river Yamuna in Agra. Its main architect was Ustad Isa Khan. The work started in 1631 and was finished in 1653.

(ii) The Taj Mahal was built as a monument of love. It is a testament to love from a devoted king to his beloved queen. During the Mughal dynasty reign over India in the 16th-18th century, Emperor Shah Jahan reigned over Northern India between 1628-1658. He married his most beloved queen. At the age of 36, Shah Jahan became the Emperor and a 3 years later, Mumtaz Mahal died after giving birth to their 14th child. The Taj Mahal was built as a memorial to house the remains of his cherished wife.

(iii) Refer to chapter theory page no. 155.

Chapter Assessment

Section-I

Multiple Choice Questions

1. The First Battle of Panipat was in
   (a) 1527 (b) 1526
   (c) 1528 (d) 1529
2. Which among the following were the sources of Mughal Empire?
   (a) Ain-i-Akbari (b) Taj Mahal
   (c) Red Fort (d) All of these
3. Complete the given analogy.
   Battle of Panipat : 1526 : : Battle of Khanwa : ?
   (a) 1527 (b) 1528
   (c) 1529 (d) 1530
4. Replaced the underlined word to correct the sentence.
   Aurangzeb was son of <u>Jahangir</u>.
   (a) Akbar (b) Shah Jahan
   (c) Humayun (d) Babur

Section-II

Short Questions

1. Why Mughals called themselves Timurids?
2. What was the consequence of the Second Battle of Panipat?
3. Mention two works of Sher Shah Suri.
4. Mention two steps taken by Akbar for his non-Muslim subjects.
5. What was the Deccan policy of Aurangzeb?
6. Why did the Mughal Empire decline after the death of Aurangzeb?

Structured Questions

1. With reference to the sources of Mughal Empire explain
   (i) Ain-i-Akbari
   (ii) Taj Mahal
   (iii) Jama Masjid
   (iv) Ibadat Khana
2. The Mughals had a very systematic administrative structure. With reference to this explain the role of
   (i) *Wazir*
   (ii) *Diwan*
   (iii) *Subedar*
3. With reference to the Mansabdari system in the Mughal period, answer the following questions
   (i) What was the role of *Mansab*?
   (ii) What was *Zat* and *Sawar* rank?
   (iii) How the *Mansabs* received their salary?
   (iv) What do you mean by *'zabti'*?

CHAPTER 10

Emergence of Composite Culture

SYLLABUS

Composite Culture : Factors responsible for composite culture
Principles of Bhakti and Sufi Movements; Impact of composite culture, impact of the Bhakti Movement, the Sufi Movement and Christian missionaries.

Composite Culture

The term 'composite culture' means culture drawn from various strands. Composite culture is a heterogenous mixture of multiple cultures meeting and co-existing in one single religion.

The Bhakti and Sufi movements played a crucial role in creating a new composite culture called **Indo-Islamic culture**. The composite culture was neither purely Hindu nor entirely Muslim, but a combination of the best elements of the two religions. Medieval Hindu and Muslim saints helped to develop this cultural brotherhood.

The rule of Turks and Pathans enabled the followers of two faiths to live as friendly neighbours. The Hindu population incorporated the detail of Turkish culture and public life and the Muslims adopted a variety of Hindu traditions and customs in their everyday life.

Factors Responsible for Composite Culture

The concept of composite culture is particularly prominent in regions like India, where different communities with their distinct identities have interacted for centuries. These interactions led to the creation of a shared cultural space that celebrates diversity, harmony and coexistence.

Several factors contribute to the development of a composite culture and these factors are deeply intertwined with the history and evolution of human societies. Below, there are five crucial factors that have been responsible for the development and sustenance of composite culture across the world.

Historical Interactions

One of the most significant factors responsible for the creation of composite culture is the historical interactions between different communities, civilisations and empires. These interactions have taken place through various means such as trade, conquests, political alliances, cultural exchanges and diplomatic relations. For example, ancient trade routes like the Silk Road facilitated the exchange of goods, ideas and cultural practices between the East and West. Merchants, scholars and travellers brought not just products but also languages, religious ideas and art forms which were absorbed by the local cultures.

Advent of Islamic and Mughal Era

In India, the arrival of Islamic rulers in the 12th century led to the fusion of Islamic culture with the pre-existing Hindu and Buddhist cultures. The Mughal Empire also played a crucial role in shaping the composite culture of India by combining elements of Persian, Central Asian and indigenous cultures.

Mughal rulers like Akbar promoted religious tolerance which encouraged cultural exchanges and interactions between Hindus, Muslims, Christians and other communities.

As a result, the Mughal period saw the emergence of syncretic art forms, architectural styles, cuisine and literature that reflected a blend of diverse cultural influences.

Advent of Colonial Era

Similarly, colonial interactions between European powers and the societies they colonised also contributed to the emergence of composite cultures. The British colonial period in India left behind a lasting impact on the culture of the subcontinent. English became a dominant language, Western educational systems were introduced and European cultural practices intermingled with Indian traditions which create a unique fusion of cultural elements.

Religious Tolerance and Syncretism

Religious tolerance and syncretism (the blending of different religious traditions) have been one of the essential components of the development of composite culture.

In India, the coexistence of Hinduism, Islam, Sikhism, Buddhism, Jainism and Christianity for centuries led to the growth of a composite culture. The syncretic tradition in Indian music, for instance, blends elements from both Hindu devotional music and Islamic Sufi music. Classical music forms such as Hindustani music evolved by incorporating Persian, Afghan and Mughal influences. Similarly, Indian art and architecture witnessed a blending of Hindu and Islamic styles.

Another example of religious syncretism is the emergence of the Bhakti and Sufi movements in medieval India. Both movements encouraged a direct connection with God, transcending ritualistic practices and promoting a more personal and emotional form of worship. The Bhakti movement, which originated in Hinduism and the Sufi tradition within Islam emphasised love, devotion and universal brotherhood which led to shared cultural practices and the development of a composite religious culture that integrated elements from both Hinduism and Islam.

Geographical Diversity

Geographical diversity has played an important role in fostering cultural exchange, interaction and the formation of composite cultures. Regions with diverse populations, multiple languages and a mix of different geographical environments tend to develop more complex and varied cultural identities. This diversity often leads to the sharing of customs, food, clothing, music and art forms between different communities that create a hybrid cultural landscape.

India, for instance, is a geographically diverse country with a vast array of languages, religions, ethnic groups and traditions. The North and South of India have distinct cultural identities, yet there are significant overlaps due to centuries of migration, trade and political expansion. Coastal areas, where various trade routes converged, became centers of cultural exchange, where people from different parts of the world interacted. The fusion of indigenous and foreign elements in the cuisine, architecture and clothing of these coastal regions is an example of how geography contributed to the development of composite cultures.

Similarly, the Mediterranean region, which is surrounded by diverse countries and cultures, has witnessed centuries of cultural blending due to its geographical location. The exchange between Europe, Asia and Africa, facilitated by the Mediterranean Sea led to the development of a rich composite culture that encompasses various art forms, cuisines, languages and religious practices.

Geographical proximity also encourages migration and settlement, which further contributes to cultural diversity. People from different regions bring their customs, beliefs and traditions with them, leading to a fusion of cultural elements. Urban centers, in particular, tend to be melting pots of diverse cultures, as they attract people from various parts of the country and the world.

Migration and Influx of Different Peoples

Migration is another factor that has greatly influenced the development of composite cultures. People move from one place to another for various reasons, such as seeking better opportunities, escaping conflicts or exploring new lands. This movement brings together individuals from different cultures which leads to the exchange of ideas, traditions and practices. Over time, these different cultural elements are absorbed, adapted and integrated into the host society which results in the creation of a composite culture.

In India, the migration of people from different regions has contributed to the development of its composite culture. The influx of Central Asian, Persian and Afghan people during the Mughal period as well as the arrival of Portuguese, Dutch and British colonisers added new cultural layers to the existing Indian culture. The exchange of culinary traditions, art and architecture between different communities further enriched the cultural fabric of the region.

Migration also occurred through the transatlantic slave trade which brought Africans to the Americas. In the Caribbean and parts of South America, the blending of African, European and Indigenous cultures created unique cultural identities that reflect a mix of these traditions. The development of music, dance, cuisine and religious practices in the Americas is a direct result of the migration of different peoples and their cultural exchange.

Cultural Pluralism and Social Harmony

Cultural pluralism refers to the coexistence of multiple cultural groups within a society, where each group maintains its distinct identity while contributing to the larger cultural landscape. Societies that promote cultural pluralism encourage the acceptance and celebration of diverse cultural expressions, which in turn fosters the growth of composite cultures.

The concept of social harmony is also critical in this regard. In societies that value social harmony, different cultural groups are encouraged to interact, share their customs and live together peacefully. This sense of mutual respect and understanding leads to the blending of cultural traditions and the creation of a shared cultural space.

In India, the concept of cultural pluralism has been a long-standing feature of the country's social fabric. The Indian ethos encourages the celebration of diversity, whether in terms of religion, language or regional traditions. The fusion of different cultural practices and the promotion of social harmony have allowed India to develop a rich composite culture that embraces its multiple identities.

Impact of the Composite Culture

The Indo-Islamic culture impacted all aspects of life i.e. culture, art, architecture and literature.

Culture

- The dress, manners and festivals which the Mughals introduced in India were accepted by the Indians.
- The Turks not only brought new musical instruments such as the 'rabab' and 'sarangi' with them, but also introduced new musical modes.
- Amir Khusrau introduced many Persian and Arabic ragas. He also developed the style of 'qawwalis' and 'khayals'.

Architecture

- During the reign of Akbar, there was a mixture of Persian and Indian style of painting. The Indian and Islamic systems were mixed together to give rise to a new type of Indo-Islamic architecture.
- The Islamic features introduced the concept of spaciousness, massiveness and width to Indian architectural designs.
- The Indian style of architecture was profoundly impacted by the Turkish and the Mughal style. For example, many temples of Vrindavan assimilated the Mughal style of architecture.

Language and literature

- Language and literature also saw the influence of the two traditions. Through the Persian language, India was able to develop close cultural relations with Central Asia and Iran.
- Persian was the official language of the Mughals. This enabled the country to develop close cultural contact with Persia.
- The local languages and literature were also influenced by the Indo-Islamic style of architecture.
- The origin of Urdu was developed. It developed as a mixture of Persian, Arabic, Hindi and other regional languages. It was known as *'Zaban-e-Hindvi'* as it was similar to that of Hindi. It developed rapidly during the Mughal rule.
- Many Sanskrit books were translated into Persian and Urdu. Some great Urdu poets were Amir Khusrau and Mirza Ghalib.

Check Your LEARNING...

1. What do you understand by the term 'Composite Culture'?
2. Name two musical instruments introduced by the Turks.
3. In what ways did persian and Indian styles blend during Akbar's rule in the fields of art and architecture?
4. What was the official language of the Mughals?

Bhakti Movement

The Bhakti movement was a reform movement in Hinduism. It occupies a significant composition in bringing about harmony and normal relationships between the Hindus and Muslims.

The Bhakti Movement was essentially founded in South India and later spread to the North during the late medieval period. It was led by **devotional mystics** (later revered as Hindu saints) who praised devotion and love to God as the chief means of spiritual perfection. It originated as a reaction against caste division and ritualism in India.

The Bhakti Movement in South India was led by the 63 Nayanars (Shaivite devotees) and 12 Alvars (Vaishnavaite devotees), who preached personal devotion to God as a means of salvation. The Bhakti culture originated as a reform religious movement from the philosophy of Shankaracharya (the reformer of Hinduism in 9th century AD).

Some of the Bhakti saints were Ramanujcharya, Madhavacharya, Ramananda, Kabir, Nanak, Namdev, Chaitanya Mahaprabhu and Mirabai.

Principles of the Bhakti Movement

The main features highlighting the principles of the Bhakti movement were

- Unity of God or one God though known by different names.
- Bhakti, intense love and devotion, the only way to salvation.
- Repetition of the true name.
- Self-Surrender.
- **Condemnation**[1] of rituals, ceremonies and blind faith.
- Rejection of idol worship by many saints.
- Open-mindedness about deciding religious matters.
- No distinction in different castes, higher or lower.
- Need of a guru for guidance.
- Preachings through local or regional languages and travelling from place-to-place for spreading the religious message.

Bhakti Saints

Some of the important Bhakti saints who propagated Bhakti movement were

Sant Jnaneshwar or Dnyaneshwar (1275-1296 AD)

Jnaneshwar was a 13th century Marathi saint poet, philosopher and Yogi of the Nath tradition. His *Jnaneshwari or Bhavartha Dipika* (a commentary on Bhagwad Gita) and *Amrutanubhav* are considered to be most important achivements in Marathi literature. He popularised yoga and believed in Vithala or Lord Vishnu.

Mirabai (1498-1546 AD)

She was a great saint of the Bhakti movement. She was born at the village of Kudki in the Merta district of Rajasthan. Mirabai was a Rajput princess. She was married to Rana Sanga's, eldest son and heir apparent Raja Bhojraj in 1516. Her poetry is known as **Padavali**.

Impact of Bhakti Movement

- The followers of the Bhakti movement rejected the caste distinction and began to mix together on the basis of equality. They took their meals together from the common kitchen. The movement tried to loosen the bond of caste.
- A spirit of harmony among different sections of the society and religion received encouragement.
- The status of women received more importance and the evil pratice of 'Sati' received a set-back.
- The movement aroused awakening among the Hindus and Muslims regarding the ineffectiveness of ritualism and superstitions.
- The feeling of appreciation of the difference between the thought and practices of the two religions emerged and encouraged religious toleration.
- In place of Sanskrit, Persian and Arabic, the Bhakti Saints preached through the medium of local languages which could be understood very easily.
- Some of the rulers adopted liberal religious policies under the impact of the Bhakti movement.
- The movement attempted to awake a spirit of moral conduct in the daily life of the people. It emphasised earning of wealth through hard work and honest means.
- It developed a humanitarian attitude and also encouraged the value of social service to the poor and the needy.

Sufism

Sufism was a mystic in Islam. According to some scholars, the word 'Sufi' was derived from the word 'Safa' which means pure. Those saints among the Muslims who advocated a life of purity and renunciation were called Sufi. Some other scholars view that the word 'Sufi' came out of the word 'Suf' which means *'Wool'*. Those saints who put on woollen clothes after the death of Prophet Muhammad came to be known as Sufis.

Sufism started in Persia and Arabia as a liberal reform movement to bridge the gap between Shia and Sunni sects of Islam. The Sufis were mystics who emphasised on an **egalitarian society**[2] based on universal love. They emphasised on realisation of divine unity by arousing intuitive and spiritual faculties. They started preaching oneness of God, tolerance and brotherhood. They believed that all religions have different path of reaching the same God.

In India, the Sufi saints belonged to the Chishti and Suhrawardi orders.

1 **Condemnation** It is the action of expression very strong disapproval.

2 **Egalitarian Society** It refers to a society in which all persons have equal rights.

The Chishti Silsila/Order

The Chishti order was the earliest and most liberal Sufi order in India.

The Chishti Saints lived simple and pure lives. The Chishti Saints advocated harmony between the Hindus and the Muslims.

The Chishti order was brought to India by **Khawaja Moinuddin Chishti** (1141-1236). He arrived at Lahore in 1162 AD and settled at Ajmer about 1206 AD. His view was that the greatest form of devotion to God consisted in service to humanity.

Other famous saints of the Chishti order were Nizamuddin Auliya of Delhi, Fariduddin Ganjshakar of Pakpattan, Qutbuddin Bakhtiar Kaki and Hazrat Makhdoom Ashraf Semnani of Kichhauchha Sharif.

The Chishti Silsila/Order is known for the following principles

- Obedience to *shaykh* or *pir*
- **Renunciation**[3] of the material world
- *Sarna* or musical assemblies
- Extreme prayers and fasting
- Service to humanity
- Respect for other devotional traditions

The Suhrawardi Order

Shaikh Baha-ud-din Zakariya was the founder of the Suhrawardi order in India. This order came to India with the foundation of the Delhi Sultanate. The saints of this order believed that living in luxury and active participation in political affairs were not hindrances to spiritual progress.

Principles of Sufism

The main features highlighting the Principles of Sufism were

- Instead of depriving God of form and attributes, they credit the qualities of effulgence (extreme brightness), love, mercy, generosity and firmness to him.
- Instead of inculcating fear of the wrath of God, they put forward the ideal of securing union with him by pursuing the path of perfect love.
- According to the Sufis, the most outstanding attribute of God is his effulgence and they reside upon his luster, glory and splendor in various ways.
- Many Sufis were strict vegetarians.
- Sufis recognise the value of repetition of God's name and sometimes resort to music of a loving devotional character as an aid to concentration. The passion of music often led to heightening of emotion which ended in overjoy dancing.
- Their goal is union with God.

Impact of Sufism

- The common people got enchanted by the simple ascetic lifestyle of the saints. Their humanism and unique nature pleased them. People of all creeds, caste, and religion, educational and financial levels were drawn towards them.
- Sufism neutralised the Hindu-Muslim tension in society. The belief of Sufi Saints in equality led people to protest against caste domination, consumption of alcohol, gambling and slavery.
- The Sufi Saints actually Indianised Islam as they lived and preached in India. Moreover, *Sufi Khanqaks* were centres of moral life.
- Devotional songs were composed in Urdu and Hindi. Sufi music and dance were considered as manifestation of complete submission to *Allah*.
- In the rural agricultural background of human life, Sufism became a vehicle of spiritual and cultural upliftment of people.
- Many principles of Sufism were similar to those of Bhakti culture. Hence, it led to the popularity of Bhakti movement.

Influence of Christianity

In India, the arrival of **Vasco da Gama** in Calicut in 1498 AD is a landmark in its history of Christianity. The visits of Roman Catholic Missions to India became more organised. With the arrival of Portuguese to India.

They were initially concentrated to Goa, Cochin, Tuticorin and other coastal areas.

The Portuguese were inspired by the Pope's order to **baptise**[4] people around the world. They fought wars against the local Indian rulers and also tried to enforced their Roman Catholic prayers on Syrian Christians. It paved way to the Christian missionaries.

The Portuguese Colonial Government in Goa supported the mission in India with incentives for baptised Christians.

Impact of Christian Missionaries

- The Christian missionaries brought out grammars and dictionaries of the Indian languages in order to understand Indian people and their beliefs could be understood by the Indian people. For example, an epic in Konkani and a grammar book was brought by the *English Jesuit, Thomas Stephens.*
- Western music was taught in Church schools in India. In every Church, hymns were sung accompanied by organ and instruments.

3 **Renunciation** It is the formal rejection of something, typically a belief, claim or course of action.

4 **Baptise** Admit (someone) into a specified Church by baptism.

- The Christian Missionaries patronised paintings which influenced the Mughals. These paintings influenced the Mughals. Akbar had painting of Jesus Christ and Mother Mary whereas Jahangir possessed an album of miniatures containing paintings with Christian themes.
- They also played an important role in the field of architecture. Many European architectural ideas like two-storeyed house with high-pitched roof, balconies and verandas were introduced.

Check Your LEARNING...

1. Who led Bhakti movement in South India?
2. Mention any two principles of sufism.
3. What was the purpose of Christian missionaries creating dictionaries and grammars of Indian languages?
4. Mention one feature highlighting the principles of sufism.

QUiCK Revision

- The composite culture was neither purely Hindu nor entirely Muslim.
- The Bhakti Movement was essentially founded in South India and later spread to the North during the late medieval period.
- The Bhakti Movement in South India was led by the sixty-three Nayanars (Shaivite devotees) and the twelve Alvars (Vaishnavaite devotees), who preached personal devotion to God as a means of salvation.
- The main features of the Bhakti movement are like Unity of God or one God though known by different names, Bhakti, intense love and devotion, the only way to salvation etc.
- Jnaneswar was a 13th century saint, poet, philosopher and Yogi of the Nath tradition, who criticised the religious, degeneration, sectarianism, superstition and ritualism.
- Mirabai was a great saint of the Bhakti movement. The message of Mira was that none by means of birth, poverty, age or sex can be debarred from His divine presence.
- Sufism was a mystic in Islam. The word 'Sufi' was derived from the word 'Safa' which means pure. Those saints among the Muslims who advocated a life of purity and renunciation were called 'Sufi'.
- The monastic organisation of Sufi was called 'Khanqah'.
- The Chishti order was the earliest and most liberal Sufi order in India. It was brought to India by Khawaja Moin ud din Chishti (1141-1236 AD).
- Other famous saints of the Chishti order were Nizamuddin Auliya of Delhi, Fariduddin Ganjshakar of Pakpattan, Qutbuddin Bakhtiar Kaki and Hazrat Makhdoom Ashraf Semnani of Kichhauchha Sharif.
- Shaikh Baha-ud-din Zakariya Suhrawardi was the founder of the Suhrawardi order in India. This order came to India with the foundation of the Delhi Sultanate.
- The arrival of Vasco da Gama in Calicut in 1498 AD is a landmark in the history of Christianity in India. It paved way to the Christian missionaries.
- The Portuguese Colonial Government in Goa supported the mission in India with incentives for baptised Christians. They offered rice donations for the poor, good positions in the Portuguese colonies for the middle class and military support for local rulers.
- The Christian missionaries had a great impact on the literature, language and art of India.

Chapter Practice

Section-I

Multiple Choice Questions

1. Which of the following is a major factor responsible for the development of composite culture?
   (a) Political dominance
   (b) Historical interactions
   (c) Economic growth
   (d) Technological advancements

Ans. (b) Historical interactions

2. What role did the Mughal rulers play in shaping the composite culture of India?
   (a) Promoted trade between India and Europe
   (b) Encouraged cultural exchanges between different communities
   (c) Isolated India from other cultures
   (d) Destroyed existing cultural traditions

Ans. (b) Encouraged cultural exchanges between different communities

3. What was one of the major effects of colonial interactions in India?
   (a) Promotion of caste-based practices
   (b) Creation of a unique fusion of European and Indian cultural elements
   (c) Isolation of Indian cultures
   (d) Rejection of European cultural influence

Ans. (b) Creation of a unique fusion of European and Indian cultural elements

4. Which of the following movements emphasised love, devotion and universal brotherhood in India?
   (a) The Bhakti movement
   (b) The Sufi movement
   (c) Both the Bhakti and Sufi movements
   (d) The Jain movement

Ans. (c) Both the Bhakti and Sufi movements

5. The fusion of indigenous and foreign elements in coastal regions of India is an example of the impact of
   (a) Migration (b) Colonialism
   (c) Geographical diversity (d) Religious tolerance

Ans. (c) Geographical diversity

6. Which among the following were the Bhakti Saints?
   (a) Ramajunacharya (b) Ramananda
   (c) Mirabai (d) All of these

Ans. (d) All of the above

7. Sufi Saints was divided into ...... *silsilas*.
   (a) 9 (b) 10 (c) 11 (d) 12

Ans. (d) 12

8. Who introduced the Chishti order in India?
   (a) Baba Farid
   (b) Khawaja Moinuddin Chishti
   (c) Nizamuddin Auliya
   (d) None of the above

Ans. (b) Khawaja Moinuddin Chishti

9. Which of the following is not the significance of Sufism?
   (a) Their goal is union with god
   (b) Many sufis were strict vegetarian
   (c) The sufi was derived from the word 'Safa'.
   (d) They were not interested in music

Ans. (d) They were not interested in music

10. Complete the analogy
    Mughal Era: Composite Culture :: Migration: ?
    (a) Isolation (b) Cultural Exchange
    (c) Conquest (d) Repression

Ans. (b) Cultural Exchange

11. Which of the following best describes cultural pluralism?
    (a) Exclusion of foreign cultures
    (b) Coexistence of multiple cultural groups within a society
    (c) The dominance of one culture over others
    (d) Isolation of different cultural groups

Ans. (b) Coexistence of multiple cultural groups within a society

12. Which of the following historical events greatly influenced the emergence of a composite culture in India?
    (a) The Harappan Civilisation (b) The Mughal Empire
    (c) The Gupta Empire (d) The Maurya Empire

Ans. (b) The Mughal Empire

13. Read the two statements given below about the role of Sufism in India and select the option that shows the correct relationship between (A) and (R).

    Assertion (A) Sufism played an important role in promoting religious tolerance in India.

    Reason (R) Sufi saints were largely focused on spreading the teachings of the Quran without incorporating local traditions.

    Options
    (a) R contradicts A.
    (b) R is the reason for A.
    (c) A is true but R is false.
    (d) A and R are independent of each other.

Ans. (c) A is true but R is false.

14. Which of the following statements are correct regarding the development of composite culture?
   I. The arrival of Islamic rulers in India led to the fusion of Islamic culture with Hindu and Buddhist cultures, contributing to a composite culture.
   II. The British colonial period had no impact on the cultural development of India.
   III. Religious syncretism, such as the Bhakti and Sufi movements, played a significant role in the development of composite culture in India.
   IV. Migration of people from different regions has never influenced the creation of a composite culture.

Codes

(a) Only I (b) Both I and II
(c) Both I and III (d) All of these

Ans. (c) Both I and III

15. Consider the following statements associated with impact of Christian missionaries and choose the correct option.
   (i) Western music was taught in Church.
   (ii) They also patronised paintings which influenced by Mughals.
   (iii) They also placed all important role in the field of architecture.
   (iv) They brought out grammers and dictioneries in Indian language.

Codes

(a) Only (i) (b) Both (i) and (ii)
(c) Both (ii) and (iii) (d) All of these

Ans. (d) All of these

16. Match the following.

List I	List II
A. Historical Interactions	1. The movement of people from one place to another leading to cultural exchange and fusion.
B. Advent of Islamic and Mughal Era	2. The coexistence of different religious and cultural traditions, leading to the creation of a composite culture.
C. Migration and Influx of Different Peoples	3. Interaction of different civilisations, including trade, conquests and diplomacy that leads to cultural blending.
D. Religious Tolerance and Syncretism	4. The fusion of Islamic, Persian, Central Asian and indigenous cultures, promoted by rulers like Akbar.

Codes

	A	B	C	D		A	B	C	D
(a)	3	4	1	2	(b)	4	3	2	1
(c)	3	2	1	4	(d)	2	3	1	4

Ans. (a) 3 4 1 2

Passage Based Questions

17. Read the passage given below and answer the questions that follow.

Sufism is a spiritual path that emphasises inner peace, devotion and a deep connection with the divine. It focuses on love, kindness and self-discipline as a way to achieve spiritual fulfillment. Through various forms of expression, it promotes harmony and unity among people.

Over time, its teachings have inspired many to seek a life of simplicity and compassion. The essence of this path lies in the belief that true understanding comes from within, leading to a life guided by peace and devotion.

(i) Who was the founder of the Chishti Silsila in India?
   (a) Shaikh Nizamuddin Auliya
   (b) Shaikh Nasiruddin Chirag-i-Dehlvi
   (c) Khwaja Moinuddin Chishti
   (d) Shaikh Bahauddin Zakariya

Ans. (c) Khwaja Moinuddin Chishti

(ii) The Suhrawardi Order in India was led by ....
   (a) Khwaja Moinuddin Chishti
   (b) Shaikh Bahauddin Zakariya
   (c) Shaikh Nizamuddin Auliya
   (d) Baba Farid

Ans. (b) Shaikh Bahauddin Zakariya

(iii) Which of the following principles is not related to Sufism?
   (a) Devotion and love for God
   (b) Meditation and spiritual practice
   (c) All Sufis were strict vegetarians
   (d) Promoting peace and harmony

Ans. (c) All sufis were strict vegetarians

(iv) What was one major impact of Sufism?
   (a) Spread of strict religious laws
   (b) Promotion of love, peace and unity
   (c) Decline of spiritual practices
   (d) Restriction on music and poetry

Ans. (b) Promotion of love, peace and unity

18. Read the passage given below and answer the questions that follow.

From an early age Mirabai felt an irresistible attraction and devotion to Shri Krishna. As a young child she was given a doll of Krishna, which she worshipped as if it embodied the living presence of Krishna. Although people misunderstood her, she considered Krishna to be both her best friend, lover and husband.

Mirabai was a devotee of the high, higher, highest order. Among the saints of India, she is absolutely unparalleled. She composed many, bhajans, which are prayerful songs to God. Each song of Mirabai expressed her inspiration, aspiration and sleepless self giving.

(i) Hindu mystic poet and devotee of Krishna Mirabai lived during ....

(a) 12th Century (b) 13th Century
(c) 17th Century (d) 16th Century

Ans. (d) 16th Century

(ii) Mirabai was born in

(a) Uttar Pradesh (b) Madhya Pradesh
(c) Rajasthan (d) Gujarat

Ans. (c) Rajasthan

(iii) Mirabai was married to whom

(a) Raja Bhojraj (b) Maan Singh
(c) Rana Sanga (d) Maldev Rathore

Ans. (a) Raja Bhojraj

(iv) Which of the following is/are the composition of Mirabai?

(a) Raag Soratha (b) Raag Govinda
(c) Mera Ki Malhar (d) All of these

Ans. (d) All of these

Section-II

Short Questions

1. What do you mean by composite culture?

Ans. The term 'composite culture' means culture drawn from various strands. Composite culture is a heterogenous mixture of multiple cultures meeting and co-existing in one single religion.

2. Cite the various sources of Sufism and Bhakti movement in India.

Ans. The various sources of Sufism and Bhakti movement in India are

- Bijak
- Guru Granth Sahib
- Ajmer Sharif
- St. Francis Assisi Church (Kochi)

3. What role did historical interactions such as trade and conquests play in the development of composite culture?

Ans. Historical interactions like trade, conquests and cultural exchanges facilitated the blending of diverse ideas, languages, art forms and traditions. These interactions created a shared cultural space where different communities influenced each other which leads to the emergence of composite cultures.

4. How did the arrival of Islamic rulers and the Mughal Empire influence India's composite culture?

Ans. The Islamic rulers and the Mughal Empire influenced India's composite culture by fusing Islamic, Persian, Central Asian and indigenous cultures. Under rulers like Akbar, religious tolerance was promoted, encouraging cultural exchanges which resulted in syncretic art, architecture, cuisine and literature reflecting diverse cultural influences.

5. What is the significance of religious tolerance and syncretism in the development of composite cultures, particularly in India?

Ans. Religious tolerance and syncretism were essential in developing composite cultures, particularly in India, where different religions like Hinduism, Islam, Sikhism and Christianity coexisted. These traditions blended, especially in music and art, where influences from both Hindu and Islamic cultures merged and created a unified yet diverse cultural heritage.

6. How did the British colonial period impact the cultural landscape of India?

Ans. The British colonial period left a lasting impact on India's culture by introducing Western education, the English language and European cultural practices. This fusion of British and Indian traditions created a unique blend of cultures, influencing art, architecture, language and social systems in India.

7. In what ways did geographical diversity contribute to the development of composite cultures?

Ans. Geographical diversity promoted cultural exchange by bringing together people from various backgrounds. In regions like India, diverse languages, traditions and environments led to the blending of customs, food, art and music. Coastal areas, where trade routes converged, became centers of cultural fusion and created a hybrid cultural landscape.

8. Explain the role of the Bhakti and Sufi movements in fostering a composite religious culture in India.

Ans. The Bhakti and Sufi movements emphasised direct, personal connections with God, transcending ritualistic practices. Both movements promoted love, devotion and universal brotherhood, leading to shared cultural practices. These movements integrated elements from both Hinduism and Islam, fostering a composite religious culture in India.

9. How did the Mediterranean region's geographical location promote cultural blending?

Ans. The Mediterranean region, surrounded by Europe, Asia and Africa acted as a crossroads for trade and migration. This facilitated the exchange of goods, ideas, art and religious practices that led to a rich composite culture. The blend of diverse influences from these regions contributed to the region's varied cultural identities.

10. What is cultural pluralism and how does it contribute to the growth of composite cultures?

Ans. Cultural pluralism is the coexistence of multiple cultural groups within a society, where each group maintains its unique identity while contributing to the broader cultural landscape. By promoting mutual respect and acceptance of diverse traditions, cultural pluralism encourages the blending of practices, leading to the development of composite cultures.

11. What were the circumstances which led to an emergence of Sufism and Bhakti Movement?

Ans. The circumstances which led to an emergence of Sufism and Bhakti Movement were

- Antagonism between the Hindus and Muslims continued to grow day-by-day.
- Religious supremacy made the Muslim rulers and people to exhibit mutual hatred and hostility towards their fellow Hindu citizens.

At this critical time, there appeared a group of serious religious thinkers who by their Sufi and Bhakti movement awakened the people about God and religion.

12. What was the origin of Bhakti movement?

Ans. The Bhakti movement was founded in South India and later spread to the North during the late medieval period. It was led by devotional mystics (later revered as Hindu saints) who praised devotion and love to God as the chief means of spiritual perfection.

13. Who was Sant Jnaneshwar?

Ans. Sant Jnaneshwar was a 13th century Marathi, saint, poet, philosopher and yogi of the Nath tradition. He emerged as a first original philospher who wrote in Marathi language.

14. State two important literary works of Jnaneshwar.

Ans. The two important literary works of Jnaneshwar are *Dhyaneshwari* (a commentary on Bhagwad Gita) and *Amrutanubhav*, which are considered to be milestones in Marathi literature.

15. Who was Mirabai?

Ans. Mirabai was a great saint of the Bhakti movement. She was born at the village of Kudki in the Merta district of Rajasthan. She was married to Rana Sanga's eldest son and heir apparent Raja Bhojraj in 1516. She was highly religious from her childhood and a follower of the Krishna culture of Vaishnavism.

16. How was the life of Mirabai? What was her message?

Ans. Mira gave herself up completely to a life of devotion. Her songs were full of devotion and love, written in Rajasthani and Braj Bhasha. Her poetry is known as 'Padavali'.

17. Give a brief account of Sufism.

Ans. Sufism was a mystic in Islam. The word 'Sufi' was derived from the word 'Safa' which means pure. Those saints among the Muslims who advocated a life of purity and renunciation were called 'Sufi'. Another view is that the word 'Sufi' came out of the word Suf whose meaning is wool. Those saints who put on woollen clothes after the death of Prophet Muhammad came to be known as 'Sufis'.

18. What was *Khanqah*?

Ans. The monastic organisation of Sufi was called *Khanqah*. The head of *Khanqah* was known as 'Pir'. He appointed his successor who was called *'Wali'* and their disciples were known as *'Murids'*. By 12th century Sufi Saints got divided into 12 *Silsilas*.

19. Mention two main features of Sufism.

Ans. The two main features of Sufism are

(i) The most outstanding attribute of God, according to the Sufis, is his extreme brightness and they dwell upon his luster, glory and splendor in various ways.

(ii) They recognise the value of repetition of God's name and sometimes resort to music of a loving devotional character as an aid to concentration.

20. Why the *Pir* had importance in Sufism?

Ans. The preceptor or the *pir* has a great importance because only under his guidance, spiritual progress is possible.

21. What were the basic principles of Sufism?

Ans. The basic principles of Sufism are

- Obedience to *shaykh* or *'pir'*
- Renunciation of the material world
- Sarna (or musical assemblies)
- Extreme prayers and fasting
- Service to humanity
- Respect for other devotional traditions

22. Who was the founder of the Suhrawardi order? What does the saints of this order believe?

Ans. Shaikh Baha-ud-din Zakariya Suhrawardi was the founder of the Suhrawardi order in India.

The saints of this order believed that living in luxury and active participation in political affairs were not hindrances to spiritual progress.

23. What were the two impacts of Sufism?

Ans. Two impacts of sufism were

(i) The common people got enchanted by the simple ascetic lifestyle of the saints. Their humanism and unique nature pleased them. People of all creeds, caste and religion were drawn towards them.

(ii) It neutralised the Hindu-Muslim tension in society. Their belief in equality led them to protest against caste domination, consumption of alcohol, gambling and slavery.

24. What is landmark in the history of Christianity in India?

Ans. The arrival of Vasco da Gama in Calicut in AD 1498 is a landmark in the history of Christianity in India. During this period, the Portuguese, inspired by the Pope's order to baptise people around the world. They not only fought wars against the local Indian rulers, but even tried to enforced their Roman Catholic prayers on Syrian Christians. It paved way to the Christian missionaries. The Portuguese colonial government in Goa supported the mission in India with incentives for baptised Christians.

25. What was the issue with the Christian population when Francis Xavier came to India?

Ans. When Francies Xavier came to India, the Christian population had churches, clergy, and a bishop, but there were few preachers and no priests beyond the walls of Goa. Xavier decided that he must begin by instructing the Portuguese themselves and gave much of his time to the teaching of children.

26. How did St Francis Xavier preach in India?

Ans. The first five months St Francis Xavier spent in preaching and ministering to the sick in the hospitals. After that, he walked through the streets ringing a bell to summon the children and servants to catechism. He was invited to head Saint Paul's college, a pioneer seminary for the education of secular priests, which became the first Jesuit headquarters in Asia.

Structured Questions

1. The impact of the Composite culture can be seen in various aspects of life. With reference to this, explain
   (i) Impact on social life
   (ii) Impact on architecture
   (iii) Impact on music
   (iv) Impacts responsible for the growth of composite culture.

Ans. (i) Different aspects of the social life of the Hindus were influenced by Muslims. The influence of Islam can be witnessed in the Indian ceremonies connected with marriages, customs, manners, etiquettes of daily life, dress and costume, festivals.

(ii) A new style of Indian architecture developed especially under the Mughals, from the time of Akbar onwards, due to the amalgamation of Hindu and Islamic styles. The latter was chiefly based on Central Asian and Persian styles. This amalgamated style may be called 'Indo-Islamic architecture'.

(iii) The Muslims adopted musical instruments like the sitar and the tabla of the Hindus and their dhrupad style. The celebrated singers and musicians composed and introduced new varieties of ragas and forms like tarana, thumri, ghazal, etc and some Sanskrit works on music were translated into Persian. When the Turks came to India, they inherited the rich Arab tradition of music. They brought with them not only a number of new musical instruments such as the Sarangi and Rabab but also new musical modes.

(iv) Refer to chapter theory page no. 179.

2. With reference to Sufi movement, discuss
   (i) The Chishti *Silsila* (ii) The Suhrawardi Order
   (iii) Principles of Sufism

Ans. (i) Refer to chapter theory page no. 171.
(ii) Refer to chapter theory page no. 171.
(iii) Refer to chapter theory page no. 171.

3. With reference to the Bhakti movement in India, mention the following
   (i) Background of Bhakti Movement
   (ii) Principles of Bhakti Movement
   (iii) Impact of Bhakti Movement

Ans. (i) Refer to chapter theory page no. 169.
(ii) Refer to chapter theory page no. 170.
(iii) Refer to chapter theory page no. 170.

4. With reference to the factors responsible for composite culture, explain the following
   (i) Geographical diversity (ii) Migration
   (iii) Cultural pluralism

Ans. (i) Refer to chapter theory page no. 168.
(ii) Refer to chapter theory page no. 168-169.
(iii) Refer to chapter theory page no. 169.

5. With reference to the composite culture, explain
   (i) Background of Christianity in India
   (ii) Bhakti Movement
   (iii) Impact of Christian Missionaries
   (iv) Sufi Movement

Ans. (i) The background of Christianity in India is associated with the arrival of Vasco da Gama in Calicut in 1498 AD. It is a landmark in the history of Christianity in India. With the arrival of Portuguese to India, the visits of Roman Catholic Missions to India became more organised and were initially concentrated to Goa, Cochin, Tuticorin and other coastal areas. The Portuguese Colonial Government in Goa support of the mission in India with incentives for baptised. They offered rice donations for the poor, good positions in the Portuguese colonies for the middle class and military support for local rules.

(ii) Refer to chapter theory page no. 169.
(iii) Refer to chapter theory page no. 169 and 172.
(iv) Refer to chapter theory page no. 171.

Picture Based Questions

1. With reference to the Bhakti movement, answer the following.

(i) Identify the Bhakti movement saint shown in the picture above.
(ii) Write about the major impacts of the bhakti movement.
(iii) What were the major principles of the Bhakti movement?

Ans. (i) The famous female Bhakti movement saint Mirabai is shown in the picture above. She was a great saint of the Bhakti movement who was born at Kudki in the Merta district of Rajasthan.

(ii) Refer to chapter theory page 180.

(iii) Refer to chapter theory page 180.

Q.2 With reference to a movement related picture, answer the following.

(i) Identify the major principles of the movement with which these saints as shown in the picture were attached.

(ii) When and where was the Chishti Silsila established in India?

(iii) How did these saints promote peace and harmony in society?

Ans. (i) The saint shown in the picture is related to sufi movement. These saints instead of depriving God from different form and attributes they credited the qualities of effulgence (extreme brightness), love, mercy, generosity and firmness to him. They put forwarded the ideal of securing union with god by pursuing the path of perfect love. According to the Sufis, the most outstanding attribute of God is his effulgence and they reside upon his luster, glory and splendor in various ways.

(ii) Refer to chapter theory page 171.

(iii) Refer to chapter theory page 170.- Sufism.

Chapter Assessment

Section-I

Multiple Choice Questions

1. What role does migration play in fostering composite culture?
   (a) It causes cultural stagnation
   (b) It limits the spread of new ideas
   (c) It leads to the exchange and integration of cultural elements
   (d) It creates conflict between communities
2. What is a key outcome of promoting social harmony in culturally diverse societies?
   (a) Increased cultural conflicts
   (b) Suppression of minority cultures
   (c) Blending of cultural traditions and the creation of a shared cultural space
   (d) Reduction of cultural diversity
3. Which of the following were the saints of Chishti order?
   (a) Nizamuddin Auliya
   (b) Fariduddin Ganjshakar
   (c) Qutbuddin Bakhtiyar Kaki
   (d) All of the above
4. Replace the underlined word to correct sentence.
   Hazrat Nizamuddin was the founder of Suhrawardi order
   (a) Shaikh Baha - ud - din Zakariya
   (b) Baba Farid
   (c) Khwaja Moin ud-din Chishti
   (d) None of the above

Section-II

Short Questions

1. How does geographical diversity contribute to the development of composite cultures?
2. What do you mean by the term Bhakti?
3. What was the result of Bhakti movement?
4. Who are known as Sufis?
5. Name any two Sufi Saints.
6. What are two similarities between Sufi and Bhakti movements?
7. Mention the two phases of the growth of Indo- Islamic culture.
8. What is the significance of migration in the development of composite culture?

Structured Questions

1. With reference to the Bhakti movement, explain its view about
   (i) Caste (ii) Idol worship
   (iii) God (iv) Wealth/Properly
2. With reference to the Sufi and Bhakti movements, explain
   (i) Origin (ii) Principles
   (iii) Name of two saints
3. With reference to the Sufi and Bhakti movements, explain the
   (i) Impacts of Bhakti movement
   (ii) Two principles of Sufism
   (iii) Impacts of Sufism

CHAPTER

11

The Modern Age in Europe : Renaissance

SYLLABUS

Renaissance Definition, causes (capture of Constantinople, decline of Feudalism, new trade routes, spirit of enquiry and invention of the printing press) and impact on art, literature and science (Leonardo da Vinci, William Shakespeare and Copernicus). Consequences of Renaissance.

Definition and Meaning of Renaissance

The term 'Renaissance' is derived from the French word meaning 'rebirth'. Renaissance was the revival of European art and literature under the influence of classical models.

The Renaissance period dated from 14th to 17th centuries and spread across Europe from its origin place in Italy. In this period, major changes took place in Europe which had their impact on world history. For some historians, the European Renaissance is the beginning of the Early Modern Era.

Causes for Renaissance

Capture of Constantinople

Constantinople[1] was the capital of Eastern Roman Empire (Byzantine Empire) and centre of learning for Greek and Roman culture. Although, it was under the control of the Christians, many Greek scholars were living there. They became famous by teaching Greek language and literature to the people. They also had the valuable **manuscripts**[2] of Greek and Roman writers.

In 1453, **Muhammad II** of Ottoman Empire occupied Constantinople and devastated it. As a result of this, the Greek intellectuals left Constantinople and entered into different cities of Italy like Venetia, Milan, Naples, Sicily, Rome, etc. These scholars and learned men took their precious books and manuscripts with them.

They taught mathematics, history, geography, philosophy, astronomy, medicine, etc to the people of Italy. They spread their ideas and revived the interest of the people in the study of Greek philosophy, science, art and literature. This led to the foundations of Renaissance.

Decline of Feudalism

Feudalism was a way of structuring the European society on the basis of land tenure which meant the holding of land in exchange for service and labour.

In feudalism, king was at the highest level of feudal lords, subordinated by Dukes and Earls and they were subordinated by Barons. The knights were at the lower level. In this system, there was no freedom and equality of rights.

The feudalism began to decline around 13th century in France and Italy virtually disappeared from Western European countries by the 1500.

1. **Constantinople** Largest city of Byzantine Empire. Present day, Istanbul.
2. **Manuscripts** A hand written book or text.

A major factor which played a dominant role in the decline of feudalism was the rise of the middle class comprising of traders and businessmen.

This middle class provided necessary money to king for the maintenance of armies. This enabled them to reduce their dependence on the feudal lords. The decline of feudalism led to freedom and peace which further led to growth of new learning and developments in the field of art, literature, philosophy and science.

New Trade Routes

The invention of Mariner's compass led to large number of people taking long **voyages**[3] because it was possible for them to know the exact direction in which they were sailing.

Due to the capture of Constantinople by the Turks in 1453, the trade routes between the West and East was closed. So, the European navigators and traders felt the need to discover a new sea-route. This led to the following sea expeditions or voyages

- **Prince Henry**, the Navigator was the first to discover a sea route to Africa. The main project of Henry, was exploration of the West Coast of Africa. In 1419, the Madeira Islands were discovered and in 1427, the Azores were discovered. Both of them became Portuguese colonies.
- In 1482, an expedition under **Diogo Cao** made contact with the Kingdom of Congo.
- In 1487, **Bartolomew Dias** reached the Cape of Good Hope and proved that access to the Indian Ocean was possible.
- In 1492, **Christopher Columbus** sailed with three ships and discovered the islands of Bahamas, Cuba and Hispaniola. He found the mainland of Central and South America on three later voyages.
- **Amerigo Vespucci** was an Italian sailor who followed the route of Columbus. He made four voyages to the new world during 1497-1503. America was named after him.
- In 1498, **Vasco da Gama** reached Calicut in India.
- In 1519, **Ferdinand Magellan** sailed from Spain to Brazil. He sailed into the ocean which he named the Pacific. One of his ships went on to India and finally in 1522 to Spain by way of the Indian Ocean and the Cape of Good Hope. The voyage established Magellan as the foremost navigator in history.
- Many explorers such as Captain James Cook and Sir Francis Drake searched for a North-West passage to East Asia, but they failed. However, in 1906 **Roald Amundsen** completed this journey.

Spirit of Enquiry

In the Middle Age, the human activities were guided and controlled by the authority of the Pope and the Church. But the scholars discarded the ideas and developed a sense of enquiry among people.

They advised not to accept anything blindly which is not proved properly. They taught human beings to know the 'Why' and 'How' of things. They also questioned the authority of the Church. These thoughts made the way for Renaissance.

The factors responsible for the development of the spirit of enquiry were

- **Role of Crusades** Crusades were the religious expeditionary wars with the Church's access to holy places in and near Jerusalem, Israel. The Crusades brought ideas to Western Europe from the East. It widened their views on life.
- **Role of Original Thinkers** During the medieval phase, the Church discouraged original thinking and called upon scholars to put faith in the Church dogmas (principles). However, the original thinking could not be suppressed for a long time. Some independent thinkers criticised, the Church and asked the people to develop their own thinking. The thought process was revolutionised by thinkers like Abolard, Roger Bacon and Thomos Aquinas and they laid stress on reasoning. These original thinkers were called the forerunners of Renaissance.
- **Development of Science** Development of science created the spirit of enquiry and scientific temper. Some inventions broadened the mental views of the people and ended the old beliefs and traditions. These include
  - Roger Bacon designed the use of horseless carriage and flying machines.
  - Copernicus proved that the earth moves around the sun.
  - Galileo invented the telescope.

Invention of Printing Press

The invention of printing press was responsible for Renaissance. In 1456, **Johannes Gutenberg** of Germany invented printing press and set up first printing press in Germany. **William Caxton** brought this

3. **Voyages** A long journey involving travel by sea or in space.

machine to England in 1477. With the passage of time, printing press were established in Italy, France, Belgium and other European countries. Thus, books could be published very easily at a cheaper cost and within a short span of time. People could easily get books for study and learnt many things. Printing and distribution of books influenced the attitude of people towards life and brought about a new awakening in Europe.

Check Your LEARNING...

1. What was the importance of Constantinople?
2. What is meant by term 'Voyages'?
3. America was named after which sailor?
4. Who were called the forerunners of Renaissance?

Principles of Renaissance

The three principles of Renaissance are

(i) **Individualism** It is an idea that promotes independence for people to make their own decisions while also being responsible for ideas or beliefs.

(ii) **Secularism** It is basically the idea of separation of church and state.

(iii) **Humanism** It is an idea of rationality or reason. It disagrees with the ideas of faith or believing something because you have faith in it.

Impact of Renaissance

The Renaissance had a great impact on the various field of art, architecture, painting, sculpture, literature and science.

Impact on Art and Architecture

Before Renaissance, the chief art of the middle age was essentially Christian. Art was intimately associated with religion. It did not portray nature and human life. However, the Renaissance artists and painters developed a growing interest in classical civilisation. The artists how became interested in man and his life and they began to emphasise upon nature, humanity, etc. The artist adopted new artistic methods like **frescoes**[4] or wall pictures, oil colours and woodcuts.

The architecture of Italy was largely influenced by the spirit of Renaissance. The architects rejected the old Gothic style and accepted the Greeco-classical architecture. The builders of that time constructed many Churches, palaces and massive buildings following the style and pattern of ancient Greece and Rome. The pointed arches of the Churches and palaces were substituted by round arches, domes or by the plain lines of the Greek Temples. 'Florence', a city of Italy became the main centre of art-world.

The 'St Peter's Church of Rome', the 'Cathedral of Milan' and the 'Palaces of Venice and Florence' were some of the remarkable specimens of Renaissance architecture.

Impact on Sculptures

Sculptures also underwent a significant change during the Renaissance Period. Some artists copied the works of Greek and Romans while others produced the works that could match greek works.

The famous sculptor of Italy during Renaissance period was **Lorenzo Ghiberti**, who carved the bronze doors of the Church at Florence which was famous for its exquisite beauty. Another Italian Sculptor named Donatello is remembered for his realistic statue of 'St. George' and 'St. Mark'.

Michelangelo's huge marble statue of 'David' at Florence, give an idea about his greatness as a sculptor. He had also made the grand statue of 'Moses'. He had also completed the construction of 'Basilica of St. Peter' at Rome.

He made a statue in Rome called **Pieta** showing Mother Mary in a seated posture carrying the body of Jesus across her chest. Many sculptors in Italy worked for the Popes and rich merchants. Later, they were invited to England, France or Spain through which they spread Renaissance art the to the rest of Western Europe.

Impact on Paintings

The painters of Italy during Renaissance brought excellence and became world famous. They had a humanistic secular approach and produced life-like paintings. One of the most famous painter of Renaissance period was Leonardo da Vinci.

Leonardo da Vinci (1452-1519)

Leonardo da Vinci was a great painter, sculptor, musician and a scientist. The hidden expression in his paintings made them attractive.

Leonardo has become immortal for his famous painting of **Monalisa**. The smile on the lips of Monalisa is so mysterious that it is beyond the

4. **Frescoes** Paint onto wet-plaster on a wall.

comprehension of man. 'The Last Supper', 'The Virgin of the Rocks' and 'The Virgin and Child with Saint Anne' are his other immortal paintings which are appreciated all over the world.

Monalisa by Leonardo da Vinci

Impact on Literature

During Renaissance period, a large number of good literature was produced in local languages. Greek and Latin languages were started to be taught. Drama and theatre also began to develop.

Some of the important writers and their works during Renaissance period were

- The Renaissance literature originated in Italy. The first notable creation was **Dante's 'Divine Comedy'**. This book was written in Italian language and it was meant for the common people. In the book, Dante describes about the heaven, hell and the other world. It introduced new themes like love of one's country, love of nature as well as the role of individual.
- Another pioneer of Renaissance thought was **Francesco Petrarch**. He glorified the secular or worldly interests of life and humanism through his 'Sonnet', a form of poetry. His notable works were 'Familiar Letters' and 'Lovers of Illustrious Man'.
- Another great writer of Italy during that period was **Boccaccio**. In his world famous book 'Decameron' (Ten Days), he denounced God which brought a revolutionary change in the Christian World.
- The famous philosopher of Italy was **Machiavelli** who described the principle of 'the Lion and the Fox' in his famous book 'The Prince'.
- Ariosto's 'Orlando Furioso' and Tasso's 'Jerusalem Delivered' were two other great works for the Italian literature.
- In England, Thomas Moore's 'Utopia', Milton's 'Paradise Lost' and 'Paradise Regained' were very famous which were created during that period.
- Christopher Marlowe of England wrote his famous drama 'Doctor Faustus'.
- During Renaissance period, the Spanish writer 'Don Quixote', the works of Lope de Vega and Calderon were very famous.
- By this time Martin Luther of Germany translated the 'Bible' into German language.
- The writings of famous Dutchman, Desiderius Erasmus like 'In Praise of Folly', 'Handbook of a Christian Knight' and 'Familiar Colloquies' gave new dimension to the literature.
- Rabelais' 'Gangantua' and the writings of Racine, Sevigne and La Fontaine created golden age in the French literature.
- The Portuguese writer Camoens' 'Lusiads' was admired by the people to a great extent.

William Shakespeare (1564-1616)

William Shakespeare was an English poet, playwright and actor, widely regarded as the greatest writer in the English language and world's pre-eminent dramatist. He is often called **England National Poet** and the **Bard of Avon**. His works include 39 plays, 154 sonnets, two long narrative poems and few other verses.

His early plays were primarily comedies and histories but later, he wrote mainly tragedies including Hamlet, Othello, Macbeth, King Lear, Julius Caesar, etc which are considered the finest works in English language. In his last phase, he wrote tragicomedies also known as romances and collaborated with other playwrights.

William Shakespeare

Impact on Science

In the age of Renaissance, Science developed to a great extent. The development in astrology, medicine and other branches of science made this age distinct.

Francis Bacon was a great scientist who advised to explore nature. He advised that truth was to be discerned by experiment. This idea prompted others to regard him as the **Father of Modern Science**. Another famous scientist of Renaissance period was Nicolaus Copernicus.

Nicolaus Copernicus (1473-1543)

Nicolaus Copernicus was born in Poland. He was a Renaissance and reformation-era mathematician and astronomer who formulated a model of the universe that placed the Sun rather than the Earth at the centre of the universe. This is called the **heliocentric theory of universe**.

Copernicus was a polyglot (knowing or using several languages) and polymath (a person with wide-ranging knowledge) and he obtained a degree in Canon Law. He was also a physician, classic scholar, translator, governor, diplomat and economist.

In 1517, he derived a quantity theory of money, a key concept in economics. In 1519, he formulated an economic principle that later came to be called **Gresham's Law**[5].

Consequences of the Renaissance

The **Renaissance** (14th to 17th century) was a period of cultural, intellectual and artistic revival that emerged in Italy and spread across Europe. It had far-reaching consequences that transformed Europe's intellectual, artistic, religious, political, economic and social landscapes. It laid the foundation for the scientific revolution, reformation, age of exploration and modern nation-states, shaping the contemporary world.

Some of the consequences of the renaissance were as follows

- **Revival of the Intellectuals** The Renaissance revived interest in classical Greek and Roman knowledge, promoting humanism, scientific inquiry and secular learning across Europe.
- **Scientific Advancements** It led to the scientific revolution, fostering discoveries by figures like Copernicus, Galileo and Newton, challenging traditional beliefs and encouraging empirical observation.
- **Artistic Innovation** Artists like Leonardo da Vinci and Michelangelo developed new techniques such as perspective and realism which transformed European art and architecture.
- **Political Change** It weakened feudalism, strengthened centralised monarchies and contributed to the rise of modern nation-states with structured governance.
- **Economic Growth** The Renaissance expanded trade and commerce, fostering early capitalism and the growth of powerful merchant classes in Europe.
- **Spread of Knowledge** The invention of the printing press by Johann Guttenberg facilitated the mass production of books which resulted in increasing literacy and spreading Renaissance ideas rapidly.

Check Your LEARNING...

1. Name three principles of Renaissance.
2. Who was sculptor of the marble statue 'David'?
3. What was the first notable creation of Renaissance literature?
4. What is heliocentric theory of universe?

5. **Gresham's Law** It is a monetary principle stating that 'bad money drives out good'.

QUiCK Revision

- The term 'Renaissance' is derived from the French word meaning 'rebirth'. It refers to the transitional movement in Europe between medieval and modern times. European history refers Renaissance, a period of great social and cultural change in Europe.
- There were many causes behind 'Renaissance' like Capture of Constantinople, Decline of Feudalism, New Trade Routes, Spirit of Enquiry, Original thinker and Invention of Printing machine.
- The three principles of Renaissance are Individualism, Secularism and Humanism.
- The Renaissance had a great impact on the various field of art, architecture, painting, sculpture, literature and science.
- Before Renaissance, the chief art of the middle age was essentially Christian. Art was intimately associated with religion. However, the Renaissance artists and painters developed a growing interest in classical civilisation.
- The architecture of Italy was largely influenced by the spirit of Renaissance. The builders of that time constructed many churches, palaces and massive buildings following the style and pattern of ancient Greece and Rome.
- Sculpture also underwent a significant change during the Renaissance Period. The famous sculptor of Italy during this period was Lorenzo Ghiberti.
- In painting, the painters of Italy during Renaissance brought excellence and became world famous. They had a humanistic secular approach and produced life-like paintings.
- The Renaissance literature had its birth in Italy.
- The first notable creation was Dante's 'Divine Comedy'. This book was written in Italian language and it was meant for the common people. In the book, Dante describes about the heaven, hell and the other world. It introduced new themes like love of one's country, love of nature as well as the role of individual.
- William Shakespeare was an English poet, playwright and actor, widely regarded as the greatest writer in the English language and world's pre-eminent dramatist.
- In the age of Renaissance, Science developed to a great extent. The development in astrology, medicine and other branches of Science made this age distinct.
- Nicolaus Copernicus was a Renaissance and reformation-era mathematician and astronomer who formulated a model of universe that placed the sun rather than the Earth at the centre of the Universe.
- The Renaissance had far-reaching consequences that transformed Europe's intellectual, artistic, religious, political, economic and social landscapes.
- It laid the foundation for the scientific revolution, reformation, age of exploration and modern nation-states that shaped the contemporary world.
- Revival of Greek and Roman knowledge promoted humanism and scientific inquiry which resulted in the scientific revolution with discoveries by Copernicus, Galileo and Newton.

Chapter Practice

Section-I

Multiple Choice Questions

1. The term 'Renaissance' is derived from the .... word meaning 'rebirth'.
(a) French (b) German
(c) Russian (d) Polish

Ans. (a) French

2. The Renaissance literature had its birth in ....
(a) France (b) Germany
(c) England (d) Italy

Ans. (d) Italy

3. In which year, Muhammad II of Ottoman Empire occupied Constantinople and devastated it.
(a) 1253 (b) 1375 (c) 1453 (d) 1512

Ans. (c) 1453

4. The trade routes between West and East was closed when .... captured Constantinople in 1453.
(a) Turks (b) Germany (c) Greek (d) Arab

Ans. (a) Turks

5. Who was Amerigo Vespucci ?
(a) Painter (b) Sailor (c) Singer (d) Actor

Ans. (b) Sailor

6. In which year Vasco da Gama reached Calicut ?
(a) 1320 (b) 1498 (c) 1526 (d) 1628

Ans. (b) 1498

7. Who was the inventor of printing press?
(a) Captain James Cook (b) Johannes Gutenberg
(c) William Caxton (d) Roald Amundsen

Ans. (b) Johannes Gutenberg

8. Leonardo da Vinci was great
(a) Painter (b) Sculpture
(c) Musician (d) All of these

Ans. (d) All of these

9. William Shakespeare was ...... poet, playwright, actor and greatest writer.
(a) English (b) American
(c) Irish (d) Russian

Ans. (a) English

10. Complete the given analogy.
William Shakespeare : England : : Nicolaus Copernicus : ?
(a) Poland (b) Russia
(c) Denmark (d) Hungary

Ans. (a) Poland

11. Complete the given analogy.
Leonardo-da-Vinci : Painter :: Machiavelli : ?
(a) Philosopher (b) Sailor (c) Astronomer (d) Poet

Ans. (a) Philosopher

12. Replace the underlined word to correct the statement.
The three principles of Renaissance are Individualism, Secularism and <u>Liberalism</u>.
(a) Humanism (b) Capitalism
(c) Communalism (d) None of these

Ans. (a) Humanism

13. Replace the underlined word to correct the sentence.
<u>Amerigo Vespucci</u> has become immortal for his famous painting of 'Monalisa'.
(a) Leonardo da Vinci (b) Guttenberg
(c) William Caxton (d) Sir Francis Drake

Ans. (a) Leonardo da Vinci

14. Complete the given table.

William Shakespeare	Writer
Vasco da Gama	?

Choose the correct option.
(a) Painter (b) Astronomer
(c) Scientist (d) Merchant

Ans. (d) Merchant

15. Consider the following statement about Renaissance and choose the correct option.
(i) Feudalism began to decline around 13th century.
(ii) Prince Henry was the navigator of Portugal.
(iii) Western routes were discovered by Columbus.
(iv) The men with new thought paved the way for Renaissance.

Codes
(a) Only (i) (b) Both (i) and (ii)
(c) (i), (ii) and (iii) (d) All of these

Ans. (d) All of these

16. Consider the given statement associated with the impact of Renaissance on literature.
(i) The book 'Dante's Divine Comedy' was written in Italian language .
(ii) Boccaccio was a Italian writer.
(iii) Martin Luther of Germany translated the 'Bible' into German language.
(iv) Cameons was a Portuguese writer.

Codes
(a) Only (i) (b) Both (i) and (ii)
(c) (i), (ii) and (iii) (d) All of these

Ans. (d) All of these

17. Match the following.

List-I	List-II
A. Shakespeare	1. Astronomer
B. Copernicus	2. Writer
C. Leonardo da Vinci	3. Inventor
D. Guttenberg	4. Polymath

Codes

	A	B	C	D		A	B	C	D
(a)	1	2	3	4	(b)	4	3	2	1
(c)	3	1	2	4	(d)	2	1	4	3

Ans. (d)

Passage Based Question

18. Read the passage given below and answer the following questions.

It was during this period that he experimented with radically new and different painting techniques. One of the techniques Leonardo da Vinci is famous for his ability to create a smoky effect, which was coined sfumato. Through his deep knowledge of glazes and brushstrokes, he developed the technique, which allowed for edges of color and outline to flow into each other to emphasise the soft modulation of flesh and fabric, as well as the remarkable translucence of hard surfaces such as crystal or the tactility of hair. The intimate authenticity that resulted in his figures and subjects seemed to mirror reality in ways that had not been seen prior.

(i) Who was the painter of 'Monalisa' ?
(a) Guttenberg (b) Copernicus
(c) Leonardo da Vinci (d) William Shakespeare

Ans. (c) Leonardo da Vinci

(ii) When was Leonardo da Vinci was born?
(a) 1452 (b) 1731 (c) 1512 (d) 1519

Ans. (a) 1452

(iii) Which among the following were the famous paintings of Leonardo da Vinci ?
(a) The Virgin of the Rocks (b) The Last Supper
(c) Monalisa (d) All of these

Ans. (d) All of these

(iv) When was Leonardo da Vinci died?
(a) 1472 (b) 1498 (c) 1510 (d) 1519

Ans. (d) 1519

Section-II

Short Questions

1. What do you mean by Renaissance?

Ans. The term 'Renaissance' is derived from the French word meaning 'rebirth'. Renaissance was the revival of European art and literaturature under the influence of classical models. The Renaissance period dated from 14th to 17th centuries and spread across Europe from its origin place in Italy.

2. What was the position of Italy during the Middle Ages?

Ans. During the Middle Ages, Italy was not the unified country that it is today. The Italian Peninsula was made up of a number of independent city-states, most of these were ruled by powerful families.

3. What was the time period of European Renaissance?

Ans. The time period during which the European Renaissance fell was between the end of the Middle Ages (or medieval period) and the beginning of the Modern Age.

4. How the fall of Constantinople was a major cause for the emergence of Renaissance?

Ans. The fall of Constantinople was a major cause for the emergence of Renaissance because the Greek intellectuals left Constantinople with their valuable manuscripts and entered into different cities of Italy. They taught mathematics, history, geography, medicine, etc to the people of Italy. This gave birth to Renaissance.

5. Mention any two voyages took place during the era of exploration.

Ans. Two of the voyages that took place during the era of exploration are

(i) In 1487, Bartholomew Dias rounded the Cape of Good Hope and proved that access to the Indian Ocean was possible.

(ii) In 1498, Vasco da Gama reached Calicut in India.

6. How men with new thoughts paved the way for Renaissance?

Ans. The men with new thoughts paved the way for Renaissance as they advised not to accept anything blindly which is not proved properly. They taught human beings to know the, 'Why' and 'How' of things.

7. Explain the role of one of the original thinkers in spreading the ideas of Renaissance.

Ans. Original thinkers such as Peter Abelard (1079-1142) managed to weaken the intellectual authority of the Church by setting new trails. In his opinion, the mysteries of Christianity were not to be taken for granted. They had to be tested in the light of reason and investigation.

8. Why the invention of printing machine is regarded as the cause of beginning of Renaissance?

Ans. The invention of printing machine was responsible for Renaissance because by this, books could be published very easily with a short span of time. People could easily get books for study and learnt many things.

9. How was the art before the coming of Renaissance?

Ans. Before Renaissance, the chief art of the middle age was essentially Christian. Art was intimately associated with religion. However, the Renaissance artists and painters developed a growing interest in classical civilisation.

10. Give a brief account about the architecture of Italy.

Ans. The architecture of Italy was largely influenced by the spirit of Renaissance. The builders of that time constructed many Churches, palaces and massive buildings following the style and pattern of ancient Greece and Rome. The pointed arches of the Churches and palaces were substituted by round arches, domes or by the plain lines of the Greek temples.

11. Give some examples of the architecture of Italy during Renaissance.

Ans. 'Florence', a city of Italy became the nerve centre of art-world. The 'St Peter's Church of Rome', the 'Cathedral of Milan' and the 'Palaces of Venice and Florence' were some of the remarkable specimens of Renaissance architecture.

12. What was the impact on sculpture during the Renaissance period?

Ans. Sculpture also underwent a significant change during the Renaissance period. The famous sculptor of Italy during that period was Lorenzo Ghiberti, who carved the bronze doors of the Church at Florence which was famous for its exquisite beauty. Another Italian Sculptor named Donatello is remembered for his realistic statue of 'St. George' and 'St. Mark'.

13. Mention any three famous writers of Renaissance with their works.

Ans. The three famous writers of Renaissance with their works were

- The famous philosopher of Italy, Machiavelli who described the principle of 'the Lion and the Fox' in his famous book 'The Prince'.
- Ariosto's 'Orlando Furioso' and Tasso's 'Jerusalem Delivered' were two other great works for the Italian literature.
- Rabelais' 'Gangantua' and the writings of Racine, Sevigne and La Fontaine created golden age in the French literature.

14. Mention some famous writers of England during Renaissance.

Ans. In England, Thomas Moore's 'Utopia', Milton's 'Paradise Lost' and 'Paradise Regained' were famous writers during Renaissance.

15. Mention some works of famous Dutchman writer, Desiderius Erasmus.

Ans. Some writings of famous Dutchman, Desiderius Erasmus are 'In Praise of Folly', 'Handbook of a Christian Knight' and 'Familiar Colloquies'.

16. Name some famous plays written by William Shakespeare.

Ans. Some famous plays written by William Shakespeare are 'Julius Caesar', 'Othello', 'Macbeth', 'As you Like it', 'Romeo and Juliet', 'Hamlet', 'Merchants of Venice', 'King Lear', etc.

17. State the heliocentric theory of Copernicus.

Ans. Copernicus formulated a model of universe that placed the Sun rather than the Earth at the centre of the universe. This is called the heliocentric theory of universe.

18. Mention any two consequences of Renaissance.

Ans. The two consequences of Renaissance are

(i) The period witnessed the end of the old and reactionary medieval spirit and the beginning of the new spirit of science, reasoning and experimentation.

(ii) It gave a great impetus to art, architecture, learning and literature.

Structured Questions

1. Decline of feudalism was one of the major causes for the beginning of Renaissance. With reference to this, explain

(i) What is feudalism? When did it decline?

(ii) Major factor which played a dominant role in the decline of feudalism.

(iii) Effect of decline of feudalism.

Ans. (i) Feudalism is a way of structuring the society around relationships derived from the holding of land in exchange for service and labour.

The feudalism began to decline by the close of the 13th century in France and Italy virtually disappeared from Western European countries by the 1500 AD.

(ii) The major factor which played a dominant role in the decline of feudalism was the rise of the middle class comprising of traders and businessmen. This middle class provided necessary money to king for the maintenance of armies and thereby enabled them to reduce their dependence on the feudal lords.

(iii) Due to development of trade and commerce during this period, there was great increase in prices which greatly benefitted the craftsmen, merchants and cultivators. As the feudal lords could not increase their rents, they were forced to borrow to maintain themselves. As the feudal lords were not able to repay the debts they were often obliged to sell off their lands.

2. The discovery of mariner's compass lead to large number of people taking long voyages. With reference to this, mention the voyage of

(i) Prince Henry, the Navigator

(ii) Christopher Columbus

(iii) Magellan

(iv) Bartolomew Dias and Amerigo Vespucci

Ans. (i) Prince Henry, the Navigator was the first to discover a sea route to Africa in 1419. The main project of Henry, was exploration of the West Coast of Africa. The Madeira Islands were discovered and in 1427, the Azores were discovered. Both of them became Portuguese colonies.

(ii) In 1492, Christopher Columbus, sailed with three ships. Bahamas and discovered the islands of Cuba and Hispaniola. He found the mainland of Central and South America on three later voyages.

(iii) In 1519, Magellan sailed from Spain to Brazil. He sailed into the ocean which he named the Pacific. One of his ships went on to India and finally in 1522 to Spain by way of the Indian Ocean and Cape of Good Hope. The voyage established Magellan as the foremost navigator in history. For the first time the globe was circled and the vast expanse of the Pacific was revealed.

(iv) In 1487, Bartolomew Dias reached the Cape of Good Hope and proved that access to the Indian Ocean was possible. Amerigo Vespucci was an Italian sailor who followed the route of Columbus. He made four voyages to the new world during 1497-1503. America was named after him.

3. The men with new thoughts paved the way for Renaissance. In context of the above, explain
(i) Spirit of Enquiry
(ii) Invention of Printing Press
(iii) New Trade Routes
(iv) Principle of Renaissance

Ans. (i) Refer to chapter theory page no. 180.
(ii) Refer to chapter theory page no. 180-181.
(iii) Refer to chapter theory page no. 180.
(iv) Refer to chapter theory page no. 180.

4. Art, literature and science had great impact on Renaissance. With reference to this, explain the contributions of
(i) Leonardo-da-Vinci
(ii) William Shakespeare
(iii) Nicolaus Copernicus

Ans. (i) Refer to chapter theory page no. 181-182
(ii) Refer to chapter theory page no. 182.
(iii) Refer to chapter theory page no. 182.

Picture Based Question

1. With reference to the given picture, answer the following question

(i) Identify the given image. What is unique about the picture?
(ii) What are the other works of the artist who painted this given picture?
(iii) Give a brief description about the artist of given picture.

Ans. (i) The given image is of Monalisa, a painting by Leonardo da Vinci.
The unique feature of the picture is the smile on face of Monalisa. The smile on the lips of Monalisa is so mysterious that it is beyond the comprehension of man.

(ii) 'The Last Supper', 'The Virgin of the Rocks' and 'The Virgin and Child with Saint Anne' are his other immortal paintings which are appreciated all over the world.

(iii) Leonardo da Vinci was a great painter, sculptor, musician and scientist. He has occupied a unique position in the history and has become immortal for his famous painting of 'Monalisa'. The hidden expression in his paintings made them attractive.

Chapter Assessment

Section-I

Multiple Choice Questions

1. Constantinople was the capital of ....
   (a) Greek
   (b) Eastern Roman Empire
   (c) France
   (d) USSR
2. Which was/were the cause of decline of Feudalism ?
   (a) Rise of the middle class
   (b) Rise of businessmen
   (c) Development of trade and commerce
   (d) All of the above
3. Who among the following invented the first printing press?
   (a) Johannes Kepler
   (b) Galileo Galilei
   (c) Johanness Guttenberg
   (d) Nicolous Copernicus
4. Replace the underlined word to correct sentence.
   Nicolaus Copernicus was born in Germany.
   (a) Poland (b) France
   (c) Russia (d) Denmark

Section-II

Short Questions

1. Why did Renaissance begin in Italy?
2. What are the different causes that led to the emergence of Renaissance?
3. Mention any two statues sculpted by Michelangelo.
4. What is the unique feature of a statue at Rome called 'Pieta'?
5. What was the impact of Renaissance on science?

Structured Questions

1. With reference to the causes of Renaissance, explain
   (i) Fall of Constantinople
   (ii) Spirit of Enquiry
   (iii) Development of Science
2. With reference to the impact of Renaissance, explain its impact on
   (i) Painting (ii) Literature
   (iii) Architecture (iv) Sculpture

CHAPTER

12

The Modern Age in Europe : Reformation

SYLLABUS

Reformation Meaning, causes of reformation (dissatisfaction with the practices of the Catholic Church and new learning), Martin Luther's contribution, Counter Reformation.

Meaning of Reformation

The Reformation could be described as a group of religious movement that was directed against the Church of Rome. It involved a revolt against the authority and principles of the Christian Church in Rome with the Pope as its head.

The Reformation was also a rebellion against the corruption and abuses in the Church, **monasticism**[1], Church rituals and sacraments (holy orders) as well as interference of the Pope in temporal affairs. The people that were against the Pope were called **Protestants** while the people who continued supported the Pope, were referred to as **Roman Catholics**.

The Reformation started in number of countries like England, France, Germany, Czechoslovakia, Switzerland and Scotland. It helped to put an end to this age of blind faith and dogmas (principles) prevalent in the modern times.

Causes of Reformation

There were many causes behind 'Reformation' but the two most prominent causes were dissatisfaction with the malpractices of the Catholic Church and new learning.

Dissatisfaction with the Practices of the Catholic Church

During the early medieval period, the Church had become a hierarchical organisation with Pope as its head.

The position of Pope is often described as **papal monarchy** but during the 14th century, people became dissatisfied with some of the Church practices which paved the way for Reformation. These practices were

- **Corrupt Practices** The priest and officers of higher positions in the church hierarchy received their appointments through corrupt means. They led lives of luxury and immorality. They had devised a number of practices for this purpose. Thus, the Church offices were openly sold to the higher bidder and mostly unsuitable men were appointed as priests. This practice was known as **simony**. The corrupt practices of the Church has been criticised by Erasmus in his book 'Praise of Folly'.
- **Issue of Indulgence** Priests and Church officers tried to make as much money as possible and liberally issued indulgences or pardon certificates against payment. This practice of issue of indulgences invited severe criticism and was described as 'sale of licences to commit sin'.

1 **Monasticism** Religious way of life in which one renounces worldly pursuits to devote oneself fully to spiritual work.

- **Salvation through Fees** The priests promised salvation in exchange of fees. The priests, the bishops and the wandering monks could pronounce a marriage lawful or unlawful. There were fees for every process in life such as birth, death, peace of the soul, etc.
- **Issue of Taxes** The Church imposed various kinds of taxes like **Peter's pence** and the **tithe** (one-tenth of income of each person). Taxes collected from different countries of Europe reached Rome. The Church properties and nobles were exempted from taxes. The burden of taxation was completely on the merchants.
- **Division in Church** The division in Church during the 15th century also greatly lowered its prestige. Instead of one Pope, two Popes began to be elected, one by the French cardinals and the other by the Italian **cardinals**[2]. This undermined the prestige of Pope and people lost faith and reverence for the holy institution.

  The things were further became complicated in 1409 when the cardinals at a joint sitting elected a third Pope. This is known as the **Great Western Schism**. This Schism was extended when the council at constance deposed both the Popes and elected a new Pope. But these developments certainly undermined the powers and prestige of the Church.
- **Pope's Interference in Political Affairs** The Popes interfered in the political affairs. This was opposed by the kings. The kings of Europe also had quarreled with Popes over the royal right to tax the Church property. Thus, the kings like French King Philip IV and King Henry VIII of England, strongly supported the Reformation movement in order to weaken the Church.

New Learning

The new spirit of learning and enquiry set initiated by the Renaissance also greatly contributed to the Reformation. The invention of printing press and the printing of Bible in vernacular (local) languages brought about a new view among the people. People began to assert themselves against blind faith and useless religious rituals.

People began to feel that they could reach God without the intermediary of a priest. Their reason also made them highly critical of the prevailing practices of sale of indulgences (pardon certificates), non-enforcement of the code of morality among the clergy and undue inter- ference of Papacy (office of the Pope) in the secular affairs.

Criticism by Scholars

Several scholars raised their voices in opposition to certain Catholic teachings and practices. Among them was **John Wycliffe** (1320-1384), an English priest and professor in the University of Oxford who declared that the Pope was not Christ's representative on Earth, but an anti-Christ. He also felt that individual Christians should only be guided by what they read in the Bible. He recommended that the church should be subordinate to the State. Wycliffe is regarded as the **Morning Star of the Reformation.**

Contribution of Martin Luther in Reformation

Martin Luther (1483-1546) initiate the reformation in Germany. He was the first reformer to lead a large number of people against the Church.

Luther was a native of German who became a monk at the age of 22 and was then appointed as professor of theology in the University of Wittenberg.

In 1512, he took a pilgrimage to Rome where he was shocked to see the Churchmen leading a luxurious life. This made him a strong critic of the Church. He openly questioned the sale of indulgences in 1517 by several agents of Pope Leo X, for collecting money for completing the construction of St. Peter's Church at Rome.

In 1517 he posted his **Ninety-five Theses** written in Latin on the Church door at Wittenberg. It contained statements on points of difference in the beliefs and practices of the Church.

In 1520, Pope Leo X issued a Papall Bull (a public decree issued by a Pope) against Martin Luther but he burnt this letter in the presence of public.

In 1521, the Holy Roman Emperor Charles V asked Luther to defend his case before the Diet of Worms (a General Assembly). However, Luther denied due to which Emperor ordered his arrest and his writings to be burnt. Luther was provided shelter by the Duke of Saxony, Frederick. During this period, Luther translated the Holy Bible from Latin to German.

Many German princes separated from the Catholic Church and supported Martin Luther. Lutheran Churches were established all over the Germany. Luther travelled to different parts of Europe– Germany, Sweden, Norway and Denmark to spread his ideas against the Catholic Church. This movement came to be known as **German Protestant Movement**.

2 **Cardinals** Cardinal is a leading dignitary of Roman Catholic Church. Cardinals are nominated by the Pope and they form the sacred College which elects succeeding Popes.

Luther and his followers formed the **Schmal Kaldic** League to face the challenge of Emperor. This led to a religious Civil War during 1546-1553 AD.

Finally, nine years after the death of Luther, a treaty known as the Peace of Augsburg was signed by which Lutherism was accepted as another legal form of Christianity.

The Northern states of Germany accepted Lutherism while the Southern states remain loyal to the Catholic Church.

Martin Luther

Counter Reformation

In order to restore the reputation of the Church, an attempt was made by some dedicated Christians. They included some Popes to reform the Catholic Church in Italy, Austria, France and Spain, in response to the Protestant Reformation being carried out in Germany, Switzerland and Scandinavia.

They introduced a number of reforms within the Church. This movement was known as **Counter Reformation.**

The Counter Reformation was a comprehensive effort which consisted of the following five major elements

(i) Reactionary defence of Catholic sacramental practices

(ii) Structural reconfiguration

(iii) Religious orders

(iv) Spiritual movements

(v) Political dimensions

The Counter Reformation included the following reforms

The Council of Trent (1545-1563)

As a result of Counter Reformation, Council of Trent was convened in 1545 by Pope Paul III in order to make a better statement of the doctrines of the Catholic Church and also to carry out useful reforms in money matters and education.

A revision of the service-books of the Church was carried out, together with an issue of a new edition of the Vulgate and the Latin Bible. Catholics were prohibited from reading several dangerous and heretical (religious opinion) books which were put down in a list called **the Index**.

The Church Court, known as the Inquisition, punished lapses from faith, especially those in Spain and in Italy. The Council of Trent was responsible for establishing seminaries, centres to educate and train priests. The sale of indulgence was stopped, no fees were to be charged for religious services and the use of vernacular language was advocated for preaching in the Church.

The Society of Jesus

Ignatius Loyola, a Spanish noble (1493-1556) founded the Society of Jesus in 1534. Its members were called the Jesuits, in the new movement for reforms. This society helped the Jesuits to won more followers in Europe, China, India, Africa and the Americas.

St. Francis Xavier, a follower of Jesuit Loyola went to several European countries to propogate reformed Christianity. The selfless and dedicated work done by Jesuits like Loyola and St Xavier produced significant impact on Counter Reformation. This enabled restoring of the prestige of the Roman Catholic Church.

Check Your LEARNING...

1. Who were Protestants?
2. Mention any one corrupt practice of Church.
3. Who is regarded as the Morning Star of Reformation?
4. Who was the founder of the Society of Jesus?

QUiCK Revision

- The Reformation could be described as a group religious movement that was directed against the Church of Rome. It involved a revolt against the authority and principles of the Christian Church in Rome with the Pope as its head.
- Those going against the Pope were called the Protestants while those continuing their allegiance to him, were referred to as Roman Catholics.
- During the early medieval period, the Church had become a hierarchical organisation with Pope as its head. The position of Pope is often described as 'Papal Monarchy'.
- But during the 14th century people became dissatisfied with some of the Church practices which paved the way for Reformation.
- The priest and officers of higher position in the Church hierarchy received their appointments through corrupt means. They led lives of luxury and immorality. Often the churchmen used the church as a means of business.
- Priests and Church officers tried to make as much money as possible and liberally issued indulgences or pardon certificates against payment.
- One could now gain salvation in exchange for fees. The priests, the bishops and the wandering monks could pronounce a marriage lawful or unlawful.
- The Church imposed various kinds of taxes like Peter's pence and the Tithe (one-tenth of income of each person). The Church properties were exempted from taxes. The burden of taxation was completely on the merchants.
- The Schism in Church in the 15th century also greatly lowered its prestige. Instead of one Pope, two Popes began to be elected one by the French cardinals and the other by the Italian cardinals.
- The new spirit of learning and enquiry set in motion by the renaissance also greatly contributed to the Reformation.
- Several scholars raised their voices in opposition to certain Catholic teachings and practices. Among them was John Wycliffe (1320-1384). He is regarded as the 'Morning Star of the Reformation'.
- Martin Luther (1483-1546) was the first reformer and a native of German who lead a large number of people to openly break with the Church.
- He openly questioned the sale of indulgences in 1517 by several agents of Pope Leo X, for collecting money for completing the construction of St. Peter's Church at Rome.
- In order to restore the reputation of the Church, an attempt was made to reform the Catholic church in Italy, Austria, France and Spain, while the Protestant Reformation was being carried out in Germany, Switzerland and Scandinavia.
- The Council of Trent (1545-1563) was convened in order to make a better statement of the doctrines of the Catholic Church and also to carry out useful reforms in money matters and education.
- The Society of Jesus founded by Ignatius Loyola played an important role in reviving the Church. Its members were called the Jesuits, in the new movement for reforms.

Chapter Practice

Section-I

Multiple Choice Questions

1. Reformation was a religious movement directed against the church of ....
   (a) Rome (b) England (c) America (d) Germany

Ans. (a) Rome

2. Who were called Protestants?
   (a) People against the Pope
   (b) People in favour of Pope
   (c) The officers of church
   (d) The reformers

Ans. (a) People against the Pope

3. The position of Pope is often described as ....
   (a) Dogmas (b) Papal
   (c) Schism (d) None of these

Ans. (b) Papal

4. Which among the following was the cause of reformation?
   (a) Dissatisfaction with the practice of Catholic Church
   (b) New learning
   (c) Salvation through fees
   (d) All of the above

Ans. (d) All of the above

5. Why priest were avoided when new learning was introduced in Churches?
   (a) The invention of printing press.
   (b) Availability of printing Bible in local languages.
   (c) They feel that they could reach God without the intermediary of priest.
   (d) All of the above

Ans. (d) All of the above

6. Who called that Pope was not Christ's representative on Earth, but anti-Christ?
   (a) Martin Luther (b) John Wycliff
   (c) St Francis Xavier (d) Ignatius Loyola

Ans. (b) John Wycliff

7. Complete the given analogy
   Ninety-Five Theses posted : 1517 :: Society of Jesus founded :?
   (a) 1493 (b) 1534 (c) 1545 (d) 1642

Ans. (b) 1534

8. Replace the underlined word to correct the sentence.
   Ignatius Loyola founded the 'Society of Jesus' in <u>1524</u>.
   (a) 1493 (b) 1556 (c) 1534 (d) 1563

Ans. (c) 1534

9. Replace the underlined word to correct the sentence.
   <u>Martin Luther</u> was a follower of Jesuit Loyola who went to several European countries to propogate reformed Christianity.
   (a) Francis Xavier
   (b) Ignatius Loyola
   (c) John Wycliff
   (d) Martin Luther King Jr.

Ans. (a) Francis Xavier

10. Identify the given statement about Martin Luther and choose the correct option.
    (i) He was born in 1483 in Germany.
    (ii) He became the monk at the age of 22.
    (iii) He wrote Ninety-Five Theses.
    (iv) The Theses contained points of difference in the beliefs and practices of the Church.

    Codes
    (a) Only (i) (b) Only (ii)
    (c) Both (i) and (ii) (d) All of these

Ans. (d) All of these

11. Identify the elements of Counter Reformation and select the correct option.
    (i) Structural reconfiguration
    (ii) Spiritual movements
    (iii) Religious orders
    (iv) Political dimensions

    Codes
    (a) Only (i)
    (b) Both (i) and (ii)
    (c) Both (iii) and (iv)
    (d) All of the above

Ans. (d) All of the above

12. Match the following.

List-I	List-II
A. Martin Luther	1. Ninety-Five Theses
B. St Francis Xavier	2. Propogate reformed Christianity in Europe.
C. Ignatius Loyola	3. Founded Society of Jesus
D. Wycliff	4. Regarded as the Morning Star of the Reformation

Codes

	A	B	C	D
(a)	1	2	3	4
(b)	4	3	2	1
(c)	2	1	4	3
(d)	3	4	1	2

Ans. (a)

Passage Based Questions

13. Read the passage given below and answer the following questions.

In 1501, Martin Luther became a student at the University of Erfurt. At the request of his father, he took law, but he soon abandoned law, preferring to study Aristotle and the subjects of philosophy and theology. Despite admiring aspects of Aristotle and the classics, he was unsatisfied with just reason and intellectual studies and decided to become a monk so he could devote his life to God.

In 1517, Martin Luther first protested to the Catholic Church about the sale of indulgences. (Buying an indulgence gave the person full or partial remission of temporal punishment due for sins which have already been forgiven). Martin Luther argued that his faith alone that could provide the remission of sin and not monetary payments to the church.

(i) Who was Martin Luther?
(a) Reformer (b) Painter
(c) Sailor (d) Social Worker

Ans. (a) Reformer

(ii) Martin Luther belonged to ....
(a) Poland (b) Italy (c) Spain (d) Germany

Ans. (d) Germany

(iii) Where did Luther post his Ninety-Five Theses?
(a) Germany (b) Russia
(c) France (d) Italy

Ans. (a) Germany

(iv) Who wrote the Ninety-Five Theses that questioned the practices and beliefs of the Catholic Church?
(a) Martin Luther
(b) John Calvin
(c) Martin Luther King Jr
(d) William Shakespeare

Ans. (a) Martin Luther

Section-II

Short Questions

1. Define Reformation.

Ans. Reformation was a religious movement that was directed against the authority and principles of the Christian Church in Rome with the Pope as its head.

2. State the reasons of rebellion against the Church.

Ans. The corruption and abuses in Church, monasticism, Church rituals and sacraments as well as interference of the Pope in temporal affairs are the reasons of rebellion against church.

3. Who were called the Protestants and Roman Catholics?

Ans. The people who went against the Pope were called the Protestants while those continuing their allegiance to the Pope, were referred to as Roman Catholics.

4. In what way Reformation proved beneficial to the modern world?

Ans. The Reformation helped to put an end to the age of blind faith and dogmas ushered in the modern times. For this reason, Reformation occupies an important place in the study of the forming of the modern world.

5. State the corrupt practices of the Church which led to the rise of Reformation.

Ans. The corrupt practices of the church which led to the rise of Reformation are

- The priest and officers of higher positions in the Church hierarchy received their appointments through corrupt means.
- The churchmen used the Church as a means of business and for this purpose they devised a number of practices like charging fees for every rituals.

6. Why was the issue of indulgence criticised and who brought it into light?

Ans. The issue of indulgences was criticised because by this the churchmen tried to make as much money as possible as they liberally issued indulgences or pardon certifications against payment of fees. This practice of issuing indulgences was described as 'sale of licences to commit sin'. These corrupt practices of the Church were brought into light by great scholars like Erasmus and Thomas Moore.

7. What were the kinds of taxes imposed on people by the Church?

Ans. The Church imposed various kinds of taxes like Peter's Pence and the Tithe (one-tenth of income of each person) and the taxes collected from different countries of Europe reached Rome.

8. What do you mean by 'Great Western Schism'?

Ans. In the 15th century instead of one Pope, two Popes began to be elected one by the French cardinals and the other by the Italian cardinals. This greatly lowered the prestige of the Church. The prestige was further undermined and people lost faith and reverence for the holy institution. In 1409, the cardinals at a joint-sitting elected a third Pope. This is known as 'Great Western Schism.'

9. How did the invention of printing press contributed in the Reformation process?

Ans. The invention of printing press led to the printing of Bible in vernacular languages and brought about a new outlook among the people. People began to assert themselves against blind faith and useless religious rituals and began to feel that they could reach God without the intermediary of a priest.

10. Mention the contribution of John Wycliffe in Reformation.

Ans. John Wycliffe was an English priest and professor in the University of Oxford. He discarded the Pope to be a representative of Christ on Earth.

He propounded that individual Christians should only be guided by what they read in Bible and recommended that the Church should be subordinate to the state.

11. State the background of the life of Martin Luther King.

Ans. Martin Luther (1483-1546) was the first reformer who lead a large number of people to openly break with the church. Luther was a native of German who became a monk at the age of 22 and was then appointed as professor of Theology in the University of Wittenberg.

12. What do you mean by German Protestant Movement?

Ans. Many German princes separated from the Catholic Church and supported Martin Luther. Lutheran Churches were established all over the Germany. Luther travelled to different parts of Europe, Germany, Sweden, Norway and Denmark to spread his ideas against the Catholic Church. This movement came to be known as German Protestant Movement.

13. What is Counter Reformation?

Ans. In order to restore the reputation of the Church an attempt was made by some pious and dedicated Christians. They included some Popes to reform the Catholic Church in response to the Protestant Reformation. This is called Counter Reformation.

14. State the five major elements composed for Counter Reformation.

Ans. The Counter Reformation was a comprehensive effort composed the following five elements

(i) Reactionary defence of Catholic sacramental practices.

(ii) Ecclesiastical (related to the Christian Church) or structural reconfiguration.

(iii) Religious orders

(iv) Spiritual movements

(v) Political dimensions

15. What were the major establishments born out of the Council of Trent?

Ans. The Council of Trent was responsible for many major establishments such as

- Seminaries to educate and train priests.
- Sale of indulgence was stopped.
- No fees were to be charged for religious services and advocate the use of vernacular language for preaching in the Church.

16. How were Jesuits responsible for gaining back the respect for the Catholic Church?

Ans. The 'Society of Jesus' played an important role in reviving the reverence of the Church. By founding many schools and colleges, through their wide learning and culture and also by their simple and clear sermons and instructions, the Jesuits won back considerable respect for the Catholic Church.

Structured Questions

1. Dissatisfaction with practices of the Catholic Church was the cause for Reformation. In context of the above explain

(i) Corrupt practices

(ii) Issue of Indulgence

(iii) Issue of taxes

(iv) New Learning

Ans. (i) Refer to chapter theory page no. 190.

(ii) Refer to chapter theory page no. 190.

(iii) Refer to chapter theory page no. 190.

(iv) Refer to chapter theory page no. 191.

2. Write short notes on the following

(i) St Francis Xavier

(ii) John Wycliffe

(iii) Martin Luther

Ans. (i) Refer to chapter theory page no. 192.

(ii) Refer to chapter theory page no. 191.

(iii) Refer to chapter theory page no. 191-192.

Picture Based Questions

1. With reference to the given picture, answer the following question.

(i) Explain about the personality shown in the above picture.

(ii) How he led to the German Protestant Movement?

(iii) How Lutheranism was accepted as legal form?

Ans. (i) Martin Luther is shown in the given picture. He was the first reformer who lead a large number of people to openly break with the Church. He was a native of German and become monk at the age of 22. He was appointed professor of Theology in the University of Wittenberg.

(ii) Martin Luther led to the German Protestant Movement in the following ways

- In 1512, he took a pilgrimage to Rome where he was shocked to see the Churchmen leading a luxurious life. This made him a strong critic of the Church.
- In 1517, he posted his Ninety-five Theses written in Latin on the Church door at Wittenberg. It contained statements on points of difference in the beliefs and practices of the Church.
- In 1520, Pope Leo X issued a Papall Bull (a public decree issued by a Pope) against Martin Luther but he burnt this letter in the presence of public.

Due to these events, many German princes separated from the Catholic Church and supported Martin Luther. This led to the movement which came to be known as German Protestant Movement.

(iii) Luther and his followers formed the Scheme Kaldic League to face the challenge of Emperor Charles V. This led to a religious Civil War during 1546-1553 AD. Finally, nine years after the death of Luther, a treaty known as the Peace of Ausburg was signed by which Lutherism was accepted as another legal form of Christianity. The Northern states of Germany accepted Lutherism while the Southern states remain loyal to the Catholic Church.

Chapter Assessment

Section-I

Multiple Choice Questions

1. Reformation was ...... movement.
   (a) Religious
   (b) Political
   (c) Social
   (d) None of these
2. John Wycliff was a ...... priest and Philosopher.
   (a) English
   (b) Roman
   (c) German
   (d) Polish
3. What is the meaning of 'Schism' ?
   (a) Division
   (b) Local
   (c) Theory
   (d) Argument
4. Consider the following about the beginning of Modern age in Europe and select the correct option.
   (i) Reformation broke out number of countries like England, Germany and France , etc.
   (ii) The priest of Church led lives of luxury and immortality.
   (iii) The Church imposed various types of taxes.
   (iv) Priest and Church officers tried to make as much money as possible.

   Codes
   (a) Only (i) (b) Only (ii)
   (c) Both (ii) and (iii) (d) All of these

Section-II

Multiple Choice Questions

1. Cite the immediate cause of Reformation.
2. What was the Great Western Schism?
3. What was the objective of Council of Trent?
4. What do you understand by seminaries?
5. Who founded the 'Society of Jesus'? Who were called Jesuits?
6. What do you mean by Mercantilism?

Structured Question

1. With reference to the progress of Protestant Church, discuss
   (i) Counter Reformation
   (ii) Council of Trent
   (iii) Society of Jesus
   (iv) St Francis Xavier

CHAPTER 13

Industrial Revolution

SYLLABUS

Industrial Revolution Definition of the term; Causes of Industrial revolution
Meaning of Capitalism and causes for the rise of Capitalism
Meaning of Socialism and causes for the rise of Socialism.

Definition and Meaning of Industrial Revolution

The term 'Industrial Revolution' was used for the first time in England by the English philosopher and economist **Arnold Toynbee** (1852-83). The transformation in the method of production from man-made to machine made and from small-scale production to large-scale production is called the Industrial Revolution.

The period 1750 and 1870 in England is known as the first stage of Industrial Revolution. It was marked by the change in the manufacturing processes from slow to faster and expensive hand production to cheaper machine production.

The second stage of Industrial Revolution began after 1870, which was characterised by more direct application of science to industry and by the development of mass production techniques. This phase started in England to fulfill the growing demands for goods both at home and abroad. Further, it had been spread to many other countries like France, Belgium, North America, Germany, Russia, etc.

Causes of Industrial Revolution

The Industrial Revolution began in England and spread to many other countries. Some of the important causes for the origin of the Industrial Revolution in England are

Inventions of Spinning and Weaving

- In 1733, John Kay invented 'Flying Shuttle' which increased the speed of the weaving of cloth.
- In 1764, 'The Spinning Jenny' was invented by James Hargreaves. This machine spun eight threads simultaneously.
- Two years later, Richard Arkwright invented a spinning frame called 'Waterframe' which used waterpower in place of manpower.
- In 1779, Samuel Crompton invented his 'Spinning Mule' which included good combination of both the 'Spinning Jenny' and 'the waterframe'. It spun hundreds of thread at a time and produced either fine or coarse thread.
- In 1785, Reverend Edmund Cartwright invented the 'Powerloom' which wove cloth very quickly and it was run by a big water-wheel.
- Subsequently, Eli Whitney invented the 'Cotton Gin', a machine which was used to separate the seeds from the hand picked cotton from the fields.

Invention in Iron and Steel

- In 1709, Abraham Darby discovered the art of smelting iron with coke.
- In 1790, Henry Cort developed the new method of blasting iron with steam power.
- In 1856, Henry Bessemer discovered a faster and cheaper method of producing steel. Textile and metal industries were started in British towns like Birmingham, Sheffield, Manchester, Liverpool and London.

Invention of Steam Engine

A Scottish inventor, James Watt redesigned the steam engine which produced more power with less fuel. His invention was a great success and it was patented in 1769. This steam engine was used in the steel and textile industries. Thus, steam power replaced water power.

Location and Natural Resources

The geographical location of England was suitable for world trade and all major ports were well-connected to its sea routes. The rivers were beneficial for inland transport and its coastline offered excellent harbour.

Beside this, England was fortunate in the coal, iron, steel and hydro-power which were plentifully available in addition with other important minerals like lead, copper and tin that were used in the industry. The vicinity of coal and iron-ore mines encouraged the English people to adopt new technique for the manufacture of iron.

England procured huge supply of new materials from their colonies in Asia and Africa for their factories. In contrast to this, France, Spain and Germany had to depend on their own home-market for the disposal of their manufactured goods availability of labour.

New Factory System

In England, the household industry in towns and villages was replaced by the new factory system. Many workers were needed to operate the machines and were recruited. People without jobs in the villages began to move towards cities for employment. It has totally replaced the guild system in due course.

Transport and Communication

The use of tarcoal enabled the construction of roads in many countries of Europe. In the construction of roads and canals, France led the other countries.

A British Engineer named Mc Adam showed how smooth and hard surfaced roads could be built.

An English Engineer, George Stephenson, designed the railway line and invented a locomotive called **Rocket**. In 1830, it completed forty miles of journey from Manchester to Liverpool within an hour. During the next 40 years, Britain built a network of railway line measuring 15,000 lines which revolutionised the transport.

A number of inventions were carried in field of communication like

- In 1844, an American named Samuel Morse invented the telegraph and sent a message.
- In 1876, Alexander Graham Bell invented the telephone.
- In 1899, Marconi invented the wireless which made it possible to send signals to many parts of the world. This invention paved the way for radio broadcasting and television in future.

Check Your LEARNING...

1. Who introduced the term 'Industrial Revolution'?
2. What was/were the causes of Industrial Revolution?
3. Why England was suitable for World Trade during Industrial Revolution?
4. Who was the inventor of telegraph?

Capitalism

The word 'capitalism' is derived from capital. Capitalism is an economic system in which business and industry of a country are controlled and run for profit by private individuals rather than by the government. In common language, the wealth used for making more wealth is known as **Capital** and the owner of this capital is known as **Capitalist**.

The capitalist owned the means of production such as labour, raw-materials, tools and machines. They managed industrial units and convert the workers into mere wage earner.

The motto of capitalism is profit maximisation and accumulation of wealth. As a result, the ultimate sufferers were the helpless workers who bound to work more than 12 hours a day under inhumane conditions and the gainers were the capitalists.

Capitalism increase individual productivity through 'the division of labour' which divides productive labour into its smallest components. The result of the division of labour is decrease in the value of the individual worker in terms of skill and wages.

Causes for the Rise of Capitalism

- **Increase in Population** The Industrial Revolution increased the national wealth and improved purchasing power and health care facilities, which led to increase in the population of the country. People moved from rural to urban areas in search of job opportunities, better life and some other benefits.
- **Growth of Towns** Many manufacturing sectors came to located close to the coalfields and supplied fuel to the factories. So new town and cities grew dramatically.
- **Mass Production** Machine helped in producing and manufacturing goods on large scale. Mass production enabled the capitalists to a mass huge wealth and gave rise to capitalism.

- **Disappearance of Small Farmers** Many small farmers shifted to new industrial towns for employment because their land were purchased by industrialist. Availability of abundant labour for factories helped in the development of the Industrial Revolution.

Socialism

The evil effects of capitalism and the spirit of improving the condition of workers gave birth to socialism. Socialism is defined as an economic system in which the means of production are owned not by private individuals but by the community in the order that all may share the produced wealth more fairly.

Socialism is based upon three principles. First, it is opposed to private capitalism, secondly, socialism is the voice of all workers and the working class and thirdly, socialism demands a just distribution of wealth.

Socialists maintain that all factors of production should belong to entire human race or society. The first socialists were Frenchmen namely Babeuf, Saint Simon, Charles Fourier, Robert Owen (father of the British socialism) and Louis Blanc. Karl Marx and Friedrich Engels were the scientific socialists.

Bernstein, Jean Juras, Bernard Shaw and Sidney Webb were democratic socialists. They advocated that socialism could be brought about by peaceful and democratic means.

Causes for the Rise of Socialism

- **Reaction to the Evils of Capitalism** As a result of the Industrial Revolution, the society was divided into two distant classes, the capitalists and the socialists. The capitalists had their selfish interests and they began to exploit the workers. They accumulated great wealth and began to lead a luxurious life at the cost of the workers. Thus, the socialists stood up for the workers and tried to save them from the exploitation of the capitalists.
- **Trade Union Movement** The British Government was forced by the strong trade union movement to recognise the worker's right to vote. It had brought the division of society into the rich and the poor into sharp focus. This had led to rethinking among the vast majority of workers.
- **The Chartist Movement** The Chartist Movement took place between 1836-1848 in which worker's leader put up their demands before the Parliament in the form of a charter. Hence, the movement was named the Chartist Movement. It aimed at getting the right to vote for workers. It led to many riots and strikes and the movement declined in the mid of 19th century.

This led to sharp class divisions among capitalists and workers which gave rise to socialism. Therefore, the socialists wanted to set up a society free of exploitation and class divisions. They proposed that this can be achieved through social control of means of production and distribution.

Check Your LEARNING...

1. Write any one impact of Industrial Revolution.
2. What do you mean by capitalism?
3. What is Socialism?

QUiCK Revision

- Industrial Revolution means a system of manufacturing on a large-scale with the help of machinery driven by mechanical, chemical or electrical energy.
- Industrial Revolution began first in England due to the inventions of spinning, weaving, invention in iron and steel and inventions of steam engine, suitable location and natural resources, emergence new factory system and development in transport and communication.
- Several machines relating to textiles, steam power, smelting iron, means of transport, communication and electricity were developed during the 1765 to 1900. It is through these machines and inventions that Industrial Revolution became possible. Therefore, Industrial Revolution in other countries, e.g. Belgium, France, Germany, North America and Japan, followed in due course.
- Capitalism and socialism were the two major impacts of Industrial Resolution.
- Capitalism is an economic system in which business and industry of a country are controlled and run for profit by private individuals rather than by the government.
- The factors which led to rise of capitalism were increase in population, growth of towns, mass production and disappearance of small farmers.
- Socialism means people's control on all means of production, distribution and exchange and the economic system of the country.
- Reactions to the evil of capitalism, trade Union and the Chartist Movement were the factors which led to the development of socialism.
- In 1934, Socialist Party of India was established under the leadership of Acharya Narendra Dev, Achyut Patwardhan, Jaya Prakash Narayan and Dr Ram Manohar Lohia.

Chapter Practice

Section-I

Multiple Choice Questions

1. In which year 'Flying Shuttle' was invented?
(a) 1733 (b) 1764 (c) 1779 (d) 1785

Ans. (a) 1733

2. Spinning Mule was invented by ...... in 1779.
(a) Samuel Crompton (b) Abraham Dassy
(c) MC Adam (d) Robert Owen

Ans. (a) Samuel Crompton

3. Which of the following was the causes of the Industrial Revolution?
(a) Invention of Spinning and Weaving
(b) Invention in Iron and Steel
(c) Invention of Steam Engine
(d) All of the above

Ans. (d) All of the above

4. James Watt was a .... inventer who redesigned the steam engine.
(a) German (b) Scottish
(c) Russian (d) English

Ans. (b) Scottish

5. Which of the following was not a cause of the Industrial Revolution?
(a) Growth of factories and machines
(b) Advancement in agriculture
(c) Decline in trade and commerce
(d) Availability of raw materials

Ans. (c) Decline in trade and commerce

6. What was/were the factors for the rise of the capitalism?
(a) Increase in population
(b) Growth of towns
(c) Disappearance of small farmers
(d) All of the above

Ans. (d) All of the above

7. Which of the following is a key feature of capitalism?
(a) Government control over industries
(b) Equal distribution of wealth
(c) Private ownership of businesses
(d) Elimination of competition

Ans. (c) Private ownership of businesses

8. The Chartist Movement took place during ....
(a) 1826- 38 (b) 1836- 48
(c) 1942- 46 (d) 1934 - 48

Ans. (b) 1836- 48

9. Who was Karl Marx?
(a) Painter (b) Historian
(c) Economist (d) Scientist

Ans. (c) Economist

10. Who invented the telegraph?
(a) Alexander Graham Bell
(b) Samuel Morse
(c) Thomas Edison
(d) Guglielmo Marconi

Ans. (b) Samuel Morse

11. Complete the given analogy
Telegraph : Samuel Morse : : Telephone : ?
(a) A. Graham Bell (b) Einstein
(c) Marcony (d) John Kay

Ans. (a) A. Graham Bell

12. Replace the underlined word to correct sentence
<u>Samuel Morse</u> invented the telephone in 1876.
(a) Alexander Graham Bell
(b) James Watt
(c) John Kay
(d) Louis Blanc

Ans. (a) Alexander Graham Bell

13. Replace the underlined word to correct the sentence.
The motto of <u>Socialism</u> is profit maximisation and accumulation of wealth.
(a) Capitalism (b) Liberalism
(c) Karl Marx (d) Democratic socialist

Ans. (a) Capitalism

14. Consider the following statement associated with Industrial Revolution and choose the correct option
(i) In 1764, the Spinning Jenny was invented by James Hargreaves.
(ii) In England, the household industry in towns and village was replaced by the new factory system.
(iii) Due to industrial revolution, the transport and communication system was improved.
(iv) Because of Industrial Revolution, new towns and cities were established.

Codes
(a) Only (i) (b) Both (i) and (ii)
(c) (i), (ii) and (iii) (d) All of these

Ans. (d) All of these

15. Which of the following pairs of inventors and their inventions with the correct year are correct?
I. John Kay - Flying Shuttle (1733)
II. James Hargreaves - Spinning Jenny (1764)
III. Richard Arkwright - Water Frame (1785)
IV. Samuel Crompton - Spinning Mule (1801)

Options
(a) Only I and II (b) Only II and III
(c) Only I and IV (d) Only III and IV

Ans. (a) Only I and II

16. Consider the following statements associated with socialism.
I. It focuses on private property and individual profit-making.
II. It aims to reduce income inequality and provide social welfare.
III. Socialism promotes free-market competition without government intervention.
IV. Socialism advocates for collective or government ownership of resources.

Which of the above statements are correct?
(a) Only I and II
(b) Only II and III
(c) Only I and IV
(d) Only III and IV

Ans. (a) Only I and IV

17. Match the following.

List-I		List-II
A. Flying Shuttle	1.	James Hargreaves
B. Spinning Jenny	2.	Reverend Edmund Cartwright
C. Waterframe	3.	John Kay
D. Powerloom	4.	Richard Arkwright

Codes

	A	B	C	D		A	B	C	D
(a)	1	2	3	4	(b)	4	3	2	1
(c)	2	4	1	3	(d)	3	1	4	2

Ans. (d)

18. Match the following.

List-I	List-II
A. James Watt	1. Telephone
B. Samuel Morse	2. Railway line
C. George Stephenson	3. Telegraph
D. Alaxender Graham Bell	4. Steam Engine

Code

	A	B	C	D		A	B	C	D
(a)	4	3	2	1	(b)	1	2	3	4
(c)	2	4	1	3	(d)	3	1	4	2

Ans. (a)

Passage Based Question

19. Read the passage given below and answer the following questions.

Socialism is a populist economic and political system based on public ownership (also known as collective or common ownership) of the means of production. Those means include the machinery, tools, and factories used to produce goods that aim to directly satisfy human needs. By the 1870s, socialist ideas spread through Europe. To coordinate their efforts, socialists formed an international body - namely, the Second International. Workers in England and Germany began forming associations to fight for better living and working conditions.

Socialist ideals include production for use, rather than for profit, an equitable distribution of wealth and material resources among all people; no more competitive buying and selling in the market; and free access to goods and services.

(i) Which of the following is/are the characterstics of socialism?
(a) Self managed economy
(b) Freedom of consumption
(c) Equal income distribution
(d) All of the above

Ans. (d) All of the above

(ii) Which of the following is a key characteristic of socialism?
(a) Emphasis on private property and profit-making
(b) Government control over major industries
(c) Complete absence of government intervention in the economy
(d) Promotion of individual competition over social welfare

Ans:. (b) Government control over major industries

(iii) Which statement is not associated with socialism?
(a) It demands unequal distribution of wealth.
(b) It demands equal distribution of wealth.
(c) State is the primary employer.
(d) Give equal opportunities to all classes of people.

Ans. (a) It demands unequal distribution of wealth.

Section-II

Short Questions

1. Who coined the term 'Industrial Revolution'?

Ans. The term 'Industrial Revolution' was coined by European scholars Blanqui and George Michelet in France and Friedrich Engels in Germany.

2. What was the period of first and second stage of Industrial Revolution?

Ans. First stage of Industrial Revolution period was 1750 to 1870. Second stage of Industrial revolution period was after 1870.

3. What is Industrial Revolution?

Ans. The transformation in method of production from man-made to machine-made, from small-scale production to large-scale production is called the Industrial Revolution.

4. Who invented the powerloom and when?

Ans. Reverend Edmond Cartwright invented the Powerloom in 1785 which wove cloth very quickly and it was run by a big water-wheel.

5. What do you mean by Cotton Gin?

Ans. 'Cotton Gin' is a machine which was used to separate the seeds from the hand picked cotton from the fields. It was invented by Eli Whitney.

6. Mention the developments in the iron and steel industry during Industrial Revolution.

Ans. In 1709, Abraham Darby discovered the art of smelting iron with coke followed by the new method of blasting iron with steam power in 1790 by Henry Cort. Henry Besemer invented a new method of removing impurities from iron and made steel in 1856.

7. What was the prime source of energy before Industrial Revolution? State its limitations.

Ans. Water as a hydraulic power had been the prime source of energy for centuries. However, it had certain limitation such as specific to certain areas, seasonal variations and the speed of the flow of water.

8. Who realised that steam could generate tremendous power? What was the outcome?

Ans. A Scottish inventor, James Watt realised that steam could generate tremendous power, so he redesigned the steam engine which produced more power with less fuel.

His invention was a great success and was patented in 1769. This steam engine was used in steel and textile industries and further replaced the water power.

9. How is the geographical location of England was a significant factor of Industrial Revolution?

Ans. The geographical location of England was significant factor of Industrial Revolution because

- Its geographical position was suitable for world trade and all major ports were well connected to its sea-routes.
- Coal, iron and steel and hydro-power were plentifully available in addition with other important minerals like lead, copper and tin for industrial uses.

10. How was England benefitted from their colonies in Asia and Africa?

Ans. England was benefitted as it procured huge supply of raw-material from their colonies at Asia and Africa for their manufacturing needs.

11. How is the new factory system, a cause of Industrial Revolution?

Ans. The new factory system was a cause of industrial revolution in the following ways

- The household industry in towns and villages was replaced by the new factory system.
- Wealthy capitalist bought machines and large buildings and turned them into mills.
- The unemployed people of the villages went to cities for jobs in the factories.

12. Which two means of communication revolutionised the world during this period?

Ans. The two means of communication which revolutionised the world during this period are

(i) The invention of telephone in 1876 by Alexander Graham Bell, which carried human voice on wire from one end to other.

(ii) The invention of wireless in 1899 by Marconi, which made it possible to send signals to many parts of the world. This invention paved the way for radio-broadcasting and television in future.

13. What were the immediate effect of expansion of trade and commerce?

Ans. Expansion of trade and commerce led to the growth of new cities/industrial towns like Manchester, Leeds, Birmingham, etc which had the concentration of factories, marketing and financial institutions to facilitate the exchange of products.

14. What was the impact of Industrial Revolution on the family system?

Ans. The Industrial Revolution led to the breakdown of traditional joint family system which shared loyalty and cooperation among members of family and it was replaced by the new nuclear family system, which developed on individualistic attitude.

15. What do you mean by a capitalist economy?

Ans. Capitalist economy is an economic system in which business and industry of a country are controlled and run for profit by private individuals rather than by government. The factors of production such as labour, raw-material, tools and machines are owned by the capitalists or private individuals.

16. How does capitalism promote economic growth and innovation?

Ans. Capitalism promotes economic growth and innovation by encouraging private ownership and competition. Businesses strive to improve products and services to attract customers and leading to technological advancements. The profit motive drives entrepreneurs to invest in new ideas, boosting industrial and economic development.

17. Define socialism.

Ans. Socialism is defined as an economic system in which the means of production are not owned by private individuals but by the community in order that all may share more fairly in the wealth produced.

18. What are the three principles of socialism?

Ans. Socialism is based upon three principles such as

(i) First, socialism is opposed to private capitalism.

(ii) Second, socialism is the voice of all workers and the working class.

(iii) Thirdly, socialism demands a just distribution of wealth. It maintains that all factors of production should belong to entire human race or society.

19. What does socialism and capitalism connotes in the present scenario?

Ans. In the present scenario, there seems to be balance between capitalism and socialism. It has the connotation for working further for the promotion of a just and a welfare state.

20. What is the Chartist Movement?

Ans. The Chartist Movement took place between 1836-1848, in which worker's leader put up their demands before the Parliament in the form of charter. It aimed at getting the right to vote for workers. It led to many riots and strikes and the movement declined in the mid 19th century.

Structured Questions

1. With reference to genesis of industrial revolution, explain the following

(i) The term 'Industrial Revolution'.

(ii) First stage of Industrial Revolution

(iii) Second stage of Industrial Revolution

(iii) New factory system in England

Ans. (i) The term 'Industrial Revolution' was used by European scholars Blanqui and George Michelet in France in 1837 and Friedrich Engels in Germany. It was used for the first time in England by the English philosopher and Economist Arnold Toynbee during the period 1852 to 1883. He described the changes that took place in England's industrial development between 1750 to 1870.

(ii) England's industrial development between 1750 to 1870 is considered to be the first stage of industrial revolution. It is marked by the change in the manufacturing processes from slow to faster and from expensive hand production to cheaper machine production.

(iii) The second stage began after 1870, which was characterised by more direct application of science to industry and by the development of mass production techniques. This phase started in England to fulfill the growing demands for goods both at home and abroad.

(iv) In England, the household industry in towns and villages was replaced by the new factory system. It is the area where manufacturing process is carried on with the help of power and machine. It is one of the important causes of industrial revolution as wealthy capitalist bought machines and buildings to establish factory.

2. With reference to the scientific inventions as the cause of industrial revolution, explain.

(i) Cotton spinning and weaving

(ii) Iron and steel

(iii) Steam power

(iv) Location and Natural resources

Ans. (i) Refer to chapter theory page no. 198.

(ii) Refer to chapter theory page no. 198.

(iii) Refer to chapter theory page no. 199.

(iv) Refer to chapter theory page no. 199.

3. With reference to good and ill-effects of Industrial Revolution, explain.

(i) Standard of living

(ii) Expansions of trade and commerce

(iii) Disintegration of joint family

(iv) Chartist Movement

Ans. (i) Industrial revolution resulted in the increase of standard of living as there was large-scale production of quality products at cheaper rates and most of the goods can be used by the common people. Consumer goods were available in plenty and at reasonable rates.

(ii) A large section of people engaged themselves in trade and commerce after the Industrial Revolution. This development carried on mostly in towns which led to the growth of new cities and industrial towns like Manchester, Leeds, Birmingham, etc.

(iii) Breakdown of traditional joint family system was another ill effect. The joint family system demanded obedience from children, loyality among husband and wife and co-operation among all members of the family. In town, this system was replaced by the new nuclear family system consisting of single parents and their minor children.

(iv) Refer to chapter theory page no. 200.

5. The industrial revolution in England and subsequently elsewhere in Europe during the early 19th century had great impact on society. With reference to this discuss the :

(i) General effect of industrial revolution.

(ii) Social consequences of industrial revolution.

(iii) Major causes behind the rise of industrial revolution.

Ans. (i) In general, the industrial revolution produced both good and bad effects on society. Large-scale production of quality products at cheaper rates, most of the goods can be used by the common people. These goods were available in plenty and at reasonable price. Such cities had the concentration of factories, marketing and financial institutions like banks, guilds etc. to facilitate the exchange of products.

(ii) Industrial revolution led to the breakdown of traditional joint family system. This system required obedience from children, loyality among husband and wife and co-operation among all members of the family. However, gradually, it diminished and in town, this system was replaced by the new nuclear family system consisting of single parents and their minor children.

(iii) The impacts of Industrial Revolution in rural were
- Agriculture and village handicrafts decline due to competition from machine made goods.
- In the place of tenant farmers, the rich landlords became more influential. The landless labourers fled to towns and cities in search of jobs.
- Rural unemployment raised and it laid to lowering of farm wage-levels to subsistence level.

6. With regard to rise of new social classes as a result of industrial revolution, explain the following.
   (i) Socialism
   (ii) Role of natural resources
   (iii) Capitalism

Ans. (i) Refer to chapter theory page no. 200.
(ii) Refer to chapter theory page no. 199.
(iii) Refer to chapter theory page no. 199.

7. There are various major factors which led to the development of socialism, in context of the above explain.
   (i) Reaction to the evils of capitalism
   (ii) Trade Union Movement
   (iii) Chartist Movement

Ans. (i) Refer to chapter theory page no. 200.
(ii) Refer to chapter theory page no. 200.
(iii) Refer to chapter theory page no. 200.

Chapter Assessment

Section-I

Multiple Choice Questions

1. The term 'Industrial Revolution' was used for the first time in England by ....
   (a) Adam Smith (b) Henry Cort
   (c) Arnold Toynbee (d) James Watt
2. Who invented 'Flying Shuttle'
   (a) John Kay (b) Eli Whitney
   (c) Abraham Dorby (d) Henry Bassemer
3. Karl Marx was a ...... political Philosopher and economist.
   (a) Russian (b) German (c) French (d) English
4. Replace the underlined word to correct the sentence.
   In <u>1834</u>, the socialist party was established in India
   (a) 1852 (b) 1932 (c) 1934 (d) 1954

Section-II

Short Questions

1. Mention any two reasons as why Industrial Revolution began first in England.
2. What were the advantages of Spinning Jenny and the Flying Shuttle?
3. How did the increase in the demand for the British goods led to the invention of new machines?
4. What were the three main points of the impact of Industrial Revolution?
5. Name any two consequences of the Industrial Revolution in the economic field.
6. Explain how the colonial policy of Britain contributed to the spread of the Industrial Revolution.
7. State how urbanisation took place as a result of Industrial Revolution.
8. State the contribution of immigrants/artisans to the Industrial Revolution.
9. Differentiate between Capitalism and Socialism.

Structured Questions

1. Discuss the role of the following factors in ushering in the Industrial Revolution.
   (i) Geographical location and availability of natural resources
   (ii) Age of machines
   (iii) Boost in transport system
   (iv) Growth of new cities / towns
2. The Industrial Revolution affected the economic social and cultural life of the people. With reference to this, explain.
   (i) Rise of capitalism
   (ii) Rise of socialism
   (iii) Impoverishment of the masses
3. Socialism originated as a direct reaction to the evils at Industrial Revolution and capitalism. With reference to this, discuss.
   (i) Circumstances which lead to the growth of socialism
   (ii) Meaning and feature of socialism
   (iii) Exponents of socialism

Sample
Question Papers (1-3)

SAMPLE QUESTION PAPER 1

A HIGHLY SIMULATED Sample Question Paper for ICSE Class IX

History & Civics (Solved)

General Instructions

1. Answers to this paper must be written on the paper provided separately.
2. You will not be allowed to write during the first 15 minutes.This time is to be spent in reading the question paper.
3. The time given at the head of this Paper is the time allowed for writing the answers.
4. Attempt all questions from Part I (Compulsory).
5. A total of five questions are to be attempted from Part II, two out of three questions from Section A and three out of five questions from Section B.
6. The intended marks for questions or parts of questions are given in brackets [ ].

Time : 2 Hrs **Max. Marks : 80**

PART - I

(30 Marks)

Attempt all questions from this part.

Question 1

1. Which of the following statement is correct about Fundamental Rights? (1)
   (a) The freedom of speech is mentioned in Article 14 of the Indian Constitution.
   (b) Supreme Court can issue any type of writs for enforcement of the Fundamental Rights.
   (c) The Freedom to move is not part of the Fundamental Rights in India.
   (d) The Fundamental Rights are mentioned in Part IV of the Indian Constitution.

2. Which of the following statements about elections in India is correct? (1)
   P General elections are held when the term of the legislature is completed.
   Q Mid-term elections take place when the legislature is dissolved before completing its full term.
   R By-elections are conducted for all constituencies in a state if the government resigns.
   S The Election Commission of India is responsible for conducting elections in the country.
   (a) P and Q (b) Q and S
   (c) P, Q and S (d) All of these

3. Given below are details of a few individuals. (1)

Person	Age (in years)	Description
W	21	Is a teacher
X	36	Is a businessman
Y	19	Has declared insolvency
Z	24	Has taken citizenship of another country

Who among them is eligible to become a member of the State Legislative Council? (1)

(a) W (b) X
(c) Y (d) Z

4. Which of the following options given below is not a part of the State Legislature? (1)
(a) The Governor
(b) The Legislative Assembly
(c) The Legislative Council (in some states)
(d) The Lok Sabha

5. With reference to the Election Commission of India, complete the following analogy: (1)

Direct Election: Lok Sabha :: Indirect Election: ....

(a) Rajya Sabha (b) Vidhan Sabha
(c) Lok Sabha Speaker (d) Gram Panchayat

6. Observe the given picture. In case of a similar unruly situation in the State legislature , choose the action that may be taken by the Speaker. (1)

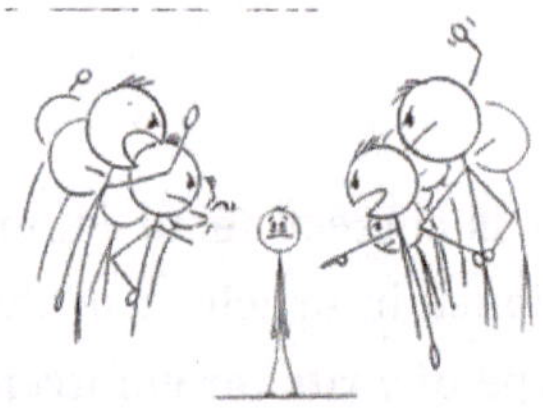

(a) Dissolve the Legislature
(b) Adjourn the House for lack of quorum.
(c) Adjourn the House for lack of discipline.
(d) disqualify the members under Anti-defection law.

7. Complete the given analogy.
Harappa : Daya Ram Sahni :: Mohenjo-Daro : .... (1)
(a) R. D. Banerji (b) John Marshall
(c) Mortimer Wheeler (d) Rakhal Das

8. Identify the correct statement related to the Vedic period. **(1)**

(a) Early Vedic society was primarily urban and trade-based.

(b) Later Vedic texts mention the expansion of agriculture and the use of iron tools.

(c) The caste system was absent during the Vedic period.

(d) The Vedas were written in Persian language.

9. Which of the following statements about the Mauryan Empire are correct? **(1)**

P : Chandragupta Maurya was the founder of the Mauryan Empire.

Q : Ashoka adopted Buddhism after the Battle of Kalinga.

R : The Mauryan administration had a well-organised spy system.

S : The empire was ruled under a democratic system.

(a) P and Q

(b) P and R

(c) R and S

(d) Q and R

10. Complete the given analogy.
Jainism : Mahavira :: Buddhism : .... **(1)**

(a) Ashoka

(b) Gautama Buddha

(c) Chanakya

(d) Mahayana

11. Which of the following statement is not related to the Sangam Age? **(1)**

(a) The Sangam literature was written in Sanskrit.

(b) The economy was in flourishing state.

(c) The rulers of this period were strong.

(d) The three major kingdoms of this period were the Cheras, Cholas and Pandyas.

12. Identify the odd one which is not related to the Gupta Empire. **(1)**

(a) Chandragupta I was the king of this dynasty.

(b) Samudragupta was the king of this dynasty and he is also called Napoleon of India

(c) Ashoka was the famous king of this dynasty who flourished Buddhism in India.

(d) Skandagupta was the last king of this dynasty

13. Read the statements given below and select the option that shows the correct relationship between (A) and (R). **(1)**

Assertion (A) The Bhakti Movement promoted devotion to a personal god and rejected rituals.

Reason (R) Bhakti saints believed that caste and social status should not determine one's relationship with God.

(a) (A) is true and (R) is false.

(b) (R) is true but (A) is false.

(c) Both (A) and (R) are independent of each other.

(d) (A) is the reason for (R).

14. Read the description and identify the person. (1)
He invented the steam engine, which played a crucial role in the Industrial Revolution by improving transportation and manufacturing.

(a) James Watt
(b) Richard Arkwright
(c) George Stephenson
(d) Eli Whitney

15. The scholars and artists in a European city during the 15th century noticed a growing interest in classical learning and artistic expression. They decided to embrace new ideas and challenge old traditions to bring about cultural and intellectual progress. (1)

Which method of the Renaissance must they follow to achieve this transformation?

(a) Feudalism
(b) Scholasticism
(c) Humanism
(d) Theocracy

16. Which of the following statements about capitalism is correct? (1)

(a) Capitalism encourages private ownership and profit-making.
(b) In a capitalist economy, the government owns all industries.
(c) Capitalism does not allow competition in the market.
(d) Capitalism ensures equal distribution of wealth among all citizens.

Question 2

(i) Why Fundamental Rights are considered as Magna Carta of the Indian Constitution? How can Parliament make amendment into it? (2)

(ii) 'The State Legislature plays a crucial role in law-making and governance, ensuring representation of the people in a democratic setup. To function effectively, it must have a well-defined structure and powers, free from undue influence'. – (*The Role of State Legislatures in Democracy*) (2)

From the passage, deduce and mention any two ways in which the Constitution ensures the proper functioning of the State Legislature. (2)

(iii) Mention any two important features of the Indus Valley Civilisation. (2)

(iv) Who was Megasthenes? Name the book written by him. (2)

(v) What do you mean by Sangam Age and what were the food habits of the Sangam Age people? (2)

(vi) Imagine you are a scholar living during the Renaissance period. Mention any two factors that you believe led to the rise of the Renaissance and how they influenced society. (2)

(vii) What is the Yajur Veda?. (2)

PART - II

(50 Marks)

Section A (Civics)

Attempt any two questions from this section.

Question 3

The Constitution contains law and rules by which a country is governed. In the light of this statement answer the following questions :

(a) Write about some salient features of the Indian Constitution. (3)

(b) What are the different types of Fundamental Rights of the Indian Constitution? (3)

(c) What are the Directive Principles of State Policy? (4)

Question 4

Democracy is a government of the people, for the people and by the people.In the light of this statement answer the following questions:

(a) What is an election and what are the needs of it? (3)

(b) What are the systems of elections in India? (3)

(c) What are the different constituencies in India? (4)

Question 5

The State Legislature plays an important role in the governance of a state. In the light of this statement, answer the following questions.

(a) Why State Legislatures are important and write any two points highlighting its importance.(3)

(b) Mention some important provisions related to the post of Speaker and Deputy Speaker.

(c) Highlight the differences between State Legislative Assembly and Council. (3)

Section B (History)

Attempt any three questions from this section

Question 6

Kalinga war has a great historical significance. In the light of this statement answer the following questions :

(a) Why is Kalinga war regarded as a turning point in Ashoka's life?

(b) Write about the main features of Dhamma.

(c) What was the impact of Dhamma?

Question 7

(a) What is Sangam Age? What are the two sources of Sangam Age? (3)

(b) What was the position of women in Sangam Age? (3)

(c) Describe the economy of Sangam Age. (4)

Question 8

Study the picture given below and answer the following questions :

(a) Identify the structure given in the picture. Name the place and the state where it is located? (3)

(b) Name the dynasty and the king who built it. When it was built? (3)

(c) Mention its architectural features. (4)

Question 9

(a) What do you mean by Bhakti Movement? (3)

(b) What are the significance of Bhakti Movement? (3)

(c) Name two Bhakti saints and describe their ways of teachings. (4)

Question 10

(a) What is Reformation of Europe? (3)

(b) What are the causes of Reformation? (3)

(c) What do you mean by Counter Reformation? (3)

Answers

1. 1 (b) Supreme Court can issue any type of writs for enforcement of the Fundamental Rights.
2. (c) P, Q and S
3. (b) X
4. (d) The Lok Sabha
5. (a) Rajya Sabha
6. (c) Adjourn the House for lack of discipline.
7. (a) R. D. Banerji
8. (b) Later Vedic texts mention the expansion of agriculture and the use of iron tools.
9. (b) P and R
10. (b) Gautama Buddha
11. (a) The Sangam literature was written in Sanskrit.
12. (c) Ashoka was the famous king of this dynasty who flourished Buddhism in India.
13. (d) (A) is the reason for (R).
14. (a) James Watt
15. (c) Humanism
16. (a) Capitalism encourages private ownership and profit-making.

2. (i) Fundamental Rights are considered the Magna Carta of the Indian Constitution because they guarantee essential freedoms and rights to individuals by which they ensure justice, equality and liberty. They act as limitations on the powers of the government and protect citizens from arbitrary actions.

Parliament can amend Fundamental Rights mentioned under Article 368 of the Constitution. However those amendments must not violate the "basic structure" of the Constitution as ruled in the Kesavananda Bharati case (1973).

(ii) Two ways in which the Constitution ensures the proper functioning of the State Legislature are as follows

- In some states, there is a Legislative Assembly and a Legislative Council to ensure better decision-making and to prevent hasty laws.
- The Governor is also a constitutional head and ensure that laws are in line with the Constitution and not influenced by political pressure.

(iii) The two important features of the Indus Valley Civilisation were as follows

- **Well-Planned Cities** Streets followed a grid pattern with advanced drainage and sanitation systems.
- **Economic Prosperity** Trade was widespread and the use of standardised weights and seals for business transactions makes it unique.

(iv) Megasthenes was a Greek ambassador to the court of Chandragupta Maurya. He wrote the book Indica which provides detailed accounts of Indian society, administration and geography.

(v) The Sangam Age (c. 300 BCE-300 CE) refers to the period of Tamil literary and cultural development. People consumed rice, millet, fish, meat, dairy products and a variety of fruits like jackfruit and mango.

(vi) Factors that leads to the rise of the Renaissance and their influence on society were as follows

- Ancient Greek and Roman texts were revived which lead to advancements in art, science and literature.
- Invention of the Printing Press helped in the spread of new ideas quickly which helped in promoting the ideas of modern education and challenging to the traditional religious and political beliefs also.

(vii) The Yajur Veda is a collection of rituals for performing different sacrifices and recited by the priests. It contains 40 chapters and 2086 hymns which throw light on the social and religious life of the Aryans.

3 (a) The Constitution of India has several salient features that distinguish it from the Constitutions of other countries. Some of these are

(i) **Written and Lengthy Constitution** Indian Constitution is one of the most lengthy and detailed Constitutions of the world. It originally had 395 Articles and 8 schedules and now have 448 Articles in 25 parts and 12 schedules. The framers of the document have written all the relevant information about the working of the Legislature, the Executive and the Judiciary.

(ii) **Single Citizenship** The Indian Constitution provides single citizenship, i.e. a person cannot be a citizen of their state as well as the country. According to Citizenship Amendment Act of 2003, any person migrated to other countries after 26th January, 1950 will be granted dual citizenship but he must be the Person of Indian Origin (PIO).

(iii) **Universal Adult Franchise** Universal Adult Franchise guarantees that every Indian citizen of the age of 18 and above, irrespective of caste, colour, creed, race, religion, faith can vote and contest in the election.

(b) The Indian Constitution has guaranteed six Fundamental Rights to all its citizens. The six rights are

(i) Right to Equality (Article 14-18)

(ii) Right of Freedom (Article 19-22)

(iii) Right against Exploitation (Article 23-24)

(iv) Right to Freedom of Religion (Article 25-28)

(v) Cultural and Educational Rights (Article 29-30)

(vi) Right to Constitutional Remedies (Article 32).

These right are binding and are enforceable in courts of law and guarded by the judiciary.

(c) The Constitution provides some very special directives to the Central and State Governments. They must keep these Directives of State Policy in mind while making and implementing any law. These directives are vital because they give direction to the state to achieve the objectives for the welfare of the people. These are

(i) They secure social and economic justice to the people.

(ii) They secure social and economic equality for the people.

(iii) They promote international peace and serenity.

(iv) They establish a welfare state.

4 (a) The mechanism or procedure by which people choose their representatives at regular intervals in a democracy is called election. If people are not satisfied with the working of the government then they can change the government in the next term of elections. Elections are necessary for following reasons

(i) In order to choose the desired representatives, elections are must. People get a greater choice of selection for whom to cast their votes.

(ii) Election is an important tool to assess the functionality of the current government by the voters.

(iii) Election is needed by democracy to perform in the way which is in the best interest of the people of the country.

(b) Three systems of elections are prevalent in India. These are

(i) **General Elections** The elections for the Lok Sabha and Vidhan Sabha in the states, that happen after every five years are called general elections.

(ii) **By Elections** When seat held by any member of the Legislative Assembly in the state or any member of the Parliament falls vacant on account of death, resignation of member before completion of the term, the elections are held to fill up this vacancy, it is known as by-election.

(iii) **Mid-term Elections** When State Legislative Assembly or Lok Sabha is dissolved before the completion of a full five year term, elections need to be held. These are called mid-term elections.

(c) There are different types of constituencies in India. These are

(i) **Single Member Constituency** There is one representative from each constituency. After the conduction of the elections, the candidate who gets the highest number of votes, becomes the one and only representative of that constituency. This simple and convenient system is adopted by India and England.

(ii) **Multi-Member Constituency** There are a multiple number of representatives from each constituency. It this system, the voter has as many usable votes as the total number of candidates. This system was adapted by Germany, France and Italy, later they moved over to single-member constituency system.

(iii) **Reserved Constituencies** In India, there are a number of reserved constituencies for both Scheduled Castes and Scheduled Tribes in Parliamentary as well as Assembly elections.

General candidates cannot contest there and the voters have to choose from the candidates those belong to Scheduled Castes or Scheduled Tribes.

5. (a) The State Legislature plays a key role in governance by following ways
   - **Law-Making** The State Legislature creates laws on subjects in the State List such as education and agriculture.
   - **Representation of the People** The State Legislature elected members voice the concerns of citizens and ensure democracy at the state level.
   - **Control Over the Executive** The State Legislature monitors the government's actions, approves budgets and ensures accountability of the ruling authority.

   (b) Some of the important provisions related to the post of Speaker and Deputy Speaker are as follows
   - **Election** The Speaker and Deputy Speaker of the Legislative Assembly are elected by its members only.
   - **Role of the Speaker** The Speaker maintains order during debates, decides on points of order and ensures the smooth functioning of the house.
   - **Deputy Speaker's Role** The Deputy Speaker takes over when the Speaker is absent and performs all necessary duties.

   (c) The differences between the State Legislative Assembly and Council are as follows

Feature	Legislative Assembly	Legislative Council
Election	Members are directly elected by people	Members are indirectly elected by various groups
Tenure	The term of the members is of 5 years	The term of the members is of 6 years.
Presence	Present in all states	Present only in a few states
Powers	Has more legislative and financial powers	Limited role in law making and other aspects

6 (a) In 261 BC, Ashoka invaded Kalinga (Odisha) and succeeded in conquering it after a bloody war in which approximate 1,00,000 men were killed and around 1,50,000 people were injured. The massive violence and devastation filled Ashoka's heart with grief and regret. Ashoka ended the military expansion of the emprie and devoted rest of his life to ahimsa (non-violence) and dhamma- vijaya (victory) through dharma) The tern 'Dhamma' corresponds to the Sanskrit word 'Dharma? Thus, Kalinga war is regarded as a turning point in Ashoka's life.

(b) The main features of Ashoka's Dhamma are

(i) Service to father and mother practice of ahimsa, love of truth, reverence to teachers and good treatment of relatives,

(ii) Prohibition of animals sacrifices and festive gatherings. Avoiding expensive and meaningless ceremonies or rituals.

(iii) Efficient organisation of administration in the direction of social welfare and maintenance of constant contact with people through the system of Dhammayatras.

(iv) Humane treatment of servants by masters and prisoners by government officials.

(v) Consideration and non-violence to animals and courtesy to relations and liberality to Brahmins.

(vi) Tolerance among all the religious sects and appropriate treatment of ascetics.

(c) The policy of Dhamma marked the end of wars and conquest in India and there came a change in the policy of the State. This allowed the kings of Mauryan Empire to concentrate on the economic and social life of the ordinary people. The following points highlight impact of Dhamma

(i) People started to lead a moral life.

(ii) People gave support to the policy of religious tolerances propagated by their Emperor.

(iii) With the end of continuous wars and conquest, the officials paid more attention to the schemes and welfare measures assigned for the common public which ultimately led to the prosperity of the nation.

(iv) The policy of 'Ahimsa' impacted the people morally, thereby decreasing crimes like theft and various illegal activities.

7 (a) The Sangam Age is considered as a landmank in the history of South India. The word Sangam in the Tamil form of the Sanskrit word 'Sangha' which means a group of persons or an association. The Sangam Age is the classical period in the history of Tamil Nadu, Kerala and other parts of South India during 3rd century BC to 3rd century AD. This age witnessed rapid development in the literary works in the southern regions. The Sangam literature speaks highly of three South Indian Kingdoms, i.e., Chola, Pandya and Chera.

The sources of the Sangam Age can be classified into two groups, viz, literary sources (Sangam literature) and archaeological sources (megalitho, hero stone and inscriptions).

(b) A lot of information is available in the Sangam literature to understand the position of women during the Sangam age. Though the women enjoyed a respectable position, but their status was not equal to men in the society. There were women poets like Avvaiyar' Nachchellaiyar and Kakkaipadiniyar who flourished and contributed to Tamil literature. Some women were educated and contributed to Tamil literature. Some of them even had knowledge of politics who even used to advise the kings. Chastity was the most important virtue of Tamil women. Love marriage was a common practice and women were allowed to choose their life partners. But life of widows was miserable. There is also a mention about the practice of Sati being prevalent in the higher level of society.

(c) Economy of Sangam Age can be described in the following points

(i) Agriculture was the chief occupation where rice was the most common crop.

(ii) The handicraft included weaving, metal works and carpentry, ship building and making of ornaments using beads, stones and ivory.

(iii) A high expertise was attained in spinning and weaving of cotton and silk clothes. These were in great demand in the Western world especially for the cotton clothes woven at Uraiyur.

(iv) Both the internal and foreign trade was extensively carried on throughout the period and most of the trade was carried on by barter system.

(v) Significant ports of commercial activity were Puhar, Tondi, Musiri, Karkai, Arikkamedu and Marakkanam.

(vi) Many gold and silver coins that were issued by the Roman Emperors like Augustus, Tiberius and Nero have been found in all parts of Tamil Nadu indicating flourshing trade.

(vii) Major exports of the Sangam age were cotton fabrics and spices like pepper, ginger, cardamom, cinnamon and turmeric along with ivory products, pearls and precious stones.

(viii) Major imports for the traders were horses, gold and sweet wine.

(ix) Both internal and foreign trade was well-organised and briskly carried on in the Sangam age.

8 (a) This is picture of Red Fort or Lal Quila. It is situated in the ancient town of old Delhi in capital state of Delhi.

(b) Mughal Emperor Shah Jahan built it. He built Red Fort when he decided to transfer his capital to Delhi. The construction of Red Fort was begun in AD 1639 and was completed in AD 1648.

(c) The architectural features of Red Fort are

(i) It is a huge structure made of red stone and marble on the bank of Yamuna. Originally, it was known as Qila-e-Mubarak.

(ii) The fort is in form of a parallelogram measuring 930 metres by 495 metres.

(iii) The fort is surrounded by a strongly fortified wall.

(iv) The Lahori Gate is the main gate of Red Fort. The Lahori Gate and Delhi Gate were used by the public, and Khizrabad Gate was for the emperor.

(v) The other important buildings included Diwan-i-Aam, Diwan-i-Khas, Khas Mahal, Rang Mahal, Mumtaz Mahal, Naubat Khana , Hamam, Moti Masjid , Hira Mahal etc..

(vi) Shah Jahan built the Red Fort, later Aurangzeb added some building like Moti Masjid in the Red Fort.

9 (a) The word 'Bhakti' means 'devotion to God'. The Bhakti Movement originated as a reaction against caste division and ritualism in Indian society. Originally, this movement was started by the Shaivite and Vaishnava saints of South India in the 8th century and later became very popular in the 11th and 12th centuries. They were known as Nayanars (Shaivite devotees) and Alvars (Vaishnavite devotees). They preached personal devotion to God as a means of salvation. This religious movement has its roots in the philosophy or Shankaracharya, the reformer of Hinduism in 9th century AD.

(b) The main features highlighting significance of the Bhakti Movement are as follows

(i) Unity of God or one God though known by different names.

(ii) Bhakti, intense love and devotion, the only way to salvation.

(iii) Repetition of the True Name , Self-Surrender are the main objectives.

(iv) Condemnation of rituals, ceremonies and blind faith.

(v) Rejection of idol worship by many saints to open-mindedness about deciding religious matters.

(vi) No distinction of different castes, higher or low. Need of a guru for guidance.

(vii) Preaching's through local or regional languages and travelling from place-to place for spreading the religious message.

(c) Two famous Bhakti saints are Kabir (AD 1440-1518) and Guru Nanak (AD 1469-1538).

Kabir tried to reunite Hindus and Muslims and establish harmony between the two sects. The main teachings of Kabir are

(i) He rejected **idolatry** and rituals and laid great emphasis on the equality of man before God.

(ii) He regarded devotion to God as an effective means of salvation.

He urged that to achieve salvation one must have a pure heart, free from cruelty, dishonesty, **hypocrisy** and insincerity.

(iii) He emphasised the essential oneness of all religions by describing Hindus and Muslims 'as pots of the same clay'.

(iv) He believed that there was only one God, who might be worshipped under many names.

The founder of Sikhism Guru Nanak Dev emphasised personal devotion to God as a means of attaining salvation. The main teachings of Guru Nanak are

(i) According to him there was no Hindu and no Muslim. He believed in unity of mankind.

(ii) He laid emphasis on the oneness or unity of God. His concept of God was **Nirguna** (attribute less) and **Nirankara** (formless).

(iii) He advocated a middle path between extreme **asceticism** and free satisfaction of the senses.

(iv) He believed in leading a normal life.

(v) He attacked the caste system of the Hindus as it was against the will of God.

(vi) He did not believe in the Vedas and the Quran.

(vii) He believed in the doctrine of **Karma** and the theory of the Transmigration of Soul.

(viii) He gave importance to morality, humility, honesty, charity, truth and mercy.

(ix) He did not believe in the **incarnation of God** and rejected idolatry in all its forms.

His teachings are compiled in a book known as '**Adi Granth**'.

10 (a) The Reformation is a set for religious movements of sixteenth century encouraged by the Renaissance of later Middle age. It involved a revolt against the authority and principles of the Christian Church in Rome with the Pope as its head. It was a rebellion against the corruption and abuses in the church, monasticism church rituals and interference of Pope in temporal affairs. This movement created a split in the Christian church between those who continued to remain loyal to the Pope at Home viz, Roman Catholics and those who broke away from the church at Rome, viz, Protestants. The Reformation broke out in number of countries like, England, France, Germany, Czechoslovakia, Switzerland and Scotland. The Reformation helped to put an end to this age of blind faith and dogmas.

(b) There were many causes behind Reformation, but the two most prominent causes were dissatisfaction with the practices of the catholic church and new learning. During the 14th century people became dissatisfied with some of the church practices which paved the way for Reformation. The church involved with corrupt practices, the practice of issue of indulgence, salvation through fees, imposing various taxes, schism or split in church by the appointment of three Popes. The new spirit of learning and enquiry set initiated by the Renaissance greatly contributed to the Reformation. The invention of printing press and the printing of Bible in vernacular language and criticism by scholars to certain Catholic teaching and practices paved the way for Reformation. Martin Luther, a German priest challenged and raised a strong voice against the authority of the Pope and the abuses of the church.

(c) In order to restore the reputation of the church, an attempt was made by some dedicated Christians, including some paper who introduced certain reforms within the church. This movement is known as the Counter Reformation. This movement led to the revision of the service books of the church with an issue of a new edition of the Latin Bible, vulgate which became the official Bible of the Roman Catholics. The Catholic church was strengthened by the society at Jesus, whose members were known as Jesuits who dedicated themselves to the services of people. This society was founded by Ignatius Loyola in AD 1534. The efforts of Jesuits were carried forward by St. Francis Xavier in Japan, China and India. His efforts helped in restoration of the Roman Catholic Church.

SAMPLE QUESTION PAPER 2

A HIGHLY SIMULATED Sample Question Paper for ICSE Class IX

History & Civics (Unsolved)

General Instructions : See Sample Paper 1

PART - I

(30 Marks)

Attempt all questions from this part

Question 1

Attempt all questions from this part

1. Which of the following statements is correct about the Indian Constitution? (1)
   (a) It was enforced on 26th November, 1949.
   (b) It provides for a dual system of citizenship.
   (c) It guarantees Fundamental Rights under Part III.
   (d) It allows the Parliament to amend Fundamental Rights without any restriction.

2. Which of the following Fundamental Rights protects citizens from discrimination? (1)
   (a) Right to Equality
   (b) Right to Freedom
   (c) Right against Exploitation
   (d) Cultural and Educational Rights

3. Identify the statement which is incorrect from the following about the Directive Principles of State Policy (DPSP). (1)
   (a) They are non-justiciable in nature.
   (b) They aim to establish a welfare state.
   (c) They were borrowed from the Irish Constitution.
   (d) They are always superior to Fundamental Rights.

4. Read the following statements and identify the correct statement about elections in India? (1)
   P The Lok Sabha elections are conducted by the Election Commission of India.
   Q The Rajya Sabha members are elected through direct voting by the public.
   R By-elections are conducted for vacant seats before the next general election.
   S The President is elected through an electoral college system.
   (a) P and Q
   (b) P and R
   (c) P, R and S
   (d) All of these

5. Which of the following elections in India does not follow direct voting? (1)

(a) Lok Sabha elections
(b) Rajya Sabha elections
(c) State Legislative Assembly elections
(d) Gram Panchayat elections

6. Given below are details of a few Indian Citizens. (1)

Person	Age (in years)	Description
W	25	Is a part of the the medical association.
X	21	Is a graduate
Y	18	Is a first time voter
Z	35	Is a Government Teacher

Which of the following is eligible to become the member of the Legislative Council in India?

(a) W
(b) X
(c) Y
(d) Z

7. Complete the analogy.
Harappa : Ravi :: Mohenjo-daro :?? (1)

(a) Saraswati
(b) Indus
(c) Sutlej
(d) Beas

8. The dockyard of the Indus Valley Civilisation was found at .... (1)

(a) Harappa
(b) Mohenjo-daro
(c) Dholavira
(d) Lothal

9. Identify the statement which is correct about the Vedic period? (1)

(a) The Early Vedic society was pastoral in nature.
(b) The Later Vedic period saw the decline of agriculture.
(c) The Vedas were written in the Persian language.
(d) The caste system was completely absent in Vedic society.

10. Read the statements given below and select the option that shows the correct relationship between (A) and (R). (1)

Assertion (A) The Later Vedic Period saw the expansion of iron tools and agriculture.

Reason (R) The use of iron tools improved farming methods and led to an increase in agricultural productivity during the Later Vedic Period.

(a) (A) is true and (R) is false.
(b) (R) is true but (A) is false.
(c) Both (A) and (R) are independent of each other.
(d) (A) is the reason for (R).

11. Identify the king who is associated with the picture given below **(1)**

(a) Mahavir Jain (b) Gautam Buddha
(c) Ashoka (d) Chandragupta Maurya

12. Who was the first Tirthankara of Jainism? **(1)**
(a) Rishabhanatha (b) Mahavira (c) Parshvanatha (d) Vasudeva

13. Which of the following statements is correct about Chandragupta Maurya? **(1)**
(a) He was the last ruler of the Mauryan Dynasty.
(b) He was the disciple of Chanakya.
(c) He wrote the Arthashastra.
(d) He was defeated by the Gupta rulers.

14. Complete the analogy.
Kundagrama : Mahavir Jain :: Lumbini : .... **(1)**
(a) Ashoka (b) Gautama Buddha (c) Chanakya (d) Mahayana

15. Which of the following factors led to the rise of the Renaissance in Europe? **(1)**
(a) Capture of Constantinople (b) The decline of Feudalism
(c) The invention of the printing press (d) All of these

16. He was a 16th-century theologian and reformer who challenged the authority of the Catholic Church and opposed the practice of indulgences. His 95 Theses, written in simple yet powerful language, sparked the Protestant Reformation. He emphasised that salvation comes through faith alone and translated the Bible into the vernacular to make it accessible to the common people. Who is he?
(a) Martin Luther (b) Thomas Newcomen
(c) George Stephenson (d) Thomas Alva Edison

Question 2

(i) What do you mean by election? How members of the Legislative Councils are appointed in States? **(2)**

(ii) "Fundamental Rights are essential for ensuring individual liberty, equality and justice in a democratic society. They protect citizens from arbitrary actions of the state and uphold the rule of law, ensuring that every individual enjoys dignity and freedom." *- The News Express.*

From the passage, deduce and mention any two ways in which the Constitution safeguards the enforcement of Fundamental Rights. (2)

(iii) Mention any two main features of the Vedic Society. (2)

(iv) Mention any two important teachings of the Mahavir Jain. (2)

(v) Mention any two contributions of the Gupta period in the fields of science and education. (2)

(vi) "Name the dynasty that promoted the Sangam literature during the Sangam Age. Which famous poets were associated with this period?" (2)

(vii) Who was the founder of the Gupta dynasty and Who saved the Gupta Empire from Hun invasion? (2)

PART - II

(50 Marks)

Section A (Civics)

Attempt any two questions from the section

Question 3

Fundamental Rights and Duties are the basic resources to social life. In the light of this statement answer the following questions.

(a) What are Fundamental Rights? Write about the importance of Fundamental Rights. (3)

(b) Write any five Fundamental Duties. (3)

(c) Explain about the Right to Equality mentioned in our Constitution. (4)

Question 4

Directive Principles of State Policy is one of the most important provisions of the Constitution of India. In the light of this statement, answer the following questions.

(a) What are the different sources of Directive Principles? (3)

(b) How many types of Directive Principles are there? (3)

(c) What is the purpose of a welfare state? (4)

Question 5

The Legislatures are the primary body of a state. With reference to the Indian State legislatures, answer the following questions:

(a) Mention any three circumstances under which the Parliament can make laws on subjects in the State List. (3)

(b) Explain the following (3)

- Indirect election of the Council Members.
- Position of the Speaker in State Legislatures.

(c) How does the state Legislature ensure accountability of the government. (4)

Section B (History)

Attempt any three questions from this section

Question 6

The archaeological sources help to understand the Mauryan empire. In light of this statement answer the following questions.

(a) Define edicts. Who was the first ruler to issue edict? (3)

(b) How many edicts of Ashoka were found? (3)

(c) Write about the importance fo Sanchi stupa. (4)

Question 7

(a) Who was known as Napoleon of India? (3)

(b) How did he expand his empire? (3)

(c) Which university was regarded as the most renowned repository of Buddhist knowledge? (4)

Question 8

Study the picture given below and answer the following questions.

(a) Identify this image and give a brief description of it. (3)

(b) What do you know about the script of Indus valley civilisation? (3)

(c) Write about two archaeological sources of Indus valley civilisation. (4)

Question 9

The Industrial Revolution had a great impact on growth of industries. In the light of this statement answer the following questions.

(a) What were some important inventions of the Industrial Revolution? (3)

(b) How did transportation and communication development helped in the growth of Industrial Revolution? (3)

(c) What is capitalism? What are its impacts on society? (4)

Question 10

(a) What is the meaning of the term Renaissance? (3)

(b) What are the causes of decline of feudalism? (3)

(c) Write short note on the invention of printing press. (4)

SAMPLE QUESTION PAPER 3

A HIGHLY SIMULATED Sample Question Paper for ICSE Class IX

History & Civics (Unsolved)

General Instructions : See Sample Paper 1

PART - I

(30 Marks)

Attempt all questions from this part

Question 1

1. Which of the following is a fundamental feature of the Indian Constitution? (1)
   (a) Dual Citizenship
   (b) Universal Adult Franchise
   (c) Unwritten Fundamental Rights
   (d) Unwritten Fundamental Duties

2. What is the maximum duration after which the fresh elections for State Legislature are organised? (1)
   (a) 2 years
   (b) 4 years
   (c) 5 years
   (d) 6 years

3. Identify the body which is responsible for conducting State Legislature elections in India? (1)
   (a) Parliament
   (b) Election Commission
   (c) State Election Commission
   (d) Judiciary

4. Complete the given analogy. (1)
   Legislative Assembly : Lower House in states:: Legislative Council : ?
   (a) Legitimate house
   (b) Upper House
   (c) Directly Elected House
   (d) None of these

5. Given below are details of a few Indian Citizens. (1)

Person	Age (in years)	Description
W	30	Is a part of the anti national forces
X	21	Is a graduate
Y	18	Is a first time voter
Z	35	Is a Government Teacher

Which of the following is eligible to become the member of the Legislative Council in India? (1)

(a) W (b) X
(c) Y (d) Z

6. The maximum number of members allowed in the Legislative Assembly of a state .... (1)

(a) 200 (b) 300
(c) 400 (d) 500

7. Identify the location from which below depicted image was found. (1)

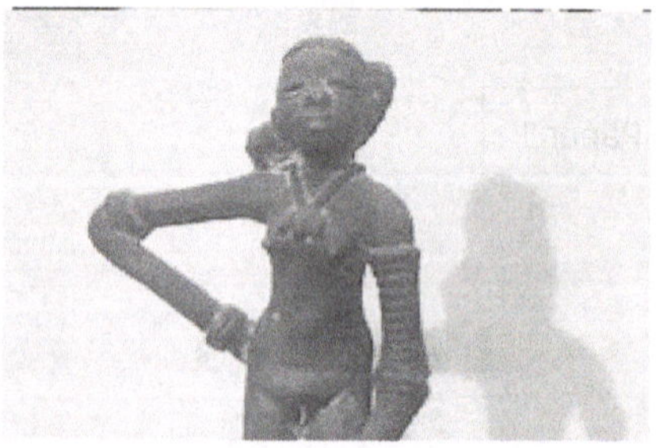

(a) Mohenjo-daro (b) Ajanta Caves
(c) Sanchi Stupa (d) Hampi

8. Which of the following statements correctly describes the main occupation of people during the Early Vedic Period? (1)

(a) People primarily engaged in trade and commerce.
(b) Agriculture and cattle rearing were the main occupations.
(c) Handicrafts and weaving were the dominant sources of livelihood.
(d) Hunting and gathering was the primary means of sustenance.

9. Identify the odd one out based on the main occupation of people during the Early Vedic Period. (1)

(a) Agriculture and Cattle Rearing (b) Trade and Commerce
(c) Handicrafts and Weaving (d) Hunting and Gathering

10. The .... text is associated with Buddhism? (1)

(a) Angas (b) Tripitikas
(c) Arthashastra (d) Indika

11. Identify the correct statement about the person who is known as the 'Napoleon of India' (1)

(a) Samudragupta was a Gupta ruler who expanded his empire through conquests and inscriptions.
(b) Ashoka was a Mauryan ruler who embraced Buddhism after the Kalinga war.
(c) Akbar was a Mughal ruler who introduced the Mansabdari system.
(d) Rajendra Chola was a Chola ruler known for his naval expeditions in South-East Asia.

12. Identify the correct statement related to the construction of the Brihadishwara Temple. (1)
    (a) The Maurya dynasty is known for the spread of Buddhism and Ashokan Edicts.
    (b) The Gupta dynasty contributed to art, science and the Nalanda University.
    (c) The Chola dynasty built the Brihadishwara Temple under Rajaraja I's rule.
    (d) The Mughal dynasty is famous for architectural marvels like the Taj Mahal and Red Fort.

13. Read the statements given below and select the option that shows the correct relationship between (A) and (R).
    Assertion (A) The Bhakti Movement encouraged the use of vernacular languages for religious teachings.
    Reason (R) Bhakti saints wanted to make spiritual teachings accessible to the common people, regardless of caste or social status. (1)
    (a) (A) is true and (R) is false
    (b) (R) is true but (A) is false
    (c) Both (A) and (R) are independent of each other
    (d) (A) is the reason for (R)

14. Which of the following statement correctly describes the impact of the Bhakti Movement? (1)
    (a) It led to the spread of rigid social hierarchies and caste-based discrimination.
    (b) It played a significant role in promoting communal harmony and simplifying religious practices.
    (c) It restricted the use of local languages in devotional literature.
    (d) It was only confined to North India and had no influence in the South

15. Which of the following statement is related to Capitalism? (1)
    (a) Capitalism promotes state control over industries and equal wealth distribution.
    (b) Capitalism encourages private ownership, profit motive and free-market economy.
    (c) Capitalism was first introduced during the Industrial Revolution by Karl Marx.
    (d) Capitalism eliminates competition by allowing government monopolies over businesses.

16. Which of the following statement is incorrect and not related to the Renaissance (1)
    (a) The Renaissance was a period of religious decline with no impact on art and science.
    (b) The Renaissance led to a revival of classical learning, humanism and scientific discoveries.
    (c) The Renaissance was limited to Italy and had no influence on the rest of Europe.
    (d) The Renaissance rejected new ideas and supported medieval feudal practices.

Question 2

2. (i) "Fundamental Rights protect the freedoms and dignity of individuals, ensuring equality, justice and non-discrimination. They act as a safeguard against arbitrary actions of the State and provide legal remedies in case of violation".
   From the passage, deduce and mention any two ways in which the Constitution guarantees the protection of Fundamental Rights. (2)
   (ii) Mention any two qualifications which are necessary to become the member of the State Legislative Assembly. (2)
   (iii) Mention any two ideas of Karma according to Jainism and Budhism. (2)
   (iv) Name any two dynasties that ruled Magadha before the Mauryan dynasty. Highlight some important war. (2)

(v) Mention any two reason for the emergence of Bhakti and Sufi movement in India. (2)

(vi) Who was Senguttuvan? Mention any two of his achievements. (2)

(vii) What are the different Vedic literatures? (2)

PART - II

(50 Marks)

Section A (Civics)

Attempt any two questions from this section.

Question 3

Preamble is considered the soul and spirit of our Constitution. In the light of this statement answer the following questions.

(a) What do you mean by the Preamble of Indian Constitution? (3)

(b) How is India described in our Preamble? (3)

(c) State the main principles of Preamble. (4)

Question 4

Election is necessary for a democracy. In the light of this statement, answer the following questions.

(a) What is an election? How many types of elections are there? (3)

(b) What do you mean by Election Commission? Write about its composition. (3)

(c) Explain the powers and functions of Election Commission. (4)

Question 5

5. The State Legislature plays a crucial role in the governance of a state. In the light of this statement, answer the following questions.

(a) What is a State Legislature? How many types of State Legislatures exist in India? (3)

(b) What do you mean by a Bicameral Legislature and also mention the types of presiding officer found in such legislatures. (3)

(c) Explain the following powers of the State Legislature. (4)

(i) Legislative Powers (ii) Financial Powers

Section B (History)

Attempt any three questions from this section.

Question 6

The Harappan Civilisation is considered as one of the greatest civilisation of all times. In the light of this statement answer the following questions.

(a) In which area the Harappan Civilisation was extended? (3)

(b) What are the important sources of the Harappan Civilisation? (3)

(c) Describe the town planning features of the Harappan civilisations. (4)

Question 7

The Sangam Age is the classical period in the history of Tamil Nadu, Kerala and other parts of South India. In the light of this statement answer the following questions.

(a) Write about the caste system prevalent in the Sangam Age. (3)

(b) What were the food and dress habits of the Sangam period? (3)

(c) What are the literary sources of the Sangam Age? (4)

Question 8

Study the picture given below and answer the following questions.

(a) Identify the monument. Who was responsible to construct the monument? (3)

(b) Name another three important monuments of Delhi Sultanate period. (3)

(c) Write about the special features of Qutab Minar. (4)

Question 9

(a) Who was the founder of the Gupta Empire? (3)

(b) Write about the achievements of Chandragupta I. (3)

(c) Who was known as Vikramaditya? What do you know about him? (4)

Question 10

With reference to Industrial Revolution in Europe answer the following questions.

(a) What were the major causes of capitalism? (3)

(b) What is socialism? Name some main exponents of socialism. (3)

(c) How do socialism and Capitalism differs in their origin? (4)

